Cultural Influences on the Law of the Sea

Cultural Influences on the Law of the Sea

History, Legacy, and Future Prospects

Edited by

JAMES KRASKA

Charles H. Stockton Professor of International Maritime Law, Stockton Center for International Law, US Naval War College

HAYOUN RYOU-ELLISON

Assistant Professor, College of International Security Affairs, National Defense University

OXFORD
UNIVERSITY PRESS

OXFORD
UNIVERSITY PRESS

Great Clarendon Street, Oxford, OX2 6DP,
United Kingdom

Oxford University Press is a department of the University of Oxford.
It furthers the University's objective of excellence in research, scholarship,
and education by publishing worldwide. Oxford is a registered trade mark of
Oxford University Press in the UK and in certain other countries

Published in the United States of America by Oxford University Press
198 Madison Avenue, New York, NY 10016, United States of America

British Library Cataloguing in Publication Data
Data available

Library of Congress Control Number: 2024948880

ISBN 9780198944133

DOI: 10.1093/9780198944140.001.0001

The manufacturer's authorised representative in the EU for product safety is
Oxford University Press España S.A. of El Parque Empresarial San Fernando
de Henares, Avenida de Castilla, 2 – 28830 Madrid (www.oup.es/en or
product.safety@oup.com). OUP España S.A. also acts as importer into Spain
of products made by the manufacturer.

This book is dedicated to the Korea Institute for Maritime Strategy (KIMS), in recognition of their generous support, without which this study and release of this volume would not have been possible.

Foreword: The World's Major Regional Cultures and Oceans Law and Governance

Human history is formed and continues to evolve in the littoral oceans or waters surrounding the land. This intercoastal area is used to transport everything from people and goods to less desirable cargoes, like disease. Throughout history, the relevant 'sea area' for many of the most pivotal human events lies at the interface of the sea and land. Human history has unfolded throughout the sea, and maritime history is intertwined with the human experience. By presenting perspectives arising from the different maritime cultures, we can think about history and the world as a network of relationships across sea and land areas. The focus on maritime cultural geography rather than relationships among states or political geography is a new lens.

This cultural network is not linear, simply connecting nodal points in the sea and land areas, but expands into a broader system or web that brings the hinterland and the outside world to the littoral regions. As human activities at various levels take place throughout this network of relationships along myriad points, lines, and planes, a three-dimensional image of the world may be constructed. This structure or model of the world evolves and transforms over time, forming human history. The social culture and its transformation created through the interaction of people (groups) within a sea area form the history of each littoral region, and the accumulation of that process is expressed in our contemporary world.

Culture is one of the most important factors in forming laws and norms. Naturally, we must be able to think about the role of culture in creating maritime laws and patterns of behaviour. Nevertheless, exploring the connection between culture and maritime law has been insufficient. This volume is the result of important research examining the maritime culture of various regions and how these cultural influences shaped and continue to influence international maritime law. The chapters identify the historical process of formulating and developing the international law of the sea and oceans governance. We uncover and analyse experiences of contact and negotiation and uncover intercultural methods of resolving conflicts. The book is a transcultural toolkit for how to move forward in shaping oceans law and governance.

The Korea Institute for Maritime Strategy (KIMS) is a private, non-profit think tank that raises awareness of the sea's importance, contributes to the development of sound maritime policies, and ultimately strives to create a safer and more peaceful world. Founded in 1997, KIMS has been dedicated to identifying and analysing emerging and pressing problems related to the maritime domain.

This book, produced under the sponsorship of KIMS, shows how close teamwork has been achieved among renowned experts from Western Europe, Eastern Europe, Russia, East Asia, South Asia, Africa, South America, North America, and Oceania. Each chapter provides a breathtaking wealth of knowledge that helps readers understand the contributions of regional cultures to the international law of the sea, from historic development to contemporary practice. I would like to thank all chapter contributors for their dedication. I acknowledge Professor James Kraska, Professor Hayoun Ryou-Ellison, Professor Robin Churchill, Judge Stanislaw Michal Pawlak, Mr. Alexander S Skaridov, Professor Seokwoo Lee, Dr. Aniruddha Rajput, Attorney Tafadzwa Pasipanodya, Judge María Teresa Infante, and Professor Karen N Scott, in the order in which the contributions appear in this book. I am especially grateful to Professor Kraska for his leadership in the project and editing and proofreading the volume.

Chung, Eui-Sung
Chairman
Korea Institute for Maritime Strategy

Preface

This book emerged from an enquiry made by contributing editor Hayoun Ryou-Ellison, while she served as a visiting scholar at the Korea Institute for Maritime Strategy (KIMS) in Seoul. She wondered how the world's major cultures have influenced the law of the sea. In discussions with contributing editor James Kraska, they realized that this question had not been closely examined. How have the world's great cultures impacted the historical evolution and contemporary development of the law of the sea? What are the commonalities and differences among cultures, and how have they shaped oceans law and policy? With the kind support and direction of Chung, Eui-Sung, Chairman of KIMS, and the engagement of Sam-man Chung, also of KIMS, the editors embarked on the project.

The idiom that the land dominates the sea is a foundation of oceans law and governance. Geography is destiny, but culture is too. How people perceive their reality is as important as their physical location and topography. This volume explores the contributions of regional cultures to the international law of the sea, from historic development to contemporary practice. The continental-sized civilizations in this volume cover Western Europe, Eastern Europe, Russia, East Asia, South Asia, Africa, South America, North America, and Oceania. In assessing the influences of these cultural regions, the book concludes with a normative evaluation of what each of the world's civilizations has contributed to the law of the sea and how they can promote oceans governance today.

We assembled a team of prominent international legal jurists and scholars to unpack how major cultural regions of the world have shaped and influenced the emergence of the law of the sea and how they are expressed in contemporary oceans governance and initiatives to regulate the Blue Economy. This group includes authors from Chile, Korea, India, New Zealand, Poland, Russia, the United Kingdom, the United States, and Zimbabwe. The group of contributors includes two sitting judges on the International Tribunal for the Law of the Sea, a former member of the International Law Commission, and prominent practitioners and scholars who come from the regions on which they are writing their respective contributions, ensuring authenticity and genuinely global representation. Half of the editors or contributors are non-white people and/or are from the Global South. Three of the contributors are men from Western Europe, Eastern Europe, and North America. Three chapters are written by women, including one from Africa, one from New Zealand, and one from Latin America. The contributors each have native insight into their respective areas of cultural expertise. The co-editor is a woman from Asia who, until recently, served on the faculty of a leading historically Black university in the United States. One contributor is from East Asia, one from Africa, one from Latin America, and one from South Asia. One scholar is from Russia, offering a rare perspective that is often not included in English-language publications today because of geopolitical tensions.

The contributors conducted a broad and inclusive analysis of the cultural norms of major civilizations and how these traits contribute to preferences that are reflected in the law of the sea. This original study lies between the two most common units of analysis for understanding the law of the sea: first, the purely global approach to oceans governance, such as what might be observed through the conferences of the United Nations and initiatives including the 1995 Fish Stocks Agreement, the 2023 High Seas Treaty (also known as the Biodiversity Beyond National Jurisdiction Agreement), and the effort to negotiate a plastics treaty; and, second, more regionally focused mechanisms, such as the 15-country Convention for the Protection of the Marine Environment of the North-East Atlantic (also known as the OSPAR Convention) in the European Union.

This intermediate or regional level of analysis illuminates the impact of cultural norms evident in civilizations and how they have shaped the law of the sea. These continent-sized influences are often ignored by law of the sea scholars, who have preferred to study law-making at either the global level or the individual state level. The global level obfuscates different approaches to the law of the sea, while the national level elides meaningful international cultural norms that more broadly shape oceans law and governance. This edited volume reflects the contributions and impacts of regional cultural influences in shaping the international law of the sea. These cultural strands demonstrate the complex background and set of human experiences that have informed the development of the law of the sea and that continue to shape it today.

The Global South is a big part of this story but not the complete story. Although using these regions and cultures is somewhat subjective, and other scholars might be drawn to include or exclude certain cultural areas (often based on the nationality or origin of the scholar), we believe that the division we adopt offers greater fidelity to the authority and influence that actually shapes the law and provides a richer tapestry than a purely North–South focus, while avoiding the inclusion of so many regions that the book becomes an unwieldy encyclopaedia of national approaches.

The weakness of national approaches is that the analysis of the impact of the law of the sea is atomized or becomes so granular that it prevents drawing on similarities or appreciating the differences among the world's major cultures. Our choice of a balanced approach includes the major civilizational influences on the law of the sea, and it underscores common or shared interests and inflection points for disagreement. We also analyse how the global regime of oceans law has navigated the cultural polarities, without becoming bogged down by them.

Although international law and the law of the sea are regarded as arising mostly from Western conceptions of law, the Global South achieved its first dispositive impact on global governance with its participation at the Third UN Conference on the Law of the Sea (1973–1982). The North–South dichotomy is a feature of the UN Convention on the Law of the Sea and resonates through the three implementing agreements on seabed mining, high seas fish stocks, and high seas biodiversity.

While the North–South dimension still resonates today, the realities of geographic position or strategic alignment, such as whether a state has an expansive continental margin or is landlocked and geographically disadvantaged, often drive immediate goals. Many states in the Global South are bypassing the West to take the lead on overdue reforms or erecting alternative institutions in global governance, convinced that the Western-led governance model is no longer addressing their concerns.

Cultural influences reflect the unique social elements that have informed civilizations and their interests in the law of the sea, complementing and interacting with geography and economics. The chapter contributions provide signposts along the range of civilizational perspectives in an approachable volume to raise awareness among diplomats, negotiators, and scholars on how regions express and understand the law of the sea through a cultural lens, and how and why regions have sought to shape the law to fit their cultural models and expectations.

James Kraska
Charles H Stockton Professor of International Maritime Law
Chairman, Stockton Center for International Law
US Naval War College
Newport, Rhode Island

Hayoun Ryou-Ellison
Assistant Professor
College of International Security Affairs
National Defense University
Washington, DC

December 2024

Acknowledgements

The editors express their sincere appreciation to the Korea Institute for Maritime Strategy (KIMS) for its generous support of this book, especially its CEO Chung Eui-Seung, who endorsed this project from the start; Dr. Chung Sam-man, the Director of the Center for Maritime Security at KIMS, who encouraged the editors in their work; and Dr. Ye Seul Kim, also of KIMS, for her administrative support.

We also thank the Oxford University Press team for their professionalism and enthusiasm for this project. We also appreciate the two anonymous reviewers and their valuable comments. The editors are indebted to Michelle Nicols's excellent indexing and copy-editing assistance for the final project. Christopher Ellison, a senior editor at the George Washington University, also contributed his knowledge of the literature on culture and development, as well as on Latin America, to the introduction and conclusion chapters of this book.

Finally, we appreciate the scholars and practitioners who study the impact of culture on many aspects of global affairs and hope this book contributes to ongoing scholarship in the field. We hope this book sheds new light on invisible values' tangible impact on the development of the law of the sea and that it will inspire further research into the ways in which culture matters in international development.

The views presented in this volume are those of the contributors and do not represent the official policy or position of any institution they are affiliated with, including for both contributing editors, the Department of Defense.

James Kraska — Newport, Rhode Island

Hayoun Ryou-Ellison — Washington, DC

September 2024

Contents

Contributors

Robin Churchill, PhD, is Emeritus Professor of International Law, School of Humanities, Social Sciences and Law, University of Dundee, Dundee, United Kingdom

María Teresa Infante, PhD, is Professor of International Law, University of Chile, Santiago, Chile

James Kraska, JD, LLM, SJD, is Charles H. Stockton Professor of International Maritime Law, Stockton Center for International Law, US Naval War College, Newport, Rhode Island

Seokwoo Lee, DPhil, is Professor of International Law, Inha University, Incheon, South Korea

Tafadzwa Pasipanodya, JD, MPA, is Partner, International Litigation and Arbitration Department, Foley Hoag LLP, Washington, DC, United States

Stanislaw Michal Pawlak, PhD, is Judge, International Tribunal for the Law of the Sea, Hamburg, Germany

Aniruddha Rajput, PhD, is Distinguished Professor of Law; Barrister; Consultant, National Law University Delhi, India; Withers LLP, London, United Kingdom

Hayoun Ryou-Ellison, PhD, is Assistant Professor, College of International Security Affairs, National Defense University, Washington, DC, United States

Karen N Scott, LLM, is Professor, Faculty of Law, University of Canterbury, Christchurch, New Zealand

Alexander S Skaridov, Doctor of Law, is Professor, Head, International and Maritime Law Department, Admiral Makarov State University of Maritime and Inland Shipping, St. Petersburg, Russia Federation

About the Contributors

Robin Churchill

Robin Churchill began his academic career in 1970 at the British Institute of International and Comparative Law in London, where he was research officer in international law. In 1977, he joined the staff of the Law Department of what was then the University of Wales Institute of Science and Technology (subsequently Cardiff University), eventually becoming Professor of International Law. In 2006, Churchill was appointed Professor of International Law at the University of Dundee in Scotland. Since his retirement in 2016, he has continued as an Emeritus Professor at the University. Churchill has also held visiting positions at the University of Tromsø (Norway), the University of Wollongong (Australia), and the European University Institute, Florence (Italy). He has researched and written on the international law of the sea for many years and is the author of four books and over a hundred journal articles and book chapters on the subject, including *The Law of the Sea* (4th edn, 2022) (with Vaughan Lowe and Amy Sander) and *The EC Common Fisheries Policy* (2010) (with Daniel Owen). For the past 20 years, Churchill has contributed an annual survey on dispute settlement in the law of the sea to the *International Journal of Marine and Coastal Law*. His other research interests include international human rights and international environmental law, on both of which he has published quite widely. Churchill has advised on law of the sea questions for a number of governments, the European Parliament, and various environmental and fishery NGOs, as well as providing written evidence to a number of parliamentary committees in the United Kingdom.

María Teresa Infante

María Teresa Infante is a Judge of the International Tribunal for the Law of the Sea, elected in 2020. She has held several other positions, including Professor in the Faculty of Law at the University of Chile, Professor of the Diplomatic Academy of Chile, and Director of the Institute of International Studies at the University of Chile. She was Co-Agent of Chile in disputes before the International Court of Justice (maritime dispute, 2008–14; obligation to negotiate, 2013–18; status and use of the waters of the Silala, 2016–20). She was also Ambassador of Chile to the Kingdom of the Netherlands, Permanent Representative to the Organization for the Prohibition of Chemical Weapons (OPCW), Chair of the Sub-Working Group on Non-State Actors of the OPCW, and Co-Chair of the Study Group on Governance (together with Japan and Switzerland) of The Hague Working Group of the Assembly of States Parties. Infante was Chair of the Working Group of the Bureau on the Implementation of Article 97 of the Rome Statute. She has advised and participated in research programmes for, among others, the Permanent Commission of the South Pacific, the Ministry of Foreign

Affairs of Chile, the UN Development Programme, and the National Commission of the Environment. Infante participated in diplomatic negotiations on maritime and Antarctic matters, and with neighbouring and South American countries on issues of integration, limits, international law, and cooperation on border policies.

James Kraska

James Kraska is Visiting Professor of Law and John Harvey Gregory Lecturer on World Organization at Harvard Law School, where he teaches a popular course on the law of the sea. Kraska is also Charles H. Stockton Chair of International Maritime Law and Department Chair of the Stockton Center for International Law at the US Naval War College and Visiting Professor of Law at Reading University. Previously, he served as Visiting Professor at the College of Law at the University of the Philippines and as Distinguished Visiting Professor at Gujarat National Law University. Kraska was also the Mary Derrickson McCurdy Visiting Scholar at Duke University Marine Laboratory and Chief of Naval Research Fellow at Woods Hole Oceanographic Institution. He is General Editor of *International Law Studies*, the oldest journal of international law in the United States, and Editor-in-Chief of the three-volume treatise *Benedict on Admiralty: International Maritime Law*. A permanent member of the Council on Foreign Relations, Kraska served as a US Navy officer and lawyer, including as Director of the International Negotiations Division of the Joint Staff. He earned a JD from Indiana University Maurer School of Law in Bloomington and an LLM and JSD from the University of Virginia School of Law.

Seokwoo Lee

Seokwoo Lee is Professor of International Law at Inha University Law School in Korea (since 2003). He was Chairman of the Foundation for the Development of International Law in Asia (2012–17) and is Co-Chair of the International Law Association Study Group, Asian State Practice of Domestic Implementation of International Law (since 2018). Lee was Vice President of the Korean Society of International Law (2019), also serving as Executive Board Member (since 2010) and Director of International Relations (2010–11). He also served as Chairman of the Research Committee, SLOC (Sea Lanes of Communication) Study Group—Korea (2010–13). Lee is General Editor of the *Encyclopedia of Public International Law in Asia* and the *Encyclopedia of Ocean Law and Policy in Asia-Pacific*, Co-Editor-in-Chief of the *Asia-Pacific Journal of Ocean Law and Policy* and the *Asian Yearbook of International Law*, Executive Editor of the *Korean Journal of International and Comparative Law*, Co-Series Editor of the book series *Maritime Cooperation in East Asia*, and Associate Editor of *Brill Research Perspectives in the Law of the Sea*, all published by Brill. He has authored more than a hundred publications in English and more than a hundred more in Korean. His representative publications in English are 'Yeo Woon Taek v. New Nippon Steel Corporation' ((2019) 113(3) *American Journal of International Law* 592); *Regulation on Navigation of Foreign Vessels: Asia-Pacific State Practice* (Brill Nijhoff 2019); and *The Making of International Law in Korea: From Colony to Asian Power* (Brill Nijhoff 2016). Lee received his undergraduate law degree from Korea University; master's degrees from Korea University, the University of Minnesota, and New York University; and a doctorate from Oxford University. In addition, he has completed the required coursework for his doctoral degree programme in Modern and Contemporary Korean History at the Department of Korean History, Korea University.

Tafadzwa Pasipanodya

Tafadzwa Pasipanodya is a partner in the international litigation and arbitration department of the law firm Foley Hoag LLP and chair of its Africa practice. She has represented sovereign states from all over the world in more than 30 interstate and investor-state disputes concerning the law of the sea, territorial boundaries, mining, hydrocarbons, the environment, human rights, and infrastructure, including before the International Court of Justice, the International Tribunal for the Law of the Sea, and ad hoc arbitration tribunals. Pasipanodya also represents foreign states in US federal court proceedings. She is a member of the International Chamber of Commerce Court of Arbitration, vice president of the African Society of International Law, and a member of the Executive Council of the American Society of International Law. Pasipanodya was named to Africa's 30 Arbitration Powerlist 2020 by the Africa Arbitration Academy, Africa Arbitration, and the Association of Young Arbitrators. She has been ranked by Latinvex as one of the top 32 female international arbitration lawyers working on Latin American matters and is also recognized by Who's Who Legal: Arbitration and by The Legal 500: USA and Latin America. Pasipanodya obtained a Juris Doctor from New York University School of Law, a master's degree in Public Affairs from Princeton University, and a bachelor of arts in Economics and French from Macalester College. She has authored numerous publications on a variety of issues on international law and is currently co-editing a book entitled *The Law of the Sea—Contemporary Norms and Practice in Africa*. Pasipanodya understands English, Shona, Spanish, French, German, and Portuguese.

Stanislaw Michal Pawlak

Stanislaw Michal Pawlak has served as a Judge of the International Tribunal for the Law of the Sea since 2005 (re-elected in 2014), including as President of the Chamber for Marine Environment Disputes (2017–20), President of the Chamber for Fisheries Disputes (since 2020), and member of the Special Chamber formed to deal with the dispute concerning delimitation of the maritime boundary between Mauritius and Maldives in the Indian Ocean. He has also served as a member of the International Law Commission (1987–91). Pawlak is the author of books and articles on international law and international relations concerning the activities of the United Nations, the law of the sea, international terrorism, disarmament, and the foreign policy of states, related mostly to the Far East. He was a Judge in the Arbitral Tribunal in the case of the *Philippines v China* (2013–16). At the University of Warsaw, Pawlak served as Professor of International Law and International Relations (2002–14) and as Emeritus Professor (since 2014). He was a member of the Polish diplomatic service (1955–2005), including as Ambassador to Canada (1978–83), Ambassador and Permanent Representative to the United Nations (1989–91), and Ambassador to Syria and Jordan (1996–2001). Pawlak was an adviser to the President of Poland (2001–05), with the rank of Titular Ambassador.

Aniruddha Rajput

Aniruddha Rajput was a member of the International Law Commission (2017–22), serving as Chairperson of the Drafting Committee at its 69th Session in 2017. The topic he proposed, 'Evidence Before International Courts and Tribunals', was put on the Long-Term Programme of Work of the Commission in 2017. A practising barrister, Rajput advises and appears on behalf of states and private entities before international courts and tribunals. His areas of research, writing, and practice are general international law, the international law of the sea, international boundary disputes, international trade, and investment law. He has also published and lectured in these areas. Rajput is a Visiting Fellow and Lecturer at the University of Vienna. Previously, he was a Visiting Fellow at the Max Planck Institute Luxembourg for International, European and Regulatory Procedural Law and a Practitioner-in-Residence at the KFG programme 'The International Rule of Law—Rise of Decline?' at Humboldt University in Berlin in 2017. Rajput is a member of the Governing Council of the Indian Council of World Affairs. He was a member of the study group constituted by the Law Commission of India to revise the Model Bilateral Investment Treaty and a member of the Fifth Haryana State Finance Commission constituted under Articles 243(I) and 234(Y) of the Constitution of India.

Hayoun Ryou-Ellison

Hayoun Ryou-Ellison serves as Assistant Professor in the College of International Security Affairs at National Defense University in Washington, DC. She has also taught at Howard University, Virginia Commonwealth University, and the Catholic University of America. Ryou-Ellison is a non-resident research fellow at the Korea Institute for Maritime Strategy. Previously, she worked in New Delhi, where was an Associate Fellow at the Observer Research Foundation, a Visiting Fellow at the Institute of Peace and Conflict Studies, and a Visiting Scholar at the Institute for Defence Studies and Analyses. She earned a PhD in Political Science and a master's degree in Statistics from the University of Tennessee, a master's degree in Political Science from the George Washington University, a master's degree in China Area Studies from Seoul National University, and a bachelor's degree in Chinese language from Hankuk University of Foreign Studies (Seoul Campus). Ryou-Ellison also holds a diploma from the Korea Maritime Institute's Yeosu Academy of the Law of the Sea and a certificate in National Security Law from the University of Virginia School of Law.

Karen N Scott

Karen N Scott is a Professor of Law at the University of Canterbury in New Zealand. She also serves as President of the Australian and New Zealand Society of International Law and as Editor-in-Chief of the journal *Ocean Development & International Law*.

Scott is a board member of seven journals, including *Brill Research Perspectives on the Law of the Sea* and the *Australian Yearbook of International* Law. She researches and teaches in the areas of public international law, the law of the sea, and international environmental law. Scott has published more than a hundred edited books, journal articles, and book chapters in these areas. A University Proctor and a former Head of the School of Law at the University of Canterbury (2015–18), Scott previously taught at the University of Nottingham in the United Kingdom.

Alexander S Skaridov

CAPT Alexander S Skaridov enlisted in the Russian Navy in 1977 and held various positions in the Pacific Fleet. In the late 1980s, he was assigned to the Mediterranean Command as a fleet exercise planner and staff legal adviser, and in 1985 he became a senior staff legal adviser to the Commanding Officer of the Black Sea Fleet. In 1986, Skaridov reported to the Command faculty of the International Law Chair of the Russian Naval Academy. He graduated from the Defense Language Institute in Lackland, Texas, in 1995, and from the Naval Command College in Newport, Rhode Island, in 1996. In early 1997, he was promoted to Chief of the International Law Chair of the Russian Naval Academy, making him the second-ranking attorney in the Russian Navy. Skaridov retired as a captain in 2001. For several years, beginning in 2000, he lectured at the Rhodes Academy of Oceans Law and Policy. From 2009, he was head of the Maritime Law faculty at the Admiral Makarov Maritime Academy. In 2015, he was appointed Rector of the State Polar Academy. Currently, Skaridov serves as the Chair of International Law and Maritime Law at the Admiral Makarov State University of Maritime and Inland Shipping in St Petersburg. He is the Editor-in-Chief of the journal *Ocean Management* and Director of the Maritime Law Agency (St Petersburg), a private law practice.

1

Introduction: Cultural Geography and the Law of the Sea

James Kraska and Hayoun Ryou-Ellison

1.1 What is meant by 'culture'?

This study focuses on the different cultural contributions to the formation and progressive development of the international law of the sea. Although this is the first attempt to explore the contours of cultural influences in oceans law and policy, the importance of culture has long been recognized as a central feature of other aspects of human development and an expression of the human experience. Culture makes us who we are and is our broadest category of identity as members of a group, beneath the level of our species.

The Constitution for the United Nations Educational, Scientific, and Cultural Organization (UNESCO) states that education, science, and culture contribute to peace and security and assist in furthering the rule of law.[1] UNESCO defines culture as the distinct spiritual, material, intellectual, and emotional features characterizing a society. It encompasses arts, lifestyle, human rights, value systems, traditions, and beliefs.[2] The widespread diffusion of culture is essential for building the rule of law and indispensable for the dignity of man.[3] The study of culture and associated ethnography is fundamental to understanding who we are as humans, how we engage in collective decision-making, and how we interpret the present and the past.

This book explores regional cultural differences and how they have affected and continue to shape the international law of the sea. Culture and ethnography are related concepts in anthropology, but they refer to different aspects

[1] Article 1(1) of the UNESCO Constitution (16 November 1945) states:

The purpose of the Organization is to contribute to peace and security by promoting collaboration among the nations through education, science and culture in order to further universal respect for justice, for the rule of law and for the human rights and fundamental freedoms which are affirmed for the peoples of the world, without distinction of race, sex, language or religion, by the Charter of the United Nations.

[2] UNESCO, 'About the Culture Sector' <www.unesco.org/en/culture/about> accessed 7 July 2024.

[3] UNESCO Constitution (n 1) preamble.

James Kraska and Hayoun Ryou-Ellison, *Introduction: Cultural Geography and the Law of the Sea* In: *Cultural Influences on the Law of the Sea*. Edited by: James Kraska and Hayoun Ryou-Ellison, Oxford University Press.
 DOI: 10.1093/9780198944140.003.0001

of understanding human societies. Culture refers to the shared beliefs, values, norms, behaviours, and symbols that characterize a particular group of people. It can encompass everything from language, religion, customs, traditions, and social institutions to material objects and artefacts. Culture is learned and transmitted from one generation to another, shaping the perceptions, behaviours, and interactions of individuals within a society. It is a broad concept that encapsulates the entire way of life of a group of people.

Lawrence Harrison and Samuel Huntington, in the foreword to their co-edited volume, *Culture Matters*, acknowledge different definitions of culture. They note that one conventional definition in most people's minds refers to 'the intellectual, musical, artistic, and literary products of a society, its "high culture"'.[4] They further note anthropologist Clifford Geertz's academically minded understanding of culture as 'the entire way of life of a society: its values, practices, symbols, institutions, and human relationships', characterized as the 'thick description' definition.[5]

Ethnography is a research methodology used by anthropologists and sociologists to study and understand cultures. It involves immersive fieldwork, where researchers directly observe and participate in the daily lives of the people they are studying. This often includes living among the people in a community, learning their language, participating in their rituals and activities, and documenting their behaviours, beliefs, and practices. Ethnographers aim to provide detailed descriptions and interpretations of cultural phenomena within specific social contexts. Ethnographic research typically results in detailed ethnographic texts or studies that offer insights into the complexities of human societies.

For the purpose of focusing on comparative patterns of human development across the world, as shaped and informed by these different worldviews, Harrison and Huntington focus their definition of culture on 'the values, attitudes, beliefs, orientations, and underlying assumptions prevalent among people in a society'.[6] In line with their definition, this introduction suggests that culture is a shared worldview, a set of interpretations of why things happen the way they do in society, and an array of behavioural norms regarding what to do and when. Also, there are different levels at which culture can be understood: the individual, organizational, national, and universal levels. We focus on culture at the regional or civilizational level. The chapters in this book

[4] Lawrence E Harrison and Samuel P Huntington (eds), *Culture Matters: How Values Shape Human Progress* (Basic Books 2000) xv.
[5] ibid.
[6] ibid.

explore differences among regional or civilizational groups and discern their *shared* expectations of how things should be done.

Many scholars have published on the influence of cultural values and worldviews on contrasting development patterns of societies. Over a century ago, German social scientist Max Weber observed that the Protestant Reformation had resulted in long-lasting divergences in work culture and motivations between Protestants and Catholics, as well as patterns of Jewish achievement.[7] In the 1960s, Daniel Patrick Moynihan (who would later serve as US Ambassador to India and to the United Nations before being elected senator from New York) produced a government report that caused unusually widespread debate in the public media regarding the role of family structure in citizen well-being.[8] Similarly, political sociologist Edward Banfield published an anonymized study of a town in southern Italy, documenting people's pathological social relationships and how these contributed to the south's poverty as contrasted with the material progress seen in the much more modernized north of the country.[9] A quarter-century later, political scientist Robert Putnam demonstrated how these same divergent social patterns produced disparate qualities of governance as the country went through a process of administrative decentralization.[10]

The end of the Cold War opened up the world to scholars and policy experts in a new way, giving rise to increased interest in comparisons between the patterns of national performance of different countries, and the period from the late twentieth through the early twenty-first centuries saw considerable growth in expertise on the role of cultural worldviews in conditioning such performance. At the time of the Asian financial crisis of the late 1990s, a bestselling work by economic historian David Landes refocused attention on the role of culture in economic growth, going far beyond Weber's smaller scope of analysis to look at the subject from a global perspective.[11] This detailed and lengthy work of economic historiography was followed a few years later by a much slimmer and more theoretically parsimonious volume by another economist, the Nobel laureate Douglass North, which laid out the framework for how successful

[7] Max Weber, *The Protestant Ethic and the Spirit of Capitalism* (first published 1904–05, Talcott Parsons tr, George Allen & Unwin 1930).

[8] Daniel Patrick Moynihan, *The Moynihan Report: The Negro Family—A Case for National Action* (first published 1965, Cosimo Reports 2018).

[9] Edward C Banfield with Laura Fasano Banfield, *The Moral Basis of a Backward Society* (The Free Press 1967).

[10] Robert D Putnam, *Making Democracy Work: Civic Traditions in Modern Italy* (Princeton UP 1993).

[11] David S Landes, *The Wealth and Poverty of Nations: Why Some Are So Rich and Some So Poor* (2nd edn, WW Norton 1999).

societies have been able to erect what he called the institutional 'scaffolds' necessary for sustained economic growth, with reflections on why not all societies have managed to achieve this.[12]

The foregoing works were all published by scholars who also worked on other subject matter. However, in the twenty-first century, several works would be published by specialists who devoted their entire policy and scholarly aims to the subject of the influence of culture on human social development. These have included Lawrence Harrison, a chief of mission for US Agency for International Development in Costa Rica, the Dominican Republic, Guatemala, Haiti, and Nicaragua; the Mexican Ambassador to the United States, Miguel Basáñez; and the latter's long-time research colleague, the leader of the World Values Survey, Ronald Inglehart. Building upon the works of Weber, Banfield, and Landes, Harrison's own body of work highlights not just the role of culture itself but also the importance of processes that kick-start progress-prone cultural change as a means of propelling a society forward.[13] Inglehart's work on the World Values Survey—which covers most of the world's population, with hundreds of survey questions per respondent going back to the late 1970s and early 1980s in order to track the underlying causes of changes in societies' values systems—has brought the analysis of culture into the realm of big data. It demonstrates that cultural values evolve within certain predictable parameters, but also that societies follow certain trajectories that they share in common with other countries from their same civilizational cluster.[14] Inglehart's work has garnered over one hundred thousand academic citations and won him a Johan Skytte Prize, the highest honour in political science. The culmination of a life's work alongside Inglehart has been Basáñez's synthesis of the various civilizational–cultural regions of the world under three umbrella categories: those cultures that prioritize attaining honour, maximizing personal achievement, or engaging in the pursuit of joy in making decisions about life's trade-offs.[15] In sum, these authors bring to bear a

[12] Douglass C North, *Understanding the Process of Economic Change* (Princeton UP 2005).

[13] See, for example, Lawrence E Harrison, *The Central Liberal Truth: How Politics Can Change a Culture and Save It from Itself* (OUP 2006); Lawrence E Harrison, *Jews, Confucians, and Protestants: Cultural Capital and the End of Multiculturalism* (Rowman & Littlefield 2013).

[14] See especially Ronald Inglehart, *Modernization and Postmodernization: Cultural, Economic, and Political Change in 43 Societies* (Princeton UP 1997); Ronald Inglehart and Christian Welzel, *Modernization, Cultural Change, and Democracy: The Human Development Sequence* (CUP 2005); Ronald F Inglehart, *Cultural Evolution: People's Motivations Are Changing, and Reshaping the World* (CUP 2018).

[15] Miguel E Basáñez (foreword by Ronald F Inglehart), *A World of Three Cultures: Honor, Achievement and Joy* (OUP 2016).

large body of evidence demonstrating the far-reaching power of cultural values in shaping the social, political, and economic outcomes of societies.

Drawing on an interdisciplinary understanding, our point of departure for the chapter contributions in this volume is that the interpretations by states of their own social history and practices fit patterns shared by fellow states within the same civilizational and cultural zone. In this book, we follow regional cultural definitions similar to those outlined in Huntington's classification of political culture in terms of civilizations on the basis of geography and history, as seen in his seminal work *The Clash of Civilizations and the Remaking of World Order*.[16] Huntington divided the world into the following civilizations: Western, Orthodox, Latin American, Hindu, greater Chinese (the Confucian Sinosphere), African, Buddhist, and Muslim. While there are countries that are predominantly Buddhist without a mixture of other major traditions (mainly in Southeast Asia) and Islamic countries, we did not include them explicitly for the sake of brevity and because their impact on global oceans law and policy has been more limited and their intellectual approaches and policy preferences are reflected in other civilizations.

In a slight departure from Huntington's civilization-based categories listed above, we divide the world into regions based on geographical considerations. Our regional categories are Western Europe, Eastern Europe, Russia, East Asia, South Asia, Africa, South America, North America, and Oceania. While religion is Huntington's key factor in understanding the nature of modern conflicts, our study on the influence of culture on the law of the sea is focused more on geography or shared historical legacies, such as hierarchies of social construction or colonization patterns, though there certainly is a logical overlap in the two approaches.

The regional cultural zones in our analysis are reflected in similar understandings that inform their own unique approaches to law and policy and tend to be consistent among states with a shared cultural worldview, as opposed to those from traditions outside the civilizational zone in question. For example, Western traditions have focused more on individuality and liberalism, whereas Eastern traditions have placed comparatively greater emphasis on group stability and social harmony. Furthermore, broader patterns are evident beyond their respective cultural spheres and are manifest in the Global North–South developmental dynamic.

[16] Samuel P Huntington, *The Clash of Civilizations and the Remaking of World Order* (2nd edn, Simon & Schuster 2011) 27–28.

The earlier work sets the stage for the first comparative study of these issues in the formation of the law of the sea and in oceans law and governance more broadly. The law is a form of discursive rationality based on clarification of the thought process of authoritative decision-making,[17] while culture is not purely rational in its origins. Culture serves as a key insight for answering otherwise puzzling questions about observable state behaviour patterns in the law of the sea, from geographic questions to process questions.

1.2 East and West

There are major cultural cleavages between East and West or, broadly speaking, between East Asian cultures and societies that arose from or are grounded in the cultures of Europe. Each of these cultures has produced cognitive traits that provide indicators reflected in the law of the sea. In order to grasp the major strands of thinking in the global law of the sea, we must understand the contributions and cognitive–cultural approaches embedded within the major contributions of influential civilizations. Cognitive processes are not necessarily universal, and there are natural limits to understanding the law of the sea from a single cultural ethnography.[18]

Cultural communities have arisen in major world civilizations, and their approach to the law of the sea is shaped by both their physical geography and the geography of the mind. As Richard E Nisbett has demonstrated, '[h]uman cognition is not everywhere the same'.[19] Members of different cultures differ in their fundamental beliefs about the nature of the world, and the characteristic thought processes of different groups vary widely.

People use cognitive tools that make sense to them in order to help make sense of the world, and these tools have shaped their approaches to the law of the sea. At a high level of generalization, the independent or individualistic nature of Western society views particular objects in isolation from their context. It supports a belief that we can know the rules governing objects and therefore control their behaviour.[20] This sense of individual identity emerged from a Greek perception of personal agency.[21] Personal freedom manifests in the

[17] Myres S McDougal and Trevor J Burke, *The Public Order of the Oceans: A Contemporary International Law of the Sea* (Yale UP 1987) 28.

[18] Richard E Nisbett and others, 'Culture and Systems of Thought: Holistic Versus Analytic Cognition' (2001) 108(2) Psychological Review 306.

[19] Richard E Nisbett, *The Geography of Thought: How Asians and Westerners Think Differently… and Why* (Free Press 2004) xvii.

[20] ibid.

[21] Nisbett and others (n 18) 292–93.

value of vigorous debate to solve problems.[22] Statistical analysis, cost–benefit analysis, formal logic, and other composite cognitive tools were constructed in the West on the basis of rules-based empirical observation.[23]

1.3 The peg that stands out is pounded down: cultural cognition in the East

Where the West emphasizes individual agency, in the East the emphasis is placed on social harmony. In China, Japan, and Korea, an individual is first and foremost a member of a collective, or rather several collectives—the clan, the village, and especially the family.[24] '[F]or Confucius I *am* my roles. Taken collectively, [the different roles] weave, for each of us, a unique pattern of personal identity, such that if some of my roles change, others will of necessity change also, literally making me a different person.'[25] This emphasis on collective rather than individual agency resulted in greater value being placed on group harmony.[26]

Contextual factors in relation to one another and a tendency to focus on relationships in a complex, interconnected world operate in a manner that is less deterministic and rules-based than in the West. East Asians tend to be holistic and comfortable when presented with contradictions of yin and yang. For example, if someone wants to construct a building, they might seek a feng shui master to take into account the positioning of the structure in relation to the altitude, sun, prevailing wind, proximity to water, and other geographical features.[27] While Westerners have a strong sense of rules and categorization, East Asians view objects more within their broader context.[28] This approach has evolved into more sophisticated dialectical notions of change, moderation, and relativism, as well as awareness of multiple viewpoints.[29] A seeming contradiction is unacceptable to Westerners but not to Easterners.[30] The typical East Asian approach does not mean that people feel like helpless pawns in the hands of their superiors and family members, but rather that they enjoy

[22] ibid 292.
[23] ibid 306.
[24] Nisbett (n 19) 5.
[25] Henry Rosemont, 'Rights-Bearing Individuals and Role-Bearing Persons' in Mary Bockover (ed), *Rules, Rituals, and Responsibility: Essays Dedicated to Herbert Fingarette* (Open Court 1991) 90.
[26] Nisbett and others (n 18) 292–93.
[27] Nisbett (n 19).
[28] ibid xvi.
[29] Nisbett and others (n 18) 306.
[30] ibid.

a sense of collective agency. The obligations between emperor and subject, parent and child, husband and wife, elder brother and younger brother, and friend and friend form a large and complex social organism with clear mutual obligations that guide ethical conduct.[31] Carrying out prescribed roles in an organized hierarchical system reflects each individual's stake or share in the community as a whole, in contrast to the Greek sense of personal liberty to do as one pleases.

In East Asia, the optimal approach is to be less concerned with personal goals or self-aggrandizement and more focused on group goals and coordinated action. Maintaining harmonious social relations is likely to be seen as preferential to achieving personal success, and success is valued as a group goal rather than a personal goal.[32] Patrick Gambrel and Rebecca Cianci argue that the Chinese have preferences that are different from those of Westerners, prioritizing collective identity over individual identity.[33] By applying Abraham Maslow's hierarchy of needs model, they found that, unlike the original model, which sees basic needs such as physiology, and then safety and security, social belonging, self-esteem, and self-actualization (individual development) as the ascending list of priorities to be built upon in moving up the pyramid of well-being, Chinese society perceives basic needs as social belonging first, and then the needs of physiology, safety and security, and, lastly, self-actualization (understood as being in service of society, rather than the individual self alone). The Chinese view of social belonging as the primary need, coming prior to any other needs, implies that if a person faces a potential conflict that can jeopardize his or her sense of social belonging, then efforts to avoid such conflict would be more intensely pursued than they would be in Western societies, where other needs come before that of social belonging.

The Western approach is evident in the most basic text of learning, the reading primer called *Dick and Jane*. Dick and Jane were two children who played, often with their dog named Spot. The book first appeared in the 1930s and was used well into the 1960s. It begins with these sentences: 'See Dick run. See Dick play. See Dick run and play.' The first page of a Chinese reading primer of the same era shows a little boy sitting on the shoulders of a bigger boy. It says: 'Big brother takes care of little brother. Big brother loves little brother. Little brother loves big brother.' Rather than individual action, the book begins with the relationship between two people.[34] This contextual or

[31] Nisbett (n 19).
[32] ibid.
[33] Patrick A Gambrel and Rebecca Cianci, 'Maslow's Hierarchy of Needs: Does It Apply in a Collectivist Culture?' (2003) 8(2) Journal of Applied Management and Entrepreneurship 143–61.
[34] Nisbett (n 19).

relational position is different from a merely logical orientation. As Nisbett and colleagues observe:[35]

> There is a long Western tradition—from the ancient Greeks, to the medieval Scholastics, to the propositional logic theoreticians of the late 19th and early 20th centuries—of analyzing argument structure apart from content and of reasoning on the basis of the underlying abstract propositions alone. Such a tradition has never been common in the East, where instead there has been an explicit disapproval of such decontextualizing practices and an emphasis on the appropriateness of plausibility and sense experience in evaluating propositions. Several studies suggest that East Asians do indeed rely less on formal logic and more on experiential knowledge in reasoning than do Americans—at any rate when logic and experience are in conflict.

The written Chinese language is pictographic in nature, which makes Chinese speakers 'tend to see the whole picture at once'. It is a language with a relatively high context culture, which implies several meanings even in a single word, such that it is less clearly defined or there may be more meanings. This makes Chinese culture one that is led by 'the indirect style of Chinese philosophy', in which 'aphorisms, apothegms, allusions, and illustrations' are common features in its language.[36]

The Western penchant for categorization helps to explain classes of events and the ability to form rules that govern things that are in the same class. The Greeks found it necessary to categorize objects in order to apply rules to them. In order to apply rules to the greatest array of objects, they began to generalize at higher and higher levels of abstraction.[37]

1.4 Ways to deal with conflicts

James Wall, Michael Blum, and Dengjian Jin find that mediation is a popular means of dispute resolution, and Bee Chen Goh argues that mediation is the preferred method of conflict resolution in China, with a long history of

[35] Nisbett and others (n 18) 301.

[36] Christine A Locke, *Chinese Methods of Interpersonal Conflict Management* (School of Advanced Military Studies, United States Army Command and General Staff College 2007) 23.

[37] Nisbett (n 19).

practice.[38] Goh argues that the Chinese think mediation makes people in conflicts less likely to be hurt by helping them avoid public shame, since the Chinese think *mianzi* (reputation saving) and *renqing* and *ganqing* (emotions and sentiments) are especially important in personal relationships. Mediators are respected members of the community with whom ordinary people find themselves comfortable and whom they respect, rather than strangers (as are judges in the courts). This view prefers to avoid formalized judicial processes as more painful than informal methods of conflict resolution. Not only the outcome but also the legal process itself is hurtful to people: therefore, reducing such conflict through the use of the least hurtful method—mediation—is preferred.

Goh argues that while mediation is found both in China and in Western society, the latter is focused on the vindication of personal justice, which is reflected in litigation. Seeking justice is the embedded value within individual rights. As individual rights need to be protected, the court is their ideal guardian. Justice—not compromise—is the goal, while for the Chinese the preferred outcome of mediation is the restoration of harmony: 'The formal law could perhaps achieve legal justice, but not social harmony.'[39] A large part of mediation occurs based on compromise rather than the calculation of costs and benefits.

1.5 Goal-setting

These differences are further manifest in differences in perception across civilizations. Among Asians, there is a strong tendency to look at many different aspects of a situation and determine the potential consequences of alternative solutions. Nisbett's *The Geography of Thought* captures how the Eastern approach differs from the much more goal-oriented approach by which Americans decide in advance a preferred conclusion and then move forward in a highly effective manner to make their desired goal a reality. The shortfall of the Asian approach is that it is easy to get bogged down in the details and in 'what if' thinking. The weakness of the Western approach is that action is often taken without thorough consideration of the full range of potential consequences.

[38] James A Wall Jr, Michael Blum, and Dengjian Jin, 'Response to Diamant's "Conflict and Conflict Resolution in China"' (2000) 44(4) Journal of Conflict Resolution 547; Bee Chen Goh, *Law Without Lawyers, Justice Without Courts: On Traditional Chinese Mediation* (Routledge 2016).

[39] Goh (n 38) 113.

1.6 North and South

Furthermore, North–South cultural cleavages were also significant in shaping the negotiations for the UN Convention on the Law of the Sea (UNCLOS)[40] beginning in the 1970s, and they still resonate today. The nations of the Global South—consisting of countries in Africa, Latin America, the Caribbean, and much of Asia—have influenced the law of the sea in ways shaped by their cultural perspectives, historical experiences, and socio-economic realities. Many countries in the Global South were formerly colonized by European powers, which shaped their perspectives on sovereignty and territorial integrity. The struggle for independence and self-determination influenced how these states relate to maritime boundaries, offshore resources, and maritime security. Their experiences have contributed to the development of principles of sovereignty and equitable access to marine resources in international law. In many cultures of the Global South, there is a strong tradition of communal ownership and stewardship of natural resources, including marine resources. Indigenous and traditional communities often possess valuable knowledge and practices related to sustainable fishing, marine conservation, and maritime navigation. These cultural perspectives have influenced discussions on sustainable development, Indigenous rights, and the protection of traditional knowledge in the law of the sea.

States in the Global South have long advocated for more equitable distribution of benefits from marine resources by taking positions that maximize their access to and benefits from natural resources in areas beyond national jurisdiction and then advocating policies that leverage the wealth in those areas for the benefit of developing states. In the past, they emphasized the importance of ensuring that developing countries have access to and benefit from high seas fisheries, deep seabed mineral mining, and, more recently, marine genetic resources. This approach has prompted the establishment of mechanisms for benefit-sharing and technology transfer in international agreements.

Because of their claimed affinity with, or close relationship to, the natural environment, states in the Global South are particularly vulnerable to the impacts of climate change and environmental degradation, including rising sea levels, ocean acidification, and the loss of biodiversity. As a result, they generally seek strong measures to protect the marine environment and mitigate climate change within the framework of the law of the sea. The cultural values of stewardship and respect for nature have informed their positions on issues

[40] UN Convention on the Law of the Sea, 10 December 1982, 1833 UNTS 397 (UNCLOS).

such as marine pollution, marine protected areas, and sustainable fisheries management. In pursuing their development goals, the affected states recognize strength in numbers and emphasize the principles of solidarity, cooperation, and mutual assistance in international relations. This perspective has influenced their approach to maritime governance, leading to calls for enhanced cooperation, capacity-building, and technology transfer to support sustainable development and maritime security in the region. These views are expressed unilaterally, at the regional level, and in global negotiations. Regional organizations in the Global South include the African Union, the Association of Southeast Asian Nations, and the Organization of American States.

1.7 Africa as an element of the Global South

The positions of Africa and the West provide a helpful lens through which to view how this dynamic has unfolded over the past half century. Despite recently having emerged from colonialism, Africa held outsized influence on the negotiations at the Third UN Conference on the Law of the Sea (1973–82). Africa was especially influential in creating the regime of the exclusive economic zone and the regime of the deep seabed. The idea that the mineral resources of the deep seabed, or international seabed area, are the common heritage of mankind was derived from Africa's emphasis on communal ownership of property by a village, community, or family under native law and custom.[41]

During the negotiations, the First Committee was chaired by Paul Bamela Engo, an African from Cameroon, and it had responsibility for crafting the governance architecture of deep seabed mining beyond national jurisdiction. Speaking before the Third Conference convened, Engo said: 'Absolute sovereignty is anachronistic in this age of universal desperation in the quest for meaningful and lasting peace.'[42] In arguing for a new approach to seabed mining that accommodated the interests of all humans, he claimed the inevitability of the arc of history and normative authority:[43]

> It would be folly for any nation to fail to recognize the writing on the wall. The illusions of power—which some mistake for the bases of virtue—have

[41] Edwin Egede, *Africa and the Deep Seabed Regime: Politics and International Law of the Common Heritage of Mankind* (Springer 2011) 241.

[42] Paul Bamela Engo, 'Current International Issues Relating to the Law of the Sea' (1971) 4 Natural Resources Lawyer 622, 623.

[43] ibid 623–24.

> more dangerous consequences today. . . . The arrival of new nations on the international scene cannot be ignored. Their numbers, together with the vast areas they occupy, and the vastness of their untapped resources (both human and material), completely alter the character of the magnitude of the problems of the international community.

African states sought not only joint management but also joint ownership of the international seabed area and its resources under the concept of the common heritage of mankind.[44] Similarly, they advocated for the mandatory transfer of marine technology in Parts XI and XIV of UNCLOS, which are consonant with the traditional African outlook that innovation should not be credited to a single inventor, but rather intellectual property rights inure to the community as a whole.[45] These African cultural norms depart from Western standards of individualism and private ownership of land and technology. Furthermore, cultural as well as material characteristics underpin negotiating positions in the law of the sea. For example, Engo asked: 'Why must we adopt industrial advancement as a basis of awarding privileged seats of decision-making, such as the Council of the International Seabed Authority, when the potential for economic strength is equally valid?'.[46]

The influence of Africa became more evident in the intergovernmental conference sessions to negotiate an international legally binding instrument under UNCLOS and on the conservation and sustainable use of the marine biological diversity of areas lying beyond national jurisdiction.[47] The final agreements concerning marine genetic resources, the fair and equitable sharing of benefits derived from those resources, and the transfer of marine technology include special dispensation for developing state parties, particularly coastal African states.[48]

1.8 Theory versus practice

Although it may be apocryphal, Yogi Berra is credited with the quip 'In theory there is no difference between theory and practice—in practice there is.' This

[44] Egede (n 41) 241.
[45] ibid 89–98.
[46] Engo (n 42) 623–24.
[47] Agreement Under the United Nations Convention on the Law of the Sea on the Conservation and Sustainable Use of Marine Biological Diversity of Areas Beyond National Jurisdiction, UN Doc A/CONF.232/2023/4* (19 June 2023).
[48] ibid arts 9, 17, 27, 40, 41, 52.

highlights another distinction between East and West. In the East, scientific advances were connected more to practicality than to scientific theory and investigation. The embodiment of the Western height of scientific enquiry has been discovery for its theoretical sake in the form of basic research, which was even foreshadowed in ecclesiastical debates by medieval scholastics about how many angels can dance on the head of a pin. Such arcane intellectual speculation was a theoretical trope for the power of God to add an infinite number of angels in a finite world if He were indeed all-powerful.[49]

This approach is also evident in debates within Cartesian rationalism on the emergence of the scientific method and the pursuit of basic science. Cartesian rationalism is focused on the innate value of enquiry and reason springing forth from the human mind. This curiosity contributed to, or even produced, the 'fields of physics, astronomy, axiomatic geometry, formal logic, rational philosophy, natural history, history and ethnography'.[50] While ancient Mayan, Mesopotamian, and Egyptian civilizations made systematic observations about the natural world and science, only the Greeks attempted to model these observations in a manner that presumed their underlying physical causes.[51] In the Confucian tradition of East Asia, there was no value in exploring knowledge that did not entail 'some consequence for action'.[52]

In the East and West, these differences have been apparent for millennia and are impervious to change. Globalization has worked on the margins to ameliorate the sharp cultural divisions, although their persistence is remarkable. In Japan, for example, the adoption of individualistic capitalism has been adapted to the local culture and has had less effect on many enduring socio-cultural practices than might have been anticipated.[53]

While these differences are real and evident, humans from all cultures still share common experiences and are motivated by the same biological impulses. As Europe reverted to being primarily agricultural with the collapse of the Western Roman Empire and the onset of the Middle Ages, it became less individualistic. European peasants had shared experiences with Asian peasants in that they were the lower participants in a system of daily life that lacked freedom or personal autonomy.[54]

[49] Natasha Lushetich, 'How Many Angels Can Dance on the Head of a Pin? Understanding "Alien" Thought' (2022) 37 AI & Society 1411.
[50] Nisbett and others (n 18) 292.
[51] ibid.
[52] DJ Munro, *The Concept of Man in Early China* (Stanford UP 1969) 55.
[53] Nisbett and others (n 18) 306.
[54] Nisbett (n 19).

1.9 International human rights law

Scholars are only beginning to unpack the cultural dimensions of international law-making and norm creation. The relationship between culture and international law has not been examined closely, except in the field of human rights.[55] However, 'Culture lies at the heart of international law. The international community comprises culturally diverse countries, and international law governs relations among states and civilisations.'[56] 'The relationship between law and culture is rooted in values. This connection is underlined by the phrase—*ius est ars boni et aequi*—used by the ancient Romans, which means law is the art of goodness and justice. If law was an art, it has certainly also been an element of the culture.'[57]

In this case, we may debate whether cultural relativism and universal rules are inconsistent. The 1993 Vienna Conference on Human Rights in its declaration and program of action stated that, in accordance with the Charter of the United Nations, international law, and international human rights treaties, the universal nature of human rights and fundamental freedoms is 'beyond question.'[58] Nonetheless, this area of law has regional and national peculiarities. In this regard, China and Singapore have asserted that Asian values produce a distinct version of human rights law.

1.10 Protection of the marine environment

Similarly, Roda Mushkat has examined how Asian cultural values interact with international environmental law. In this respect, global norms and Asian values mostly converge in striving to protect the natural environment.[59] Westerners believe more in the controllability of the environment than Easterners. The two groups also disagree on tacit assumptions about stability and change, with Westerners seeing stability as valuable, whereas Easterners see change as inevitable. These two groups also have different experiences with dialectical approaches, with Easterners being inclined to seek a middle ground when

[55] Ved P Nanda, 'Foreword' in Roda Mushkat, *International Environmental Law and Asian Values: Legal Norms and Cultural Influences* (University of British Columbia Press 2004) ix.

[56] Valentina Vadi, *Cultural Heritage in International Economic Law* (Brill Nijhoff 2023) ch 1.

[57] Tamar Frankel and Tomasz Braun, 'Law and Culture' (2023) 101 Boston University Law Review Online 157, 160 <https://scholarship.law.bu.edu/faculty_scholarship/3560> accessed 7 July 2024.

[58] UN General Assembly, Vienna Declaration and Programme of Action, UN Doc A/CONF.157/23 (12 July 1993) par I.1.

[59] Roda Mushkat, 'Culture and International Law: Universalism v. Relativism' (2002) 6(2) Singapore Journal of International & Comparative Law 1028.

confronted with apparent contradictions. At the same time, Westerners are more inclined to insist on the correctness of one belief over another.[60]

The oceans are facing a cascade of threats to the marine environment, increasing naval risks, and growing economic uncertainties surrounding international maritime shipping. Addressing these challenges requires a continual focus on collective action, which necessarily involves an engagement with, and often working through a clash of, the cultural visions that inform our interpretations of the international law of the sea and the structure of oceans governance.

[60] Nisbett (n 19); Nisbett and others (n 18).

2
Western Europe

Robin Churchill

2.1 Introduction

On the banks of the River Tagus, a few kilometres downstream from the centre of Lisbon, stands a stone structure in the shape of the prow of a caravel, the sailing ship developed by the Portuguese in the fifteenth century for the purpose of exploring distant waters. This structure is the Padrão dos Descobrimentos, the Monument of the Discoveries. On it are statues of some of Portugal's most notable maritime explorers, including Pedro Álvares Cabral (the first European to discover Brazil), Bartolomeu Dias (the first European to round the Cape of Good Hope), Ferdinand Magellan (the first person to circumnavigate the Earth), and Vasco da Gama (the discoverer of the sea route from Europe to India via the Cape of Good Hope). It was the consequence of this Portuguese seafaring—in particular, the growth of the lucrative spice trade with the East Indies and the rivalry engendered thereby with other European seafaring nations, notably England, the Netherlands, and Spain—that was a major catalyst for the development of the law of the sea in Western Europe.

While seafaring prowess may have been a spur to that development, the form that the latter took was due, at least in part, to broader cultural influences. The aim of this chapter is to examine how those influences helped to shape the development of the law of the sea in Western Europe. The chapter does not consider—except in passing in Section 2.3.5—the influence of Western European culture on the interpretation of the substantive rules of the law of the sea. That would be a very different exercise and would require a different framework of discussion from that used in this chapter. In carrying out its aim, the chapter takes a broad view of what constitutes culture,[1] considering it to include legal, political, and economic philosophy; ideas about the role of science and the scientific method; religion; and language.[2]

[1] cf the discussion of 'culture' in Section 1.1 of this book.

[2] For a similarly broad view of culture, see Alison Dundes Renteln, 'Cultural Bias in International Law' (1998) 92 American Society of International Law Proceedings 232, 233.

Robin Churchill, *Western Europe* In: *Cultural Influences on the Law of the Sea*. Edited by: James Kraska and Hayoun Ryou-Ellison, Oxford University Press. © Robin Churchill 2025. DOI: 10.1093/9780198944140.003.0002

For the purposes of this chapter, Western Europe is taken to be that part of the European continent (including its offshore islands, such as the British Isles) to the west of the former Iron Curtain, which ran from the terminus of the border between East and West Germany on the Baltic Sea to the border between Italy and the former Yugoslavia on the coast of the Adriatic Sea.

Following this introduction, the chapter is divided into two broad parts. The first (Section 2.2) considers whether there is a common Western European culture, as the discussion thus far has rather assumed, and, if so, what its characteristics are. The second (Section 2.3) attempts to identify a number of aspects of the development of the law of the sea where the influence of Western European culture can be discerned. It should be stressed at the outset that in undertaking this enterprise, it is difficult to disentangle cultural influences from more obvious political, economic, and military influences. Indeed, Western European states were able to impose many of their cultural values on the international community and the law of the sea, especially in the eighteenth and nineteenth centuries, because of their political, economic, and military superiority and as a result of their colonization of much of the non-European world. However, over time, it has become increasingly difficult to distinguish Western European (cultural) influence from Western influence more generally. For that reason, this chapter focuses on Western European cultural influences on the development of the law of the sea during the period between the beginning of the sixteenth century—when a recognizably modern system of states began to emerge in Western Europe[3] and discussion of the legal status of the sea by Western scholars was beginning to take place—and the Hague Codification Conference of 1930.[4] Thereafter, Western European states became an increasingly small minority in the international community, largely because of decolonization. Their influence accordingly waned and largely merged with that of other Western states.

One drawback with a chapter that focuses on Western European cultural influences on the law of the sea is that it feeds into the dominant Eurocentric narrative of the history and development of the law of the sea,[5] when there are

[3] By the early sixteenth century, a majority of Western European coastal nations (Denmark–Norway, England, France, Portugal, Scotland, Spain, and Sweden) would have fulfilled the Montevideo criteria of statehood, had they then existed. The exceptions were Belgium, Ireland, and the Netherlands (all under foreign rule, although the Netherlands became independent by the latter part of the sixteenth century) and the numerous polities of what are now Germany and Italy, which did not become united in single states until the 1870s.

[4] For that reason, nothing is said in this chapter about environmentalism as a possible Western cultural attribute. Environmentalism in its modern form, as distinct from a love of the natural world, developed in Western Europe only in the 1960s.

[5] For modern examples of a Eurocentric narrative, see, for example, David J Bederman, 'The Sea' in Bardo Fassbender and Anne Peters (eds), *The Oxford Handbook of the History of International Law*

other narratives.[6] Hopefully, this apparent bias will be offset by other chapters in this book.

2.2 Is there a common Western European culture?

It is widely accepted, although not uncontested, that there has been a common culture in Western Europe, at least among educated elites (from whose ranks scholars and policymakers on the law of the sea have been drawn), since at least the sixteenth century.[7] The roots of that common culture lie in the shared heritage of the civilizations of Greece and Rome and a predominant religion, Christianity.

The ancient Greeks were an intensely questioning, reasoning, and analytical people. They laid the foundations of Western moral and political philosophy and made seminal contributions to the study of mathematics, astronomy, and medicine. The Romans, although they absorbed much of Greek culture, appear to have been very different people, less interested in abstract thought and more practically minded. They emphasized the importance of law, which applied equally to all free men throughout the Roman Empire, and good administration. The Romans gradually expanded their rule through conquest beyond central Italy. For more than 400 years, the Roman Empire included not only the whole of Italy but also modern-day Belgium, England, France, Portugal, Spain, and the southern Netherlands. The Roman Empire in Western Europe collapsed in the fifth century, following invasion by Germanic peoples. In the succeeding centuries, there was little interest in the culture of the Greeks and Romans in Western Europe. However, that culture survived in the Eastern Empire until the capture of Constantinople by the Turks in 1453. Much of Greek culture and learning was also preserved in the Islamic world.

(OUP 2013) 359–79; Tullio Scovazzi, 'The Evolution of International Law of the Sea: New Issues, New Challenges' (2000) 286 Recueil des cours 39, especially at 53–87; Tullio Treves, 'Historical Development of the Law of the Sea' in Donald R Rothwell and others (eds), *The Oxford Handbook of the Law of the Sea* (OUP 2015) 1–23.

[6] See, for example, CH Alexandrowicz, *The Law of Nations in Global History* (OUP 2017) chs 6–8; RP Anand, *Origin and Development of the Law of the Sea* (Martinus Nijhoff 1983); RP Anand, 'Law of the Sea in Historical Perspective' (lecture, Xiamen Academy of International Law, China, September 2006); Erdem Denk, 'An Amodernist Approach to International Law: The Law of the Sea in the Armana Letters' in Jacques Hartmann and Urfan Khaliq (eds), *The Achievements of International Law: Essays in Honour of Robin Churchill* (Hart 2021) 21–47.

[7] Peter Rietbergen, *Europe: A Cultural History* (4th edn, Routledge 2021) xxxii–xlv. Much of the earlier part of Section 2.2 is based on chapters 2–8, 10, and 12 of Rietbergen's book.

Two aspects of Roman culture that did survive the collapse of the Roman Empire in the West were its language, Latin, and its religion, Christianity, which became the dominant and then the official religion of the Empire during the fourth century. Latin was a lingua franca among educated people in most of Western Europe until at least the first half of the seventeenth century. It was the sole language of the Bible until translations into vernacular European languages began to be made from the late fourteenth century onwards. Almost all the early works on the law of the sea, until the early eighteenth century, were written in Latin. The main languages spoken in Southern Europe—French, Italian, Portuguese, and Spanish—are all based on Latin, and in the remaining, mainly Germanic, languages of Western Europe, there are many words of Latin origin.

From its earliest beginnings in Rome, Christianity gradually spread outwards and became the dominant religion throughout Western Europe, although it took almost a millennium to be fully embraced by the whole of Western Europe. Until the sixteenth century, Christianity in Western Europe was united in the Catholic Church, headed by the Pope, and governed by canon law. The latter, largely based on Roman law, helped to preserve and promote the Roman emphasis on the importance of law and good administration through the centuries of the so-called Dark Ages, when it had little significance for secular society. However, the dominance of the Catholic Church ended when Martin Luther challenged many of its practices in his *Ninety-Five Theses*, published in 1517. That led fairly rapidly to a permanent schism in Western Christianity, between Catholicism (predominant in Southern Europe) and Protestantism (predominant in Northern Europe). In Protestant countries, the church was much less powerful than in Catholic Europe. This allowed a more liberal and questioning society to flourish in Northern Europe that proved to be especially important in the development of science and economics. Nevertheless, common to both religious halves of Europe was the Bible, on which many of the early writers on international law, including the law of the sea, drew and which strongly influenced ideas of natural law.

Other aspects of Greek and Roman culture were gradually reintroduced into Western Europe. In part, this was due to the Moors (Islamic by religion, North African by ethnicity), who, to varying extents, ruled the Iberian Peninsula between 711 and 1492, and Sicily and the southern part of mainland Italy between 827 and 1224, and brought with them the knowledge of Greek culture that had been preserved in the Islamic world.[8] In addition, from the thirteenth

[8] ibid 149–52, 202–04, 241, 408; Bertrand Russell, *History of Western Philosophy* (George Allen & Unwin 1961) 267–68.

century onwards, a growing interest in the culture of the ancient world was a prominent feature of the Renaissance.

The development of a common European culture was facilitated by the dissemination of knowledge and ideas throughout Western Europe in various ways.[9] From around the thirteenth century, there was a substantial development in university education in Western Europe and students and scholars began to study in universities outside their home country. Handwritten books, obviously very limited in number, were gradually replaced by books produced by mass printing, following the invention of the printing press by Johann Gutenberg around the mid-fifteenth century.[10] Culture was also disseminated by travel, especially along trade routes. For example, Albrecht Dürer (1471–1528), who was not only an outstanding artist but also an astute businessman, sold multiple prints of his woodcuts and engravings by utilizing the trade routes passing through his home city of Nuremberg and leading to many of the major European cities.[11] Other means of cultural dissemination included exchanges of diplomatic missions (which 300–400 years ago were much larger than they are today) and royal marriages. European monarchs, for reasons of politics rather than love, commonly chose a spouse from another European royal family. The new spouse and their entourage often infused new cultural influences into their adopted country. European culture was disseminated not only within Europe but also beyond, through the colonization by Western European states of much of the rest of the world and the practice of elites from many of those (former) colonies pursuing their tertiary education in Western Europe.

What, then, are the specific characteristics of this common Western European culture that have been relevant to the development of the law of the sea from the sixteenth century onwards? A first characteristic, inherited from the Romans, has been a strong belief in the importance of law and good administration. Translated to the law of the sea, this has meant an emphasis on activities at sea being regulated by common rules and not subject to a state of anarchy.

Related to the European belief in the importance of law and good administration is a common political culture, whose essential features are a commitment to democracy, the rule of law, and the protection of human rights. This is a culture of relatively recent origin. Although its roots go back three or four

[9] See further Rietbergen (n 7) 199–206, 349–81.

[10] Gutenberg's invention occurred separately from, and was superior to, the then existing means of printing in China and Korea.

[11] Neil MacGregor, *Germany: Memories of a Nation* (Penguin Books 2016) 305–09.

centuries, this political culture did not fully exist in any Western European state until the late nineteenth century, and not in Western Europe as a whole until the 1970s, when the dictatorships in Portugal and Spain were overthrown and women obtained the right to vote in Switzerland. While Western European political culture has had a degree of influence on some other branches of international law, notably international human rights law, it has had no discernible influence on the law of the sea—except perhaps that a belief in the rule of law at the national level has translated into rules of state responsibility and dispute settlement at the international level, including Part XV of the UN Convention on the Law of the Sea (UNCLOS).[12] While the latter may reflect Western European legal and political culture, it is the product of the influence of many different groups of states, not just those of Western Europe.[13]

A rather different aspect of Western European culture that has been important for the development of the law of the sea has been a profound interest in science and the scientific method. Modern science, which has been described as empirically gained knowledge based on critical observation and rational experimentation, allied with 'great boldness in framing hypotheses',[14] originated in Western Europe during the seventeenth century.[15] Up until the sixteenth century, the sum of scientific knowledge in Western Europe was not much greater than that of the ancient Greeks. However, during the seventeenth century, groundbreaking discoveries were made in nearly all branches of science, mathematics, and medicine, aided by the invention of numerous scientific instruments such as the microscope, the telescope, and the barometer.[16] Although addressed specifically to Isaac Newton, Alexander Pope's famous couplet epigrammatically captures the essence of the seventeenth-century scientific revolution in Western Europe:[17]

> Nature, and Nature's laws lay hid in night:
> God said, *Let Newton be!* and all was light.

Bertrand Russell puts it rather more prosaically: 'the outlook of educated men was completely transformed' during the seventeenth century. In 1600, it was 'largely medieval'; by 1700, it was 'completely modern'. Furthermore,

[12] UN Convention on the Law of the Sea, 10 December 1982, 1833 UNTS 397 (UNCLOS).
[13] AO Adede, *The System for Settlement of Disputes Under the United Nations Convention on the Law of the Sea* (Martinus Nijhoff 1987).
[14] Russell (n 8) 514.
[15] ibid 512; Rietbergen (n 7) 272.
[16] For details, see Russell (n 8) 512–22.
[17] Alexander Pope, 'Epitaph: Intended for Sir Isaac Newton' (1730).

science led to the 'reign of law' taking 'its hold of men's imagination'.[18] The development of modern science in Western Europe during the seventeenth century coincided with the relative decline of an interest in science in that other great culture of the time, China.[19] After 1700, major scientific discoveries continued to be made almost uniquely in Western Europe until well into the nineteenth century. With its emphasis on the importance of close observation of what actually occurs, the scientific method that developed in Western Europe has also encouraged evidence-based policymaking and, in the field of international law, the collection and critical analysis of state practice by academics when seeking to formulate rules of customary international law.

A further aspect of a common European culture has been in the field of economics. Since at least the beginning of the Industrial Revolution in the eighteenth century, capitalism, which originated in Western Europe (exactly where and when is disputed), has been its dominant economic philosophy, although tempered since the early twentieth century, to varying degrees, by the welfare state and social democracy, as well as being challenged by other economic ideas and models, such as Marxism (itself of European origin) and environmentalism. Western European states also exported their philosophy of capitalism to their colonies in many parts of the world. Capitalism has left its mark on the law of the sea, as explained in Section 2.3.4.

A highly regrettable feature of Western European culture has been its belief until well into the twentieth century, and even today by no means extinct, that Europeans are superior to other peoples—or, to put it bluntly, its racism. That is illustrated, if illustration were needed, by the treatment of the native populations of the territories that Western European states conquered and colonized, engaging at times in what today would be labelled and condemned as genocide, and the barbaric practice of slavery and the slave trade. That belief in European superiority has had a profound impact on the development of international law. After the Congress of Vienna (1814–15), held at the conclusion of the Napoleonic Wars, international law became Eurocentric, 'the preserve of the civilised, Christian States, into which overseas and foreign nations could enter only with the consent of and on the conditions laid down by the Western powers', and 'a reflection of European values'.[20] That position

[18] Russell (n 8) 522. Russell's gendered language is to be expected from a person of his time (he was born in 1872), but it is no doubt the case that the overwhelming majority of educated people during the seventeenth century were men.

[19] Rietbergen (n 7) 272.

[20] Malcolm N Shaw, *International Law* (6th edn, CUP 2008) 27. See also Anand, *Origin and Development* (n 6) 135–37; Martti Koskenniemi, 'International Law in the World of Ideas' in James Crawford and Martti Koskenniemi (eds), *The Cambridge Companion to International Law* (CUP 2012) 54.

could be maintained due to the extraordinary economic and military power of Western European states and their colonial domination of much of the rest of the world during the nineteenth century. It was ended only by the First World War and the establishment of the League of Nations in its aftermath. The Eurocentricity of international law until the 1920s meant that in the development of customary international law, the practice of non-European (or at least non-Western) states was largely ignored. That is particularly important, as far as the law of the sea is concerned, because before 1958 its basic rules were contained only in customary international law.

Western European society was not only racist but also patriarchal until the late twentieth century. In that it was not unique. Most non-European societies have also been patriarchal. Insofar as the law of the sea has a gender bias in favour of men, as some have argued,[21] Western Europe's patriarchal culture must have influenced that bias. However, that is not an influence that can be solely attributed to Western Europe; it is due to the influence of the majority of states.

In some ways, it is remarkable that a common European culture, at least among elites, developed and has persisted and thrived, given that between the beginning of the sixteenth century, when the modern Western European state system was coming into existence, and 1945, Western European states engaged in frequent and protracted wars with each other.[22] Although there has been no conflict in Western Europe since 1945, some Western European states, notably France and the United Kingdom, have frequently used force in other parts of the world. One could say that the use of military force as an instrument of policy, albeit nowadays subject to the constraints of the UN Charter (which has often been rather broadly interpreted), is also a feature of Western European culture. It is not, however, evident that this has translated into a distinctly Western European influence on the law of the sea. While it is true that the militarily strongest Western Europe states have pressed for guaranteed passage rights for warships, and the United Kingdom successfully gained support for that position by instituting proceedings in the *Corfu Channel* case in 1947,[23] at the First and Third UN Conferences on the Law of the Sea, their influence was subsumed in that of militarily stronger states, namely the United States and, at the Third Conference, the then Soviet Union.

[21] See, for example, most of the contributions in Irini Papanicolopulu (ed), *Gender and the Law of the Sea* (Brill 2019). The merits or otherwise of that argument lie far beyond the compass of this chapter.

[22] Notable examples include the Thirty Years War (1618–48), the Franco-Dutch War (1672–78), the War of the Grand Alliance (1688–97), the War of Spanish Succession (1701–14), the War of Austrian Succession (1740–48), the Seven Years War (1756–63), the Napoleonic Wars (1803–15), and the First (1914–18) and Second (1939–45) World Wars—both of which originated in Western Europe.

[23] *Corfu Channel (United Kingdom v Albania) (Judgment)* [1949] ICJ Rep 4.

2.3 The influence of Western European culture on the law of the sea

In this section, the influence on the development of the international law of the sea of some of the features of Western European culture identified in Section 2.2 is discussed in more detail. Those features include two aspects of the legal culture ultimately derived from Roman law, namely codification and the legal status of the sea; the role of science and the scientific method; the influence of capitalism; and language.

2.3.1 Codification of the law of the sea

One of the notable features of the law of the sea has been the attempts at its periodic codification: first, but unsuccessfully, at the Hague Codification Conference in 1930 and then, and more successfully, at the First (1958) and Third (1973–82) UN Conferences on the Law of the Sea. Western European legal culture has had a discernible influence on this process.

The idea of codifying law dates back to the Roman Empire. From time to time, Roman law was codified, most notably by Gaius in the mid-second century[24] and Justinian in 533 CE.[25] In Western Europe, influenced by Roman law and probably also by eighteenth-century rationalism and the European 'Age of Enlightenment', codification of the law began in the latter part of the eighteenth century, with the adoption of codes in Bavaria (1756) and Prussia (1794). Most notable was the Code Napoléon (or, as it was officially known, the Code Civil des Français), adopted in 1804. That Code was a significant influence in many other European states, especially those with civil law systems (ie based on Roman law), which proceeded to engage in codification throughout the nineteenth century.

The desirability of codifying international law developed in the late nineteenth century, when it was widely believed that such codification would promote international peace and security by clarifying international law, thereby removing possible causes of friction and enhancing its authority.[26] Early proposals for codification were made by private bodies and individuals. The two most important bodies were the International Law Association (ILA) and

[24] In the *Institutes*, published around 161 CE.
[25] In the *Corpus Juris Civilis*.
[26] James Harrison, *Making the Law of the Sea* (CUP 2011) 28.

the Institut de Droit International (IDI), both founded in 1873 in Belgium, at Brussels and Ghent respectively.[27] Their early membership was dominated by Western Europeans. In the case of the ILA (whose official title until 1895 was the Association for the Reform and Codification of International Law), its objective was, and remains, the 'study, clarification and development of international law, both public and private'. The ILA's early work devoted to codification focused largely on issues of private international law (including a good deal of maritime law), but it adopted in 1895 Rules on Jurisdiction in Territorial Waters and in 1926 a Draft Convention on Maritime Jurisdiction in Time of Peace.[28]

The aim of the IDI was to 'favour the progress of international law' and to aid 'any serious attempt at gradual and progressive codification'.[29] As far as its early work on the law of the sea is concerned, the IDI produced a declaration on the high seas in 1927.[30]

Intergovernmental moves to codify international law did not really begin until the Second Peace Conference, held at The Hague in 1907. Several of the leading participants at the Conference were from Western Europe. In its Final Act, the Conference called for the convening of a third conference, for which a preparatory committee should ascertain 'what subjects are ripe for embodiment in an international regulation'.[31] The outbreak of the First World War in 1914 put a stop to the arrangements for the third conference that were then being made. Instead, in 1924, the League of Nations established a Committee of Experts for the Progressive Codification of International Law. That Committee—9 of whose 17 members, including its chairman, were from Western Europe[32]—was charged with preparing a list of subjects 'the regulation of which by international agreement would seem to be most desirable and realizable', and thereafter examining the comments of governments on the list and reporting on the questions that were 'sufficiently ripe', as well as on the procedure to be followed in preparing for conferences 'for their solution'.[33] The Committee studied four law-of-the-sea topics—territorial waters, the status

[27] On the establishment of these two bodies, see Irwin Abrams, 'The Emergence of the International Law Societies' (1957) 19 Journal of Politics 361.

[28] 'List of ILA Conferences 1873–2016' <https://www.ila-hq.org/en_GB/documents/ila-conferences-1873-2016> accessed 28 November 2024.

[29] As quoted by Abrams (n 27) 375.

[30] C John Colombos, *The International Law of the Sea* (6th edn, Longmans 1967) 64–65.

[31] Final Act of the Second Peace Conference, The Hague, 18 October 1907.

[32] For a list of the Committee's members, see the letter of 1 April 1925 from the Director of the Legal Section of the League of Nations to the President of the American Society of International Law, reprinted in (1926) 20(special supp 3) American Journal of International Law 1.

[33] Resolution of the Assembly of the League of Nations of 22 September 1924, reprinted in (1926) 20(special supp 3) American Journal of International Law 12.

of state-owned ships engaged in international commerce, piracy, and the exploitation of marine resources—but found that only the first of them was 'sufficiently ripe' for codification.[34]

The codification conference envisaged in the resolution of the Assembly of the League of Nations was held at The Hague in 1930. The regime of territorial waters was one of the three topics considered at the conference, along with two non-law-of-the-sea topics. Before the conference took place, its Preparatory Committee produced 'Bases of Discussion' and a set of proposals for consideration. However, during the conference—at which 17 of the 48 participating states were from Western Europe—no convention relating to territorial waters was concluded, mainly because of disagreement over the breadth of such waters and whether a state could claim a contiguous zone beyond them.[35] Nevertheless, the conference did produce a set of draft articles on the legal status of the territorial sea[36] that was to have a considerable influence on the subsequent development of the law.[37]

Another World War interrupted any further attempt to codify the law of the sea. However, in 1947, the UN General Assembly established the International Law Commission (ILC) with the task of promoting 'the progressive development of international law and its codification'.[38] Following its establishment, the ILC selected the regime of the high seas as one of its priority topics, but it was urged by the General Assembly to add to that the regime of the territorial sea as being 'closely related'.[39] A Dutch international lawyer, JPA François, was appointed as the rapporteur for both topics. François had been a member of the Preparatory Committee and rapporteur for the Territorial Waters Committee at the 1930 Hague Codification Conference and therefore came to his task with a wealth of experience. It is often the case that the rapporteur for a topic plays a seminal role in the preparation of draft articles adopted by the ILC—one thinks, for example, of Sir Humphrey Waldock and the draft articles on the law of treaties and of James Crawford and the draft articles on state responsibility.

[34] Harrison (n 26) 28–29.

[35] Jesse S Reeves, 'The Codification of the Law of Territorial Waters' (1930) 24 American Journal of International Law 486.

[36] The text of the draft articles is reproduced in Shabtai Rosenne (ed), *League of Nations Conference for the Codification of International Law (1930)* (Oceana 1975) 833–36.

[37] Harrison (n 26) 30–31; Treves (n 5) 8–9.

[38] UN General Assembly, Resolution 174 (II), Establishment of an International Law Commission, UN Doc A/RES/174(II) (21 November 1947).

[39] UN General Assembly, Resolution 374 (IV), Recommendation to the International Law Commission to Include the Régime of Territorial Waters in Its List of Topics to Be Given Priority, UN Doc A/RES/374(IV) (6 December 1949).

That appears also to have been the case with François and the draft articles on the law of the sea adopted by the ILC in 1956.

Those draft articles were considered at the first UN Conference on the Law of the Sea, held at Geneva in 1958, at which four conventions on the law of the sea were adopted. By that time, Western European states were becoming very much a minority grouping—they comprised only 20 of the 86 states represented at the Conference—and their influence was accordingly waning. That trend continued with the final codification of the law of the sea to date, which was undertaken at the Third UN Conference on the Law of the Sea (1973–82), where Western European states comprised an even smaller minority. Nevertheless, while Western European influence on the codification of the law of the sea had markedly declined by this stage, the whole idea of codifying the law of the sea derives from the legal culture of Western Europe.

2.3.2 The legal status of the sea: the distinction between areas within national jurisdiction and the high seas

One of the key features of the law of the sea for at least the past two centuries has been the distinction between areas within national jurisdiction (notably the territorial sea) and the high seas beyond. Western Europeans have had a notable influence on elaborating this distinction. Roman law appears to have been ambivalent as to whether the sea was capable of occupation or was open to use by all,[40] perhaps because the Romans were not great seafarers and Roman lawyers were primarily interested in the private law, rather than public law, aspects of maritime law.[41] Nevertheless, Roman law was to have a considerable influence on the early European writers on the law of the sea, as explained below.

Following the collapse of the Roman Empire in the fifth century, there appears to have been little interest in Western Europe in the law concerning the sea for many centuries. That began to change from around the end of the fifteenth century, with the beginnings of colonialism in the Western hemisphere and the East Indies by Portugal and Spain, in the wake of the European voyages of discovery by Columbus (1457–1506), Vasco da Gama (1469–1524), Magellan (1480–1521), and others, and the development of an embryonic system of states in Western Europe. A lively debate arose among Western European scholars about the legal nature of the sea, encouraged by the

[40] Bederman (n 5) 362–63.

[41] Douglas M Johnston, *The International Law of Fisheries* (Yale UP 1965) 158–59.

intellectual spirit of the Renaissance. Although all these writers drew on essentially the same set of sources—Roman law, natural law as derived from the Bible and Roman writers such as Cicero,[42] and, in some cases, the state practice of the time—they reached different conclusions. Some writers argued that the sea was incapable of occupation and therefore was free for use by all. They included the Spaniards Alfonso de Castro (1495–1558) and Fernando Vázquez de Menchaca (1512–69),[43] and, most notably, the Dutchman Hugo Grotius (1583–1645).[44] Other writers took the opposite position and argued that the sea adjacent to the coast of a state was capable of occupation by that state, although their views differed as to the nature of states' rights in such a zone and how far the zone extended from land. Writers in this camp included, among others,[45] the Italians Bartolus of Sassoferrato (1314–57) and his pupil, Baldus of Ubaldis (1327–1400);[46] the Anglo-Italian Alberico Gentili (1552–1608);[47] the Dutchman Johanes Pontanus;[48] the Britons William Welwood (1578–1622) and John Selden (1564–1654);[49] and the Portuguese Serafim de Freitas (1570–1633).[50] Even Grotius modified the extreme position of *Mare Liberum* in a later work, *De Iure Belli ac Pacis, Libri Tres* (1625), where he accepted that the waters of a bay or a strait bordered by a single state could be acquired by that state.[51]

While some of the works produced by these writers were the product of disinterested scholarship, much was commissioned advocacy.[52] That was

[42] On the intellectual origins of natural law in Western Europe, see Koskenniemi (n 20) 50–51; Shaw (n 20) 17.

[43] Fernando Vázquez de Manchaca, *Controversiarum illustrium aliarumque usu frequentium libri tres* (1563) bk II, chs 36–39, as referred to by Scovazzi (n 5) 63.

[44] Hugo Grotius, *Mare Liberum* (1609). For a modern English translation, see Robert Feenstra (ed), *Hugo Grotius Mare Liberum 1609–2009* (Brill 2009). In *Mare Liberum*, Grotius acknowledges his intellectual debt to Vázquez: see Feenstra's edition at 43. According to Anand, Grotius was also influenced by the freedom of navigation and commerce that had been practised by Asian states in the Indian Ocean for centuries. See Anand, *Origin and Development* (n 6) x, 5, 81–82, 87–88.

[45] For overviews of other writers, see Scovazzi (n 5) 66–67.

[46] On these two writers, see Johnston (n 41) 161–62.

[47] See ibid 162.

[48] JI Pontanus, *Discussiones Historicae de Mari Libero* (1637), as referred to by Johnston (n 41) 166.

[49] See, respectively, William Welwood, *An Abridgement of All Sea-Lawes* (1613) and John Selden, *Mare Clausum seu de Dominio Maris, Libri Duo* (1635).

[50] Serafim de Freitas, *De Justo Imperio Lusitanorum Asiatico* (1625). The book was written at the request of the King of Spain (who at that time was also King of Portugal) to refute Grotius's views. See Jeroen Vervliet, 'General Introduction' in Feenstra (n 44) ix–xxx, xxiv. See also Alexandrowicz, *The Law of Nations* (n 6) ch 8, originally published as CH Alexandrowicz, 'Freitas Versus Grotius' (1959) 35 British Yearbook of International Law 162; Mónica Brito Vieira, '*Mare Liberum* vs. *Mare Clausum*: Grotius, Freitas, and Selden's Debate on Dominion Over the Seas' (2003) 64 Journal of the History of Ideas 361.

[51] Vervliet (n 50) xxv–xxvi.

[52] Anand, *Origin and Development* (n 6) 104–07. See also WSM Knight, 'Seraphin [sic] de Freitas: Critic of *Mare Liberum*' (1925) 11 Transactions of the Grotius Society 1.

especially true of the two best known of these writers, Grotius and Selden. Grotius's *Mare Liberum* was originally part of a much longer work, what we would today call a legal opinion, requested by the Dutch East India Company to examine the legality of its capture of a Portuguese vessel and the retention of its valuable cargo. The longer work, *De Jure Praedae Commentarius*, was written in 1604–05 but never published until it was found, by chance, with a collection of Grotius's papers in 1864.[53] *Mare Liberum* was published separately, and anonymously (in order to protect Grotius's position as public prosecutor at the Court of Appeal in The Hague), in 1609, its publication being delayed until that date in order not to jeopardize ongoing negotiations over an armistice in the hostilities between the Netherlands and Spain.[54] That Grotius was very much an advocate is also exemplified by his presence as a prominent member of a Dutch delegation sent to negotiate with the English in 1613–15 over the access of the English East India Company to the lucrative spice trade in the East Indies. Grotius denied that the English company could have the same freedom of navigation and commerce that he had argued in *Mare Liberum* the Dutch company should have, and he was disconcerted to have his own book quoted back at him by the English to support their position.[55] It was not only Grotius who was inconsistent. Although, in their negotiations with the Dutch, the English argued for freedom of navigation and commerce in the East Indies, a few years earlier, in 1609, King James (I of England, VI of Scotland) had issued a proclamation, in response to increased fishing by Dutch vessels off the coasts of England and Scotland, requiring any foreign vessels fishing in the waters off those coasts (the extent of which was not specified) to obtain a licence.[56] The failure of the Dutch to observe that requirement led to a further, and similar, proclamation by James's son, Charles I, in 1636.[57] In 1619, King James commissioned Selden to provide him with legal support in his fisheries dispute with the Dutch, but publication of Selden's resulting work, *Mare Clausum*, was put off because James did not want to offend his brother-in-law, King Christian IV of Denmark–Norway. It was eventually published in 1635, at the request of Charles I.[58]

[53] Scovazzi (n 5) 63.

[54] Vervliet (n 50) ix. The Netherlands came under Spanish rule in the early sixteenth century but declared itself independent in 1581, leading to protracted hostilities with Spain.

[55] ibid xx; Bederman (n 5) 367.

[56] The proclamation is reproduced in Scovazzi (n 5) 59–60. From 1603, England and Scotland had the same monarch, but they remained separate kingdoms until 1707.

[57] ibid 60–61.

[58] Vervliet (n 50) xxvi–xviii.

By the end of the seventeenth century, the 'battle of the books' was over, and the orthodoxy in the literature, as exemplified by writers such as the German Samuel von Pufendorf (1632–94),[59] the Dutch Cornelius van Bynkershoek (1673–1743),[60] and the Swiss Emer de Vattel (1714–67),[61] was that a state could claim a territorial sea, out to the distance that shore-based artillery could fire (the cannon-shot rule), through which all ships enjoyed a right of (innocent) passage: beyond were the high seas, which were open to use by all. That position was increasingly reflected in Western European state practice from the eighteenth century onwards, not least because it supported the economic and colonial interests of the major European powers[62]—although uncertainty persisted about the precise legal nature of the territorial sea and its breadth, as well as whether states could claim a contiguous or other zone beyond the territorial sea. Those uncertainties were not finally resolved until the UN codification conferences in the second half of the twentieth century. Nevertheless, the basic distinction between the territorial sea and the high seas had long been established by Western European legal scholarship and state practice.

2.3.3 The role of science and the scientific method in the law of the sea

UNCLOS[63]—especially in comparison with the previous codification of the law of the sea, the 1958 Geneva Conventions—puts considerable emphasis on the role of science in the law of the sea. Its preamble recognizes 'the desirability of establishing . . . a legal order [that] . . . will promote . . . the study . . . of the marine environment'.[64] The importance that UNCLOS attaches to science is most evident from the fact that it dedicates the whole of one of its 13 substantive parts, Part XIII, to the topic of marine scientific research. Part XIII not only regulates the way in which marine scientific research is to be conducted, it also calls on states and competent international organizations to 'promote and facilitate the development' of marine scientific research,[65] 'promote international cooperation' in such research,[66] 'create favourable conditions for the

[59] Samuel von Pufendorf, *De Jure Naturae et Gentium* (1672).
[60] Cornelius van Bynkershoek, *De Dominio Maris Dissertatio* (1702).
[61] Emer de Vattel, *Le droit des gens, ou Principes de la loi naturelle* (1758). Further on these three writers, see Johnston (n 41) 171–72.
[62] Anand, *Origin and Development* (n 6) 126, 129–36, 152.
[63] See n 12.
[64] UNCLOS, preamble para 4.
[65] UNCLOS, art 239.
[66] UNCLOS, art 242(1).

conduct of' such research,[67] and 'promote the flow of scientific data and information'.[68] In addition, Part XII, on the protection and preservation of the marine environment, calls on states to cooperate on programmes of scientific research and the exchange of data relating to pollution of the marine environment, and, based on the knowledge thus acquired, to establish 'appropriate scientific criteria' for developing rules to prevent, reduce, and control marine pollution.[69]

None of the provisions of UNCLOS mentioned so far appears to have been directly influenced by the European concern with science and the scientific method described in Section 2.2, although ultimately the emphasis on science in UNCLOS derives from the scientific revolution in Western Europe in the seventeenth century. There are, however, three features of UNCLOS that do appear to be, through a process of historical and legal evolution, directly the product of Western European scientific culture. The first is the system of measurement—nautical miles—used for determining the breadths of maritime zones.[70] The second is the use of coordinates of longitude and latitude to specify points at sea and on the coast from which the breadth of a maritime zone is to be measured, and its outer limit and the boundary with the zones of neighbouring states delimited.[71] The third is the obligation on states, both in the exclusive economic zone (EEZ) and on the high seas, to take into account 'the best scientific evidence available' when adopting measures to conserve and manage living resources.[72]

Turning first to the question of measurement, the Englishman Robert Hues, in 1594, appears to have been the first person to have used the term 'nautical mile' as a unit of measurement.[73] He defined this as being equal to one-sixtieth of 1 degree of latitude—that is, 1 minute of latitude. Since the Earth is not a perfect sphere, 1 minute is not a consistent length. It varies between 1,861.6 metres at the poles and 1,843 metres at the equator. In the nineteenth century, the French defined a nautical mile by utilizing the original 1791 definition of a metre as one ten-millionth of a quarter meridian, thus making 1 nautical mile equal to 1,852 metres.[74] That definition was adopted at the International

[67] UNCLOS, art 243.
[68] UNCLOS, art 244(2).
[69] UNCLOS, arts 200, 201.
[70] For references to nautical miles, see UNCLOS, arts 3, 33(2), 47(2), 57, 76.
[71] The use of coordinates is referred to in UNCLOS, arts 16(1), 47(8), 47(9), 75, 84.
[72] UNCLOS, arts 61(2), 119(1)(a).
[73] See 'Nautical mile', *Wikipedia* <https://en.wikipedia.org/wiki/Nautical_mile> accessed 31 July 2022.
[74] ibid.

Hydrographic Conference held in Monaco in 1929.[75] Although UNCLOS, like the 1958 Conventions, does not define a nautical mile, it is generally understood to have the same meaning as in the 1929 definition.[76]

Once it became generally accepted by Western European states that a coastal state was entitled to claim a zone of sovereignty or jurisdiction off its coast, there was a need to establish the breadth of such zones. Early definitions of that breadth were vague. They included the cannon-shot rule, meaning the range of a shore-based cannon firing out to sea, and the line-of-sight rule, meaning the distance visible with the naked eye from land. There is some doubt as to when breadth began to be expressed in terms of nautical miles. Some writers have argued that it was by Denmark–Norway in the mid-eighteenth century, when it claimed a breadth of 1 Scandinavian marine league, which equated to 4 nautical miles.[77] However, that claim related to jurisdictional zones for fisheries and neutrality purposes, rather than for a territorial sea as such, which was not claimed until 1812.[78] Others have cited France, which in 1761 equated the cannon-shot rule to 3 nautical miles in diplomatic correspondence with Denmark–Norway.[79] Yet others have claimed that the honour should go to the Italian polymath Ferdinando Galiani, who in a 1782 publication proposed that the cannon-shot rule should be replaced by a fixed measure of 3 nautical miles. Thereafter, in Scovazzi's striking phrase, 'geometry was ready to enter the international law of the sea and play the role that Galiani had assigned to it'.[80]

The term 'nautical mile' as such appears not to have been used in international legal texts until the twentieth century. Nineteenth-century treaties occasionally referred to 'marine miles',[81] a marine mile apparently being the

[75] International Hydrographic Organization, *A Manual on Technical Aspects of the United Nations Convention on the Law of the Sea—1982 (TALOS)* (6th edn, International Hydrographic Organization 2020) chs 3–13, 20–22.

[76] ibid.

[77] Thomas Baty, 'The Three-Mile Limit' (1928) 22 American Journal of International Law 503, 516; Tommy TB Koh, 'The Origins of the 1982 Convention on the Law of the Sea' (1987) 29 Malaya Law Review 1, 4. A non-Scandinavian marine league was equivalent to 3 nautical miles.

[78] HSK Kent, 'The Historical Origins of the Three-Mile Limit' (1954) 48 American Journal of International Law 537, 544–47, 551–52. Kent also points out that Denmark–Norway used the Scandinavian marine league as a unit of measurement for zones of fisheries jurisdiction during the seventeenth century: see ibid 539.

[79] ibid 539–40; Koh (n 77) 4, quoting Sayre Archie Swarztrauber, *The Three Mile Limit of Territorial Seas* (Naval Institute Press 1972) 51–63.

[80] Scovazzi (n 5) 72. See also Treves (n 5) 6.

[81] See, for example, Convention Respecting Fisheries, Boundary and the Restoration of Slaves, 20 October 1818, 8 Stat 248, TS 112 (between the United States and the United Kingdom). However, later treaties between the United States and Mexico continued to use the increasingly archaic term 'league': see Treaty of Peace, Friendship, Limits, and Settlement between the United States of America and the United Mexican States, 2 February 1848, 9 Stat 922, TS 207, art 5; Treaty of La Mesilla (Gadsden Purchase), 30 December 1853, 10 Stat 1031, TS 208, art 1; United Nations, *Laws and Regulations on the Regime of the Territorial Sea* (UN Legislative Series B/6, 1957) 745, 746.

same as a nautical mile, or, more commonly, simply to 'miles', with a mile then being defined as 1 minute of latitude (ie 1 nautical mile).[82] The parties to those treaties were preponderantly Western European states.

The second issue that is the product of Western European scientific culture is the use of coordinates of latitude and longitude to identify the precise location of a point on the Earth's surface, both on land and, more importantly, at sea. The Greek astronomer Hipparchus (190–120 BCE) is believed to have been the first person to specify the location of a place on land using coordinates of latitude and longitude, although latitude was already known to the Phoenicians, who inhabited roughly what is modern-day Lebanon, by about 600 BCE.[83] Instruments that could give an approximate reading of latitude at sea were used in the Islamic world from around the second century CE and adopted by the Europeans in the Middle Ages. However, it was Western Europeans who found the means for precisely identifying points of both latitude and longitude at sea, particularly through the development of the telescope by the Dutch at the beginning of the seventeenth century, the invention of the pendulum clock by the Dutchman Christiaan Huygens in 1657, and the invention of the marine chronometer by the Englishman John Harrison around 1760. From the early nineteenth century onwards, coordinates of longitude and latitude began to be used increasingly in international legal texts,[84] particularly in treaties and the judgements of international courts and tribunals delimiting maritime boundaries. There is no preponderant or specific Western European contribution to that state practice.

A third, and rather different, matter where Western European scientific culture has influenced the international law of the sea relates to the development of fisheries science and the obligation in UNCLOS for fisheries managers to take such science into account when deciding on conservation and management measures. Grotius famously asserted that the living resources of the sea were inexhaustible,[85] a view echoed and endorsed by some of the later classical writers on international law, such as Vattel.[86] That view was challenged,

[82] See, for example, Convention between Great Britain and France for Defining and Regulating the Limits of the Exclusive Rights of the Oyster and Other Fishery on the Coasts of Great Britain and of France, 2 August 1839, 27 British and Foreign State Papers 983, arts IX, X; Convention for Regulating the Police of North Sea Fisheries, 6 May 1882, 73 British and Foreign State Papers 39, arts II, III.

[83] Open University, 'Latitude and Longitude' (1 March 2019) <www.open.edu/openlearn/history-the-arts/history/history-science-technology-and-medicine/history-science/latitude-and-longitude> accessed 31 July 2022.

[84] For early examples, see the United States–Mexico treaties of 1848 and 1853 referred to in n 81.

[85] This view is stated more explicitly in Grotius's *Defensio capitis quinti Maris Liberi* than in *Mare Liberum*: see Anand, *Origin and Development* (n 6) 101; Albert W Koers, *International Regulation of Marine Fisheries* (Fishing News (Books) 1973) 17.

[86] Vattel (n 61), as quoted in Johnston (n 41) 172.

however, by Welwood, who argued that fisheries could be exhausted 'as a result of the free use of them by everybody'.[87] It appears that Welwood's view was based on the fact that the catches of Scottish fishermen at the time were declining, which Welwood attributed to Dutch overfishing close to the coast of Scotland.[88]

The views of Grotius, Welwood, and others were not based on any empirical evidence, which did not exist at the time that they were writing. Given that fishing vessels were propelled by sail and used quite simple gear, it probably was the case that the vessels of the time were incapable of fishing at unsustainable levels, except perhaps in a few particular localities. That was all about to change in the nineteenth century as a result of developments in Western Europe.

In 1731, an Englishman, Thomas Newcomen, invented the first steam engine. Some 40 years later, it was refined and made far more efficient by the Scottish engineer James Watt. From around 1810, the steam engine gradually replaced sail as the means of propulsion for ships. That transition is graphically illustrated in Turner's famous painting *The Fighting Téméraire* (1838), which shows a former warship that had been propelled by sail being towed to a shipyard to be broken up by a tug belching black smoke. The first steam-powered fishing vessels came into operation in the 1870s, in the United Kingdom. At the same time, developments in technology led to more efficient fishing gear, particularly trawls. As a result, catches in the North Sea and elsewhere in northwest Europe began to increase dramatically.

Those developments occurred at about the same time as the beginning of modern fisheries science, which again had its origins in Western Europe and also on the east coast of the United States. This early science began to provide empirical evidence that fish stocks could be—and, in some cases, actually were being—fished at unsustainable levels.[89] In 1902, in order to make such scientific evidence more widely available and to provide a forum for the encouragement and coordination of fisheries research, a number of Western European states set up the International Council for the Exploration of the Sea (ICES),[90] the world's first intergovernmental science organization. ICES has served as a

[87] Welwood (n 49), as quoted by Colombos (n 30) 147. See also Johnston (n 41) 166–67.
[88] Anand, *Origin and Development* (n 6) 101, 145–46; Johnston (n 41) 166–67.
[89] DH Cushing, *The Provident Sea* (CUP 1988) ch 9.
[90] Koers (n 85) 77–79.

model for, and has stimulated the establishment of, a number of other intergovernmental organizations, notably the International Commission for the Scientific Exploration of the Mediterranean Sea (now the Mediterranean Science Commission) in 1919, the North American Council on Fishery Investigations (which terminated in 1938) in 1920,[91] and, very much later, the North Pacific Marine Science Organization, founded in 1990.[92] In tribute to ICES, the last of these is known as PICES, although that is not its natural acronym.[93]

After 120 years, ICES is still going strong.[94] It currently provides scientific advice on appropriate conservation measures for all the international cooperative fisheries management bodies of Western Europe. It is noteworthy that of those bodies, the North-East Atlantic Fisheries Commission (like its predecessors) is required not only to base its conservation measures on the best scientific advice available to it but also, in doing so, to seek the advice of ICES.[95] While one cannot show that this practice directly influenced the obligation under Articles 61(2) and 119(1)(a) of UNCLOS for states to take into account 'the best scientific evidence available' when adopting fisheries conservation and management measures, or the somewhat similar obligation in respect of high seas fisheries in the 1958 Fisheries Convention,[96] it was part of the background, along with similar practice elsewhere,[97] of which the negotiators of both UNCLOS and the 1958 Convention would have been aware.

[91] ibid 79–80.

[92] By the Convention for a North Pacific Marine Science Organization, 12 December 1990 <https://meetings.pices.int/about/convention> accessed 28 November 2024.

[93] North Pacific Marine Science Organization, 'Journey to PICES' <https://meetings.pices.int/about/history> accessed 31 July 2022.

[94] In 1964, the organization was put on a more formal basis with the adoption of the Convention for the International Council for the Exploration of the Sea, 12 September 1964, 652 UNTS 237.

[95] Convention on Future Multilateral Cooperation in North-East Atlantic Fisheries, 18 November 1980, 1285 UNTS 129, arts 4(1), 14(1). For the equivalent obligations on the Commission's predecessor bodies, see, in chronological order, International Convention for the Regulation of the Meshes of Fishing Nets and the Size Limits of Fish, 23 March 1937, Cmd 5494 (1937), art 11; Convention for the Regulation of the Meshes of Fishing Nets and the Size Limits of Fish, 5 April 1946, 231 UNTS 199, art 12(5); North-East Atlantic Fisheries Convention, 24 January 1959, 486 UNTS 157, arts 6(1)(d), 11(1).

[96] Convention on Fishing and Conservation of the Living Resources of the High Seas, 29 April 1958, 559 UNTS 285, arts 7(2)(b), 10(1)(a). Those provisions were based almost verbatim on Draft Articles 55(2)(b) and 58(1) of the International Law Commission's 1956 Draft Articles Concerning the Law of the Sea. The Commission's commentary on those Draft Articles does not explain the origins of, or reasons for, those provisions: see International Law Commission, Draft Articles Concerning the Law of the Sea with Commentaries, reprinted in (1956) 2 Yearbook of the International Law Commission 254, 290–92.

[97] See Koers (n 85) 212, stating that most pre-UNCLOS international fisheries commissions were required to base their conservation measures on scientific findings.

2.3.4 The influence of capitalism

As explained in Section 2.2, capitalism had its origins in Western Europe and was the dominant economic philosophy there until well into the twentieth century. The philosophy was also gradually exported to other parts of the world, notably North America. Capitalism has had an influence on the international law of the sea in a number of ways. Three of the most obvious aspects of that influence will be examined here: namely, the regime of the high seas, navigational rights, and the regime of the international seabed area (the Area).

Once the high seas became unambiguously established as a distinct concept and area, as a result of the work of Western European scholars and the practice of Western European states, its regime was characterized as one of freedom (Grotius's *Mare Liberum* translates as 'the free sea'), a terminology used in the 1958 Convention on the High Seas[98] and even carried forward into UNCLOS.[99] That freedom was for two centuries or so one of unbridled use, a classic feature of unfettered capitalism. While the high seas were in theory open to all, in practice it was only states with the necessary capital and technology that were able to make significant use of them. Until the introduction of detailed regulation of the high seas in the latter part of the twentieth century, prompted by the depletion of the resources of those waters, their growing use as a sink for the disposal of pollutants, and the increasing levels of crime there (including piracy; drugs, arms, and people trafficking; and illegal fishing), the regime of the high seas was frequently described in the literature as having a 'laissez-faire' character,[100] an epithet that of course is widely applied to the practice of capitalism.

An important feature of capitalism has been its emphasis on the desirability of free trade in goods, both within and between states. The main means of transport for international trade in goods has been, and continues to be, ships. The states most heavily engaged in international trade, which until well into the twentieth century were Western European states, demanded the fewest restrictions possible on navigation. That goal was secured, before UNCLOS, through freedom of navigation on the high seas and a right of innocent passage through the territorial sea, both of which were the product of Western

[98] Convention on the High Seas, 29 April 1958, 450 UNTS 11, art 2.

[99] UNCLOS, art 87. It is noteworthy that Article 87 is the only provision in Part VII, on the high seas, in which the term 'freedom' is used. In other provisions, the term 'right', rather than 'freedom', is used. Rights may be, and in UNCLOS are, made subject to duties.

[100] See, for example, Anand, *Origin and Development* (n 6) 152, 230; Robin Churchill, Vaughan Lowe, and Amy Sander, *The Law of the Sea* (4th edn, Manchester UP 2022) 6, 374.

European scholarship and state practice. That freedom and that right were regarded as essential, not only for free trade but also to facilitate communications between the metropolitan territories of many Western European states (particularly France, the Netherlands, Portugal, Spain, and the United Kingdom) and their colonies on other continents.[101] Indeed, it is difficult to disentangle the influences of capitalism and colonialism, and eventually military interests, on the development of navigational rights. Freedom of high seas navigation and the right of innocent passage, although now much more regulated, are still dominant in the law of the sea. The former has been extended to the EEZ by Article 58(1) of UNCLOS, while a strengthened version of the latter now applies to passage through international straits (transit passage) and archipelagic waters (archipelagic sea lanes passage).[102]

A third issue where the influence of capitalism on the law of the sea is evident is the regime governing the Area. As originally drafted, the regime set out in Part XI of UNCLOS contained a number of non- or anti-capitalist features. They included limits on the production of seabed minerals; the establishment of an international body, the Enterprise, to engage in deep sea mining in areas designated by the International Seabed Authority from two sites of equal value put forward by would-be miners for exploration and possible exploitation; and the mandatory transfer of technology from miners to the Enterprise.[103] Influenced by the rise of neoliberalism and globalization, a number of capitalist states, led by the United States and supported by some other Western states, notably Germany and the United Kingdom, were opposed to those provisions and therefore declined to sign or ratify UNCLOS. They eventually succeeded in modifying the provisions to their satisfaction by means of the 1994 Agreement on the Implementation of Part XI.[104] Thereafter, with the exception of the United States, they ratified UNCLOS.

2.3.5 Language

As a result of colonization, three Western European languages—English, French, and Spanish—are among the most widely spoken languages in the

[101] Anand, *Origin and Development* (n 6) 129–36, 152.

[102] UNCLOS, arts 38, 53.

[103] UNCLOS, art 151; annex III art 8; and art 144 and annex III art 5, respectively.

[104] Agreement Relating to the Implementation of Part XI of the United Nations Convention on the Law of the Sea of 10 December 1982, 28 July 1994, 1836 UNTS 42. See, in particular, annex ss 6, 2, and 5, respectively.

world. They also constitute three of the six official languages of the United Nations and three of the six authentic languages of UNCLOS. English and French are the only official languages of most international courts, including the International Tribunal for the Law of the Sea,[105] and in practice are the main languages of international diplomacy. Many of the leading journals devoted to the law of the sea are published in English or French, as are the most widely cited textbooks and monographs on the law of the sea.

The dominance of these two Western European languages has two significant consequences.[106] First, it gives an advantage to scholars whose first language is English or French, many of whom will be from Western Europe or other states in the Western European and Other States Group of the United Nations. They are therefore likely to be more influential in the literature, often having an (unconscious) Western bias. Insofar as that literature helps to shape the development of the law of the sea, those scholars will therefore have more impact on that development. Second, language shapes thought processes and legal concepts. Here, Western European languages will again have a disproportionate influence in shaping legal concepts. An example is provided by the *Somalia v Kenya* maritime boundary case. During the course of the proceedings, Somalia explained that the reason why its legislation had used the rather ambiguous phrase 'a straight line towards the sea from the land', which was intended to denote an equidistance line, was because '[t]he Somali language does not contain a word precisely equivalent to "equidistance line" in English'.[107] A further example is property rights, where the Western concept of the meaning of 'property' is not shared by all non-Western states.[108] This, it has been argued, affects the interpretation of terms in UNCLOS that have property connotations, such as the 'common heritage of mankind'.[109]

[105] International Tribunal for the Law of the Sea, Rules of the Tribunal, ITLOS/8 (25 March 2021) art 43.

[106] For more on the importance of different languages in the development and practice of international law, see Anthea Roberts, *Is International Law International?* (OUP 2017) 3–4, 9–10, 46–47, ch 4 passim, 255–56, 260–75. See also Renteln (n 2) 240–41.

[107] *Maritime Delimitation in the Indian Ocean (Somalia v Kenya) (Judgment)* [2021] ICJ Rep 206, para 46.

[108] See Edwin Egede, 'The Common Heritage of Mankind and the Sub-Saharan African Native Land Tenure System: A "Clash of Cultures" in the Interpretation of Concepts in International Law?' (2014) 58 Journal of African Law 71, 79–88; AV Lowe, 'Reflections on the Waters: Changing Concepts of Property Rights in the Law of the Sea' (1986) 1 International Journal of Estuarine and Coastal Law 1, 9.

[109] Lowe (n 108) 9.

2.4 Conclusion

The international law of the sea today is the product of the interests and influences of many different states.[110] To single out and identify the influence, especially the cultural influence, of any particular state or group of states is therefore a difficult task. Nevertheless, it is possible to detect the influence of Western European culture on the development of the law of the sea in a number of ways, especially in the period between 1500 and 1930.

From Western European legal culture has come the desire, by the early twentieth century, to codify in treaty form the then largely customary international law of the sea. From that culture also developed the basic legal division of the sea into areas within national jurisdiction and areas beyond national jurisdiction. The emphasis on marine scientific research in UNCLOS derives ultimately from the development of modern science in Western Europe from the seventeenth century onwards—as, more concretely, do matters such as the use of nautical miles as the unit for measuring distances at sea, and the use of the coordinates of latitude and longitude for identifying particular points at sea and on the coast.

Capitalism, which originated in Western Europe, has left its mark on the law of the sea, notably on the laissez-faire nature of the regime for the high seas that persisted until the latter part of the twentieth century and, much more recently, on the regime of the Area as it emerged after the 1994 Implementation Agreement. A final Western European cultural influence on the law of the sea has been language. Two European languages, English and French, have dominated the medium in which the law of the sea has been developed through treaty negotiation; interpreted and applied by international courts and tribunals; and written about by academic commentators—including, of course, in this book. Speakers of those languages have therefore both dominated discourse on the law of the sea and had a disproportionate influence in shaping its substance.

[110] cf Allott's remark that UNCLOS 'is the product of a total international social process extending back, philosophically and historically, to the sixteenth century and far beyond': Philip Allott, '*Mare Nostrum*: A New International Law of the Sea' (1992) 86 American Journal of International Law 764, 765.

3

Eastern Europe

Stanislaw Michal Pawlak

3.1 Introduction

The law of the sea has been developed through centuries. That process cannot be stopped because of the growing needs of humankind, technical progress, or the fact that the ocean is probably the most important not-fully-explored of our planet's assets. It continues and is influenced by many factors, needs, cultures, challenges, claims, and interests of both global and regional characters. Among those factors, culture plays an important role in shaping the form and character of the law of the sea.

This chapter focuses on the Eastern European contribution to the law of the sea, particularly the Polish and Lithuanian impact on maritime governance in the Baltic Sea and Bulgarian and Romanian influence in the Black Sea. While reviewing the regional influence of culture on the development of the law of the sea, the chapter takes a broad view of the meaning of 'culture' because it is very difficult to separate cultural influences from legal, economic, political, and military influences, and from their values and ideas of the contemporary world.

The process of development of the international law of the sea, which was mostly influenced by the Western European legal culture derived from Greek and Roman law, as well as the practice of the states of the Old Continent, has materialized in periodic codification attempts. The final one to date, undertaken by the Third UN Conference on the Law of the Sea, ended in 1982 with the adoption of the UN Convention on the Law of the Sea (UNCLOS), which entered into force in 1984.[1] The Convention became the main instrument of a maritime branch of international law and a universal legal framework for the adoption of other treaties related to the oceans.

During the Third Conference, which was held in Montego Bay, Poland, and other Eastern European states were very active. They assisted in achieving

[1] UN Convention on the Law of the Sea, 10 December 1982, 1833 UNTS 397 (UNCLOS).

Stanislaw Michal Pawlak, *Eastern Europe* In: *Cultural Influences on the Law of the Sea*. Edited by: James Kraska and Hayoun Ryou-Ellison, Oxford University Press.
DOI: 10.1093/9780198944140.003.0003

the acceptance of many crucial provisions of the Convention and in attaining compromise on many issues that were dividing the participants.

Today, almost every state accepts the provisions of UNCLOS, but many states and regions also insist on the need to adapt the Convention to reflect contemporary challenges posed by climate change, sea level rise, pollution of the sea, seabed mining, and the protection of biodiversity.

The process of such adaptation is proceeding slowly, but, at the same time, UNCLOS should be implemented and preserved. This depends upon the willingness of states to uphold the Convention in all its dimensions. The annual UN General Assembly Resolutions on the oceans and the law of the sea reaffirm the vital importance of the Convention and the preservation of its integrity. It should be remembered that the Convention established a set of rules that provide a stable system for regulating activities at sea and for sustainable oceans management through provisions delimiting and defining maritime zones—provisions that had not previously existed in the law of the sea. As a framework treaty, the Convention acts as a flexible base for the adoption of a number of other treaties related to the sea—such as implementation agreements and treaties regarding fisheries, shipping, the protection of the marine environment, criminal activity on the high seas, and many other issues—without resort to a formal amendment procedure. UNCLOS established as well a working system for the compulsory settlement of disputes concerning the interpretation and application of its provisions.

The development of the law of the sea, like that of any other branch of international law, is a complex and continuous process involving the willingness and practice of states, the activities of international organizations, the judicial decisions of international courts and tribunals, and the resolutions and doctrines of the International Law Commission. All these factors are important, but the most important role is played by states. It was states that codified the fundamental part of the law of the sea at the Third Conference, and states are the principal actors responsible for the implementation of UNCLOS and for the further development of the law of the sea.

The state parties to the Convention have concrete rights and obligations. Article 192 of UNCLOS, for example, states the legal requirement: 'States have the obligation to protect and preserve the marine environment.' This is a very mandatory language without any exceptions and qualifications that would weaken or negate the obligation.

The Convention sets out in some provisions the means by which states should implement their obligations. Many of these provisions create problems with their implementation that were left deliberately ambiguous or vague during the 'package deal' negotiations of UNCLOS—for example, the ability of small islands or rocky features that are above water at high tide to generate maritime zones, the rights of passage of warships and vessels carrying hazardous substances through territorial waters, and the legality of conducting military exercises in the exclusive economic zones (EEZs) of other states. The implementation of the Convention and other related international agreements is a complex process in which individual states remain first and foremost responsible entities. They have to translate international agreements into their national legislation and policies. In fulfilling those obligations, they must take into consideration not only their own interests but also the position of their neighbours and regional conditions. Without regional cooperation, it would often be impossible to solve important problems related to the law of the sea, such as the protection of the maritime environment, fisheries, maritime security, and many others. The Convention itself encourages states to adopt on a regional basis–specific regulations for cooperation in protecting the maritime environment; establishing appropriate scientific criteria for preventing, reducing, and controlling pollution at sea; and harmonizing their policies in this regard at the appropriate regional level.[2] This encouragement applies to all regions, including the Baltic Sea and the Black Sea, which are the subject of this chapter.

During the Third Conference, the Eastern European states joined the group of geographically disadvantaged states. They did so—except the then Soviet Union—because all of them either are landlocked states, like Hungary, or have access only to semi-enclosed seas, like Poland or Bulgaria. That disadvantaged group, comprising 54 states (27 landlocked and 27 disadvantaged), was very active and did achieve at Montego Bay an acceptance of many postulates, including some but not all of those proposed by the Eastern European states. The group successfully assisted in achieving compromise on many crucial issues that were dividing the participants at the Conference. Poland and the other Eastern European states insisted, in particular, on preserving freedom of navigation, access to the living resources on the high seas, principles of exploitation of the seabed minerals in the areas beyond national jurisdiction, and the delimitation of sea boundaries. They also opposed all attempts to transform EEZs into the territorial sea or to expand the continental shelf beyond 350 nautical miles.[3]

[2] UNCLOS, arts 197, 201, 207.

[3] Janusz Symonides, 'Poland and the New Law of the Sea' (1983) 12 Polish Yearbook of International Law 57.

In this chapter, because of its scope, the influence on the law of the sea will be discussed with regard not to all Eastern European states but only to Poland and Lithuania representing the Baltic Sea region and to Bulgaria and Romania representing the Black Sea area. It seems that these states, despite their national interests, also well represent the regional approach to maritime problems. To better understand the position and maritime policy of those states, it will be necessary to present some basic information on the Baltic Sea region and, later, the Black Sea region.

3.2 The Baltic Sea region

The Baltic Sea region is a special part of Northern Europe with a rich history and recognized economic potential. The sea itself is, in fact, an arm of the Atlantic Ocean. It is linked to the North Sea and the Atlantic Ocean through the Skagerrak Strait. The Baltic Sea is about 600 kilometres long, covering a surface of about 415,000 square kilometres, and is much shallower than most of the world's seas. It is enclosed by nine states: Denmark, Estonia, Finland, Germany, Latvia, Lithuania, Poland, Russia, and Sweden. The Baltic Sea is one of the most heavily used maritime transportation areas in the world, with more than 70,000 ships—mostly flying flags of non-Baltic states—navigating within it each year.

The history of the Baltic Sea and the region as a whole is old and very interesting. Since the time of the Roman Empire, the Baltic region has been an area not only of trade and commerce, along with other forms of cooperation between the people living there, but also of wars, conquests, and power struggles. Connecting many parts of Europe, the Baltic Sea was the economic and trade centre of the Hanseatic League, a federation of many merchant cities operating in Europe from the thirteenth to the seventeenth centuries.

The countries of that area provided many goods for trading. They exported, by ship, lumber, wood tar, flax, hemp, furs, and grains. Sweden, from medieval times, delivered iron and silver. Poland was selling some food products, as well as salt from its efficient mines. Merchant ships, for a long time, were crossing the Baltic Sea. The people living on the eastern shore of the Baltic were among the last converted to Latin Christianity: Finland in the twelfth century; people in the area now constituting territories of Estonia and Latvia at the beginning of the thirteenth century; and Lithuania, closely connected with Poland, in the early fourteenth century.[4]

[4] Paul Srodecki and Norbert Kersken (eds), *The Expansion of the Faith: Crusading on the Frontiers of Latin Christendom in the High Middle Ages* (Brepols 2022).

From the beginning of the Middle Ages, the Baltic area was dominated by Scandinavians, who created a strong trade empire that practically controlled the region. That period is often referred to as the Viking Age. For a long time, Vikings (the Norse) fought for the control of the Baltic against Wendish (Slavic) tribes living at the southern shore of the sea and paying tributes to the Polish kings in the tenth and eleventh centuries. Vikings and their descendants in the central Baltic Sea region were not the stereotypical invaders connected with Norse raids, as this was mainly a problem of the English coast. Rather, in the period between the ninth and eleventh centuries, the southern coasts of the Baltic Sea were frequently visited by Vikings and other people from Scandinavia. Many of them probably came as traders, hoping to sell and exchange foreign goods in the vibrant and multicultural ports of trade and emporia situated there. Some of the Scandinavians, however, had different roles to play. To achieve their goals, they had to sail up the Oder and Vistula rivers or travel on foot or by horseback through the interior of the emerging Poland and its vast forests and fields. In Polish Pomerania and other coastal areas of today's Poland, archaeologists have found the remains of traditional Viking longhouses, longboats, and typical Scandinavian graves. The Vikings never launched a substantial invasion of Poland, as they did of the British Isles, although they established settlements in the region of the Baltic Sea's southern coast, which now belongs to Poland. From time to time, however, the Vikings raided other Polish territories and traded with the local people. One of the best-known Viking settlements is Truso in the vicinity of Gdansk. The Vikings also settled in Slavic fortified towns on Wolin, now a Polish island in the Baltic Sea just off the Polish coast in West Pomerania. They were engaged mostly with trade. Archaeological findings have confirmed the establishment of the legendary stronghold of Jomsborg.[5]

It is also worth noting a medieval trade route used by the Vikings, from Scandinavia through Kyivan Rus' to the Byzantine Empire, which is mentioned in the historical chronicles as the route from the Varangians to the Greeks. The trade route consisted of a series of waterways and portages covering nearly 3,000 kilometres from the Baltic Sea.[6]

Starting in the eleventh century, Denmark gradually gained control over most of the Baltic Sea shore. Later, it lost many of its possessions to Sweden, which made the Baltic an all-Swedish Sea in the seventeenth century. Sweden achieved this following long wars with Poland and Denmark in the sixteenth

[5] Gwyn Jones, *A History of the Vikings* (OUP 2001) 127.

[6] 'Varangian Route', *Internet Encyclopedia of Ukraine* <www.encyclopediaofukraine.com/display.asp?linkpath=pages%5CV%5CA%5CVarangianroute.htmSea> accessed 12 May 2023.

and early seventeenth centuries over the domination of the Baltic. As a result of the Great Northern War and Sweden's defeat, Russia, under Peter I (the Great), became—as it remains—a dominating power over the Baltic. During that time, Prussia also increased its influence in the Baltic region.

In the wake of the First World War, which was partly fought on the Baltic and ended with the defeat of Germany and the weakening of Russia, Poland regained access to the Baltic Sea in the form of a narrow corridor between the West and East Prussian provinces. To gain access to international maritime trade routes when the historic Polish port in Gdansk (Danzig) was denied to Poland, as it became an independent entity (the Free City of Danzig), Poland built a new port in Gdynia.

Many changes occurred in the Baltic region after the Second World War. On the basis of the 1945 Potsdam Agreement of the Allied Powers, access by Germany to the Baltic Sea was limited. The new borderline between Poland and Germany was established on the Oder-Neisse rivers, and the German population was transferred from the areas east of that line to the Allied zones in occupied Germany. The Soviet Union took a part of the East Prussia province and created the Kaliningrad Oblast. Poland gained a long stretch of the southern shore of the Baltic between Germany and the Soviet Union.[7]

The East–West division of the world and the iron curtain, which divided Europe soon after the war, also brought about a physical division of the Baltic Sea region into the north-western capitalist states and the south-eastern socialist states. The sea then became a border between opposite military blocks—that is, the Warsaw Pact states and the North Atlantic Treaty Organization (NATO). That confrontation impacted trade, travel, and other forms of cooperation between littoral states.

The situation drastically changed with the collapse of the Soviet Union and the disintegration of the former socialist block. Further changes came with the extension of the European Union in 2004 by the accession of Poland, Estonia, Latvia, and Lithuania, with the Baltic Sea thereby becoming an 'inner lake' of the European Union. Russia is the only remaining state on the Baltic shore that does not demonstrate an intention to join the European Union.[8]

In this situation, the European Union, after extensive public consultations, adopted the EU Strategy for the Baltic Sea Region, which was launched in 2009.[9] The Strategy is an agreement between member states of the European

[7] 'Baltic Sea', *Internet Encyclopedia of Ukraine* <www.encyclopediaofukraine.com/2display.asp?linkpath=pages%5CB%5CL%5CBlackSea.htm> accessed 12 May 2023.
[8] Witold Maciejewski (ed), *The Baltic Sea Region: Cultures, Politics, Societies* (Baltic UP 2002) 15–19.
[9] EU Strategy for the Baltic Sea Region <www.balticsea-region-strategy.eu/> accessed 28 June 2022.

Union and the European Commission to strengthen cooperation between the eight Baltic states (Denmark, Estonia, Finland, Germany, Latvia, Lithuania, Poland, and Sweden). It combines EU actions with local initiatives and facilitates broad regional cooperation. The Strategy is implemented in collaboration with European Commission member states, regional and local authorities, and intergovernmental and non-governmental institutions. It comprises three objectives: saving the sea, connecting the Baltic region, and increasing prosperity. The Strategy is providing input to fulfil the duties, obligations, and encouragements contained in UNCLOS for regional cooperation among the states of the Baltic region.[10]

In addition, the Strategy impacts many other objectives, not only influencing economic and political cooperation among Baltic states but also helping to solve many problems related to the protection of the marine environment, fisheries, freedom of navigation, regional security, legal developments, cultural exchange, tourism, and other issues.

Besides the European Strategy for the Baltic Sea Region, there are two other undertakings: the Council of Baltic Sea States (CBSS) and the Northern Dimension. The CBSS comprises not only the eight Baltic states that are members of the European Union but also Russia. On 3 March 2022, the Council announced its decision to suspend Russia's membership in light of the Russian invasion of Ukraine.[11]

All this indicates that the Baltic Sea region has experienced a remarkable transformation over the last three decades, from an area of confrontation and instability to one of deep European integration.

However, despite many efforts of the Baltic states, as well as European, international, and transnational governance arrangements, the Baltic Sea is regarded as one of the world's most polluted areas. There are two sources of this environmental degradation: the first is strictly geographic and the second derives from human activities.

The water in the Baltic Sea is brackish, and the average depth is shallow in comparison to other regional European seas. The surface area is 415,000 square kilometres. The saline water inflow to the Baltic Sea comes from the North Sea through the Danish straits in irregular intervals of 5 to 10 years, and fresh water flows from several European rivers. Due to slow water exchange,

[10] For example, UNCLOS, arts 200, 209.

[11] Ministry of Foreign Affairs, Republic of Poland, 'Russian Federation Suspended From Work of Council of the Baltic Sea States' (3 March 2022) <www.gov.pl/web/diplomacy/russian-federation-suspended-from-work-of-council-of-the-baltic-sea-states> accessed 12 May 2023.

the Baltic Sea is vulnerable to different types of pollution and environmental degradation.[12]

Satellite images taken in 2010 revealed a massive algal bloom covering 377,000 square kilometres of the Baltic Sea. This was a consequence of the agricultural activities in the area, exacerbated by fertilizer runoff, but it is only one example of the pollution caused by the activities of the more than 85 million people living in the drainage basin of the Baltic Sea. The other threats to the integrity of the Baltic Sea ecosystems are caused by eutrophication, overfishing, chemical pollution, invasive alien species, pollution from marine transportation, and climate change. Additionally, after the Second World War, the United States and the United Kingdom deposited large quantities of ammunition and chemical weapons directly into the Baltic Sea and the North Sea. These dumps pose a major environmental risk with potentially life-threatening consequences to the health and safety of inhabitants on the coastlines of those seas.[13]

Every year at the end of summer, specialist units from Poland, Denmark, Estonia, the Netherlands, Lithuania, and Germany visit the sea to detect and, if possible, neutralize unexploded ammunition and other deposits. But these undertakings are only partially addressing this threat.

All the sources of pollution around the entire area of the Baltic region were made subject to the Convention on the Protection of the Marine Environment of the Baltic Sea Area (Helsinki Convention) of 1974.[14] The Convention, signed by the then seven coastal states, entered into force on 3 May 1980. But political changes of the late 1980s and early 1990s, as well as progress in international environmental and maritime law, inspired states to draw up a new Convention, which was signed by all nine states bordering the Baltic Sea and by the European Union. The Helsinki Convention of 1992 entered into force on 17 January 2000.[15] Poland ratified the Convention in 1999 and Lithuania in 1997. The governing body of the Convention is the Baltic Marine Environment Protection Commission, also known as HELCOM.

The influence of Poland and Lithuania and their culture on the law of the sea, which is the main subject of this section of the chapter, is deeply rooted in

[12] Federal Ministry for the Environment, Nature Conservation, Nuclear Safety and Consumer Protection, 'HELCOM Adopts 10-Year Plan for the Baltic Sea to Reduce Litter, Noise and Fertiliser Input' (Press Release No 260/21, 20 October 2021) <www.bmuv.de/en/pressrelease/helcom-adopts-10-year-plan-for-the-baltic-sea-to-reduce-litter-noise-and-fertiliser-input> accessed 12 May 2023.

[13] Harald Franzen, 'Ticking Time Bombs in the North and Baltic Sea' *Deutsche Welle* (23 August 2017) www.dw.com/en/ticking-time-bombs-on-the-bottom-of-the-north-and-baltic-sea/a-40200208 accessed 12 May 2023.

[14] Convention on the Protection of the Marine Environment of the Baltic Sea Area, 22 March 1974, 1507 UNTS 166 (Helsinki Convention of 1974).

[15] Convention on the Protection of the Marine Environment of the Baltic Sea Area, 9 April 1992, 2009 UNTS 197 (Helsinki Convention of 1992).

the history, as well as in the global and regional regulations, presented above. On the one hand, those two states implement and follow the provisions of UNCLOS and other related international agreements of a global character. On the other hand, as members of the European Union, they participate in the formulation and implementation of the regional and subregional regulations. In both instances, they are, of course, guided by their national interests and by policy requirements. They add to all of this their cultural and historical experience, as well as their legal expertise.

3.2.1 Poland

To discuss the influence of Poland on the law of the sea, it is necessary to consider its geographical position and other important factors. Poland, as a coastal state, occupies the southern shore of the Baltic Sea. Because of the semi-enclosed character of that sea, Poland is deprived of a full 200-nautical-mile EEZ and a continental shelf of larger dimensions. Poland is also a transit country through which three landlocked states—the Czech Republic, the Slovak Republic, and Hungary—can gain access to the sea.

For Poland, located between Germany and Russia, access to the Baltic Sea was a vital necessity for centuries. Free access to the sea was a driving force of Polish economic development and security.

From the very beginning of its existence in the second half of the tenth century, the Polish state established and defined its border on the Baltic Sea running from the mouth of the Oder River to the mouth of the Vistula River. The first historical Polish ruler, Mieszko I, the founder of the Piast dynasty, united the land that covered roughly all of the present territory of Poland. He strengthened Polish access to the Baltic Sea by, for example, defeating the invasive forces of the Saxon Margrave Odo I at Cedynia on 24 June 1972.

The 'birth certificate' of the Polish sea border is the historical document *Dagome Iudex*, dated 911, in which Mieszko I placed the Polish state, himself, his wife, and his sons under the protection of the Roman Pope. In describing the borders of the Polish state, the document mentions, among others, Longum Mare, or the Baltic Sea.[16] Subsequently, Poland had access to the Baltic Sea until 1793, by which time the country had been partitioned by Russia, Prussia, and Austria.

[16] Karol Olejnik, 'Polityczne i militarne problemy polsko-zachodniopomorskie do XIII wieku' in Paweł Bartnik and Kazimierz Kozłowski (eds), *Pomorze Zachodnie w tysiącleciu* (Archiwum Państwowe w Szczecinie 2000) 41–46.

Access to the Baltic Sea over many centuries helped Poland to establish its position as an important state in Europe. That position was strengthened by the Christianization of the pagan Polish tribes commenced by Mieszko I in 966. Accepting Latin Christianity, Poland, to some extent, became part of Western Europe in a cultural sense. Religion, ideas, legal institutions, and scholarly traditions came predominantly from the West throughout the last millennium. For most of Poland's history, however, its economic systems and social structures differed from Western patterns. Polish lands and society were, as in other countries of the region, under significant influence of traditions that were not Western. As a result of Poland's geography and distinct historical evolutions, however, its culture forms an important part of Western civilization and the Western world. Poland has made significant contributions to art, music, philosophy, mathematics, international law, politics, and literature.

Over time, the culture of Poland has been influenced by Christianity and by German, Italian, French, and Baltic culture, as well as, to a lesser extent, by Byzantine and Ottoman culture. During the Jagiellonian dynasty (from the fourteenth to the sixteenth centuries), Polish culture developed extensively. Poland had ties with Western Europe, particularly Italy, during the Renaissance, when it also developed close relations with Lithuania and continued its territorial expansion to the east. The Polonization of Lithuania culminated in the establishment of the Polish–Lithuanian Commonwealth in 1569. It was one of the largest and most populous states in Europe, with an area approaching one million square kilometres and a population of about one million. Its economy was dominated by export-oriented agriculture.

The reigns of King Sigismund I the Old (1506–48) and his son Sigismund II Augustus (1548–72) saw a golden age of the Renaissance in Poland, of which the astronomer Nicolaus Copernicus (1483–1543) is the best-known representative. There were other influential Polish scientists, philosophers, and legal scholars, such as Paweł Włodkowic (1370–1435, Latinized as Paulus Vladimiri), who, along with Stanisław of Skarbimierz (1360–1431, Latinized as Stanislaus de Scarbimiria), strongly supported the idea of conciliarism in solving international disputes and pioneered the notion of peaceful coexistence among nations. Through his political, diplomatic, and academic career, Włodkowic expressed the view that the world is guided by the principles of peace and mutual respect among nations and that pagan nations have the rights to peace and to possession of the land.[17]

[17] Stanislaus F Belch, *Paulus Vladimiri and His Doctrine Concerning International Law and Politics* (Mouton 1965).

For the economy and security of the Polish–Lithuanian Commonwealth, unlimited access to the Baltic Sea was very important. Such access was granted in 1466 by the Treaty of Thorn,[18] which ended the Thirteen Years' War between Poland and the Teutonic Order. The Treaty added all of western Prussia, called Royal Prussia, to Poland, including Gdansk, while the remaining areas of Prussia continued to be held by the Teutonic Order as the fief of the Polish crown. By this solution, Poland was granted the 110-kilometre-long coast. Consequently, the Polish sea border was stable for the following 300 years, until the aforementioned partition of Poland.[19]

It is noteworthy that the last kings of the Jagiellonian dynasty, Sigismund I and Sigismund Augustus—conducted a very active maritime policy. In 1517, during the war with Russia, Sigismund I formed the first Polish Royal Navy. By cruising on the Baltic Sea, he demonstrated his authority in the waters, which he considered to be his *dominium iuris*.[20] Sigismund Augustus continued the policy of his father even more dynamically. He established the Maritime Commission (Commisio Maritime), one of the first admiralties in Europe. During his reign, the term *dominium Maris Baltici* as the name of the Baltic Sea entered into use in Polish official diplomatic correspondence. It was used for the first time by Sigismund Augustus in his letters to the city of Gdansk and Lubeck, to the princes of Western Pomerania, Brandenburg, Mecklenburg, and Brunswick, and to the Prussian Prince Albert, when he was accusing Eryk XIV, the King of Sweden, of intending to capture the whole Baltic Sea.[21] The same term was later used by all the Baltic states in their diplomatic language. By adopting the term, the Polish king demonstrated that his authority over the water of the Baltic Sea was broad and covered not only the Polish seashore but also the south-western part of the Baltic, leaving other parts to Sweden and Denmark.[22] In an exercise of that authority, on 20 April 1565, Sigismund Augustus issued an edict in which he ordered all foreign vessels crossing the

[18] Peace of Thorn, 19 October 1466 (also known as the Second Peace of Thorn).

[19] 'Treaty of Toruń', *Britannica* <www.britannica.com/topic/Treaty-of-Torun> accessed 12 May 2023.

[20] According to some researchers, *dominium iuris* at that time relied on, among other factors, controlling navigation on Polish waters, imposing and lifting embargoes, enforcing salutes to vessels of the Polish Navy, and combatting foreign navies and piracy: Kazimierz Lepszy, 'Dominium Iuris Baltici' (1967) 1(2) Nautologia 3–18.

[21] Dietrich Schäfer, 'Der Kampf um die Ostsee im 16. und 17. Jahrhundert' (1899) 83(1) Historische Zeitschrift 423.

[22] Stanislaw Bodniak, *Kongres szczeciński na tle bałtyckiej polityki polskiej* (Prace Krakowskiego Oddziału Polskiego Towarzystwa Historycznego 1929).

Polish waters to salute the vessels of the Royal Navy by lowering their sails and to explain the purpose of their passage. Some Polish historians see in the maritime policy and practice of Sigismund Augustus elements of the promotion of *mare liberum*.[23] It is necessary to understand that in those times the Polish understanding of the *dominium Maris Baltici* meant not only political or military activities but also the utility of the sea resources and navigation. Poland was then called the 'granary of Europe', because 75 per cent of grain transported through the Danish strait originated from the port of Gdansk. But only 82 per cent of Polish grain was exported via Gdansk; the rest moved through Elbląg (7 per cent), Riga (6.5 per cent), Königsberg (2.5 per cent), and Szczecin (1.6 per cent).[24]

The maritime policy of Sigismund Augustus was continued by the elected king Władysław IV (1595–1648). On his order, the Polish shore was fortified and the Polish navy was strengthened. He insisted on acquiring the benefits from the sea. In a letter to the citizens of Gdansk, he wrote: 'No state or no monarchy should neglect plans and preparations to ensure benefits from the sea.'[25]

Władysław's efforts and policy were not continued effectively by his successors. They did not prevent the military build-up conducted by the Prussian rulers and the strengthening of their position in the Baltic Sea by Denmark and Sweden and later by czarist Russia.

From the mid-seventeenth century, the Polish–Lithuanian Commonwealth entered a period of decline caused by devastating wars with Sweden, Turkey, and the Cossacks, as well as a deteriorating political system. Significant reforms were introduced in the late eighteenth century, such as Europe's first constitution on 3 May 1791, but all three neighbouring powers did not allow the reforms to advance. The existence of the Commonwealth ended in 1795, after a series of foreign invasions and the partitions of Polish soil carried out by Russia in the east, Prussia in the west, and Austria in the south. The Polish Baltic coast was incorporated into Prussia and Russia. From 1795 until 1918, no truly independent Poland existed, although there were strong Polish resistance movements, like the uprisings of November 1830 and January 1863. Poland gained sovereignty and materialized access to the sea after the First World War, when the three partitioning powers were defeated and weakened in the wake of war and internal revolutions. Poland returned to the map of Europe as an independent state and existed until 1939, when Germany and the Soviet Union

[23] Kazimierz Białkowski, 'Mare liberum czy dominium maris Baltici?' (1968) 1(2) Nautologia 47–52.
[24] S Gierszewski, 'Polska na morzu od XV do XVIII wieku' (1979) 1(5) Nautologia 206–15.
[25] Lepszy (n 20) 266–67.

invaded it, thus launching the Second World War. Afterwards, Poland restored access to the Baltic Sea, which had been lost in 1793.

The restoration of Polish access to the Baltic Sea was celebrated by the Wedding to the Sea, which symbolized Poland's marriage to the Baltic Sea just as Venetians symbolize their city's marriage to the Adriatic Sea. The ceremony was first performed on 10 February 1920 by General Józef Haller, the commandant of the Pomeranian Front of the Polish army at the seaport of Puck (Putzig). The symbolic event was witnessed by high-ranking Polish officials, a local crowd, a unit of uhlans, and naval personnel. At the main point of the ceremony, Haller threw into the sea a platinum ring funded by the Polish families of Gdansk. While doing so, he said: 'In the name of the Holy Republic of Poland, I, general Józef Haller, am taking the control over this ancient Slavic Baltic Sea shore.'[26]

In the early spring of 1945, still under the war situation, the First Polish Army units organized their own weddings with the sea when they reached the Baltic Sea shore. The main ceremony of both the First and Second Polish Armies took place in Kołobrzeg. There, the following oath of the general Michał Rola-Żymierski was pronounced:[27]

> I swear to you, the Polish Sea, that I, the soldier of the Homeland, faithful son of the Polish nation, will not abandon you. I swear that I will always follow this road, the road which has been paved by the State National Council, the road which has led me to the sea. I will guard you, I will not hesitate to shed my blood for my Fatherland, neither will I hesitate to give you my life so that you do not return to Germany. You will remain Polish forever.

After a dramatic struggle under German Nazi occupation, during which one-fifth of the population perished, Poland was liberated by the Soviet Army in 1945. Fighting alongside the Soviets was the Polish Army, which had formed in the Soviet Union. Consequently, Poland fell under the communist regime for over 40 years. Through the efforts of the whole population, the country was rebuilt from the devastation of war and a system-centralized economy was introduced.

By the terms of the 1945 Potsdam Agreement, signed by the three victorious Great Powers, Poland was shifted west in relation to its prewar location, to the area between the Oder-Neisse rivers in the west and the Curzon

[26] 'Poles Symbolize Union With Sea' *New York Times* (13 February 1920).

[27] *Zwyciężymy* (Polish Army newspaper, 10 March 1945).

Line in the east, with much broader access to the sea. Although Poland lost its eastern territories and 70 per cent of its prewar oil capacity to the Soviet Union, it gained not only broader access to the Baltic Sea but also an industrial base and the infrastructure that made industrial development possible. In response to the 1945 Yalta Conference directives, the Polish provisional government of the National Unity was formed in June of that year. However, the domination of the Soviet Union was apparent and, after elections in 1947, that government ceased to exist. The communists moved towards replacing the established postwar partial *people's democracy* with a state socialist system. The following years saw, on the one hand, the progress of industrialization and the slow development of the country and, on the other hand, periodic economic instability and a deterioration in the living conditions of the Polish population. Combined with the authoritarian communist rule and the conditions of the Cold War, this led to growing opposition and protests, culminating in the formation of the Solidarity trade union (Solidarność) in 1980. During the imposition of martial law in 1981, Solidarity became an underground movement enjoying popular support. Student protests and continuing economic decline led to strikes across the country in the spring of 1988. The government felt compelled to negotiate with the opposition. The fitful bargaining between the negotiators and inter-ruling-party squabbling led to the official Round Table negotiations of 1989. These were followed by legislative elections in June of that year, which resulted in the fall of communism in Poland.

In the 1990s, Poland charted a path leading to integration with Western Europe and the Western defence system. It became a member of the Council of Europe in 1991 and joined NATO in 1999. On 1 May 2004, Poland became a member state of the European Union; however, it has not adopted the euro as its currency.

The access to the Baltic Sea obtained in 1918, though very limited, allowed Poland gradually to develop seaborne trade, ports, a merchant fleet, and a navy, as well as shipbuilding and fishing industries. Those developments gained new dimensions after the Second World War. With wider access to the sea and a more advanced economy, Poland has increased its presence in maritime operations. It has also created better conditions for studies of the sea and has developed a wider interest in the international law of the sea.

Because of its geographical position, Poland joined the group of geographically disadvantaged states at the Third UN Conference of the Law of the Sea. Those states—including Poland—insisted on including in UNCLOS provisions that would meet their specific rights and interests. Many of those rights and interests were recognized and reflected in several articles of the Convention.[28]

For geographical, economic, social, and security reasons, Poland is vitally interested in preserving freedom of navigation, ensuring access to the living resources on the high seas and in the economic zones of other states, and participating in the exploitation of the seabed beyond the limits of national jurisdiction. These three issues and problems of the delimitation in the Baltic Sea, as well as some aspects of security in that area, are unquestionably most important to Poland.

For Poland, freedom of navigation is one of the fundamental principles of the law of the sea. In the sixteenth and early seventeenth centuries, under Władysław IV, the Polish fleet was fighting on the Baltic Sea for free access to trading routes leading to Western Europe. Access to the sea has historically been a driving force for Polish economic and social development. It has also provided additional security for the country. That is why, at the Third Conference on the Law of the Sea, Poland was for the utmost preservation of the freedom of navigation.[29]

The important issue facing Poland in the Baltic Sea area is the question of its own—as well as regional—security, which is closely related to freedom of navigation and other aspects of the law of the sea. At the end of 2019, the Polish Ministry of Defence published on its website an article titled 'Together With the Baltic States, We Care About Security in the Region'. That article analyses many aspects of military challenges and military cooperation.[30]

The Russian invasion of Ukraine makes security issues even more pressing. In particular, Poland fears the constant military threat posed by Russia's heavily militaristic enclave of Kaliningrad, home to combat forces, including the Baltic Fleet, advanced air forces, and the Iskander mobile nuclear-capable missile system installed in 2016, as well as a battery of missiles with a range that includes all of Poland.[31]

Polish authorities have developed strong bilateral relations, including with regard to maritime issues, with the other three Baltic states: Lithuania, Estonia, and Latvia. In 2011, the Polish Minister of Foreign Affairs signed with his Swedish partner a declaration on political cooperation in areas of strategic

[28] Symonides (n 3) 58.

[29] ibid 59.

[30] Ministry of National Defence, Republic of Poland, 'Together With the Baltic States, We Care About Security in the Region' (16 December 2019) <www.gov.pl/web/national-defence/together-with-the-baltic-states-we-care-about-security-in-the-region> accessed 12 May 2023.

[31] Aleksander Król, 'Kaliningrad's Island of Misfortunes—A Russian Offensive From Kaliningrad' *Warsaw Institute Review* (1 May 2018).

importance as a starting point for 'deeper cooperation in terms of foreign, security and defence policy'.[32] In 2014, in Szczecin, at the initiative of Poland, a tripartite Polish–Lithuanian–Ukrainian brigade was established.

Polish efforts in the region are also focused on energy security issues, in particular the diversification of energy supply sources. Poland actively participates in the Baltic Energy Market Interconnection Plan, which aims to desynchronize the Baltic states from the Russian and Belarusian electricity grids. The project was initiated by the European Commission in 2009. Poland also coordinates 3 of the 17 work themes carried out by the EU Strategy for the Baltic Sea Region.[33]

Seeking new energy resources, Poland is pursuing wind energy that can be exploited in the Baltic Sea. Already, three offshore wind farms are under development by a Polish company. In March 2020, the Lithuanian Ignitis Group received a €60 million loan from the European Investment Bank for the construction of a wind farm off the Polish coast.[34]

Nevertheless, wind energy is not sufficient. In cooperation with other EU member states, Polish authorities are striving for new energy sources and eliminating dependence on Russian gas and oil supplies. Poland has established the Gas Interconnection Poland–Lithuania pipeline and the North Gate project for shipping Norwegian gas to its territory via Denmark. In addition, Poland is developing its capabilities for storing imported liquefied natural gas (LNG) from Qatar, Norway, and the United States. The major LNG terminal is operating in Świnoujście and another will be built in Gdansk.[35]

While on the subject of energy issues, a brief note should be made on a very controversial question related to the Nord Stream gas pipelines in the Baltic Sea between Russia and Germany. Nord Stream 1 was operating since its completion in 2011. Nord Stream 2 was almost completed when Germany suspended operation of both pipelines in protest against the Russian invasion of Ukraine. Three of the transit states—Finland, Sweden, and Denmark—granted permission for laying Nord Stream 2 in 2018. From the very beginning, however, Poland, Lithuania, Estonia, and Latvia strongly opposed the project because it threatens to bypass them, ignores existing Ukrainian pipelines, increases

[32] Kafkadesk Kraków, 'Poland's Vested Interests in the Baltic Sea, Explained' (*Kafkadesk*, 17 August 2022) <https://kafkadesk.org/2020/08/17/polands-vested-interests-in-the-baltic-sea-explained/> accessed 12 May 2023.

[33] European Commission, 'EU Strategy for the Baltic Sea Region' <https://ec.europa.eu/regional_policy/pl/policy/cooperation/macro-regional-strategies/baltic-sea/> accessed 22 March 2022.

[34] Kafkadesk Kraków (n 32).

[35] ibid.

Europe's dependence on deliveries of Russian gas, and undermines Europe's overall security and stability.[36]

The Nord Stream projects have affected many interests and were also considered in light of legal conditions applying to submarine pipelines under UNCLOS. The conclusions of those considerations indicate that while, with respect to the seabed and subsoil, the coastal state's sovereign rights and jurisdiction are to be exercised in accordance with Articles 58(1) and 79(1) of UNCLOS, all states are entitled to lay submarine cables and pipelines in the EEZ and on the continental shelf.[37]

Poland is attaching great importance to the substantial reduction of pollution in the Baltic Sea area. Over the last decades, the environmental situation of the Baltic Sea has degraded—especially with regard to eutrophication, which is caused primarily by pollution from industry, agriculture, wastewater, and forestry. Because of the composition of the coastal states, the management of the Baltic Sea environment is regulated mainly by EU law, in particular the Marine Strategy Framework Directive 2008/56/EC and the Water Framework Directive 2000/60/EC. Along with Poland and the eight other states bordering the Baltic Sea, the European Union is a party to the Helsinki Convention of 1992. The diversity of legal regimes requires each party to implement and enforce legal measures at a national level to abate the eutrophication of the sea through rules and other instruments that aim to reduce the release of discharges into marine waters.

Poland is fulfilling its obligations with regard to those requirements. However, despite undeniable progress in reducing pollutant emissions and discharges into the environment, Poland lags behind most other Baltic states. Polish authorities are aware of this situation and have undertaken many measures in response. Along with efforts at a national level, Poland has closely cooperated with neighbouring states, especially Denmark, Germany, Lithuania, and Sweden. There is a strong focus on environmental measures, including investments in green technologies to reduce pollution discharges into the Baltic Sea.[38] For example, in cooperation with the Polish government and Taiwanese authorities, Polish scientists involved in environmental research are working to construct a modern ecological ship specially designed to clean debris from the Baltic waters.[39]

[36] Nord Stream <www.nord-stream.com/> accessed 29 June 2022.

[37] See UNCLOS, chs V and VI.

[38] Organisation for Economic Co-operation and Development, *OECD Environmental Performance Reviews: Poland* (23 April 2015).

[39] See *Angora Weekly* (3 May 2022) 29.

Turning to the legal issues related to Poland's maritime policy and legislation, it is advisable to begin with the provisions of the Act Concerning the Maritime Areas of the Polish Republic and the Marine Administration of 21 March 1991, which follows the UNCLOS regulations. The Act defines the legal situation of the maritime areas of the Polish Republic, the coastal areas, and the authorities of the marine administration and their scope of jurisdiction. According to Article 2 of the Act, the marine areas of the Polish Republic are the internal waters, the territorial sea, and the EEZ. The territorial water consists of a marine area of 12 nautical miles measured from the baseline of the sea. The baseline of the territorial sea is constituted by the low-water line along the coast or the outer limit of the internal waters (Article 5). The EEZ is established and situated beyond and adjacent to the territorial sea.[40]

The 1991 Act omitted then the establishment of the contiguous zone provided by UNCLOS. The Act states that international treaties define the boundaries of the EEZ continental shelf (Articles 15 and 16). Poland concluded such a treaty on the territorial sea with the former Soviet Union in 1958, followed in 1969 by an additional agreement concerning the continental shelf and in 1985 by an agreement on the entire sea border line related to territorial waters, the contiguous zone, the EEZ, and the continental shelf.[41]

In 1989, Poland signed an agreement with Sweden concerning a small disputed zone in the Baltic Sea, attributing 75 per cent of the zone to Sweden and 25 per cent to Poland.[42]

The negotiations with Denmark on the sea delimitation lasted for a long time, ending in Brussels in 2018 with the signing of the Agreement Concerning the Delimitation of Maritime Zones in the Baltic Sea.[43] During the signing ceremony, the Danish Minister for Foreign Affairs, Anders Samuelsen, stated:[44]

> I am very pleased with today's historic signing of the treaty on maritime delimitation between Poland and Denmark. We have now closed the

[40] Act Concerning the Maritime Areas of the Polish Republic and the Marine Administration, 21 March 1991.

[41] See United Nations Oceans & Law of the Sea, 'Poland' <www.un.org/depts/los/LEGISLATIONANDTREATIES/STATEFILES/POL.htm> accessed 28 March 2022.

[42] E Franckx, 'Maritime Delimitation in the Baltic Sea: What Has Already Been Accomplished?' (2012) 6(3) TransNav (International Journal on Marine Navigation and Safety of Sea Transportation) 437.

[43] Agreement Concerning the Delimitation of Maritime Zones in the Baltic Sea, 19 November 2018.

[44] 'Poland and Denmark Sign Agreement on Maritime Boundary in the Baltic Sea' (European MSP Platform, 28 November 2018) <https://maritime-spatial-planning.ec.europa.eu/news/poland-and-denmark-sign-agreement-maritime-boundary-baltic-sea> accessed 12 May 2023.

negotiations that were started more than 40 years ago and taken the first step in formalizing the agreement. This is great news indeed and shows our common commitment to solve difficult issues through negotiations.

The Polish Minister for Foreign Affairs, Jacek Czaputowicz, responded: 'Today's signing ceremony marks an important day in our bilateral relations. It signifies that with commitment, mutual trust and respect it is possible to successfully end even longstanding disputes.'[45]

The Polish contiguous zone was established in November 2015. It extends to 24 nautical miles from the baselines in accordance with Article 33(2) of UNCLOS. It is an area of the sea adjacent to the territorial sea, covering a part of the Polish EEZ.[46]

The delimitation of the maritime border between Poland and Germany was established after long negotiations by the 22 May 1989 Agreement between Poland and the former German Democratic Republic. This Agreement was recognized by united Germany in the following year by the Treaty Between the Republic of Poland and the Republic of Germany on the Confirmation of the Existing Border Between Them.[47]

When writing about cultural influences on the law of the sea, it is necessary to mention amber, the paramount treasure of the southern shore of the Baltic Sea—which belongs to Poland. Amber is known as the 'Gold of the North' or the 'Gem of the Baltic', due to its beautiful colour. Made of fossilized tree resin that is about 40 million years old, amber nuggets are the remnants of a vast forest in what is now Scandinavia—although a popular Polish legend tells that the nuggets are debris from the palace of the sea goddess Jurata, which was shattered to pieces by the mighty god Perkun. Amber was well known in the era of the Roman Empire. In Poland, the amber route from the shores of the Baltic Sea to Rome went through the area where the Polish city of Kalisz, under the Roman name Calisia, now lies.[48]

[45] ibid.

[46] D Pyć, 'The Polish Contiguous Zone—The Exercise of the Coastal State Jurisdiction and Control' (2017) 11(3) TransNav 453.

[47] Treaty Between the Republic of Poland and the Republic of Germany on the Confirmation of the Existing Border Between Them, 14 November 1990, 1708 UNTS 377.

[48] Marek Kępa, 'Amber & Poland: A History Crafted in Resin' (*Culture.pl*, 15 May 2018) <https://culture.pl/en/article/amber-poland-a-history-crafted-in-resin> accessed 12 May 2023.

3.2.2 Lithuania

Lithuania is one of three Baltic states on the eastern shore of the Baltic Sea. It shares borders with Latvia to the north, Belarus to the east and south, Poland to the south, and Kaliningrad—Russia's westernmost oblast—to the southwest. On the Baltic Sea, Lithuania has a short maritime border with Sweden. It has around 99 kilometres of coastline, of which only 38 kilometres face the open Baltic Sea.[49]

Lithuania has a long tradition of close relations with Poland. In 1386, having accepted Poland's offer to become its king, the Grand Duke Jogaila was crowned Władysław II Jagiełło. He embarked on the gradual Christianization of Lithuania and established a personal union between Poland and Lithuania. In 1569, the Polish–Lithuanian Commonwealth was created, although Lithuania retained its institutions—including a separate army, currency, and statutory law. In 1397, the borders of the Grand Duchy of Lithuania were expanded by the so-called Ochakiv Field (Yedisan)—that is, the area between the mouths of the Dnieper and Dniester rivers. At that time, the Principality of Moldavia was also a fiefdom of the Polish kingdom, with ports in Kilia and Bilhorod (Białogród), which, together with the Lithuanian port in Ochakiv, were important trade centres of the Jagiellonian dynasty. Goods were exported through the Black Sea ports, which were accessible to merchants from other countries. The goods then went to Polish and Lithuanian cities and—of course—to manor houses.[50]

But, due to several wars which devastated its territory as well as internal political weakness and divisions, the Polish–Lithuanian Commonwealth was partitioned by the neighbouring states—Russia, Prussia, and Austria. In 1795, it ceased to exist as a state. Between the end of the First World War and the time of the presidency of Michail Gorbachev in the Soviet Union, Lithuania was an independent republic but was twice incorporated into the USSR.

Lithuania regained its independence from Soviet rule in 1990, upon the Declaration of its Supreme Council announced on 11 March 1990, which was recognized by the Soviet Union on 6 September 1991.[51] The restoration of independence was achieved, in fact, as a result of an intense peaceful struggle conducted by Lithuanians together with Estonians and Latvians. In 1992, this

[49] VASAB, 'Country Fiche, Lithuania' (updated May 2021).
[50] Jakub Bartosik, 'Poland on the Black Sea' (*Strategy and Future*, 29 May 2021) <https://strategyandfuture.org/en/poland-on-the-black-sea/> accessed 12 May 2023.
[51] Jamestown Foundation, 'Skrunda Shuts Down, Publication: Monitor Volume: 4 Issue: 159' (1 September 1998) <https://jamestown.org/program/skrunda-shuts-down/> accessed 12 May 2023.

cooperation led to the creation of the Council of the Baltic Sea States, composed of Lithuania, Estonia, and Latvia.[52]

After achieving independence, Lithuania, Estonia, and Latvia became NATO members on 29 March 2004. They were admitted to the European Union on 1 May of that year. Lithuania joined the World Trade Organization in 2001 and the Organisation for Economic Co-operation and Development in 2018. In 2015, it adopted the euro as its single currency.

A signatory of UNCLOS, Lithuania has more than 20 laws and governmental resolutions guiding the use of sea space. According to Article 47 of the Lithuanian Constitution, the exclusive right for the Lithuanian maritime space belongs to the Republic of Lithuania. Current governance of the sea space is defined by legislation relating to the use of the sea space and the responsibilities of Lithuania under the international agreements in which it participates.[53]

The 1992 Law on the State Boundary, among others, provides the rules of peaceful navigation in Lithuania's territorial sea. Although that law does not use the UNCLOS term 'innocent passage', Article 10 states: 'During peaceful navigation, a ship may stop or anchor if it is necessary for ordinary navigation or for rendering assistance to persons, ships or aircraft in distress.' Thus, it does not automatically cover the passage of warships. According to that article, such passage could be established on the basis of reciprocity. The government of Lithuania may designate sea lines for tankers, ships carrying dangerous cargo, and ships with nuclear engines.[54]

3.3 The Black Sea region

Since ancient times, the Black Sea has been a crossroads of civilizations, cultures, trade, navigation, and strategic interests. Thracians, Scythians, Greeks, Romans, Bulgarians, Tatars, Turks, Russians, and many others shaped the area. In the tenth century, the famous Bulgarian poet Exarch wrote: 'The Sea brings together all which is at a distance.' This motto is still alive in the Black Sea area, despite many divisions and particular interests, because people living there are dependent on the sea for their survival. This is why their states must

[52] Gustav N Kristensen, *Born into a Dream: Eurofaculty and the Baltic Sea States* (BWV Berliner Wissenschafts-Verlag 2010).

[53] VASAB (n 49).

[54] Law of the Republic of Lithuania on the State Boundary of the Republic of Lithuania, 25 June 1992 (No 1-2671).

cooperate to preserve the Black Sea, which is the prime source of existence in the region.[55]

For a long time, the Black Sea area was considered the far edge of Europe, divided between Russia and Turkey, and then, during the Cold War, between East and West. This region is now more of a bridge between Europe, the Middle East, and Asia than a European border zone. Since Bulgaria and Romania became members of the European Union in 2007 and of NATO in 2004, the situation has changed. The European Union has strengthened regional cooperation with and between the countries surrounding the Black Sea.

It is important to note that the Black Sea constitutes a natural inland water basin situated between Europe and Asia. Six countries share the Black Sea coast: Bulgaria, Georgia, Romania, Russia, Turkey, and Ukraine. The lengths of their respective coastlines are 354 kilometres for Bulgaria, 310 kilometres for Georgia, 225 kilometres for Romania, 800 kilometres for Russia (including the Azov Sea), 1,329 kilometres for Turkey, and 2,782 kilometres for Ukraine (including the Azov Sea). Approximately 16 million people inhabit the coastal zones of the six countries. The total area of the Black Sea is 422,000 square kilometres (or 441,000 square kilometres if the shallow Azov Sea is included).[56]

The main difficulty in delimiting the sea spaces of the Black Sea countries stems from the elliptical shape of that sea and its limited size. For that reason, Black Sea states can claim a maximum width of 200 nautical miles in their EEZs.

The end of the Cold War and the collapse of the Soviet Union led to important changes in the Baltic Sea region. Two new states—Ukraine and Georgia—emerged and those states, along with Bulgaria and Romania, entered into a period of political and economic transformation. During these processes, the Russian Federation has attempted to re-establish a sphere of influence over the post-Soviet countries. At the same time, Bulgaria and Romania established relations with NATO and the European Union, becoming member states of both.

The Black Sea region has thus become of great interest to the European Union, due not only to the accession of Bulgaria and Romania but also to many other reasons, from security and economics to energy and transportation. Many pipelines and fibre-optic cables cross the bed of the Black Sea.

[55] Marusya Lyubcheva, *The Black Sea Region in EU Policies* (Black Sea Institute and Friedrich Ebert Stiftung 2010).

[56] Black Sea NGO Network, 'Commitment to the Black Sea' <hwww.bsnn.org/black_sea.html> accessed 29 June 2022.

The Black Sea region is also important for strategic and political reasons. The accelerated modernization of the Russian Black Sea Fleet and its hostile activity in the region as well as the Russian occupation of Crimea increase the threat to smaller Black Sea states. Without external support, those states would lack the necessary resources and capabilities to resist regional hegemony ambitions. In this complex situation, Bulgaria and Romania need increased Allied support to manage the risks arising from the security environment in the Black Sea region.[57]

The area has become subject to political conflicts, tensions, and even wars, including the current one in Ukraine. It is not only the European Union that understands the strategic importance of the region. The US Secretary of Defense, Lloyd Austin, recently stated:[58]

> Security and stability of the Black Sea are in the U.S. national interest and are critical to the security of NATO's Eastern Flank.... Russia's destabilizing activities in and around the Black Sea reflect its ambitions to regain a dominant position in the region and to prevent the realization of a Europe that is whole, free and at peace.

Bulgaria, Romania, and other littoral states of the Black Sea focus their joint efforts on fisheries, environmental sustainability, maritime affairs, and the blue economy. A collaborative approach to addressing Black Sea fisheries issues was underlined in the Bucharest Ministerial Declaration of 2016[59] and later reinforced in the Sofia Declaration of 2018.[60] EU management measures addressing fishing opportunities and the conditions relating to certain fish stocks applicable in the Black Sea refer only to Bulgaria and Romania, while fishery management requires the involvement of all Black Sea coastal states.[61]

In 2019, Bulgaria, Georgia, Moldova, Romania, Russia, Turkey, and Ukraine endorsed the Bucharest Declaration on the Common Maritime Agenda for the Black Sea, a voluntary regional cooperation framework on maritime affairs and

[57] Lubomir Ivanov, 'A Bulgarian Perspective on the Black Sea Region' (NATO Defense College Foundation, 22 June 2021) <www.natofoundation.org/food-for-thought-2021/a-bulgarian-perspective-on-the-black-sea-region/> accessed 12 May 2023.

[58] US Department of Defense, 'Secretary of Defense Lloyd J. Austin III's Remarks at Romanian Ministry of Defense Post-Bilat Joint Press Event' (20 October 2021) <www.defense.gov/News/Transcripts/Transcript/Article/2816800/secretary-of-defense-lloyd-j-austin-iiis-remarks-at-romanian-ministry-of-defens/> accessed 12 May 2023.

[59] Declaration of the High-Level Conference Towards Enhanced Cooperation on Black Sea Fisheries and Aquaculture, October 2016.

[60] Declaration of the High-Level Conference on Black Sea Fisheries and Aquaculture, 7 June 2018 (Sofia Declaration).

[61] ibid.

the blue economy carried out by the seven countries involved. The Declaration addresses the sustainability of marine sources, better data collection and improved scientific advice, the sustainable development of aquaculture, compliance, and the fight against illegal, unreported, and unregulated fishing.[62] It aims to address jointly the challenges and opportunities of the area, ensuring environmental sustainability while fostering growth and promoting the blue economy and coastal ecosystems.[63]

The Black Sea ecosystem has been the subject of intense scrutiny. Changes over the last 50 years clearly indicate its vulnerability to anthropogenic effects. Marine resources in the Black Sea have declined due to overfishing, the unplanned development of coastal zones, and intense maritime traffic.[64] The amount of marine litter in the Black Sea is twice that in the Mediterranean Sea. The concentration of some toxins exceeds their threshold value, according to the results of the Joint Black Sea Surveys presented by the EU/UNDP project and the Ministry of Ecology and Natural Resources of Ukraine. Due to environmental pollution, the Black Sea is dying—and it is posing a danger to the many millions of people living in the coastal countries.[65]

3.3.1 Romania

Romania, the twelfth-largest country in Europe, has good access to the Black Sea. It is a well-developing country and a very active member of the European Union. As an independent state since 1877, Romania has experienced many historical and political changes. After the Second World War, it was first occupied by the Soviet Union and then joined the Warsaw Pact as a member of the socialist community. After the 1989 revolution, Romania began the transition towards a Western democratic system and a market economy. It is a signatory to UNCLOS and is well engaged in maritime activities and law-of-the-sea issues.

The Act Concerning the Legal Regime of the Internal Waters, the Territorial Sea, and the Contiguous Zone of 1990[66] is a basic document regulating the

[62] Declaration on a Common Maritime Agenda for the Black Sea, 21 May 2019.

[63] European Commission, 'Black Sea' <https://ec.europa.eu/oceans-and-fisheries/ocean/sea-basins/black-sea_en> accessed 29 March 2022.

[64] European Environment Agency, 'Black Sea Region Briefing—The European Environment—State and Outlook 2015' (18 February 2015; last modified 11 May 2020) <www.eea.europa.eu/soer/2015/countries/black-sea> accessed 12 May 2023.

[65] N Quazi, 'Black Sea Pollution' (*Countercurrents.org*, 20 April 2020) <https://countercurrents.org/2020/04/black-sea-pollution/> accessed 12 May 2023.

[66] Act Concerning the Legal Regime of the Internal Waters, the Territorial Sea and the Contiguous Zone of Romania, 7 August 1990, with later amendments and supplements related to the EEZ.

maritime space of Romania and activities in the seawater under its jurisdiction. In many of its 45 articles, the Act reflects the provisions and requirements of UNCLOS. It also addresses, in Chapter VI, the prevention, reduction, and control of maritime environment pollution.[67]

Following its accession to the European Union, Romania has consistently advocated for increased EU involvement in the Black Sea region. In cooperation with the other member states, primarily Greece and Bulgaria, Romania has contributed to the launch by the European Union of the forum Black Sea Synergy and the advancement of the processes initiated under it. The region's importance would subsequently be considered in several EU policies and instruments, including the Eastern Partnership (2009), the Strategy for the Danube Region (2010), and the EU Strategy for Connecting Europe and Asia.[68]

In the first half of 2019, the Romanian presidency of the Council of the European Union focused on promoting regional cooperation in the Black Sea region with the support of the European Union. The most notable result of this period was the adoption on 21 May 2019 of two framework documents: the Common Maritime Agenda for the Black Sea and the Black Sea Strategic Research and Innovation Agenda. Both Agendas are subsumed to the Black Sea Synergy, contributing to its substantiation and implementation.[69]

During the last period of its presidency of the Council, Romania continued to act towards the goal of intensifying regional cooperation on the Black Sea, with the active involvement of the European Union, as well as placing the Black Sea on the Union's long-term agenda. In 2019, the Romanian Minister of Foreign Affairs acted as the national coordinator for the Common Maritime Agenda for the Black Sea.[70]

Consolidating territorial claims and access to maritime resources, Romania, after unsuccessful negotiations with Ukraine about the delimitation of the EEZ around Snake Island, brought the case to the International Court of Justice (ICJ) in 2004.[71]

On 3 February 2009, the ICJ handed down its verdict, establishing a maritime boundary including the continental shelf and EEZs for Romania and

[67] ibid.

[68] Ministry of Foreign Affairs (Romania), 'Results of the Romanian Presidency of the EU Council, for the Black Sea Region' (December 2021) <www.mae.ro/en/node/52667> accessed 12 May 2023.

[69] ibid.

[70] ibid.

[71] International Court of Justice, 'Maritime Delimitations in the Black Sea (Romania v. Ukraine): Conclusion of the Public Hearings, Court Begins Its Deliberation' (press release, 19 September 2008) <https://web.archive.org/web/20160303204609/http://www.icj-cij.org/docket/files/132/14755.pdf> accessed 12 May 2023.

Ukraine.[72] The court divided the Black Sea with a line between each country's claims. On the Romanian side, the ICJ found that the landward end of the Sulina dyke should be the basis for the equidistance principle. The court noted that a dyke has a different function from a port. On the Ukrainian side, the court found that Snake Island did not form part of Ukraine's coastal configuration, explaining that '[t]o count [Snake] Island as a relevant part of the coast would amount to grafting an extraneous element onto Ukraine's coastline; the consequence would be a judicial refashioning of geography'.[73] The ICJ concluded that Snake Island 'should have no effect on the delimitation in this case, other than that stemming from the role of the 12-nautical-mile arc of its territorial sea'.[74]

While the judgment drew a line that was equitable for both parties, Romania received nearly 80 per cent of the disputed area, allowing it to exploit a significant but undetermined portion of an estimated 100 billion cubic metres of natural gas deposits and 15 million tons of oil under the seabed.[75]

3.3.2 Bulgaria

The Republic of Bulgaria—bordered by Romania to the north, Greece and Turkey to the south, and Serbia and the former Yugoslav Republic of Macedonia to the west—has, to the east, a 414-kilometre coastline with the Black Sea. It established the territorial waters, the contiguous zone, and the 200-nautical-mile EEZ agreed with Turkey in 1997. The delimitation of the territorial sea, the EEZ, and the continental shelf with Romania is pending.[76]

Bulgaria enacted its very detailed Maritime Space, Inland Waterways and Ports Act in 2000.[77] Article 2 of the Act 'aims at ensuring the use of the Black Sea and the river Danube in the interests of cooperation of countries of the Black Sea, the Danube and other countries'. The Act provides that the Bulgarian sea space is comprised of internal waters, the territorial sea, the contiguous zone, the continental shelf, and the EEZ. The breadth of the territorial sea is 12 nautical miles measured from the baselines. The contiguous zone

[72] *Black Sea Case (Romania v Ukraine) (Judgment)* [2009] ICJ Rep 101.
[73] ibid para 149.
[74] ibid para 188.
[75] Philippa Runner, 'EU's Black Sea Border Set in Stone' *EUobserver* (3 February 2009) <https://euobserver.com/world/27525> accessed 12 May 2023.
[76] Siemon T Wezeman and Alexandra Kuimova, 'Bulgaria and the Black Sea Security' (SIPRI Background Paper, December 2018).
[77] Maritime Space, Inland Waterways and Ports of the Republic of Bulgaria Act, 28 January 2000.

extends to a distance of 24 nautical miles from the baselines. The outer limit of the continental shelf, according to Article 40 of the Act, 'extends beyond the territorial sea up to the lines of delimitation of the continental shelf with States with adjacent and opposite coasts'. And, according to Article 45, the EEZ 'extends beyond the limits of the territorial sea to a distance of up to 200 nautical miles from the baselines'. It is evident that Bulgaria has followed the basic provisions of UNCLOS.

Bulgarian history and culture are rich and, in many instances, related to the sea. Since ancient times, the Black Sea has been a pillar of the Bulgarian economy and culture.

Until 2018, Bulgaria's maritime spatial planning followed a sectoral approach. Some general measures are also mentioned in the Development Strategies of the various coastal districts, the National Strategic Plan for Aquaculture in Bulgaria (2014–20), the National Regional Development Strategy (2012–22), and the Marine Strategy for Conservation of the Environment in the Marine Waters of Bulgaria (2016–21) and its Programme of Measures.[78]

The Maritime Space, Inland Waterways and Ports Act established the legal regime for the maritime space and maritime spatial planning. In March 2018, Section VII—titled 'Use of the Maritime Space and Protection of the Marine Environment'—was introduced into the Act. According to new Article 51a, the maritime space of the Republic of Bulgaria is to be used in accordance with the principle of integrated maritime management. To promote sustainable growth of the marine economy, sustainable growth of the Bulgarian Black Sea region, and sustainable use of the natural resources, maritime spatial planning is applied as an instrument of the Integrated Maritime Policy of the European Union. This includes an analysis of all activities related to the use of maritime space and organizing them in a way that allows their joint existence to achieve environmental, economic, and social objectives.

The Maritime Spatial Plan of Bulgaria, adopted in May 2023, is based on the analysis of existing environmental, geological, geomorphological, and physical information; data accessible through the National Spatial Data Portal; and data on social and economic activities. The Plan takes into account issues including the specific features of the Black Sea region; the status of biological, mineral, and energy resources; existing and future activities related to the use of marine spaces, as well as their impact on the environment and underwater

[78] European MSP Platform, *Maritime Spatial Planning Country Information: Bulgaria* (2021) <https://maritime-spatial-planning.ec.europa.eu/sites/default/files/download/bulgaria_november_2021.pdf> accessed 12 May 2023.

cultural heritage; land–sea interactions; and cross-border cooperation in the Black Sea region. In implementing the Plan, Bulgaria has been cooperating with other countries in the Black Sea region, including those within the Organization of the Black Sea Economic Cooperation and the Commission on the Protection of the Black Sea against Pollution.

In the framework for spatial planning, Bulgaria and Romania focus on fields related to the blue economy, which can contribute to the sustainable economic development of the region—especially the coastal areas. Its main goals are healthy marine and coastal ecosystems; a competitive, innovative, and sustainable blue economy for the Black Sea; and fostering investment in the Black Sea blue economy.[79] Cooperation with Romania is aimed at promoting consistency and coordination of the national maritime spatial plans on all issues of a transnational nature. For example, Bulgaria's Maritime Spatial Plan could be developed as part of cross-border maritime spatial planning in the Black Sea. Numerous cross-border projects have also been conducted. The endorsement of the Common Maritime Agenda for the Black Sea in May 2019 is the latest example of concrete transboundary cooperation in the Black Sea.[80]

In December 2016, the Council of Ministers adopted the Marine Strategy of the Republic of Bulgaria, along with a programme of measures for its implementation. The Strategy assesses the current status of the marine waters (in compliance with Article 8 of the EU Marine Strategy Framework Directive), determines 'Good Environmental Status', and establishes environmental targets (in compliance with Articles 9 and 10 of the Directive), in accordance with 11 descriptors.

The programme contains both existing and new measures for implementation of the Strategy. Among the existing measures are the monitoring of marine waters to assess the resources stock, preventive measures against invasion by alien species, and strengthening the Black Sea coast for protection against landslides.

Bulgaria has demonstrated a commitment to enhancing capabilities and improving regional security through alliance exercises and multinational military cooperation. It has benefited from an increasingly close security relationship with the United States, led by a Defense Cooperation Agreement that between 2017 and 2022 provided more than $238 million in security assistance to Bulgaria.[81] However, Bulgaria needs to modernize outdated conventional

[79] ibid.

[80] Ministerial Declaration on a Common Maritime Agenda for the Black Sea (May 2019).

[81] Defense Cooperation Agreement between the United States and Bulgaria, 28 April 2006; US Department of State, *U.S. Security Cooperation with Bulgaria: Fact Sheet* (23 February 2021) <www.state.gov/u-s-security-cooperation-with-bulgaria/> accessed 12 May 2023.

capabilities, many of which are obsolete vestiges of the Soviet era. According to NATO, a positive sign is Bulgaria's adoption of Program 2032, which outlines a capability development strategy and indicates that Bulgaria will be spending 2 per cent of its gross domestic product (GDP) on defence by 2024.[82] Bulgaria also developed a National Cyber Security Strategy in 2020 but needs a more comprehensive effort to enhance national and regional resilience against broader hybrid threats.

3.4 Conclusion

The examples of Poland and Lithuania representing the Baltic Sea states, and Bulgaria and Romania representing the Black Sea states, demonstrate the rich and complex history of the region and its relationship to the sea. As this chapter has shown, the coastal states of Eastern Europe, as parties to UNCLOS, have been guided by its provisions, which they helped to negotiate. These states have also adapted the Convention to reflect both national and regional interests, including the protection of the marine environment. The Eastern European states have implemented the Convention within their own unique regional, geographic, ethnic, cultural, political, and economic realities. These realities have also shaped—and continue to shape—the attitudes of the Eastern European states towards the law of the sea and its ongoing development.

[82] Dimitrinka Metodieva, 'Modernization of the Bulgarian Military: Recent Developments and New Opportunities' (*CEE Legal Matters*, 6 September 2021) <https://ceelegalmatters.com/bulgaria/17781-modernization-of-the-bulgarian-military-recent-developments-and-new-opportunities> accessed 12 May 2023.

4
Russia

Alexander S Skaridov

4.1 Introduction

Culture should be seen as a set of distinctive characteristics—spiritual and mundane, intellectual and emotional—inherent in a society or social group, with the addition that, as well as art and literature, it also encompasses the way of living and the 'art of coexistence', as well as systems of values, traditions, and beliefs.[1] 'Culture' is such a multifaceted notion that one would be unable to speak about it as a specific subject of research without first determining a conceptual framework of sorts. We understand Russian culture on rule-making in maritime law to mean the historically formed views of the Russian state leadership on the values, goals, and practices that were (and possibly will be) implemented in the efforts to establish international relations in the field of maritime law.

Rule-making in maritime law has taken many centuries to form, passing through several formational stages that shaped certain traditions based on the historical experience of Christianity and other religions—the representatives of which contributed to the population of the multinational country.

From the historical point of view, the Russian legal system was formed under the influence of Roman law. It should be noted, however, that Russian legal awareness is tightly interwoven with the traditional values transmitted from generation to generation, thanks to the definitive role that the Orthodox faith has played in the life of the Russian people.[2]

[1] This definition is drawn from the preamble to the UNESCO Universal Declaration on Cultural Diversity, 2 November 2001.

[2] TA Senyushkina, 'Orthodox Values and Russian Legal Culture' (2017) 4(30) Journal of Cultural Research 1 <http://cr-journal.ru/rus/journals/423.html&j_id=33> accessed 16 August 2022. In this chapter, titles of Russian-language works have been translated into English.

Alexander S Skaridov, *Russia* In: *Cultural Influences on the Law of the Sea*. Edited by: James Kraska and Hayoun Ryou-Ellison, Oxford University Press. © Alexander S Skaridov 2025. DOI: 10.1093/9780198944140.003.0004

4.2 Background

The historical evidence suggests that Russian maritime law-making and legal relations with foreign countries have a history spanning thousands of years. The oldest of the extant historical documents is the treaty between Rus' and Byzantium, concluded in the year 911 by Kiev prince Oleg and Byzantine emperors Lev and Alexander.[3] The treaty contained quite specific norms of the so-called Coast Law,[4] including the protection of wrecked trade ships from plunder and the rendering of assistance to survivors. The treaty culture of that era was based on appropriating the existing Roman and Byzantine traditions—a trend that grew stronger after the adoption of Christianity and the Christianizing of Rus' in the Byzantine fashion, culminating in Russia becoming the world centre of Orthodox faith after the conquest of Constantinople by the Osmanli Turks in 1453.

The impact of the Byzantine legal culture on that of Russia was negligible, spreading only so far as the superficial form of the legal acts and their structure. The manner of writing largely corresponded to that of the 'Russian Law'—that is, the customary law of the ancient Rus' society. Furthermore, while the laws were composed in two languages (Greek and Russian), the Russian legal vocabulary in the early tenth century was already quite adequate to outline all the legal conditions without the need to resort to borrowing foreign notions.[5]

The various editions of *Russkaya Pravda*,[6] the church charters of Vladimir and Jaroslav, and other church charters and princely statutes of the twelfth century are early examples of imitating the synoptic Byzantine codification, whether descending directly from the clergy or otherwise carried out under the influence of, and with assistance from, church tutors-in-law. Naturally, these experimentations fell rather short of their models in terms of both the

[3] Compiled in two languages—Middle Greek (the Greek text is not preserved) and Old Church Slavonic—the treaty is preserved in the lists as part of the Russian chronicles—notably in *The Tale of Bygone Years*, the oldest written source of Russian law.

[4] At that time, 'Coast Law' (in Latin, *jus litoris, seu litorale, seu naufragii*; in French, *droit de naufrage*; and, in German, *Strandrecht*) was understood as a set of customs according to which the inhabitants of marine coasts, lake shores, and river banks had the right to appropriate coastal resources and everything growing on the shore, as well as the remains of wrecked ships, their cargoes, and, in general, everything that the waves threw ashore—for example, agate and amber on the shores of the Baltic Sea, pearls in Persia, or gold on the African coast.

[5] The Church Slavonic language, which was initially used in the legal acts of the Old Russian society, was gradually phased out by the colloquial Russian language and later by a specialized form of the Russian language that was taking shape in large Old Russian cities, characterized by mixed ethno-social composition. Having been put into writing, this language began to be used in Russia not only in the annals but also in recorded norms of Russian law.

[6] *Russkaya Pravda* (Russian Justice or Russian Truth), written in Old East Slavic, is a major source of early Russian law. It's origins date back to the beginning of the eleventh century.

codification technique and the formulation of legal principles. However, they awakened the legal thought by tearing it free from any immediately observed phenomena and teaching the art of finding similar legal cases and deriving from them universal rules and legal norms.

Scientists note that the culture of managerial decision-making at the formational stage of Russian statehood contained elements of democracy, insofar as it accounted for the opinion of the majority of equals—the majority that needed to be swayed to one side or another in order to reach a common solution. It is a known fact that the notion 'people of the Russian land', found in the Treaty of 945 between Russians and Greeks, encompassed not just Slavic people but also Finno-Ugric tribes on equal terms. Moreover, princes gathered at special meetings, where decisions were reached in a collective fashion that also took into account the opinion of the 'wise boyar'.[7] The Novgorod Principality[8]—which concluded border treaties as early as the thirteenth century with the Norwegians and later with Hanseatic cities to regulate relations in the event of shipwrecks, formulate the principles of dividing losses upon losing common cargo, and establish responsibility for marine robbery—was a characteristic example of the culture of collective decision-making and the elaboration of legal norms.

On 20 October 1696, Russia's boyar duma (the council of boyars and junior boyars) made a historic decision to establish the Russian regular fleet, marking a new milestone not just for Russia's marine forces but also for its maritime law. Early on, a need arose for clear legal regulation of the activities of the military fleet. This became especially apparent when Peter I put the instruction 'On the Procedure of Naval Service' in effect during the second Azov campaign. The Military Statute was adopted in 1716, and the Maritime Statute was issued in 1720, the same year that the Statute of Ewers[9] was adopted, becoming one of the first systemized legislative measures to regulate relations in the maritime transportation of goods with regard to the rules previously adopted by Germany

[7] In the period of feudal fragmentation, the wise boyar were the richest and most influential feudal lords, to some extent rivalling the power of princes. At the courts of the grand princes, they were in charge of certain branches of the palace economy and the administration of state territories. From the fifteenth century onwards, they represented the highest ranks of the service class, occupying leading administrative, judicial, and military positions, heading regiments, and serving as warlords. They also entered aristocratic circles. Peter I annulled the title at the beginning of the eighteenth century, following the liquidation of the boyar duma. *Large Encyclopaedic Dictionary* (2002).

[8] A feudal state with a republican form of government that existed in Russia during a period of political fragmentation that began in 1136.

[9] A ewer is a flat-bottomed, single-masted cargo sailing ship that was handed over 'by his royal majesty's decree . . . to merchants for the transportation of goods from the Chancellery . . . both from St. Petersburg to Kronschlot, and from Kronschlot to St. Petersburg': Charter of Ewers, concluded at the College of Commerce in 1720.

and Holland. As for the regulation of maritime trade, however, Russia has long lacked a uniform law in this regard. The seafarers had to rely on isolated statutes issued at various times by Peter I and his successors on the matters of merchant shipbuilding, sea fishing, and the transportation of goods.[10] The Statute of Ewers was the first document to set forth in legal form the terms on which owners of ships were to provide their vessels for loading, the terms for unloading ships by contractors, the liability of ship-owners, and the order of issuance for shipping documents. The Maritime Trade Regulations were issued in 1724, prescribing, among other things, customs interaction procedures for merchants and captains.

The law-making practices of this period can hardly be labelled with the term 'culture'. Rather, law-making was an adventurous process of ensuring that the military and industrial demands of a rapidly developing state were met. Numerous statutes, regulations, and charters were issued—occasionally duplicating the norms adopted earlier without formally declaring them null and void, which led to controversies and hindered legal proceedings.

However, it should be noted that the foundation for various state and commercial legal entities began to emerge during this period: a professional environment for the preparation of legislation. The drafts were distilled from a dedicated chamber of boyars with the involvement of okolnichies, boyar duma representatives, stolniks, and sextons, and later with the establishment of special boards[11]—essentially, the prototypes of modern ministries. For the first time on record, 'commission-based' drafting[12] of legal acts began to be practised with a view to evaluating current legislation and producing new codified acts.

At the top of the modern hierarchy of Russian legal sources, including those regulating the use of the sea, stands the so-called normative legal act—that is, a written form of law. Legal custom is not recognized as a source of law. However, this has not always been the case. *Russkaya Pravda* also contained norms of customary law in the form of the judicial practice of princedoms,[13] as well as certain provisions of trade customs that could be relevant to the

[10] VP Puzyrev, 'On the History of Russian Maritime Law' in *Maritime Law Yearbook* (1997) 5.

[11] In eighteenth-century Russia, the term 'board' referred to a central government agency or ministry.

[12] The first such commission was established in 1714. It was the first method of regulatory design in that era—and quite an up-to-date one, at that.

[13] Examples include the court charters of Pskov and Novgorod, as well as Belozersk and Dvina statutory charters.

implementation of maritime transportation—for example, customs regulating the liability of the merchant and the carrier, depending on the circumstances from which damages arose. The Code of Laws,[14] which came to replace *Russkaya Pravda*, contained provisions setting forth the liability of the merchant for the embezzlement of entrusted property, while trade decrees dated 1653 and 1667 imposed restrictions on foreign merchants with regard to trading certain kinds of goods considered 'protected'.

Various editions of *Russkaya Pravda* and the church charters spanning the period from the times of Vladimir and Jaroslav to the princes of the twelfth century were all, to a certain degree, formulated under the influence of the Byzantine codification culture and with the assistance of church tutors-in-law. As Russian historicist Vasiliy Klyuchevsky wrote:[15]

> These experiments fell rather short of their models in terms of both the codification technique and the formulation of legal principles. However, they awakened the legal thought by tearing it free from any immediately observed phenomena and teaching the art of finding similar legal cases and deriving universal rules and legal norms from them.

Beginning in the late seventeenth century, the culture of making managerial decisions and adopting state laws underwent significant change. Such democratic forms as the Novgorod veche, gatherings of princes, zemstvos, and church assemblies could no longer ensure swift decision-making regarding the control of a territory that by that time far surpassed that of Europe and was continuing its expansion. Peter I efficiently cancelled election institutions, discontinued the boyar duma, which had the power to disagree with the tsar, and saw to it that the Synod's patriarchal administration of collegial decisions was also dissolved. Given the continued wars, the reformation of state institutions, and the annexation of considerable new territories, the old order of legal decision-making was unable to provide efficient management. An authoritative style of state governance was formed, conclusively proclaimed the Russian Empire by Peter I.

[14] Code of Laws of the Russian State, adopted in 1497.

[15] VO Klyuchevsky, 'Contribution of the Church to the Successes of Russian Civil Law and Order' in *Essays and Speeches: Second Collection of Articles* (PP Ryabushinskys 1913).

4.3 The Russian Empire

The legal culture of eighteenth-century Russia was influenced by the infatuation of the tsar's entire court with all things Western. The Russian nobility strived to imitate Western aristocracies in every respect, including in status and entitlement, which at the law-making level boiled down to the blunt copying of relevant legal norms. This, in turn, rather quickly demolished the very modernization-focused development paradigm for Russia on which Peter I had toiled. However, a strictly formal, reason-dictated attitude to legal norms so characteristic of peoples born under the Protestant and Catholic branches of Christianity has nonetheless been alien to the historical culture of the Russian people. Russian philosopher and publicist Ivan Ilyin characterized the Russian idea as one of the heart, arguing that love was the most crucial thing in life for Russian individuals:[16]

> The Russian–Slavic soul, since ancient times organically predisposed to feeling, compassion and kindness, historically adopted this idea from Christianity . . . When a Russian believes, he believes not with his will or his mind, but with the fire of his heart. Believing in nothing, the Russian becomes an empty creature, bereft of ideal and goal. It is love and faith that drive the mind and the will of the Russian into spiritual and artistic motion.

Unlike the rule of Peter I, during which the culture of law-making was implemented in a strict and imperative manner, the rule of Catherine II (known as Catherine the Great) was marked by a partial return to the collective making of legislative decisions. The shift was dictated by the need to liberalize economic relations and boost the economy. A push in this direction came from a manifesto of 1775 that authorized the establishment of private ventures, simultaneously incentivizing the growth of commercial shipping and the development of appropriate legislation.

The growing complexity of maritime trading relations led to the issuance of a Charter of Merchant Shipping on Rivers, Waters and Seas in 1781, a normative act that heralded the coming of the future Maritime Code. The Charter was created using a compilation of foreign sources based on the adoption experience of the French Maritime Charter of 1681 (Ordonnance de la marine).

[16] '"Perceive Russia with the Heart": What Ivan Ilyin, the Chief Philosopher of the Russian Emigration, Wrote' *Cyrillitsa* (19 September 2020) <https://cyrillitsa.ru/history/134491-vosprinimat-rossiyu-serdcem-o-chem-p.html> accessed 16 August 2022.

However, this could not be called blunt copying because the scope of applicability of the 'constructed' document also stretched to the relations arising from navigating internal waterways.

The Charter listed general provisions with regard to navigation and enumerated the rights and responsibilities of crew members (boatmen) on the ship, ranging from shipman (skipper) and steersman (ship's master) to common seaman (sailor), along with procedures for their hiring and dismissal. It also dealt with the issues of insurance against naval incidents and losses, as well as recovery of the crew and cargo. Further improvement of the Russian maritime legislation found reflection in the Code of Laws of the Russian Empire.

All subsequent efforts of legal state-building were based on military successes scored by the army and the fleet. The victories of the fleet during the war with Turkey in 1768–74 and the annihilation of Napoleon's army as a result of the Patriotic War of 1812 led to changes in the political geography of the Black Sea and the Sea of Azov, necessitating their subsequent consolidation with international law. Russian diplomacy had probably never before been so fervent as it was in its efforts to consolidate the results of these successes, as reflected in the Treaty of Värälä.[17] In early 1780, Russia stepped forward with the incentive to create the First League of Armed Neutrality,[18] thus contributing to the development of naval military law.[19]

The reign of Catherine II saw a number of exceptionally talented Russian naval commanders—including Grigory Spiridov, Fyodor Ushakov, Vasily Chichagov, Dmitry Senyavin, Fedot Klokachev, and Andrey Yelmanov—complement the Russian army and fleet. Foreign officers also took honourable positions in the development of the Russian navy, among them Samuel Greig, hero of the Archipelago Expedition; admirals EE Tete and Robert Crown; and French officers Jean-Baptiste de Traversay (rear admiral and future Minister

[17] Treaty of Värälä, 14 August 1790 (Russia–Sweden).

[18] In 1780, Russia offered Denmark (subsequently joined by Sweden, the Netherlands, Prussia, Austria, Portugal, the Kingdom of the Two Sicilies, France, Spain, and the United States) the opportunity to conduct joint operations to protect neutral shipping, closing the Baltic and the Iberian Atlantic to the warships of the warring powers. Of all the major maritime powers, Great Britain was the only one not to acknowledge the armed neutrality. After the conclusion of the Treaty of Versailles in 1783, the first armed neutrality fell apart.

[19] Specific provisions were set out in five articles in the main body of the document: (1) neutral ships may freely visit the ports of belligerent powers; (2) the property of the belligerent powers on neutral ships, with the exception of military contraband, shall be granted inviolable passage; (3) only items listed in Articles 10 and 11 of the treaty between Russia and England of 1766 (such as weapons and military supplies) are recognized as military contraband; (4) only a port to which access is actually barred by naval forces falls under the definition of a blockaded port: Declaration of Armed Neutrality in the Revolution, 11 March 1780. See FF Martens, *Collection of Treaties and Conventions Concluded by Russia with Foreign Powers*, vol 9 (Tipograiya Ministerstva putei soobshcheniya 1900) 307–10.

of the Navy), Osip Deribas (or José de Ribas, rear admiral), and Karl Nassau-Siegen (vice admiral).

Considerable involvement of foreign specialists in state administration and education inevitably affected the development of scientific thought, including theoretical legal science, with regard to the legal tradition of Europe. Many works of European philosophers and legal jurists were translated into Russian, including those of Samuel von Pufendorf, Hugo Grotius, and Montesquieu, sparking the development of humanist and democratic traditions. At the same time—despite active discussion of the ideas of personal autonomy and the viability of applying the principles of personal freedom to the governmental and legal reality of Russia—the formation of a civil society was impeded by a part of the population lacking political and civil rights: the nobility was in a state of serfdom before the Emperor and the peasants before their landlords. It was not until 1762, under the rule of Peter III, that the Russian nobility received freedom.[20] The peasantry followed suit nearly a full century later, thanks to a manifesto issued by Alexander II.[21] However, the matter of the political reorganization of the state was not on the agenda. It was absolutism that determined the basis of the culture of statehood, with a fairly broad intellectual recognition of the necessity of civil liberties, election-based political rights, and, ultimately, constitutional rights as well. This was the period when the civil system began to take on distinct outlines as a sphere of individual freedom and subjective law under the conditions of transparency of the state administrative system, decentralization, and the division of state power among different state bodies as a guarantee of self-imposed limitation.

In 1766, Catherine II issued a manifesto calling upon all social classes of the Empire—except for the clergy—to participate in composing a new statute covering all parts of the legislation. She proceeded in 1767 to establish a committee tasked with formulating the project to devise the optimum political system for the state. All these efforts were aimed at the 'Europeanization' of the state system and law-making rules, but ultimately failed to give birth to a new culture of legal design. As before, the main tools used were borrowing, compilation, committee discussions at the preparation stages, and authoritarian decision-making on whether to enact the norms proposed.

The Russian legal culture of the eighteenth century developed in the vein of the Western European legal tradition, operating pan-European legal ideas and

[20] Manifesto on Granting Liberty and Freedom to the Entire Russian Nobility, 1762. The Russian legislation secured the right for landlords to own land without imposing state service liabilities on them.

[21] Manifesto on the Most Merciful Granting of Free Rural Inhabitant Rights to Serfs, 1861, as well as Regulations on Peasants Emerging from Serfdom, 1861.

theories, using a pan-European framework of concepts and categories, and staying nearly entirely within the legal environment of Europe. However, the individualism inherent in the Western European consciousness was in stark collision with the Russian sobornost.[22] Works surfaced in academic circles that insisted on the importance of conducting a general 'people's survey' (ie a plebiscite) prior to making any important regulatory decisions. Ideas began to be formulated that the law must express the country's universal interests—that 'the entire state be invited to participate in creating its own welfare; then will the laws be of action, prudence, justice and order'.[23]

The development of maritime trade was an important factor in the formation of the Russian legal culture of the nineteenth century. It is worth pointing out that the development of Russian commercial law—spurred on by the state-side incentivization of trade and industrial activity arising from attempts to introduce market forms of business—took place in the context of strengthening serfdom and command-and-control principles in the organization of business practices, which led to the formation of a fiscal-policy (administrative) principle of legal business regulation. This was predominantly manifested through constant attempts to set forth such business principles that would first guarantee the serving of state interests, often at the expense of entrepreneurs.[24] However, conducting law-making in the interests of the state was impossible in the maritime realm, as the entire maritime industry was absolutely internationalized. One had to respect international norms and use regulatory procedures based on the already established Western European legal traditions.

The defeat of Napoleon elevated the international prestige of Russia to great heights, with the country having a decisive say at the Congress of Vienna and projecting effective influence on Europe in the decades that followed. At the same time, the foreign-political strengthening of Russia was not matched by the development of its domestic way of life. Although the victory inspired and united the entire Russian society, the war's successes failed to bring any improvements to the social and economic aspects of Russian life.

Alexander I realized the necessity of reforms, but never brought himself to implement them. No sooner had his successor, Nikolai I, officially ascended to

[22] In Russian philosophy, 'sobornost' refers to the free-willed spiritual unity of people, both in their church life and in their secular community, communion in brotherhood, and love. In legal terms, the term implies the application of the principle of joint discussion and resolution of the most important national issues at a *sobor* (a meeting of people's representatives). See VV Lazarev, 'Sobornost' in *New Philosophical Encyclopedia*, vol 3 (Mysl' 2010) 580–81.

[23] AG Moskvina, 'Formation of Russian Jurisprudence' (thesis, St Petersburg 1999) 129.

[24] YB Shubnikov, 'On the Periodization of the Legislation Formation History of Merchant Shipping in Russia' (2018) 1 Leningrad Law Journal 119.

the throne than he faced an uprising by a group of like-minded nobles, many of them officers of the Guard.[25] The Decembrist Revolt convinced Nikolai I that Russia needed order and a firm rule, which only a monarch was able to provide. This period was not rich in new international agreements on the use of the sea, but it brought a technological breakthrough in the maritime industry: sailboats gradually became history, with steamships replacing them; paddle wheels were phased out by screw propellers; iron instead of wood was used for shipbuilding; trans-Atlantic cruises began on a regular basis; a sailing military fleet fought its last major battle;[26] and the first technical solutions for submarines emerged.

In 1825, Russia and Great Britain entered into the Treaty of Saint Petersburg to delimit their claims in North America. The Treaty defines the border between Russian possessions, in what eventually became Alaska, and the British claim, in what is now part of British Columbia.[27] As far as contemporaneous reports allow us to judge, the parties resolved a rather complicated delimitation issue with remarkable calmness and professionalism, taking into account all the bends of the coast and ensuring that the naval border was kept within 10 nautical miles from the coast.[28] Another important circumstance was the establishment of regulations for Russian–English trade in North America, as well as regulations for seafaring near the Russian–American coastline, in Russian territorial waters for English ships taking advantage of the same benefits as those enjoyed by Russian ships. Rules were also set forth for Russian and British subjects engaging in commercial fishing in the Russian coastal regions of Alaska and the North American west coast, as well as in the waters of Russian colonies and the Aleutian Islands.

As for the Mediterranean basin, the Treaty of London of 1827[29] provided for collective action by states against Turkey to force it to cease military action against the Greek people and to grant Greece autonomy on the condition of an annual tribute to the Sultan. Britain and France believed that they should reduce the influence of Russia in the region, but Russia insisted on including a

[25] The Decembrist Revolt took place in Senate Square on 14 December 1825, marking the first attempt at a coup d'état in the capital of the Russian Empire.

[26] This was a naval battle between the combined squadron of Russia, England, and France, on the one hand, and the Turkish–Egyptian fleet, on the other. It occurred on 20 October 1827, in the Navarino Bay of the Ionian Sea on the south-western coast of the Peloponnese.

[27] Convention Concerning the Limits of Their Respective Possessions on the Northwest Coast of America and the Navigation of the Pacific Ocean, 28 February 1825. The Convention is known as the Treaty of Saint Petersburg and, alternatively, the Anglo-Russian Convention.

[28] Although, as we know, no border agreement in this region has yet been reached between the United States and Canada.

[29] Treaty of London, 6 July 1827. The Treaty was signed by representatives of Russia, Great Britain, and France on the establishment of peace conditions between Greece and the Ottoman Empire.

provision that the truce be subject to termination should the Sultan refuse the mediation. Sultan Mahmud II's subsequent waiver of the peace treaty led to the Battle of Navarino. That conflict resulted in the annihilation of the Turkish–Egyptian fleet by a combined squadron of three states and culminated in the signing of the London Protocol of 1830, which acknowledged the independence of Greece from the Ottoman Empire.[30]

By the mid-nineteenth century, three components of Russia's new ideology—autocracy, orthodoxy, and nationality—came to replace the old ideology and the politics of 'enlightened absolutism' that Catherine II and Alexander I had sought to instil in Russian society. The *Complete Collection of Laws of the Russian Empire*, comprising forty-five volumes, was adopted in the intranational legal practice in 1830.[31]

During those years, an amendment was made to the Code of Laws of the Russian Empire[32] (Book 3, Part 2, Volume 11), titled 'On Agreements and Special Obligations in Merchant Shipbuilding and Seafaring'. The added norms comprised four sections: on agreements and obligations in merchant shipbuilding, on agreements and obligations in merchant navigation, on respondentia and incidents or maritime losses, and on maritime insurance. The provisions of the Code of Laws, including the 'sea norms', spread to the territories of the tsardom of Poland, the Baltic governorates, and beyond. Certain special regulatory provisions were dictated by discrepancies with the customary law of these regions and represented substantial systemization difficulties for the Russian legislation.

Russia's unfortunate performance in the Crimean War of 1853–56 ended with its interests compromised. Nonetheless, the diplomatic effort of the Treaty of Paris of 1856[33] minimized territorial losses. Freedom of navigation on the Danube was granted, and the previously claimed towns and fortifications were returned to Turkey. The 'marine part' of the Treaty was especially important for Russia. On the one hand, a ban was imposed on foreign (non-Black Sea) military vessels entering the straits of Bosphorus and Dardanelles in times of peace. On the other hand, all Black Sea powers were prohibited from having military fleets on the Black Sea (Article XI), and the creation of naval arsenals and fortifications on the coastline was also prohibited (Article

[30] London Protocol, 3 February 1830, signed following the conclusion of the Treaty of Adrianople between Russia and Turkey on 14 September 1829.

[31] The Code of Laws of the Russian Empire was published in 1832. The Code of Criminal and Correctional Punishments—the main source of criminal law—was approved in 1845.

[32] The amendments entered into force on 1 January 1835. The Code existed until the October Revolution of 1917.

[33] Treaty of Paris, 30 March 1856.

XIII). Russia managed to reclaim most of its lost territories in 1878 under the Treaty of Berlin,[34] signed within the framework of the Berlin Congress.[35] In April 1856, a few weeks after the conclusion of the Treaty of Paris, the Paris Declaration Respecting Maritime Law was signed,[36] putting a legal end to privateering on the sea. Like some other countries in Europe (such as France and Spain), Russia was actively discussing the viability of adopting some of its provisions, but the departure from French law was apparently substantial and the experts ultimately decided against forcing it upon the authorities of Russia.

The cession of Alaska in 1867 marked one of the most outrageously incompetent pages in the history of the imperial statehood. Discovered in 1732 by the joint efforts of Russian expeditions led by Mikhail Gvozdev and Ivan Fedorov, developed originally by private individuals and, after 1799, also by the state-sponsored Russian–American Company, Alaska remained an asset yet to be appreciated. From today's perspective, it is difficult to say whether it was sheer ham-handedness or betrayal that primarily guided the actions of Nikolay Muravyov-Amurskiy, Governor-General of Eastern Siberia; Baron Eduard de Stoeckl, Russian envoy to Washington; Prince Konstantin Nikolayevich, brother of Emperor Alexander II; and Aleksandr Gorchakov, Minister of Foreign Affairs. One thing is clear: decisions of this kind testify not to a foreign policy culture of any specific kind but rather to its absence.

The judicial reform of 1864 led by Alexander II introduced two parties into the criminal process: the prosecution and the defence, acting separately and independently of the court, and in competition with each other. Publicity of the judicial investigation was introduced, and the participation of members of society as jurors and class representatives in the administration of justice was established. Principles of oral proceedings, publicity, competitiveness, a more independent assessment of evidence by the court, and the resolution of cases based on law and according to the inner conviction of the judges were also introduced into the foundations of civil proceedings. These judicial novelties did not lead to the creation of specialized sea courts, but 'maritime rule-making' led to the development and adoption in 1887 of the Trade Charter, the second book of which was directly related to the use of the sea. It was called *On Maritime Trade* and comprised six sections ('On Seaworthy Merchant Ships', 'On Merchant Seafaring', 'On Respondentia and Maritime Supply Loans', 'On Incidents', 'On Assistance and Rescue in Cases of Shipwrecks and

[34] Treaty of Berlin, 13 July 1878.
[35] Held following another Russian–Turkish war in 1877–78.
[36] Paris Declaration Respecting Maritime Law, 16 April 1856, 115 CTS 1.

on the Ownership of Flotsam', and 'On Maritime Insurance'), which testified to a rather detailed regulation of issues in the maritime commercial law of the time. In 1903, four more sections were added to this book: 'On the Local Management of Primorye Commercial Ports', 'On the Collection of Ship and By-the-Pood Dues', 'Regulations on Shipowners' Congresses', and 'Regulations on the Dobroflot'. All these sections eventually crystallized, in one form or another, into the main structural elements of Russia's Merchant Shipping Codes of the twentieth century.

The period of the late nineteenth century saw the emergence of initiative and leadership in Russia's culture of participation in international law-making. Nikolai II convened what came to be known as the Hague Peace Conferences of 1899 and 1907. The conferences saw the adoption of international conventions on the laws and customs of war, laying the foundation for regulatory provisions aimed at the humanization of armed conflicts.

The Russian Revolution of 1905 led to the issuance of a manifesto granting civil liberties on the basis of individual inviolability, as well as freedoms of conscience, speech, assembly, and association. A Parliament was established, consisting of a State Council and a State Duma. The Fundamental Laws of the Russian Empire were amended accordingly in April 1906.

4.4 The Soviet Union

After the revolution of 1917, the Soviet Republic[37]—having coopted into its government many tsarist officials, scientists, and experts—almost immediately switched its attentions to the revival and re-issuance of maritime regulations, despite vehemently denying the validity of many leftover treaties from the Russian Empire and denouncing most of them as enslaving. Among the new rules were decrees of the Council of People's Commissars of the Soviet Republic—including On the Protection of Fish and Animal Territories in the Arctic Ocean and the White Sea (24 May 1921),[38] On the Fishing Industry and Fishing (31 May 1921),[39] and On Transportation Using Inland Waterways (11 April 1921)[40]—and Regulations on Port Dues (20 May 1921).[41]

[37] The Russian Soviet Federative Socialist Republic. The socialist state was formed on 25 October 1917. From 1922 until 1991, it was a union republic within the USSR.

[38] *Collection of Legalizations and Orders of the Workers' and Peasants' Government of the Russian Socialist Federative Soviet Republic*, no 49 (1921) 351–52.

[39] *Collection of Legalizations and Orders of the Government for 1921* (Administration of the Affairs of the Council of People's Commissars of the USSR 1944) 509–11.

[40] ibid 285–87.

[41] ibid 478–79.

During this time, legislators in many countries were actively discussing the rights of crewmembers and were either adopting or amending regulations by defining the relationships between the crewmen and ship-owners. The US Congress passed the Merchant Marine Act of 1920,[42] which allowed injured sailors or certain surviving family members of deceased sailors to sue employers for negligence that led to the injury or death of the sailor. The Act—a response to the US Supreme Court's decision in *The Osceola* in 1903[43]—provided for the filing of legal claims over suspected negligence by a ship's captain or crewmembers.

However, the law of the sea was the last thing on Soviet Russia's mind. The bulk of the state's foreign policy effort was directed at gaining international recognition within the framework of the Genoa Conference of 1922.[44] The first two decades of Soviet rule were a period of relatively unrestricted and multifaceted development for the spiritual culture of the Soviet people. Particular attention was paid to public education, the elimination of illiteracy, and the expansion of national schools. The most crucial feature of this process was the democratization of the culture, which found expression in scientific, educational, and artistic achievements becoming more accessible to the masses. Regarding the use of the sea, the country made a significant breakthrough in the codification of maritime law when it adopted the Merchant Shipping Code of 1929, which ultimately played a fundamental role in the development of the modern legal framework of maritime transportation in the Russian Federation.

Throughout the nascent era of Soviet Russia and during the pre-war development stage of the USSR, a policy of 'healthy pragmatism' shaped the Soviet culture of legal objectivism in relations with the United States and European countries. Playing along with the British Admiralty in its efforts to entice new participants into the Second London Naval Treaty,[45] the Soviet delegation waived its right to build certain types of cruisers.[46] In return, the USSR received the right to strengthen its Pacific Fleet without limitations.[47]

[42] Merchant Marine Act of 1920, Pub L No 66-261, 41 Stat 2135, also known as the Jones Act after the senator who introduced it.

[43] *The Osceola* 189 US 158 (1903).

[44] Some of the issues raised at the Genoa Conference were not resolved, and their consideration was postponed until the Hague Conference of 1922, which failed to arrive at any decisions.

[45] Treaty for the Limitation of Naval Armament, 25 March 1936, 50 Stat 1363; TS 919 (Second London Naval Treaty).

[46] The USSR abandoned the construction of cruisers under Project 26, which did not prevent the further construction of cruisers under Project 68 and the Soviet Union-class battleship, whose dimensions far exceeded the standards envisioned by the Second London Naval Treaty. This circumstance did not contradict the obligations under the Treaty, since the Soviet Union had the right to build such ships for its Pacific Fleet.

[47] The English–Soviet agreement was signed on 17 July 1937.

The legal framework of the Black Sea straits was—and still is—of vital importance to Russia. Throughout its history, Russia has found itself within varying distances of attaining the most favourable legal framework in the straits zone. Despite their diametrically opposed views, Russia and Turkey managed, from time to time, to reach compromise agreements on the control of the straits,[48] but the occasional intervention of France and Great Britain ruined those agreements. The First World War brought Allied troops to Istanbul, which temporarily enabled navigation management in the straits and allowed the Allies to turn the Lausanne Conference of 1922–23 in their favour. The resulting Treaty of Lausanne[49] fully met the interests of Great Britain while essentially failing to restore Turkey's sovereignty over the straits. Realizing that success in the reconvened Straits Conference of 1936 would be possible only if Turkey's interests were taken into account. Maksim Litvinov, who led the Soviet delegation in Montreux, fought not just for every word but quite literally for every letter in the new Convention regarding the Regime of the Straits.[50] He did not succeed in completely banning entrance to the Black Sea for the warships of non-coastal states, but what was achieved was nonetheless a triumph of Soviet and, equally, Turkish diplomacy.

In 1945, in the aftermath of the Second World War, President Harry Truman issued two proclamations that made the United States the innovation leader in the field of maritime law.[51] Well-formulated concepts of continental shelf and fish protection zones emerged, prompting a number of countries, primarily in Latin America, to step forward with unilateral claims on expanding their sovereignty over adjacent water areas.[52]

The maritime aspect of legal regulation during the Cuban Missile Crisis[53] was minimal, boiling down to good maritime practices of merchant ship

[48] The Treaty of Küçük Kaynarca, signed on 21 July 1774, allowed free passage between the Black Sea and the Mediterranean Sea for Russian merchant ships. Russian warships were granted the same right in 1799. By the Treaty of Paris of 1856, the Bosphorus and Dardanelles were closed to the military vessels of all states.

[49] Treaty of Lausanne, 24 July 1923.

[50] See 'Press Statement of the Soviet Delegation Chairman M. M. Litvinov at the Montreux Conference on the Regime of the Straits, June 25, 1936' (1936) 147 (6004) Izvestia (26 June); Convention Regarding the Regime of the Straits, 20 July 1936, 173 UNTS 213.

[51] US Presidential Proclamation 2667, Policy of the United States With Respect to the Natural Resources of the Subsoil and Sea Bed of the Continental Shelf, 10 Fed Reg 12303 (28 September 1945); US Presidential Proclamation 2668, Policy of the United States with Respect to Coastal Fisheries in Certain Areas of the High Seas, 10 Fed Reg 12304 (28 September 1945).

[52] GE Gigolaev, 'USSR, USA and Maritime Law Issues in the International Security Context, 1945–1973' (2015) 4 Bulletin of the Nizhny Novgorod University 15.

[53] The Cuban Missile Crisis was an extremely tense political, diplomatic, and military confrontation between the Soviet Union and the United States in October 1962. It was caused by the deployment by the United States of medium-range missiles in Turkey in 1961. With their short flight time, the missiles could reach cities in the western part of the USSR. In response, the Soviet Union deployed ground-based tactical ballistic missiles on the island of Cuba.

captains and military commanders, as well as restraint on the part of both sides. On the other hand, the culture of decision-making demonstrated by the leaders of the superpowers testified to their ability to assess the situation and ditch their initial desire for armed resolution of conflict in favour of constructive restraint, which later became characteristic of the relations between the two countries until the 'thaw' of the 1970s.

The year 1972 was important for both the USSR and the United States. The countries were at the peak of the Cold War, yet an adequate reassessment of capabilities led to the conclusion of Strategic Arms Limitation Talks (SALT) and the signing of the Anti-Ballistic Missile Treaty (SALT I)[54] and, seven years later, the Strategic Arms Limitation Treaty (SALT II).[55] The Incidents at Sea Agreement (INCSEA)—probably the most extended of all agreements in the field of naval activity and sea—was also signed in 1972.[56] The United States and the USSR both demonstrated a responsible attitude towards the regulation of naval force activities. This served as a legal basis and transformed the culture of naval–military relations on the high seas, amending the international regulatory regime with yet another accord—the Agreement on the Prevention of Dangerous Military Activities of 1989.[57]

The Soviet–American experience of INCSEA turned out to be so precisely on point that it not only allowed the conclusion of similar agreements with the fleets of eleven or so states but also served as a legal model in relations between other countries, in particular between the United States and China. Perhaps most importantly, such agreements established a culture of trusting and professional relations at the level of navy leaders, which made it possible to improve the INCSEA regime and ensure the predictability of naval activities.

As always, however, no rule is without exception—such as the Black Sea bumping incident of 1988,[58] the passing of the British destroyer HMS *Defender* through Russia's territorial waters in 2021,[59] and the 'bum rush' of the Dutch Navy frigate HNLMS *Evertsen* towards the Kerch Strait the day after the *Defender* incident. It is hard to say on what legal culture the US and

[54] Treaty on the Limitation of Anti-Ballistic Missile Systems, 26 May 1972.

[55] Treaty on the Limitation of Strategic Offensive Arms, 18 June 1979.

[56] Agreement on the Prevention of Incidents On and Over the High Seas, 25 May 1972, 852 UNTS 151 (INCSEA). A protocol to the agreement was signed in Washington on 22 May 1973.

[57] Agreement on the Prevention of Dangerous Military Activities, 12 June 1989.

[58] The incident during which two Soviet warships, patrollers SKR *Bezzavetny* and *SKR-6*, carried out an assault on two US warships, the missile cruiser USS *Yorktown* and the destroyer USS *Caron*, in order to squeeze them out of the territorial waters of the USSR near the Crimean Peninsula.

[59] On 23–24 June 2021, the British destroyer HMS *Defender*, despite the announcement by the Russian Federation that certain areas of the territorial sea were temporarily closed for navigation, defiantly passed through those waters, ignoring the warning shots of coast guard ships.

British navy commands based their decisions, but the command of the Black Sea Fleet based its decisions on resorting to force for squeezing the ships out, but without the use of weapons, on both accounts. Since then, the technique of 'calculated and controlled assault' directed at the intruder has found its place in the practice of countering illegal actions of foreign navies in Russian territorial waters.[60]

The events that became known as the 'Kerch Strait incident', involving the detention of three Ukrainian warships by the Russian Coast Guard in November 2018,[61] are particularly characteristic in this regard. Ukraine brought a case before the International Tribunal on the Law of the Sea, the issue being whether Russia's actions constituted 'military activities'. The Tribunal found that the Russian ships belonged to the armed forces of the state, but its ruling did not imply that the suppression of attempts by Ukrainian ships to enter the Kerch Strait without authorization could be deemed military activity.[62] Yet Russian legal doctrine and naval science do not support categorizing as 'law enforcement activity' the efforts by Navy and Coast Guard ships to protect the maritime border and prevent its violation by foreign navies.[63]

In the Soviet period, the culture of regulatory decision-making and directing diplomatic efforts in the development of international law norms was inseparable from the decision-making of the Central Committee of the Communist Party of the Soviet Union.[64] A decision was formally considered collegial and was preceded by an information letter (a note) to the Central Committee, in which the event was professionally assessed and appropriate recommendations were made on the country's participation in the relevant international conference. After the Twentieth Congress of the Communist Party, a course was taken for more active interaction with developing countries, regardless of their socio-economic structure. This further affected the standing of the USSR when discussing and adopting the provisions of both the 1958 Geneva Conventions on the Law of the Sea and the 1982 UN Convention on the Law of the Sea (UNCLOS).[65]

[60] Similar actions were taken against the ships of the Ukrainian Navy during the incident that occurred on 25 November 2018 on the approaches to the Kerch Strait, as discussed below.

[61] The detention concerned suspected violation of the rules for passage through the strait and the crossing of the Russian maritime border.

[62] *Detention of Three Ukrainian Naval Vessels (Ukraine v Russian Federation)*, ITLOS Case No 26, 25 May 2019.

[63] For more information, see AS Skaridov, 'Military and Law Enforcement Activities in the Context of the Use of Armed Forces for Naval Defence of the State Border' (2019) 2(5) Ocean Management 4.

[64] The Central Committee is the highest organ between party congresses.

[65] UN Convention on the Law of the Sea, 10 December 1982, 1833 UNTS 397 (UNCLOS).

Time inexorably takes us away from the events surrounding the adoption of the Geneva Conventions in 1958.[66] The mood of the UN Conference on the Law of the Sea[67] that year was influenced by international circumstances, as it took place in the context of the ongoing Cold War and the confrontation between the two camps. The universal issues on the international relations front could not but influence the flow of the Conference. Today, it can be difficult to reconstruct the instructions received by the head of the Soviet delegation, Grigory Tunkin[68]—instructions that shaped the position of the USSR at the (first) Conference and also, two years later, at the Second Conference on the Law of the Sea.[69] As a rule, the composition and structure of the Soviet delegation at any negotiations were determined according to a rigid hierarchical principle. Reaching a decision necessitated coordinating issues with Moscow, which could take much time. During the negotiations, the Soviet side preferred to act cautiously to avoid risks. If there was a choice between more risky and less risky solutions, the latter were often chosen. This risk aversion led to curbed initiative. The Soviet participants in the negotiations were more likely to react to what the other party offered rather than suggesting solutions of their own.

It can be difficult to discuss the decision-making culture in the context of formulating regulatory positions when working on draft convention provisions. However, testimonies of the participants and transcripts of the meetings of the relevant project development committees demonstrate that ideology prevailed over the practical sea use interests in the bases of many negotiating positions. The opportunity to express oneself and to strengthen one's influence in the international political arena, to demonstrate one's dedication to international duty aimed at supporting the Council of Mutual Economic Assistance countries[70] and developing states, imposed limitations on making critical assessments.

An obvious example is the standpoint regarding the width of the territorial sea. Deployed by the time that the Third UN Conference on the Law of the Sea[71] began its work in 1973, the Soviet Navy lacked a basing system

[66] See Final Act of the United Nations Conference on the Law of the Sea, UN Doc A/CONF.13/L.58 (1958).

[67] Held between 24 February and 27 April 1958.

[68] Grigory Tunkin was head of the legal department of the Ministry of Foreign Affairs from 1957 to 1966.

[69] Held between 17 March and 26 April 1960.

[70] The Council of Mutual Economic Assistance (1949–91), which was led by the Soviet Union, comprised Eastern Bloc countries and other socialist states.

[71] Third UN Conference on the Law of the Sea, 1973–82.

in remote areas of the oceans and direly needed to legitimize its presence in anchorage areas. Consequently, having a minimum-width stretch of the territorial sea as an international legal norm was of paramount importance for anchoring to be possible in the first place. The persistence of the Russian delegation in establishing a 12-mile limit on the outer boundary of the territorial sea, which flew in the face of the interests of the Navy, was inexplicable—especially since the Soviet delegation included Piotr Barabolya, the Major General of Justice[72]—and the reference to a long-standing historical tradition was unfounded since the first formalized claim to this limit did not occur until 1896.[73]

The submission for review in 1972 of the Draft Articles on Fisheries to the Committee on the Peaceful Uses of the Sea-Bed and the Ocean Floor Beyond the Limits of National Jurisdiction—in which the Soviet delegation proposed acknowledging special rights to exploit the living marine resources of coastal areas only for developing countries—was also inexplicable from the standpoint of the state's own interests.[74]

At the same time, the Soviet party system was quite capable of learning from its mistakes, since it possessed a culture of mandatory consideration of appeals and decision-making at the level of the Central Committee—with decisions having a 'governing' significance for the legislative and executive authorities. In 1976, the Presidium of the Supreme Soviet issued a decree, On Temporary Measures for the Conservation of Living Resources and Regulation of Fisheries in the Sea Areas Adjacent to the Coast of the USSR, which consolidated the sovereign right of the country over the fish and other living marine resources of the 200-mile coastal sea belt for the purposes of exploration, development, and conservation. In accordance with the decree, foreign legal entities and individuals were permitted to fish within these territories only insofar as the agreements between the USSR and their states of nationality allowed.

[72] Piotr D Barabolya was head of the International Legal Department of the Navy Main Headquarters from 1970 to 1982.

[73] The Instruction for the Russian Military Cruiser Sent to Protect Marine Industries in the Bering Sea, dated 1896, was the first document of the Russian Empire to make unambiguous use of the concept of 'territorial waters' and provided the method for their measurement. See *Complete Collection of Laws of the Russian Empire* (1830), Law No 22206.

[74] However, the proposal was not approved and, by the mid-1970s, due to a sharp increase in the number of cases of individual states extending their sovereign rights, jurisdiction, and even sovereignty over the natural resources of coastal waters, the USSR was forced to take the necessary measures to legally protect the wealth of the sea belt adjacent to its own territory.

4.5 The Russian Federation

The culture of so-called legal nihilism and authoritarian governance began to take shape in Russia after 17 March 1991, when state policy ran afoul of the results of a Referendum on the Preservation of the Renewed USSR and the Establishment of the Office of the President of Russia. The Belovezha Accords—signed by the leaders of the Republic of Belarus, the Soviet Republic, and Ukraine on 8 December 1991—established the Commonwealth of Independent States to replace the USSR. The Soviet Union thus ceased to exist, not so much because of its own weaknesses but, more crucially, because the ruling elite—which had engaged in rivalry and power seizing—was mortally afflicted. The decline of the legal culture that followed the collapse of the USSR was caused not just by the inherent difficulties of the transition period but also by the traditional Russian tendency to not discriminate between legislation and law and to deny its role as a regulator of relations within society.

The most crucial agreements of the last years of the USSR and the first two decades of the new Russian statehood include those that led to the division of the navies in the Baltic and Black Seas and the Caspian flotilla between the former Soviet republics, as well as the untimely disposal of most of the submarine fleet, and those containing territorial concessions, which exhibited what could be called the 'anti-culture of lawmaking'. With regard to that last group of agreements, it is worth considering in particular the Maritime Boundary Agreement Between the United States and the USSR of 1990[75] and the Agreement Concerning Maritime Delimitation and Cooperation in the Barents Sea and the Arctic Ocean between Norway and the Russian Federation of 2010.[76] Those two instruments still attract criticism from government officials and from representatives of the professional communities of both lawyers and users of the sea.

Regarding the Maritime Boundary Agreement of 1990, for 30 years and counting, the executive and representative branches of power—ranging from the former Supreme Soviet of the USSR to the State Duma and the Federation Council of Russia—have been conducting a discussion on whether the Agreement is in line with national interests. Although the Agreement contained

[75] Maritime Boundary Agreement, 1 June 1990. The Agreement, which was signed by US Secretary of State James Bakes and Soviet Minister of Foreign Affairs Eduard Shevardnadze, is also referred to as the 'Baker-Shevardnadze line agreement'.

[76] Agreement Concerning Maritime Delimitation and Cooperation in the Barents Sea and the Arctic Ocean, 15 September 2010; Order of the President of the Russian Federation No 627-rp, 2 September 2010.

a provision stating that it was 'subject to ratification and shall enter into force on the day of the exchange of ratification instruments', Eduard Shevardnadze[77]—in violation of the provision and the relevant Soviet legislation—gave his consent to US Secretary of State James Baker for its temporary application in full pending ratification.[78] Under the Agreement, by the sole decision of its Minister of Foreign Affairs, the USSR effectively ceded 34,000 square miles of presumably oil-bearing area to the United States. There existed no procedure for mandatory ratification of the Agreement in accordance with the Soviet Constitution[79]—in fact, there is still no such procedure in existence on behalf of the Russian Federation. Because of fears that the Agreement would fail to pass ratification, Boris Yeltsin never submitted it to the Russian Parliament. Therefore, the Agreement has now been applied on a temporary basis for more than three decades, in violation of Russian law.[80]

For many years, the USSR/Russia and Norway have been negotiating the delimitation of maritime areas in the Varanger Fjord and Barents Sea regions. Temporary agreements were enacted between the countries, enabling reciprocal fishing and other activities in the disputed areas. In 2010, in the worst tradition of silent approval by the public, the Agreement Concerning Maritime Delimitation and Cooperation in the Barents Sea and the Arctic Ocean between Norway and the Russian Federation was adopted. According to various estimates, Russia ceded approximately 175,000 square kilometres of the Barents Sea to Norway.

Another sensitive issue related to, among other things, the culture of regulatory decision-making is the Russian Arctic and navigation along the Northern Sea Route (NSR). It must be noted that Russia perceives its 'North' as something that is absolutely and inherently Russian. If we were to talk about the emergence of maritime culture, then—at the risk of sparking controversy—I dare say that it was there that Russia emerged as a maritime power. From about the tenth century onwards, the lands from Lake Onega to Lake Beloye had begun to be settled by the 'Pomors', a name for the Slavs who populated the White Sea coast. The sea was their main source of food and, later, trade. The Pomors have been honing their expertise in shipbuilding and navigation

[77] Shevardnadze served as the final Soviet Minister of Foreign Affairs from 1985 to 1990.

[78] When the Agreement was being signed, an understanding was reached and confirmed via exchange of notes on its temporary application from 15 June 1990, as provided for by Article 25 of the Vienna Convention on the Law of Treaties, 23 May 1969, 1155 UNTS 331.

[79] USSR Constitution, 7 October 1977 (revised 26 December 1990), art 108(3).

[80] The United States ratified the Agreement on 16 September 1991. The US State Department indicated that, as a result, approximately 70 per cent of the Bering Sea will be under the jurisdiction of the United States, giving the country 13,200 square nautical miles more space than if the line were drawn at an equal distance between the coasts, as proposed by the USSR.

in high latitudes for centuries, passing it from generation to generation. Only irrepressible curiosity could push the Pomors to expand their habitat in the harsh Arctic region and hence to explore coastal areas. By the thirteenth century, their expertise enabled them to create the so-called Yamal portage, known as the ancient 'sea passage' along which the Pomors in the Middle Ages 'went beyond the stone' (the Ural Mountains) and onwards to the Ob Bay.

From the beginning of the sixteenth century—spurred by the assumption that it was possible to go much further from west to east, up to another ocean—expeditions were no longer being made exclusively by Russian navigators[81] but also by others. Among them, Willem Barents (1594–97) and Semyon Dezhnev (1648) achieved the greatest success in navigating the entire route. The only expedition to pass the entire NSR in a single navigation was that of Otto Schmidt, manning the icebreaking steamer *Alexander Sibiryakov* in 1932. This brief enumeration of relatively successful expeditions should be supplemented by a huge number of both organized and private efforts of people who, throughout many centuries, have forged not only the character but also the culture of perceiving the North as something extremely Russian—something accessible and belonging exclusively to the Russian people.

It is possible that this belief was what delayed by many years the formalization of the legal status of these areas as Russian regions. The repeated attempts to establish the boundaries of the Russian Arctic territories reveal the lack of any kind of overarching doctrine and reasonable legal framework.[82] It was in 1916 that the Russian Empire formalized its claims to these territories for the first time, submitting by a note of the Ministry of Foreign Affairs a provision on the inclusion of all lands stretching to the north of the Empire into its state territory.[83] The document was a reaction to a state act issued by Canada in 1909, containing a similar claim to possession of all lands and islands, both discovered and with the potential of being discovered, residing west of Greenland between Canada and the North Pole.[84]

[81] Starting with the expedition of Hugh Willoughby (1553–54) and followed by the high-latitude voyages of Adolf Erik Nordenskiöld (1878–79), Fridtjof Nansen (1893), Eduard Toll (1901), and others.

[82] According to some estimates, the Arctic currently provides Russia with up to 15 per cent of its GDP and up to 25 per cent of its exports. It accounts for 80 per cent of Russia's natural gas production, along with 30 per cent of the fish catch and much of Russia's reserves of nickel, diamonds, and rare earth metals. Up to 40 per cent of the total population living in the coastal areas of the subarctic countries resides in the coastal regions of the Russian Arctic. See 'Icebreaking Fleet of Russia—From the Coal-Powered Ermak to the Nuclear Lenin' (*Engineering_ru*, 30 September 2021) <https://engineering-ru.livejournal.com/597898.html> accessed 16 August 2022.

[83] Note of the Ministry of Foreign Affairs of the Russian Empire, 20 September 1916.

[84] In 1922, the Prime Minister of Canada made a statement that Wrangel Island belonged to Canada. In 1925, Canada passed an amendment to the law that prohibited all foreign states from engaging in any activity within the Canadian Arctic lands without first obtaining special permission from the Canadian government.

In 1921, the already-Soviet Russia secured the extension of Soviet Republic sovereign rights to a 12-mile strip of territorial waters by a decree of the Council of People's Commissars of the Soviet Republic, On the Protection of Fish and Animal Lands in the Arctic Ocean and the White Sea. The same decree established the exact boundary of coastal sea waters on the Barents Sea and reaffirmed the exclusive right of the Soviet Republic to the exploitation of fish and animal areas of the White Sea south of the straight line connecting Capes Svyatoy Nos and Kanin Nos, as well as in the Arctic Ocean along the coast from the Finnish border[85] to the northern tip of Novaya Zemlya, and up to 12 nautical miles inland from the low tide line both along the mainland coast and along the coast of the islands.[86] In 1926, the Soviet government again returned to the issue of legal title to the Arctic territories, issuing a decree titled On Declaring the Lands and Islands in the Arctic Ocean the Territory of the USSR.[87] Given the inconsistencies inherent in the approaches of the near-Arctic states to delineating their borders, the Soviet approach cannot be considered acceptable; moreover, it failed to avoid some obvious mistakes.[88]

In 1985, the USSR established a list of geographical coordinates referring to the points determining the baselines from which the width of the territorial sea was to be measured, including in the Arctic Ocean.[89] The author is personally familiar with the decision-making procedure that saw this document enter into force—and it had nothing to do with legal culture. For almost 30 years, Russia failed to issue a similar decree, doing so only in 2021 by adopting the corresponding government decree.[90]

[85] Finland had access to the Arctic at that time.

[86] In 1924, the Soviet Union confirmed the provisions of the note of 1916 on all the lands and islands of the Arctic sector belonging to Russia. By a decree of the Council of People's Commissars of the USSR in 1925, the Karskie Vorota, Yugorsky Shar, Matochkin Shar, Vilkitsky, Shokalsky, and Krasnoy Armii Straits were declared territorial waters of the Soviet Union, while the waters of the Dmitry Laptev and Sannikov Straits were declared as 'historically belonging to the USSR'.

[87] The Decree of the Presidium of the Central Executive Committee of the USSR, 15 April 1926, On Declaring the Lands and Islands in the Arctic Ocean the Territory of the USSR, provided that the territory of the USSR 'extends to all lands and islands, both discovered and with the potential of being discovered in the future, that do not constitute, by the publication time of this Decree, the territory of any foreign states recognized by the Government of the USSR, located in the Arctic Ocean north of the coast of the Union of Soviet Socialist Republics to the North Pole within the limits between the meridian 32°4'35" E., passing along the eastern side of Vaida-Guba, and the meridian 168°49'30" W., passing through the middle of the Bering Strait'. The status of those territories as belonging to the USSR was never officially disputed by any of the Arctic countries.

[88] In 1979, the Soviet Union, following an earlier inaccurate determination of the coordinates of the line passing through the middle of the Bering Strait and dividing the islands of Ratmanov and Krusenstern, changed the eastern borders of its Arctic holdings. See Decree of the Presidium of the Supreme Soviet of the USSR No 8908-IX, 21 February 1979.

[89] Decree of the Council of Ministers of the USSR No 56-22, 15 January 1985.

[90] Decree of the Government of the Russian Federation No 1959, 16 November 2021, On Approval of the List of Geographical Coordinates of Points Determining the Positions of the Baselines for Measuring the Width of the Territorial Sea of the Russian Federation, the Adjacent Zone of the Russian

The issue of taking state interests protected by the abovementioned regulatory measures into account is beyond the scope of this chapter and cannot be characterized as a constituent of the legal culture of regulatory decision-making. Having established the starting points by the aforementioned resolution, the state effectively outlined the boundaries of its national interests—which, of course, does not preclude members of the expert community from having their own opinions on the matter.

As for the use of the NSR, in the Soviet era, it was mainly coastal and served the ports of the Arctic and the large rivers of Siberia (for the import of fuel, equipment, and food, and for the export of timber and minerals), essentially implementing the so-called Northern Delivery. Although the Northern Delivery retains its significance to this day, modern NSR development efforts are more focused on ensuring international transport operations and the management of its areas by national companies. One would think that Russia spent enough years perfecting the NSR—among other things, developing navigation rules—and yet critical concerns remain regarding the clarity of border delimitations and the procedure for managing navigation along the NSR routes.

Likewise, the never-ending reforms within the NSR management did not further the goal of establishing a reliable international transport route. Since 1919, with the creation of the first management body—the Committee of the Northern Sea Route, headed by Admiral Alexander Kolchak—and throughout the entire Soviet history, the NSR had been undergoing a never-ending transformation in terms of its status, departmental affiliation, and functions. In 2012, the Administration of the Northern Sea Route was established, based on an existing federal law, as a federal state-owned institution.[91] But the issues did not end there. In December 2018, a law was signed appointing the State Atomic Corporation (Rosatom) as the infrastructure operator of the NSR, which it was empowered to control by means of centralized management—including providing icebreaking assistance to ships and escorting them along

Federation Near the Mainland Coast and the Islands of the Russian Federation in the Arctic Ocean, and on the Invalidation of the 'Arctic Ocean' Section of the List of Geographical Coordinates of Points Determining the Positions of the Baselines for Measuring the Width of the Territorial Waters, the Economic Zone and the Continental Shelf of the USSR Near the Mainland Coast and Islands of the Arctic Ocean, the Baltic and Black Seas, approved by a resolution of the Council of Ministers of the USSR No 56-22, 15 January 1985.

[91] See Federal Law No 132-FZ, 28 July 2012, On Amendments to Certain Legislative Acts of the Russian Federation Regarding the State Regulation of Merchant Shipping in the Waters of the Northern Sea Route, *Collected Legislation of the Russian Federation*, No 31, 30 July 2012, art 4321; Decree of the Government of the Russian Federation No 358-r, 15 March 2013, On the Establishment of a Federal State Public Institution, *Collected Legislation of the Russian Federation*, No 12, 25 March 2013, art 1365.

their navigation routes in NSR waters. From a commercial use perspective, the idea of creating a means by which ship-owners can quickly reach out to a single contact centre that is capable of handling all their requests seems quite viable. However, it remains unclear just how well the state corporation specializing in atomic energy will be able to handle this complex, multifaceted maritime task.

In 2012, when the State Duma of the Russian Federation adopted the law On Amendments to Certain Legislative Acts of the Russian Federation Regarding the State Regulation of Merchant Shipping in the Waters of the Northern Sea Route, the changes were few: the concept of 'route' used in the earlier document was phased out by the word 'water territory', and a corresponding change was made to Article 5 of the Merchant Shipping Code of 1999. Article 5 recognizes the water territory of the NSR as the water area adjacent to the northern coast of the Russian Federation, which, aside from the country's internal waters and its territorial sea, also includes the exclusive economic zone (EEZ) of the Russian Federation. In 2013, the Ministry of Transport adopted the Rules for Navigation in the NSR Waters,[92] paragraph 2 of which stipulates that the navigation of vessels in the waters of the NSR occurs on a permission basis. Any vessel in respect of which permission to navigate the NSR water territory has not been obtained in the manner prescribed by the Rules may not enter the territory. This raises the question of enforceability of the provisions of Article 58(1) of UNCLOS, which stipulates that all states enjoy freedom of navigation and overflight in the foreign EEZ. On 18 September 2020, the Russian Federation issued a new edition of the NSR Rules for Navigation,[93] which again establishes the permission-based navigation procedure and again leaves hanging the question of how this requirement correlates with the provisions of UNCLOS.

Plans existed in 2018 to adopt a new law containing the rules for the provision of services and the list of port dues applicable to the seaports within the water territory of the NSR. Restrictions were planned regarding the use of ships navigating under foreign flags. In particular, restrictions on the navigation of foreign-built ships in the Russian waters of the NSR and in coastal waters were planned for adoption from 1 January 2019. If the country's leadership still plans to increase the cargo turnover along the NSR to 80 million metric

[92] Order of the Ministry of Transport of the Russian Federation No 7, 17 January 2013 (void since 30 August 2022).

[93] Decree of the Government of the Russian Federation No 1487, 18 September 2020, On Approval of the Rules for Navigation in the Waters of the Northern Sea Route, *Collected Legislation of the Russian Federation*, No 39, 28 September 2020, art 6064.

tons and make shipping international, then such initiatives seem unreasonable at best.

Arguably, the reason for such erratic rule-making lies in the fact that there is no 'open professional discussion' stage in the existing decision-making culture. Every ministry tasked with developing regulatory acts tends to coordinate its own draft of the document with other interested parties through its own internal corporate law body. However, the lack of any public discussion renders such documents extremely vulnerable to adjustment in accordance with practical needs. There is an obvious cultural lacuna here. Even so, blaming the absence of a formal procedure for the preparation of regulatory instruments would be unfounded. Granted, there is a procedure for interdepartmental approvals; as soon as a complaint is filed regarding the poor quality of regulatory design activities, an opponent will immediately reply that the document has passed the examination of the Government Committee on Legislative Activities. But who are those specialists entrusted with quality assessment, including the quality of marine rule-making? Their list is determined by the relevant government decree.[94] There are no names in the list, just positions, including the Chairman of the Committee (the head of the Russian Federation), authorized representatives of the government from both chambers of the Federal Assembly, the assistant to the President of the Russian Federation, the head of the State Legal Administration of the President of the Russian Federation, the Commissioner for Human Rights, the Chief of Staff of the Accounts Chamber, the Deputy General Director of Rosatom, and a representative of the all-Russian public organization Delovaya Rossiya and the Association of Lawyers of Russia.

Once again, it is a fact that wherever the normative act being adopted happens to affect the interests not only of its national users, its narrowly specialized interdepartmental development hurts its prospects of stable and long-term application. The attempt to regulate military navigation in the waters of the NSR is quite characteristic in this regard.

Media reports indicate that the Government Committee on Legislative Activities approved a draft amendment to the federal law On the Internal Sea Waters, Territorial Sea, and the Adjacent Area of the Russian Federation. The amendment concerned the legal regulation of the procedure for the passage of foreign warships and other vessels used for non-commercial purposes. In accordance with a suggestion by the Ministry of Defence, the current law will

[94] For example, the Decree of the Government of the Russian Federation No 737, 24 June 2017, On Amending Clause 5 of the Regulations Regarding the Legislative Activities Commission of the Government of the Russian Federation, *Collected Legislation of the Russian Federation*, No 27, 3 July 2017, art 4040.

be supplemented with a clause according to which foreign military and government ships will be allowed to enter internal marine waters only with permission, which is to be requested through diplomatic channels 90 days before the intended entry. It is assumed that the authorities will be able to suspend the entry of foreign warships and other government ships into the internal sea waters in the NSR in the interests of ensuring security over a certain period. The right of a coastal state to lay down rules for foreign warships intending to enter the internal waters of another state cannot be challenged. But the Russian military command still considered it necessary to eliminate the 'legal vacuum' and regulate foreign military navigation in all NSR waters.[95] As early as 2019, a draft government decree was published on a regulatory website that proposed changing the Rules for the navigation and stay of warships and other government ships. According to that document, foreign warships and government ships must notify the Russian authorities 45 days before the intended passage through the NSR, take Russian marine pilots on board, and additionally report the name of the ship, its main specifications, and the military rank and last name of the captain. A separate paragraph of the draft resolution was devoted to foreign submarines, which were supposed to navigate the NSR in a surfaced state and under their own flag.[96]

It is patently obvious that the requirements for warships proceeding into the internal waters of a foreign state follow from its sovereignty; however, there is the question of the legitimacy of demands addressed to foreign warships located in the EEZ to follow established routes or report on some issue or another, especially their intentions. These demands appear quite excessive and inconsistent with the provisions of UNCLOS.

The culture of Russia's involvement in international relations in the period from 1993 to 2007 can be summarized as 'dependent independence'. It was a period of Western companies actively integrating themselves into the Russian economy and acquiring assets, including those crucial for naval security; the unjustified retirement of defence-capable ships and vessels from the Navy; and the elimination of naval bases in Cuba and Cam Ranh (Vietnam), which inevitably affected the activity of the state in the World Ocean.

[95] 'Russia Will Restrict the Passage of Foreign Ships Along the Northern Sea Route' (NTV, 30 November 2018) <https://www.ntv.ru/novosti/2114981/> accessed 16 August 2022.

[96] In July 2022, the Ministry of Defence of the Russian Federation proposed to restrict completely the navigation of any foreign military vessels along the NSR.

4.6 Recent developments

In 2007, Russia began to break free from its 'submissive partner' role, and its foreign policy began to be determined largely by economic modernization goals. It adopted a state program for the development of the armed forces, which notably envisioned the construction of new ships—making it possible to return to military service in September 2013[97] and conclude agreements on the fleet's naval bases in Syria and Sudan.[98]

Since the beginning of the twenty-first century, novelties have been making their way into Russian legal and managerial culture. These include publications on the fundamentals of state policy, as well as doctrines on various aspects of state aspirations considered as a set of public views that can, in the near future, be distilled into regulatory acts or departmental rules and instructions.

Initially, there was no 'culture' in the formation of Soviet doctrines. Starting in 1991, the Russian doctrine became a collective effort destined to grant the Russian Federation as a nation its own 'weapon of consciousness'—a tool that would prevent the destruction of the national mentality.[99] Ranging from the Food Doctrine to the Arctic Doctrine, all kinds of doctrines were adopted by Russia going forward. For the purposes of this chapter, a few references to the relevant maritime doctrinal acts will suffice.

In 2000, the state adopted the Fundamentals of Russian Policy in the Field of Naval Activities for the Period Until 2010,[100] which provided the basis for determining the main goals, principles, and priority areas for Russia's activities aimed at studying, developing, and using the World Ocean in the interests of national defence and state security.[101] The document defines Russia's interests in the oceans, including the maritime spaces to which it extends both sovereignty and jurisdiction. Among the key components are ensuring access by the Russian Federation to the resources and spaces of the World Ocean;

[97] In Russian military terminology, 'military service' refers to the deployment and continued operation of an operational formation of the Navy, which is entrusted with a wide range of tasks in peacetime to ensure Russia's naval presence in various regions of the world's oceans.

[98] Agreement Between the Russian Federation and the Syrian Arab Republic on the Territorial Expansion of the Russian Federation Navy's Logistics Center in the Area of the Port of Tartus and on the Entry of Russian Federation Warships into the Territorial Sea, Internal Waters, and Ports of the Syrian Arab Republic, 2017; Agreement Between the Russian Federation and the Republic of Sudan on the Establishment of a Logistics Center for the Navy of the Russian Federation on the Territory of the Republic of Sudan, 23 July 2019 to 1 December 2020. In 2019, a military coup took place in Sudan. At the time of this writing, the current legal status of the agreement remains uncertain.

[99] 'Russian Doctrine' (*Rusdoctrina.ru*, 22 January 2019) <http://www.rusdoctrina.ru/page95556.html> accessed 16 August 2022.

[100] Approved by Decree of the President of the Russian Federation, 4 March 2000.

[101] Defined as 'naval activity'.

excluding discriminatory actions against Russia or its allies by any individual states or military–political blocs; preventing the dominance of any state or military–political bloc in the spaces of the World Ocean deemed essential for the implementation of Russia's state interests, especially in its adjacent seas; and the favourable settlement of existing political and international legal issues relating to the use of the World Ocean. The document concludes that Russia must possess adequate naval potential in order to protect its interests in the World Ocean.

These circumstances affected the professional thoroughness and clarity in the formulation of goals and objectives. The Maritime Doctrine of the Russian Federation for the Period Until 2020[102] was adopted in 2001, but as early as 2010 the Security Council had demanded the development of a new document. And, although the superficial reason was quite justified (there were significant changes in the international situation, with new challenges and security threats), in the end, the attempts to create a uniform, well-appointed, and professionally structured document have failed.

In July 2022, President Vladimir Putin signed a new Maritime Doctrine of the Russian Federation. The Doctrine represents another stage in the culture of formulating the main provisions of the state's maritime national policy, from the conceptual framework (risks, challenges, threats, and maritime potential); through the principles of maritime policy, strategic goals, and naval activities;[103] to the development of maritime transports, pipeline systems, commercial fishing activities, and scientific research. Analysing the provisions of the Doctrine warrants a separate study, but for present purposes it is worth considering one particular section, titled 'International Legal Support for Maritime Activities and International Cooperation in the Field of Maritime Activities'.[104] Unfortunately, the section lacks any consideration of the prospects of the Russian Federation with regard to the country's participation in international legal activities. Instead, it uses general provisions that apply to the various directions of national maritime policy.

The Maritime Doctrine of 2022 provides for the intensification of maritime activities in the northern archipelagos, increasing the naval potential and developing the basing system for the Northern Fleet, the Federal Security Services, and the National Guard. There is novelty in the fact that the national

[102] Approved by the President of the Russian Federation, 27 July 2001.

[103] Defined as state activities aimed at preventing aggression against the Russian Federation, as well as implementing and protecting its national interests in the oceans: Maritime Doctrine of the Russian Federation, 31 July 2022, s 46.

[104] ibid s 59.

interests of the Russian Federation extend not to coastal areas or individual sea areas but rather to the entire World Ocean and the Caspian Sea.

From a pragmatic point of view, the Doctrine involves holding joint naval exercises between the Russian Navy and the fleets and coast guards of foreign states, expanding the geography of annual calls to foreign ports, conducting joint regular exercises and drills on search-and-rescue operations at sea with the forces and search-and-rescue assets of foreign states, expanding the areas of international cooperation to ensure the safety of maritime activities, and fulfilling the international obligations of the Russian Federation to provide ships and vessels with navigational and meteorological information within the framework of the Global Maritime Distress and Safety System. Furthering these areas of cooperation will require developing and improving the international contractual legal framework, including the conclusion of intergovernmental agreements on the prevention of incidents at sea, on the prevention of dangerous military activities, on the simplified procedure for ships to enter foreign state ports, and on other issues.

Among the doctrinal shortcomings inherent in the Russian culture of forming the future foundations of state policy in various areas, including maritime, is the introduction of sanctioning methods that later prove unfeasible to enforce, as well as the low quality of the implementation of such doctrines in legislation.

A detailed analysis of the involvement of the USSR/Russia in international rule-making cannot be undertaken here. The country has assumed obligations under approximately 50 maritime conventions developed within the framework of the United Nations and the International Maritime Organization (IMO) to regulate the use of the sea.[105] Russia is persistently implementing the idea of ensuring environmental security in its international legal doctrine following the signing[106] of the Paris Agreement of 2015.[107] However, with regard to the marine component of the environmental problem, Russia is striving to somewhat loosen the legal regulation of decarbonization—in particular, the banning of the use of heavy fuels in ships traversing the Arctic waters. The

[105] Including UNCLOS; the International Convention for the Safety of Life at Sea, 1 November 1974, 1184 UNTS 2 (SOLAS); the International Convention for the Prevention of Marine Pollution from Ships, 2 November 1973, 1340 UNTS 184 (MARPOL); the International Convention on Standards of Training, Certification and Watchkeeping for Seafarers, 7 July 1978, 1361 UNTS 2; and the Convention on the International Regulations for Preventing Collisions at Sea, 20 October 1972, 1050 UNTS 16.

[106] Decree of the Government of the Russian Federation No 670-r, 14 April 2016.

[107] Paris Agreement to the United Nations Framework Convention on Climate Change, 12 December 2015, TIAS No 16-1104. The Paris Agreement was the final document of the Twenty-first Conference of the Parties to the United Nations Framework Convention on Climate Change: UN Doc FCCC/CP/2015/L.9/Rev/1 (12 December 2015).

efforts made by Russian experts helped tame the wording of the prohibitive legislation,[108] essentially postponing its enforcement by seven years from what had initially been scheduled. Vessels designed for oil spill response and ensuring the safety of other vessels were made exempt from the ban. Deferrals were provided for ships with structural protection of the fuel tank until 1 July 2029, and permissions were granted for flag administrations of states whose waters border Arctic waters (as defined in the Polar Code) to issue temporary exemptions for ships flying their own flag and operating in waters under the sovereignty or jurisdiction of those states until 1 July 2029. Russia is a supporter of the IMO's efforts to tighten control over plastic waste management.[109]

With regard to the improvement of provisions of the International Convention for the Safety of Life at Sea (SOLAS),[110] Russia advocates the adoption of a new Chapter XV on the safe operation of ships carrying a 12-strong or larger crew of operational staff. Russia has also expressed interest in evaluating the possibility of using maritime autonomous surface vessels (MASVs) and is actively involved in developing relevant regulatory projects within the IMO's Maritime Safety Committee in order to identify gaps that will need to be filled with the view of developing an IMO Code on MASV.[111]

The participation of the Russian Federation in international efforts to improve the norms of maritime law has lately been taking place against the background of the United States and EU countries drastically weakening their own responsibilities with regard to previously accepted international obligations, including those related to maritime use. To a certain extent, the European Union's ban on tanker deliveries of Russian oil to Europe can be explained as a matter of choice. However, the ban on all ships entering US and European ports if they are suspected of having cargo associated with Russian owners and the closure of the insurance services market are complete novelties belonging to the realm of legal nihilism. The termination of the Russian operational direction by the largest container operators—including Maersk (Denmark), CMA CGM (France), and MSC (Italy)—will only result in increased profits for the COSCO Group (China) and, eventually, in FESCO and SASCO also receiving new and larger opportunities. The market will change, as will the

[108] In 2020, the seventh session of the Subcommittee on Pollution Prevention and Response approved relevant amendments to the MARPOL Convention.

[109] In October 2021, the seventy-seventh session of the Marine Environment Protection Committee developed and approved a strategy for the IMO to combat marine plastic waste from ships. The strategy outlines the main goal: to improve the international legal framework with the view of eliminating all plastic waste discharge from ships by 2025.

[110] SOLAS (n 105).

[111] According to information found on the IMO website: <http://www.imo.org> accessed 16 August 2022.

logistics landscape, but—most crucially—trust in the agreement as the key factor and basis of all international maritime projects will falter. No matter how weird the outcome, the construction of the Nord Stream along the bottom of the Baltic Sea was a truly grand project[112] from both the technical[113] and the legal perspectives.[114] Another project, the TurkStream gas pipeline[115] along the bottom of the Black Sea, had a completely different fate: it continues to function properly, ensuring the interests of all parties to the agreement.[116] Both pipeline projects followed corresponding agreements. However, the Nord Stream agreements fell victim to politics, while the TurkStream agreements continue to demonstrate stable international legal relations.

The triumph of politics over law is perceived by many experts as a very troublesome sign of the end of international law. However, there is hope. Of the 193 sovereign states of the United Nations and the 175 member states of the IMO, only 45 countries supported sanctions against Russia. Unfortunately, those states are all former partners with which Russia had formed long-term economic ties, including key maritime powers whose efforts are now destroying the post-war world order—including in the field of maritime use. But, if we are to talk about culture, then hardly anything can be considered a more genuine part of the Russian culture than its ability to endure in challenging times and to piece together a new puzzle.

4.7 Conclusion

To sum up these reflections, it is always the leader of the state who makes the governing decision. However, the actual legal design of such decisions depends on the adopted rule-making traditions. Although it is possible to expose the leader's initiative almost entirely to the debate of lawmakers and, in doing so, either doom it to lengthy discussion or downright destroy it, this style is often

[112] The laying of the first branch of Nord Stream commenced in April 2010 and was completed in June 2011. The construction of the second branch lasted from May 2011 until April 2012.

[113] At around 760 nautical miles, Nord Stream 1 was the longest underwater gas pipeline in the world until the construction of Nord Stream 2.

[114] In addition to the 'crowding' of the jurisdictional zones of the Continental Shelf and the inconsistent relations between the coastal countries, the Nord Stream 2 construction was opposed by Denmark. This led to the length of the pipeline increasing by around 8 nautical miles due to the need to bypass the waters of that state.

[115] The offshore section was built in 2017–19, setting a new world record of 6.27 kilometres per day for offshore gas pipeline construction speed.

[116] The TurkStream pipeline enters the Black Sea near Anapa in Russia's Krasnodar region and has its onshore terminal in the town of Kiyiköy in the European part of Turkey.

approvingly called 'democratic' and considered the most acceptable. At the other extreme of the decision-making culture is the authoritarian style, which implies strict compliance with the requirements for regulatory support of the higher authority's will. In practice, in most countries—including Russia—we observe the use of a mixed legal support culture in decision-making, which is especially evident in the law of the sea. So, where does Russian uniqueness manifest itself? In answering that question, the factor of Russia's enormous territorial span comes to the fore. This inevitably affects any emerging political concepts, claims, and even aesthetic ideas. From the Arctic Ocean, the Baltic Sea, the Black Sea, and the Caspian Sea to the Pacific Ocean, this is true for numerous ethnic formations—including the East Slavic, Finno-Ugric, Turkic, Iranian, and Mongolian peoples, as well as those inhabiting the Russian North.

The Russian legal tradition has evolved over many centuries. Its formation and development were originally influenced by numerous historical and cultural factors. Describing the features of the national character, the Russian scientist Dmitry Likhachev emphasized that, for many centuries, Russia had been at the crossroads of trade routes running from north to south (from the Baltic Sea to the shores of the Mediterranean—'from the Varangians to the Greeks') and from west to east (from Europe to China and India). As a result, Russian culture—by virtue of its incorporation of the cultures of dozens of other peoples and its long-term association with the neighbouring cultures of Scandinavia, Byzantium, the southern and western Slavs, Germany, Italy, the peoples of the East, and the Caucasus—represents a universal culture that is tolerant of the cultures of other peoples. The ability to live and get along in a vast country as a single—albeit multinational and interfaith—people is a major component of Russian national pride. It is probably for this reason that Russians are so receptive—not just of other languages but also of the standards and ways of life of other peoples. Hence, Russians are able to conduct business easily with representatives of various countries and nationalities, being open to their negotiating styles. On the other hand, as Likhachev wrote, the Russian character is also characterized by the desire to bring everything 'to extremes, to the limits of the possible', manifested, on the one hand, as a constant adherence to a very firm negotiating position (or otherwise) and, on the other hand, as a full acceptance of the partner's proposed terms coming as a surprise to the partner.[117] Generally speaking, the emotional aspect represents an important

[117] DS Likhachev, 'On the National Character of Russians' (1990) 4 Matters of Philosophy 3.

component of Russian culture, and it also applies to the adoption of regulatory acts. Another important feature of the Russian style of regulatory design is that, when discussing issues, the country's negotiators tend to pay more attention to the goals in general and relatively little attention to the particular ways of achieving them. If one were to suggest a brief characterization of the very essence of the Russian decision-making culture, at least three crucial components come to mind: spirituality, love, and justice.

In criticizing the traditions of managerial decision-making in the Soviet era—sometimes not without good reason—many Russian authors nevertheless forget that it was an era of defence from, and confrontation with, a powerful rival that did not conceal its intentions to destroy the Soviet Union. The party system, clumsy as it was, nonetheless was no worse than any other, as we now realize. It was the Soviet Union that paved the way for the destruction of colonialism, ensured the balance of international cooperation on security issues, and made significant efforts to preserve and strengthen peace. The Soviet Union also contributed to the creation of an international legal framework—one that still cannot be considered to have been completely destroyed. The Soviet Union played a most prolific role in the development of the Geneva Conventions of 1958, UNCLOS, and other key maritime conventions, securing leadership among the Eastern Bloc countries and assisting the delegations of African countries.

Along with 45 other countries, the Soviet Union signed the 1958 Convention on the Territorial Sea and the Contiguous Zone,[118] amending two of its articles with reservations.[119] Indeed, the matter of whether it should be possible for foreign warships to enter a country's territorial waters without permission has always been difficult to rationalize. Having never invaded the waters of foreign states without a justified goal, the USSR has always been wary of military fleets navigating near its own waters.

Fundamental principles were formulated during the development of the national maritime law that regulated legal relations in all aspects of maritime use, and maritime transportation was also legislated and systemized. Maritime commercial law was codified through the adoption of the Merchant Shipping Code.

Modern historical processes pose new tasks in accordance with the new challenges. The return of Crimea to the Russian Federation in 2014 and the

[118] Convention on the Territorial Sea and the Contiguous Zone, 29 April 1958, 516 UNTS 205.
[119] Articles 20 and 23.

stated wish of people living in the coastal regions of the Sea of Azov and the Black Sea to become part of the Russian Federation in 2022 dramatically transformed the territorial title to those territories and changed the legal regime of the Kerch Strait. Despite the controversy of these circumstances as perceived internationally, it should be noted that Russia has always become stronger in overcoming such circumstances. It has always been the difficulties—or, rather, the efforts directed at overcoming them—that have enabled Russia to achieve the highest results throughout its history. Sanctions give rise to the formation of anti-Western cultural opposition, prompting the formulation of alternative purposes that enable the shifting of the development vector.

The current international events demonstrate with great clarity that international law is unable to dampen all the emerging threats. The maritime commercial law tied to London insurance institutions or to the recognition of the freedom of commercial turnover for seaports will no doubt undergo substantial revision. Apparently, the fundamental conventions setting forth the rules for the transportation of goods (the Hague-Visby Rules,[120] the Hamburg Rules[121], and the Rotterdam Rules[122]), while remaining the legal basis of the regime, will be subject to amendment. Other international maritime insurance and dispute resolution centres will emerge, most likely with addresses in the Asia-Pacific region.

At the same time, with regard to the fundamental international maritime acts related to the law of the sea, the application of UNCLOS, SOLAS, and the International Convention for the Prevention of Marine Pollution from Ships (MARPOL)[123] will remain unchanged.

The culture of regulatory decision-making has taken shape in the Russian state over many centuries and has undergone many stages, from copying the religious and legal foundations of the Byzantine civilization; to imperial autocracy, Soviet party management, and 'independent dependence' from Western traditions following the collapse of the USSR; and to the 'discretionary management' of the first decade of the current century, which became 'constructive pragmatism' starting from 2014.

[120] International Convention for the Unification of Certain Rules of Law relating to Bills of Lading, 25 August 1924 (Hague Rules). After being amended in 1968 (Protocol Amending the International Convention for the Unification of Certain Rules of Law Relating to Bills of Lading, 23 February 1968, 1412 UNTS 128), the Hague Rules became known colloquially as the Hague-Visby Rules.

[121] UN Convention on the Carriage of Goods by Sea, 31 March 1978 (Hamburg Rules).

[122] UN Convention on Contracts for the International Carriage of Goods Wholly or Partly by Sea, 11 December 2008 (Rotterdam Rules).

[123] MARPOL (n 105).

Waiving any claim to its absolute veracity,[124] the following extract from the spiritual will of Alexander III to his son Nikolai II eloquently conveys the Russian culture of serving the Motherland:

> I hereby bequeath you to love everything that serves the welfare, honour, and dignity of Russia.... Be staunch and courageous, never show weakness. Hear everyone out, there is nothing shameful in it, but listen only to Your Own Self and Your conscience. In foreign politics, maintain an independent position. Remember: Russia has no friends. They are afraid of our immensity. Avoid wars. In domestic politics, patronize the Church first of all. It has saved Russia more than once in times of trouble. Strengthen the family, as it is the foundation of any state.

Although uttered long ago, these words remain relevant.

[124] Although I am unable to provide a link to the specific document, these words were quoted by Patriarch Alexiy II and we do not doubt their authenticity.

5
East Asia

Seokwoo Lee

5.1 Introduction

The world's oceans, vast and enigmatic, have been a cradle of civilization, an arena of exploration, and a conduit for cultural exchange for millennia.[1] As maritime societies flourished along the shores of East Asia, they cultivated a profound connection with the seas, shaping their collective identity and influencing their approach to governance.[2] The cultural heritage of East Asia—encompassing philosophical beliefs, ancient maritime traditions, and profound reverence for the natural world—has left an indelible mark on the development and evolution of the law of the sea. The law of the sea, a pivotal framework governing the rights and responsibilities of nations over oceanic spaces, has emerged as a reflection of diverse cultural narratives and historical experiences. Within this context, East Asia stands as an exceptional case study, where cultural values and traditions have intricately intertwined with modern legal principles, crafting a unique maritime legal landscape.

Embodied in the cultural fabric of East Asia lies Confucianism, a philosophical system emphasizing respect for authority and the pursuit of harmony within hierarchical relationships.[3] Such values have permeated the region's approach to maritime governance, leading to a quest for harmonious interactions and adherence to mutually agreed-upon rules in oceanic affairs. Moreover, East Asia's historical emphasis on collective harmony and diplomacy has profoundly impacted the establishment of multilateral agreements and organizations, shaping the region's cooperative approach to addressing maritime challenges. Beyond philosophical tenets, ancient maritime traditions

[1] RP Anand, *Studies in International Law and History: An Asian Perspective* (Martinus Nijhoff 2004) 26.

[2] Tonio Andrade and Xing Hang (eds), *Sea Rovers, Silver, and Samurai: Maritime East Asia in Global History, 1550–1700* (University of Hawai'i Press 2016).

[3] Jeffrey L Richey, *Confucius in East Asia: Confucianism's History in China, Korea, Japan, and Việt Nam* (Association for Asian Studies 2022); Sungmoon Kim (ed), *Confucianism, Law and Democracy in Contemporary Korea* (Rowman and Littlefield 2015).

Seokwoo Lee, *East Asia* In: *Cultural Influences on the Law of the Sea*. Edited by: James Kraska and Hayoun Ryou-Ellison, Oxford University Press. © Seokwoo Lee 2025. DOI: 10.1093/9780198944140.003.0005

embedded in East Asian cultures have significantly shaped customs and norms concerning marine resource management. Fishing rights, sustainable practices, and the preservation of traditional fishing grounds are manifestations of this cultural heritage in maritime affairs. International cases addressing Japan's whaling activities have demonstrated how ancient traditions and cultural perspectives intertwine, influencing a nation's stance on marine conservation. Moreover, East Asia's cultural landscape is adorned with the tenets of Buddhism and Taoism, promoting interconnectedness and reverence for all life forms. These profound cultural values have inspired environmental protection and conservation efforts within the region, influencing international cases related to maritime disputes with underlying environmental considerations.

Intricately woven into the cultural fabric of East Asia are historical claims and territorial identity, intertwining narratives that have shaped the region's stance on sovereignty and maritime rights. Maritime territorial disputes, such as the complex and intricate South China Sea dispute, exemplify how cultural ties to the sea intensify the complexities of applying the law of the sea. Cases at the International Tribunal for the Law of the Sea (ITLOS) concerning the claims of the Philippines and China over the South China Sea underscore the interplay of cultural narratives in shaping positions on maritime boundaries.

In the modern era, East Asian nations have embraced international legal frameworks, including the UN Convention on the Law of the Sea (UNCLOS),[4] while preserving their cultural perspectives on the seas. The delicate balance between adhering to international law and safeguarding cultural interests has been illuminated in international cases at ITLOS and the International Court of Justice (ICJ), which have explored interpretations and applications of UNCLOS in the context of East Asia's rich cultural heritage.

This chapter endeavours to illuminate the intricate connections between East Asia's cultural heritage and the evolution of the law of the sea. By exploring international cases, it aims to unravel the enduring influence of cultural values, ancient traditions, and philosophical outlooks on maritime governance in the region. As the world grapples with maritime challenges in an ever-changing global landscape, a profound appreciation of East Asia's cultural underpinnings will undoubtedly enrich our understanding of the complex and evolving legal tapestry of the seas.

It is commonly recognized that the law of the sea was influenced by European civilization (Eurocentrism). However, the exclusive focus of Western legal theory on European history largely ignored the developments in

[4] UN Convention on the Law of the Sea, 10 December 1982, 1833 UNTS 397 (UNCLOS).

India, Southeast Asia, China, and Japan.[5] In 1609, Hugo Grotius, the father of international law, published *Mare Liberum*, through which he proclaimed the freedom of seas. Surveying the subsequent development of international law, RP Anand argued that there is 'no doubt that peoples or countries in their outlook and behaviour in international relations are affected by their cultures or cultural traditions which reflect their history, values, habits and accumulated social and political mores of their societies'.[6] Accordingly, it is indisputable that cultures (East and West) influence each other.[7] It is therefore essential to understand the history, culture, and traditions of Asia, along with their contributions to the development of modern international law.

The question of whether European civilization exclusively shaped international law has been a subject of debate.[8] It is contended that Asian countries have also exerted significant influence on international law, particularly concerning the law of the sea. The fourteenth and fifteenth centuries witnessed a fervent quest for spices in Asia, with a particular emphasis on the high demand for aromatic spices from India and the East Indies. European nations, notably Spain and Portugal, embarked on maritime expeditions to India in pursuit of collecting and procuring these coveted spices. In the discourse surrounding freedom of navigation (FON) in the Indian Ocean, Grotius draws attention to the Asian state practice of embracing unrestricted commerce and trade between diverse nations and peoples. This underscores the significance of considering the Asian perspective on FON. Grotius further highlights that Asians had long been engaged in unimpeded navigation and peaceful maritime trade in the Indian Ocean, thereby challenging the notion of European dominance in shaping these early principles of international maritime law.

Moreover, in the seventh century, China also influenced the law of the sea through its increased maritime trade with countries such as Egypt, Persia, and India.[9] The seas in East Asia were characterized by a prevailing state of tranquillity, with East Asian nations largely enjoying relative peace at sea, apart from isolated instances of piracy. In the fifteenth century, maritime shipping

[5] W Frank Newton, 'Inexhaustibility as a Law of the Sea Determinant' (1981) 16(3) Texas International Law Journal 369, 385.

[6] RP Anand, *Origin and Development of the Law of the Sea* (Martinus Nijhoff 1983) 4.

[7] Sakuye Takahashi, *The Influence of Grotius in the Far East* (Brooklyn Institute of Arts and Sciences 1908).

[8] John M Hobson, 'The Postcolonial Paradox of Eastern Agency' in Pinar Bilgin and LHM Ling (eds), *Asia in International Relations: Unlearning Imperial Power Relations* (Routledge 2017) 109–20. Ram P Anand, 'Freedom of the Seas: Past, Present and Future' in Hugo Caminos (ed), *Law of the Sea* (Routledge 2016) 263.

[9] Diane A Desierto, 'Postcolonial International Law Discourses on Regional Developments in South and Southeast Asia' (2008) 36 International Journal of Legal Information 388, 394.

and trade in the Indian Ocean witnessed a notable upsurge. It was during this period that Malaccan trade reached its peak and a written maritime code came into existence in Malacca. This achievement codified commercial and maritime usages and included rules about the rights of the captain of the ship and the sovereign at sea, and other rights and obligations at sea. These codified rules, along with practices on the seas, showed that the high seas were also accepted as free. It is contended that, with limited exceptions, Asian nations demonstrated a clear understanding of the principles governing the law of the sea. This Asian practice of free navigation and trade, characterized by peaceful conduct, also found reference in Grotius's doctrine of the freedom of the seas.[10] In the aftermath of the Second World War, Asian states gradually assumed a more influential role in shaping international law. This chapter aims to elucidate how East Asia, in particular, left an indelible imprint on the development of the law of the sea.[11]

5.2 East Asia's encounter with the modern international legal system

The cultural influence of East Asia is widely recognized, stemming from the Confucian tradition in China and Korea, as well as the Buddhist ideals that originated in ancient Japan. Confucius extolled the virtues of hierarchy and stability, and this reflected a desire to maintain an internal harmony in which participants from the level of the family to empires understood their place in the system. As encounters with the West occurred, colonial traditions intermingled with classical Eastern cultural norms, contributing to the development of nationalist and expansionist ideologies, first observed in Japan and more recently in China. It is important to note that Korea, too, experienced an amalgamation of influences from both the Western and Eastern spheres.

There is a long-standing debate, however, as to whether an East Asian concept of international law exists and what it is. Indeed, while applying a general understanding of international law to actual cases, international lawyers in East Asia have encountered notable challenges in identifying pertinent source materials and addressing specific aspects, leading to difficulties in conceptualizing the relevant issues.[12] A case in point is the law of the sea. Given the complexity

[10] RP Anand, 'Maritime Practice in South-East Asia Until 1600 A.D. and the Modern Law of the Sea' (1981) 30 International and Comparative Law Quarterly 440.

[11] Anand, *Origin and Development* (n 6).

[12] Eric Yong-Joong Lee, 'Early Development of Modern International Law in East Asia—With Special Reference to China, Japan and Korea' (2002) 4 Journal of the History of International Law 42.

of ascertaining a cohesive East Asian perspective on international law, the following essential enquiries arise concerning a plausible East Asian conception of international law and its application to the law of the sea: (i) To what extent can international law accommodate the cultural distinctions between Western states and East Asian states? (ii) what approach do East Asian states take regarding the cultural influence, if any, in their interpretation and application of the law of the sea; and (iii) if the distinct East Asian approach to international law exists, what is its contribution to the development of international law and the law of the sea in East Asia and the general development of international law? The comprehensive exploration of these questions is beyond the scope of this chapter. However, a more modest approach may involve investigating how East Asian states are applying the law of the sea in their domestic legal systems and in their foreign relations. Specifically, such an enquiry aims to determine whether a distinct East Asian approach to international law and the law of the sea emerges, either uniquely or shared among East Asian states. Consequently, this approach cautiously seeks to propose initial conclusions regarding the potential factors accounting for any similarities among East Asian states in their perspectives on international law and the law of the sea.

5.2.1 China

International law was systematically introduced into China in the nineteenth century, shortly following the Opium War, though arguably there was also some rudimentary form of international law in ancient China, especially during the so-called Spring and Autumn period (722–476 BCE) and Warring States period (476–221 BCE) in pre-imperial China. China's initial encounter with modern Eurocentric international law was widely known to be a bitter experience because of the 'unequal treaties' imposed by invading foreign powers during the 'century of humiliation' (1839–1949), leading to the almost perpetual belief in the People's Republic of China (PRC or China) that the function of international law is mainly to legitimize oppression of the 'Non-West' by Western powers.[13]

[13] Wang Jiangyu, '1. History & Theoretical Approaches, China' in Seokwoo Lee (ed), *Encyclopedia of Public International Law in Asia Online* <https://referenceworks.brillonline.com/browse/encyclopedia-of-public-international-law-in-asia-online> accessed 30 July 2023; Dong Wang, *China's Unequal Treaties: Narrating National History* (Lexington Books 2008); Henry Wheaton and Coleman Phillipson, *Wheaton's Elements of International Law* (5th edn, Baker, Voorhis 1916).

When, as recorded in history, international law was first introduced into China in the late nineteenth century by Western missionaries, WAP Martin translated Henry Wheaton's *Elements of International Law*. The Chinese version was officially published by the Tsungli Yamen in 1864.[14] Interestingly, in the same year, China invoked international law for the first time in its diplomacy when Prussia arrested three Danish vessels in Bohai. China lodged a protest that Bohai was China's 'internal sea' and the Prussian act was a violation of international law. As a result, Prussia released the Danish vessels.

After the founding of the PRC in 1949, there were further developments of China's practice in international law. During the 1950s–60s, China generally followed the former Soviet Union and viewed international law in a bifocal approach—that is, socialist international law and bourgeois international law. However, at a later time, particularly after the carrying out of the economic reform and open-door policy in 1978, China viewed international law in a more pragmatic approach without much ideological colour. Despite the many signs indicating this belief in the Chinese government and society, China has a much more nuanced approach to international law in reality and prefers to be viewed by other countries as a law-abiding citizen in the international society.[15]

China's status as the de facto second-largest global power prompts enquiry into its fulfilment of this role. How, and based on what standards and directions, does China interpret and apply international law in forming the norms required by its domestic legal system and foreign relations, or by the times? Have there been proper proposals for policy alternatives, based on those standards and directions? And, can China play a leading role in the formation of international norms?

China's dynamic engagement with international law reveals a strategic balancing act between adherence to established legal norms and a preference for bilateral negotiations driven by notions of sovereignty and non-interference. While its growing global status and involvement in international organizations reflect increased influence, tensions arise from assertive territorial claims, particularly in the South China Sea, raising questions about China's compliance with international norms. As China continues to shape the international legal order, the balance between pursuing national interests and upholding

[14] Maria Adele Carrai, 'The Politics of History in the Late Qing Era: William A. P. Martin and a History of International Law for China' in Raphael Schafer and Anne Peters (eds), *Politics and the Histories of International Law: The Quest for Knowledge and Justice* (Brill Nijhoff 2020).

[15] Xue Hanqin, 'Chinese Contemporary Perspectives on International Law: History, Culture and International Law' (1990) 221 Recueil des cours de l'académie de droit international de La Haye 41.

established principles remains a key challenge in its evolving role on the global stage.[16]

5.2.2 Japan

The use of international law in Japan after the Meiji era can be characterized by Japanese-style positivism and the distinction between Europe/America and Asia. These attributes align with Japan's imperialistic expansion and have emerged and flourished within the context of the nation's interactions with the West. Moreover, Japan's evolution as a modern state coincided temporally with the imperialist era. 'Being in Asia, having the character of Asia, but not Asian'—the so-called notion of 'de-Asianization'—has been predominant in modern Japan. Japan needed a methodological framework for establishing its relations with Europe and America in the process of accepting the space of Asia as something given. 'Civilization and Race' confirmed the integration of Asia caused by its differences with Europe and America. 'Culture and Nation' led to the hierarchization within Asia and the reshaping of the regional order based on the hierarchy, which took place under the influence of Japanese imperialism. These various discourses can be understood as aspects of the distinct characteristics of colonization by Japanese imperialism, which made use of international law and treaties.[17]

Japan's application of international law closely mirrors that of Western imperialist countries in terms of procedures, methods, and objectives. Regarding the changing perception of Japan as a latecomer among imperialist countries, the paradox of history mentioned by Okakura Kakuzō shortly after the Russo-Japanese War has meaningful implications: 'The average Westerner . . . was wont to regard Japan as barbarous while she indulged in the gentle arts of peace: he calls her civilised since she began to commit wholesale slaughter on Manchurian battlefields.'[18]

It is not easy to condemn Japan's state practice of evading its responsibility under international law through adherence to the minimum standards of legality in the interpretation and operation of international law, which has been the foundation for the relations between sovereign states since the end of the Second World War. Japan's operation of international law, which does

[16] Li (James Li) Zhaojie, 'The Impact of International Law on the Transformation of China's Perception of the World: A Lesson from History' (2012) 27 Maryland Journal of International Law 128.

[17] Anand, *Studies* (n 1) 38–51.

[18] Okakura Kakuzō, *The Book of Tea* (GP Putnam's Sons 1906) 7.

not reflect morality and the zeitgeist of the times, is attributable to the historical context of the building and collapse of empires based on military expansionism. It requires a thorough and careful preparation for the application of international law against Japan, which views international law from the perspective of 'legal injustice', meaning that something may be morally wrong without being legally problematic.

Japan is the de facto number two after the United States among so-called liberal democracies, but is Japan playing its role as number two? How does Japan interpret and apply international law in forming norms required by its domestic legal system and foreign relations, or by the times, and based on what standards and directions? Have there been proper proposals for policy alternatives based on those standards and directions? And, can Japan play a leading role in the formation of international norms?

Japan's engagement with international law is characterized by a delicate balance between upholding established norms and pursuing bilateral negotiations for safeguarding national interests. Active participation in international organizations and treaties showcases its commitment to the rule of law and multilateral cooperation. However, historical sensitivities and territorial disputes have at times strained Japan's relations with neighbouring countries, sparking scrutiny over its adherence to international norms. The Fukushima contaminated water discharge and law of the sea disputes underscore the challenges Japan faces in harmonizing international obligations with domestic concerns. Navigating this delicate interplay is vital for Japan's aspirations of responsible global leadership and for shaping its influence on the international stage.

5.2.3 Korea

After 676 CE, Korea was politically unified under Silla, but the dominant cultural influence remained Chinese. In its efforts to court China's favour, Silla had become increasingly sympathetic to the Chinese worldview. Although military and political differences forced the two apart, the cultural influence remained. Over the following centuries, Korea increased its cultural connection to China, a connection that culminated in Korea's formal inclusion in China's tributary system. The depth of the relationship allowed Korea to participate in the richness of Chinese culture and to take a privileged position under China's protective umbrella. Confucianism and the Confucian understanding of authority lay at the heart of China's tributary system. For Confucius, political stability was grounded on a strong and morally upright centre that provided a point of orientation for those in its political orbit.

The tributary system, which proved advantageous for Korea throughout much of its history, enabled the small kingdom to maintain relative peace and independence, shielded from undue interference by its larger neighbours. While Korea paid tribute to China, it retained full autonomy in managing internal and external affairs, preserving its sovereignty and trade practices. However, the onset of Western powers eroded China's influence over the region, leading to a shift from practical autonomy to nominal 'sovereignty'. As a consequence, Korea's once secure and self-determining position began to crumble, ushering in a new era of geopolitical complexities and challenges. The transformation of the tributary system's dynamics warrants closer analysis, shedding light on Korea's historical experiences with external powers and the evolution of its autonomy over time.

Korea is inherently constrained to rely on the interpretation and application of international law both historically and geopolitically. Korea–Japan relations, which stem from Japan's colonization of the Korean Peninsula, inter-Korean and South Korea–US relations, which became permanent around the time of the Korean War and the division of the Korean Peninsula, and Korea–China relations, which are becoming increasingly important due to their economic interdependence and the security situation in East Asia, are all involved in a complicated way. The stable management of highly volatile bilateral relations is a matter of state survival. Furthermore, as Korea is a member of the international community led by the United Nations, the clear interpretation and application of international law in multilateral relations is a matter of great importance. The recent trilateral security cooperation between South Korea, the United States, and Japan in response to North Korea's nuclear threat and their engagement in the global supply chain to counter China and Russia have also become important variables.

How then does South Korea interpret and apply international law in dealing with these complicated national issues, and based on what standards and directions? Have there been proper proposals of policy alternatives based on those standards and directions? And, can South Korea play a leading role in the formation of international norms?

Korea's engagement with international law is strategically pragmatic, blending established norms with bilateral negotiations to protect national interests. Active participation in international organizations demonstrates commitment to the rule of law and multilateral cooperation. However, historical tensions and territorial disputes have strained regional relationships, raising questions about adherence to international norms. Balancing obligations with domestic concerns, particularly evident in the Dokdo/Takeshima issue and disputes with Japan, presents complex challenges. Successfully navigating this interplay is vital for Korea's pursuit of responsible global leadership and shaping its international influence.

5.3 East Asia's perspectives and the law of the sea

The common narrative of contemporary East Asia is often described in the context of the political economy of rapid industrialization or from the point of view of international relations in light of the global balance of power and Cold War fault lines between the primary actors in the region. The dramatic economic growth of East Asia—in particular, Japan and Korea—during the latter half of the twentieth century and the meteoric rise of the Chinese economy in the twenty-first century have been well documented and researched. East Asia has also been the focus of much study in relation to the geopolitical climate of the Cold War. While economists and political scientists have made great contributions to the study of the region and its modern history, a frequently overlooked area of study is the function and impact of international law on the relations of the countries in the region. Indeed, the argument that is being made is that international law has had an important, if somewhat muted, role since it was introduced to the region by the West in the nineteenth century and continuing through the period of the Cold War. It has taken on an even more significant role in the post–Cold War era, reflecting the dynamism of the region and the prospects for establishing an order based upon international legal principles.

The growing importance of international law in East Asia can be attributed in large part to the forces of globalization that have animated the region in the economic, political, and cultural realms. It was not until the end of the Cold War and the flourishing of globalization that the countries in the region engaged each other on common issues of interest, but they also interacted with each other on the basis of modern principles of international law. Consequently, regional challenges that lay dormant during the Cold War, such as maritime delimitation and access to ocean resources, including fisheries and other non-security matters, have gained prominence due to the increasing influence of international law. While geopolitical factors continue to be relevant in understanding interstate relations in the region, international law and its attendant principles have become the basis through which East Asian states engage each other. The increasingly important role of international law in East Asia cannot be ignored in attempting to paint a complete picture of the international relations of the region.

Though there is general acknowledgement of the great variety of cultures among East Asian countries and the different interests existing between them, a strong, albeit rather undefined, feeling of familiarity, mutual understanding, and even coherence and solidarity persist among them as a result of the numerous mutual cultural and religious contacts and interconnections that have emerged and developed in the course of centuries. In the present day, this commonality emanates from a collective history of domination and dominance from without and within, in the form of both downright colonization and semi-colonization, as well as otherwise. This latter experience is, or at least is perceived to be, still relevant today because of its contribution to the presently prevalent conditions in the region. Although this historical experience is also shared by other regions, such as Africa, its manifestations and consequences in East Asia have diverged significantly due to the region's unique cultural foundations. As a result, a distinct approach is warranted to address the specific context of East Asia.

Consequently, there have been calls for examining and assessing international legal principles and their development from an East Asian perspective. In some fields of international law, such as human rights, an East Asian approach was seen to be necessary, given that international human rights law, as a product of Western philosophy, has gone too far in calling for the 'summary implementation of abstract concepts without regard for a country's unique cultural, social, economic, and political circumstances'.[19] In particular, the focus on whether East Asian cultural values are inconsistent with Western ones received quite a bit of attention in the debate over human rights in East Asia and has been framed in the context of cultural relativism versus universalism. Whether such a perspective can or should be applied to other areas of international law, in particular the law of the sea, is in part a subject of this chapter.

The states of East Asia have had considerable influence in the development of the law of the sea. East Asia was the location of critical maritime incidences that sparked the articulation of the competing enduring concepts of freedom of the seas and closed seas. East Asian states were instrumental in successfully advocating for a number of concepts that were to be entrenched in the modern

[19] Bilahari Kausikan, 'Asia's Different Standard' (1993) 92 Foreign Policy 24, 33.

law of the sea, most notably during the nine-year-long drafting process for UNCLOS at the Third UN Conference on the Law of the Sea (UNCLOS III).

Given the importance of the law of the sea in East Asia and its development, can a particular East Asian perspective be discerned? And, in particular, as it applies to East Asia, can it be said that there is a specific East Asian understanding and implementation of the law of the sea? If such a unique East Asian perspective exists, does East Asian culture have any impact on how the law of the sea is internalized into each of the East Asian states and how it is projected in each state's international relations? The argument presented here is that the national interest and political constraints that East Asia faces have determined the East Asian approach to the law of the sea, together with the influence of culture.

The central contention put forth here is that the East Asian approach to the law of the sea is the outcome of a multifaceted interplay between national interests, political constraints, and cultural influences. The unique confluence of these factors in the region has led to distinct patterns and practices in dealing with maritime matters. National interests, stemming from economic, security, and territorial considerations, have played a pivotal role in shaping the maritime policies of East Asian countries. Additionally, political constraints, both domestically and internationally, have exerted considerable influence on how states in the region navigate issues related to the law of the sea. Moreover, the cultural backdrop, characterized by a history of mutual interactions and shared practices, has further contributed to shaping East Asia's approach to the legal aspects of maritime affairs. As a result, a comprehensive understanding of the East Asian perspective on the law of the sea necessitates an appreciation of these multifaceted dynamics that underpin the region's maritime practices.

The law of the sea plays a significant role in East Asia, with important implications for the economy and for security. Of particular economic concern are issues such as piracy, armed robbery against ships, and the depletion of fish stocks. East Asian states have joined various bilateral, regional, and international cooperation agreements to address these issues. Moreover, East Asian states have been involved in disputes concerning territory, maritime delimitation, and fisheries resources, which has so far led to little progress in maritime boundary delimitation negotiations between each of the pertinent states.

For example, China and Korea have recently been in a standoff with Japan over the Japanese government's plan to release contaminated wastewater from the wrecked Fukushima Daiichi Nuclear Power Plant, and Korea has engaged with Japan regarding joint development of the continental shelf. Korea and

Japan have also found themselves embroiled in the confrontation between the United States and China over the Taiwan Strait. What can be deduced from these matters is that the policy approaches adopted by each state government are driven by considerations of national interest and by political considerations at home and abroad. These recent incidents highlight the centrality of national interest and domestic and international political considerations in shaping maritime and law-of-the-sea matters in the region.

5.4 East Asia and UNCLOS

5.4.1 China

China signed UNCLOS in December 1982 and ratified it in June 1996. UNCLOS III (1973–1982) was the first grand diplomatic conference to which the Chinese government sent a delegation after the PRC replaced the Republic of China (Taiwan) in 1971 for the seat of China in the United Nations. As a newcomer on the international stage, it was to be expected that China might not have been well prepared for such a conference. During this period, China was highly influenced ideologically under Chairman Mao Zedong. The first five years of UNCLOS III coincided with the Cultural Revolution (1966–76), a catastrophic era in Chinese history. During UNCLOS III, China seized the opportunity to criticize perceived superpowers—the former Soviet Union and the United States—accusing them of hegemonism in the global ocean order, rather than focusing on constructive deliberations for its national interests in the detailed provisions of the convention.

During the entire lengthy negotiating period, China submitted to the Conference only three short working papers.[20] As a prominent scholar observed, China had little involvement, and no expertise, in matters involving the law of the sea: 'The Chinese delegation sought instead to embarrass the Soviet Union wherever possible and to maintain the ideological and political integrity of the G77 coalition.'[21] Nevertheless, the negative impact from domestic

[20] The papers concerned sea areas within national jurisdiction, marine scientific research, and international sea areas. They are reprinted in Division of International Law of the Department of Law, Peking University (ed), *Collected Materials on the Law of the Sea* (1974) 73–76, 78–79, 81–82 (in Chinese).

[21] See Statement by Mr Han Xu, Third UN Conference on the Law of the Sea, 191st plen mtg, 9 December 1982, *Official Records*, vol 17 (1984) 102 (in English), reprinted in *Yearbook of International Situation* (1983) 391 (in Chinese).

politics gradually disappeared after 1978, when China began to implement economic reform and the 'open-door' policy. With diplomatic pragmatism under the leadership of Chairman Deng Xiaoping, China paid attention to provisions in the draft UNCLOS that might not be favourable to China, such as the definition of the continental shelf. Yet it was difficult for China to revise these provisions during the final stages of UNCLOS III. Thus, on the occasion of signing UNCLOS, the head of the Chinese delegation made a statement expressing disappointment with provisions concerning the continental shelf and innocent passage.[22]

China maintains an ambivalent stance towards UNCLOS, acknowledging its imperfections while adhering to the underlying principles and norms, as well as the majority of its provisions. In China's perception, UNCLOS embodies the 'new' law of the sea, distinct from the 'old' law represented by the four 1958 Geneva Conventions, during which China remained outside the UN system and unable to participate in the relevant international deliberations that resulted in the conventions.

5.4.2 Japan

One of the most significant claims made by Japan during the UNCLOS negotiations was the maintenance of the 3-nautical-mile territorial sea. This claim was based on Japan's interests in securing the freedom of fishing. Japan's 3-nautical-mile territorial sea was established when Japan opened its ports to Western powers in the nineteenth century.[23] The claim to retain a narrow territorial sea and broad high seas was based on the long history of fishing by Japanese fishermen within 200 nautical miles from the coasts of other states. Therefore, during the first (1958) and second (1960) UN Conferences on the Law of the Sea, Japan insisted that the areas beyond the 3-nautical-mile territorial sea should be the high seas, which belong to all human beings and where all states enjoy freedom of fishing. In the 1960s, while the international community increasingly expanded the territorial sea limit to 12 nautical miles, Japan still maintained a 3-nautical-mile territorial sea and objected to the establishment of 12-nautical-mile territorial seas by other states. In the early 1970s, Japan appeared isolated from the rest of the world on this issue.

[22] See Edward L Miles, *Global Ocean Politics: The Decision Process at the Third United Nations Conference on the Law of the Sea, 1973–1982* (Nijhoff 1998) 24–25.

[23] Shunji Yanai and Kuniaki Asomura, 'Japan and the Emerging Order of the Sea: Two Maritime Laws of Japan' (1977) 21 Japanese Annual of International Law 48.

Japan proposed an alternative approach at the 1971 Colombo meeting of the Asian–African Legal Consultative Organization. The proposal suggested that, beyond the 12-nautical-mile territorial sea, coastal states that are developing countries could have priority access to fishing. At the Lagos meeting in 1972, Japan submitted a proposal on the fishing regime on the high seas, which emphasized the priority of the coastal state's fishing rights and the importance of conservation of the marine living resources on the high seas. However, this proposal did not gain support from Asian and African states because they prioritized exclusive fishing rights within their own waters over priority access to fishing on the high seas with conservation obligations.

During UNCLOS III, the establishment of 200-nautical-mile economic or fishery zones by a number of states excluded Japanese fishermen from fishing within 200 nautical miles from the coasts of those states and resulted in increased fishing by nationals of other distant sea fishing nations, such as the then Soviet Union and the Republic of Korea, outside the 3-nautical-mile territorial sea of Japan. The Japanese fishing industry faced difficulties because its distant sea fishing in the 200-nautical-mile zones of foreign countries amounted to more than one-third of its total catch. The Japanese coastal fishing industry also demanded that the government extend the territorial sea to 12 nautical miles for protection against the large-scale operations by foreign fishing vessels in waters off the coast of Japan.

The Japanese delegation finally expressed its acceptance of the concept of the 12-nautical-mile territorial sea in the Caracas Session in 1974 and that of the 200-nautical-mile economic zone in the Fourth Session in 1976 for the pragmatic reason of protecting its coastal fisheries. It was against this background that Japan promulgated new laws in 1977, introducing the 12-nautical-mile territorial sea and the 200-nautical-mile fishery zone. Japan signed UNCLOS in 1983 but ratified it only in 1996 when simultaneously revising the 1977 laws.

5.4.3 Korea

UNCLOS III was held amid rising tension between maritime powers, advocating the maintenance of traditional narrow territorial seas, and newly independent states in Asia and Africa, hoping for the reform of the international maritime regime in favour of wide high seas. During the Conference, South Korea generally agreed with other Asian and African states. In an era when the country was heavily dependent on the United States in politics, economics, and national security, this stance can be assessed as the Korean government's own initiative for the country's rights and interests in the sea. The Korean government's core concerns during UNCLOS III are discussed below.

Unlike the 1958 Geneva Conventions on the Law of the Sea, where it did not give a definite opinion as to the contention of the scope of the territorial sea (3 nautical miles, 6 nautical miles, or 12 nautical miles), the Korean government was in favour of 12 nautical miles during UNCLOS III. Although Korea did not agree with the United States back in 1958 as to the notion of limiting coastal states' jurisdictional capacity, the government viewed pushing for 12 nautical miles to be too progressive.

In light of the North–South military conflict and armistice, South Korea was in favour of prior notification of innocent passage of foreign warships and government ships operated for non-commercial purposes in the territorial sea. The Korean government's proposition for prior notification or prior approval, however, was rejected during the 1958 Geneva Conventions.

As regards the right of passage in international straits, the Korean government advocated for innocent passage of warships and government ships operated for non-commercial purposes, but rejected the right of passage through airspace and supported the reinforcement of the right of coastal states to regulate pollution. This was also in light of the passage issues occurring in the Korea Strait and Jeju Strait.

Regarding delimitation of the territorial sea, the Korean government was in favour of the median line. However, between the Korean and Chinese continental shelf and the exclusive economic zone (EEZ), a median line would benefit Korea because the nation had already designated joint developmental zones with Japan using the natural prolongation of the land territory, Korea was careful in making its position. Nevertheless, the Korean government agreed that a compulsory dispute resolution measure is necessary for the peaceful resolution of conflict arising out of determining the delimitation of the EEZ and continental shelf. With regard to marine scientific research, the interests of developed states were towards claiming freedom of research, while developing states sought prior consent of coastal states. Korea took the side of the latter.

5.5 The recent trend of the attitude of Asian states towards third-party adjudication

In the realm of international law, the attitude of East Asian states towards submitting their disputes to international adjudication or litigation has been a subject of considerable scholarly interest.[24] East Asian countries have not frequently utilized the formal mechanisms of international dispute resolution, despite the potential they hold within the international legal process. They have demonstrated a varied approach towards engaging in formal international dispute settlement mechanisms. While some states within the region have actively embraced international adjudication and are willing to resort to international courts or tribunals to resolve disputes, others have exhibited a more cautious stance, preferring bilateral negotiations or non-binding alternative dispute resolution methods. Factors such as historical context, geopolitical considerations, national interests, and the perception of the efficacy and fairness of international adjudication play pivotal roles in shaping the divergent attitudes of East Asian states towards the submission of their disputes to international forums. Understanding the dynamics of East Asian states' attitudes towards international dispute settlement can shed light on the evolving landscape of international law and can contribute to the further development of effective mechanisms for resolving interstate conflicts in the region.

Despite the potentiality of the international legal process, countries in East Asia have not regularly employed the formal mechanisms of international dispute resolution. Several cases from ITLOS—including the *Southern Bluefin Tuna Cases (New Zealand v Japan; Australia v Japan)*;[25] *Land Reclamation (Malaysia v Singapore)*;[26] two cases related to prompt release, *The 'Tomimaru' Case (Japan v Russian Federation)*[27] and *The 'Hoshinmaru' Case (Japan v Russian Federation)*;[28] and *Delimitation of the Maritime Boundary Between Bangladesh and Myanmar in the Bay of Bengal (Bangladesh/Myanmar)*[29]—show some changes in terms of the attitude of Asian states, which has become more positive in recent years. Some commentators view this as a trend towards third-party adjudication. Although this question was not directly related to East Asia's cultural influence on the law of the sea, it can be considered that different ways of domestic interpretation and application of international law in different states would give rise to international disputes.

[24] Hisashi Owada, 'The Experience of Asia with International Adjudication' in Zou Keyuan and Jianfu Chen (eds), *International Law in East Asia* (Routledge 2017) 367–76.

[25] *Southern Bluefin Tuna Cases (New Zealand v Japan; Australia v Japan) (Provisional Measures)*, ITLOS Case Nos 3 and 4, 27 August 1999.

[26] *Land Reclamation by Singapore in and Around the Straits of Johor (Malaysia v Singapore) (Provisional Measures)*, ITLOS Case No 12, 8 October 2003.

[27] *The 'Tomimaru' Case (Japan v Russian Federation) (Judgment)*, ITLOS Case No 15, 6 August 2007.

[28] *The 'Hoshinmaru' Case (Japan v Russian Federation) (Judgment)*, ITLOS Case No 14, 6 August 2007.

[29] *Delimitation of the Maritime Boundary Between Bangladesh and Myanmar in the Bay of Bengal (Bangladesh/Myanmar) (Judgment)*, ITLOS Case No 16, 14 March 2012.

While Japan may have more experience in referring cases to international courts and tribunals, Korea and China are less active in this sense. For instance, the *South China Sea Arbitration*[30] clearly showed China's attitude. According to Bee Chen Goh, Western culture encourages litigation as the primary method because justice is the goal not to be compromised, while the Chinese consider mediation as the main method of dispute resolution because restoring group harmony is the main focus. She argues that law does play '*a* role, rather than *the* role'. The role of the mediator in the West and in China is different as well: Western mediators are third parties not related to the case, while the Chinese look for mediators related to the society wherein the need to mediate arises.[31] It is understood, however, that if the case is convincing, any state would not hesitate to refer the matter to third-party adjudication. It depends on the government's decision whether the dispute shall be referred to third-party adjudication or settled bilaterally. In the area of ocean and territory, many discussions about territorial disputes in Asia have noted that territorial disputes and claims in Asia had been subject to third-party adjudication. The questions require further investigation of whether this trend is a distinct feature of Asian states compared to other parts of the world.

In other words, Asian states have been more active in dispute resolution but, in terms of territorial sovereignty and maritime jurisdictional disputes, until a decade ago it was said that Asian states would only consider binding dispute resolution with respect to certain deadlocked disputes. In this regard, three cases have involved territorial sovereignty issues in Asia: *Temple of Preah Vihear (Cambodia v Thailand)*,[32] *Sovereignty Over Pulau Ligitan and Pulau Sipadan (Indonesia v Malaysia)*,[33] and *Sovereignty Over Pedra Branca/Pulau Batu Puteh, Middle Rocks and South Ledge (Malaysia/Singapore)*.[34] More recently, two cases arose related to the Bay of Bengal on maritime boundary delimitation, but these are not East Asian from the viewpoint of strict geographical location.[35]

[30] *South China Sea Arbitration (Philippines v China) (Award)*, Permanent Court of Arbitration Case No 2013-19, 12 July 2016.

[31] Bee Chen Goh, *Law Without Lawyers, Justice Without Courts: On Traditional Chinese Mediation* (Routledge 2016) ch 1.

[32] *Temple of Preah Vihear (Cambodia v Thailand) (Merits)* [1962] ICJ Rep 6.

[33] *Sovereignty Over Pulau Ligitan and Pulau Sipadan (Indonesia v Malaysia)* [2002] ICJ Rep 625.

[34] *Sovereignty Over Pedra Branca/Pulau Batu Puteh, Middle Rocks and South Ledge (Malaysia/Singapore) (Judgment)* [2008] ICJ Rep 12.

[35] *Delimitation of the Maritime Boundary* (n 29); *Bay of Bengal Maritime Boundary Arbitration (Bangladesh v India) (Award)*, Permanent Court of Arbitration Case No 2010-16, 7 July 2014.

The attitudes of Asian states towards international dispute settlement constitute a crucial aspect of their approach to international law and the law of the sea, reflecting their practice in foreign relations. Notably, some Asian states, including China and Korea, display reluctance to accept the compulsory jurisdiction of international courts or tribunals such as the ICJ and ITLOS. In contrast, they may demonstrate acceptance of the dispute settlement system within the World Trade Organization, including the compulsory jurisdiction of Panels and the Appellate Body. If, indeed, a distinctly Asian approach exists, it appears to be multifaceted rather than unified in nature.

5.6 The influence of East Asian culture on the law of the sea: case studies

5.6.1 China: the South China Sea Arbitration

On 12 July 2016, the arbitral tribunal constituted under Annex VII of UNCLOS issued its final award in the dispute between the Philippines and China over maritime claims in the South China Sea. The tribunal, in a 500-page final award, unanimously decided in favour of the Philippines and applied the rules of international law principally via UNCLOS, universally regarded as the constitution of the oceans, and other rules of international law that are not incompatible with the Convention.[36]

There is an extensive body of scholarly work that explores various facets of the arbitral award, especially commentaries that focus on its legal aspects. The arbitral tribunal categorically declared that China's 'nine-dash-line' claim and its historic rights over living and non-living resources in the South China Sea are incompatible with UNCLOS. The tribunal clarified that China does not possess historic rights over the resources within the nine-dash-line areas within the Philippines EEZ or continental shelf, and that any historic rights that China may have over these resources are incompatible with UNCLOS and have been extinguished by China's accession to UNCLOS and the Convention's entry into force. The tribunal further clarified that any claim by China to historic rights to the living and non-living resources within the nine-dash line beyond the limits of China's maritime zones, as provided for under UNCLOS, has been superseded by the entry into force of the Convention. In the tribunal's view, China's ratification of UNCLOS did not extinguish its historic rights in

[36] *South China Sea Arbitration* (n 30).

the waters of the South China Sea but rather constituted a relinquishment of the high seas freedoms it previously utilized that have been subsumed under the regime of the EEZ as defined by the Convention, for which it gained a greater degree of control.

The adoption of UNCLOS in 1982 has led to a period of relative stability in global ocean affairs by providing a legal framework for the sustainable development of the oceans and their natural resources. However, recent discussions highlight calls for amending the Convention due to its perceived shortcomings. Amid this backdrop, questions arise concerning the efficacy of UNCLOS in preventing and managing conflicts related to marine resources. Particularly relevant is its role in addressing the South China Sea dispute. Is UNCLOS playing a positive role in addressing the dispute? To what extent do the states involved in the South China Sea recognize the connection and relevance of UNCLOS and the settlement of disputes in this region?

Many South China Sea scholars, particularly those who are Chinese, exhibit scepticism concerning the role and efficacy of UNCLOS. Their arguments revolve around UNCLOS provisions exacerbating the complexity of the South China Sea dispute, such as the contention between the historic title concept and the EEZ regime, as well as the fierce competition for territorial claims in the region. UNCLOS may be perceived to have certain shortcomings, such as lacking a definition of the 'historic water' regime, the vague provision on the status of an 'island' and a 'rock', a lack of clear provisions on the legitimacy of military activities in a foreign country's EEZ, and the limitation and exclusion of third-party compulsory dispute settlements hindering the timely resolution of many disputes. Notwithstanding the challenges, the prospect of a third-party forum assuming a constructive role in resolving these issues endures.

First, Article 121(3) of UNCLOS does give the court or tribunal a role to play in this picture. Neither Article 297 nor Article 298 excludes disputes related to the definition and determination of a feature to be an island or a rock from the compulsory dispute settlement mechanism. The Philippines, in its Notification and Statement, has rightly pointed to this. Second, by closely reading the provisions of UNCLOS, it is fair to claim that the court or tribunal has a role to play in many issues, such as 'prompt release' and environmental protection. Third, a third-party forum, upon request, can determine the nature of specific military activities and thereby provide guidance on whether these activities are legitimate in a foreign country's EEZ, which will, to a large extent, reduce the potential military conflict in this regard.

All the states involved in the South China Sea dispute have developed a comparatively comprehensive marine legal system under the framework of

UNCLOS. These legislations provide a legal framework to deal with many maritime issues in a domestic context. Nevertheless, in a situation where multiple issues, such as the South China Sea, interrelate with each other, a theoretically robust legal system may not consistently yield favourable outcomes in crucial areas, such as maritime delimitation, overlapping maritime jurisdictional claims, fishing disputes, and transboundary marine environmental pollution. Consequently, a third-party compulsory dispute settlement regime is imperative in resolving these intricate matters effectively.

China consistently opposes international litigation, favouring negotiation as the preferred approach in all instances, whereas the Philippines is more inclined to involve third-party intervention. Nevertheless, in recent times, compelling arguments have emerged advocating for China to embrace the third-party dispute settlement mechanism more readily. This shift is encouraged due to China's expressed aspiration to assume greater responsibilities in addressing contemporary global challenges and its active role within international organizations.

5.6.2 Japan: Fukushima Daiichi Nuclear Power Plant contaminated water discharge

On 11 March 2011, an earthquake occurring in the seabed near the northeastern region of Japan damaged the internal facilities of the Fukushima Daiichi Nuclear Power Plant, causing the release of a significant amount of radioactive material. In March 2013, the Japanese government installed the Advanced Liquid Processing System (ALPS) and stored the radioactive wastewater in tanks near the nuclear power plant. Subsequently, on 13 April 2021, during a meeting of ministers, the Japanese government officially announced the confirmation of its plans to release the radioactive wastewater stored at the Fukushima plant's accident site into the Pacific Ocean over a period of 30 years. On 22 July 2022, the Japanese Nuclear Regulation Authority approved Tokyo Electric Power Company's plan to release the Fukushima nuclear wastewater into the ocean. Consequently, the formal release of the nuclear wastewater into the ocean commenced in August 2023, following the completion of discharge facilities including the undersea tunnel.

Japan's position can be summarized in three key assertions. First, Japan did not violate UNCLOS. Although the Convention imposes general obligations on contracting parties to protect and preserve the marine environment and mandates legislative action to prevent, reduce, and control pollution of the marine environment from land-based sources, it also recognizes the broad discretion of contracting states in such matters. Second, Japan asserts that it did not violate the London Protocol on the prevention of marine pollution, which prohibits the dumping of waste and other matter.[37] According to the Protocol, dumping means any deliberate disposal of waste or other matter into the sea from vessels, aircraft, platforms, or other human-made structures at sea. As such, the discharge of contaminated water from land-based nuclear power plants falls outside the scope of 'dumping'. Third, the contaminated water Japan wants to dispose of poses no harm to the marine environment or to human health, and is comparable to the emission practices of neighbouring countries such as Korea. As a result, Japan maintains that none of its discharge plans are in violation of international law.

Scientific and objective verification of the discharge of contaminated water is essential. While Japan emphasizes that most radioactive substances can be removed from the water through ALPS, it acknowledges that tritium would not be filtered. The scientific community has remained divided on the potential hazards and harmful effects of the accumulation of tritium on the marine ecosystem and on human health. After five separate on-site investigations in Japan, the International Atomic Energy Agency (IAEA) reported that it affirmed the independent role and function of the Japanese Nuclear Regulation Authority and stated that it would continue monitoring Japan's compliance with international standards. However, adherence to international standards alone is not evidence of conclusive scientific justification. If there are inherent risks associated with the release of the contaminated water, sufficient scientific evidence cannot be deemed to be present. For example, the IAEA highlighted the need for Japan to provide supplementary explanations regarding its radiological environmental impact assessments and the potential consequences of wastewater discharge. The issue of discharging contaminated water must be considered an international issue, since the discharged wastewater will circulate through ocean currents and to neighbouring countries such as Korea and the Pacific coastal states, which are likely to be exposed to residual radioactive materials.

In light of the lack of clear scientific evidence regarding the safety of treated contaminated water, concerns have arisen among neighbouring countries regarding the potential risks posed by the discharged wastewater. In response to Japan's unilateral decision to proceed with the discharge without prior consultation with adjacent countries, various measures are being discussed in terms of

[37] Protocol to the Convention on the Prevention of Marine Pollution by Dumping of Wastes and Other Matter, 1972, 36 ILM 1, 7 November 1996 (London Protocol).

international litigation. Such measures include interim measures and substantive proceedings before ITLOS initiated by sovereign states, as well as advisory opinions from the ICJ or ITLOS. For ITLOS to decide upon the appropriate interim measures, urgent risk and serious harm to the rights of the parties concerned need to be demonstrated.

Similarly, in the substantive proceedings, Japan's violation of international law regarding the discharge of radioactive contaminated water from Fukushima must be addressed. The plaintiff state must proceed with legal procedures premised on Japan's breach of international legal responsibility. In order to establish state responsibility, two essential elements must be satisfied: first, the problematic act must be attributable to the state under international law; and, second, the act must constitute a breach of the state's international obligations at that time. Intent or negligence is not included as an element required to establish state responsibility. Regarding the breach of international obligations, such obligations are set forth in treaties, customary international law, general principles of law recognized within the international legal order, and unilateral acts of states. It is imperative to emphasize that the establishment of state responsibility is dictated by international law, and any contention by a state that its actions were lawful under domestic law does not absolve it from responsibility for an internationally wrongful act. The issue of whether Japan has violated international law regarding the discharge of radioactive contaminated water arises from Japan's failure to fulfil procedural obligations regarding international cooperation, such as prior notification or provision of information, and conservation of the marine environment, including the execution of an environmental impact assessment. This issue is also closely related to the ongoing lack of communication among the parties involved. Ultimately, from an international legal perspective, the litigation is highly likely to focus primarily on the procedural aspect of Japan's alleged breach of international obligations rather than on the aftermath of the contaminated water.

In cases requiring scientific evidence, it is imperative to acknowledge the likelihood of protracted litigation potentially failing to prevent the discharge of contaminated water—and, even if successful, its efficacy in sanctioning Japan's actions may remain uncertain. Moreover, the ambiguity surrounding which sovereign state would initiate legal proceedings within the context of international dispute resolution adds complexity to the matter. Recent developments in climate change issues have seen the ICJ and ITLOS play significant roles in providing advisory opinions, drawing attention to the stance of Pacific Island nations that were formerly nuclear testing sites. Despite the legal significance of advisory opinions from international judicial bodies, it is difficult to consider such methods as effective means to prevent Japan's discharge of contaminated water.

Regarding the maritime areas beyond the national jurisdiction of individual states, the consistently evolving norms of the international marine environment have adopted a forward-looking stance. The argument that the discharge of radioactive contaminated water from a nuclear power plant is simply not a violation of international law and is comparable to the emission standards of neighbouring countries hinges on strategic and selective decisions made by the initiating state party during international litigation, which may be contingent on prevailing circumstances.

5.6.3 Korea: the US–China 'Taiwan Strait' confrontation and Korea

The enduring conflict between Russia and Ukraine has had extensive and profound global ramifications. China's forceful occupation of Taiwan, which was previously considered only hypothetical, is now being discussed from various perspectives.[38] The security situation on the Korean Peninsula has been rapidly evolving due to North Korea's recurring armed protests and provocations. After US House Speaker Nancy Pelosi visited Taiwan in early August 2022, despite China's threats of military retaliation over the visit, Chinese President Xi Jinping emphasized at the 20th National Congress on 16 October that he would not give up the use of force against Taiwan, causing further strain on US–China relations and pushing the Taiwan conflict to a climax.[39]

The enduring conflict between the United States and China concerning Taiwan holds significant implications for Korea, encompassing two primary aspects. First, it raises pertinent questions concerning the international legal status of the Taiwan Strait, situated between China and Taiwan. Second, it necessitates a careful examination of the roles that Korea and United States Forces Korea (USFK) may have to undertake if China resorts to force against Taiwan, a scenario that could likely prompt US intervention.

[38] Jude Blanchette and Gerard DiPippo, '"Reunification" With Taiwan Through Force Would Be a Pyrrhic Victory for China', *CSIS Briefs* (22 November 2022) <www.csis.org/analysis/reunification-taiwan-through-force-would-be-pyrrhic-victory-china> accessed 30 July 2023; Steve Tsang (ed), *If China Attacks Taiwan: Military Strategy, Politics and Economics* (Taylor & Francis 2010); Scott L Kastner, *War and Peace in the Taiwan Strait* (Columbia UP 2022).

[39] Jeremy Herb and Eric Cheung, 'US House Speaker Nancy Pelosi Lands in Taiwan Amid Threats of Chinese Retaliation' (CNN, 2 August 2022) <https://edition.cnn.com/2022/08/02/politics/nancy-pelosi-visit-taipei-taiwan-trip/index.html> accessed 30 July 2023.

The status of the Taiwan Strait within the framework of international law emerges as a key concern amid escalating tensions between China and Taiwan. The historical sensitivity and complexity surrounding Taiwan's sovereignty and territorial integrity demand thoughtful analysis of the legal principles governing territorial disputes and self-determination issues. The outcome of the international community's response to China's assertive actions towards Taiwan may set precedents and impact similar disputes elsewhere, entailing ramifications beyond the immediate region.

A strait, by definition, is a narrow natural waterway that serves as a conduit between two substantial bodies of water.[40] In this context, the Taiwan Strait assumes paramount significance as it facilitates maritime connections between the East and South China Sea, serving as a pivotal route to the Indian Ocean and the Atlantic Ocean not only for China and Taiwan but also for Korea and Japan. Spanning an average width of 180 kilometres, this crucial water passage accommodates a substantial daily traffic volume, with approximately 600 to 800 cargo ships and 900 to 1,200 aircraft traversing its expanse.

The strategic importance of the Taiwan Strait, akin to the Malacca Strait, warrants close scrutiny, given that any restrictions to maritime traffic routes along this vital passage could potentially imperil China's interests and have broader implications for the international community. Its location and significance are further accentuated by its function as a tactical military vantage point for China vis-à-vis the United States, thereby magnifying its geopolitical value manifold.

Considering these factors, the Taiwan Strait emerges as a geopolitical focal point, underpinning both economic and military interests for regional and global actors alike. Its significance as a critical maritime passageway underscores the necessity for a comprehensive understanding of the complex dynamics and implications that surround this crucial waterway.

The tension between the United States and China regarding the Taiwan Strait manifests prominently in their contrasting interpretations of the strait's legal status. This divergence of views highlights a fundamental conflict between the United States' advocacy for unhindered navigation through the strait, emphasizing the principle of free passage, and China's assertion of regulated transit passage rights, contending that coastal nations should have

[40] See, for example, Bing Bing Jia, *The Regime of Straits in International Law* (Clarendon Press 1998); Ana G López Martín, *International Straits: Concept, Classification and Rules of Passage* (Springer 2010); José Antonio de Yturriaga, *Straits Used for International Navigation: A Spanish Perspective* (Springer 1991); David D Caron and Nilufer Oral (eds), *Navigating Straits: Challenges for International Law* (Brill 2014).

control over navigation within the strait.[41] This divergence underscores the intricate and contentious dynamics surrounding the Taiwan Strait issue, with far-reaching implications for regional and international relations.[42]

In accordance with the US Navy's Commanding Guidelines on Naval Operational Law, the United States largely classifies the maritime zones into domestic (internal waters, the territorial sea, and archipelagic waters) and international (the contiguous zone, the EEZ, and the high seas) bodies of water.[43] Accordingly, the United States classifies the Taiwan Strait as international waters whereby high seas freedoms, including FON and overflight, are guaranteed to all states.[44] On the other hand, China maintains that the US position is intended to threaten China's sovereignty and assert control over Taiwan. Notably, on 13 June 2022, the Chinese Foreign Ministry spokesperson expressed China's opposition to the establishment by the United States of the Taiwan Strait as an international body of water. China claims that UNCLOS and relevant Chinese laws delineate the Taiwan Strait's waters as extending from both shores to the middle of the strait, with various zones such as the internal waters, territorial sea, contiguous zone, and EEZ. While China asserts its sovereignty and jurisdiction over the strait, it acknowledges respecting the lawful rights of other countries in relevant waters. This stance is seen as an effort to prevent US entry into the Taiwan Strait. In a similar vein, Taiwan aligns with the United States, maintaining that the Taiwan Strait is an international body of water, subject to international law beyond its territorial waters.

The US stance on high seas and international waters can be interpreted, in part, as a response to China's efforts to assert the Taiwan Strait as part of its internal waters. The United States perceives the conflicting status of the Taiwan Strait not merely as a disagreement in the interpretation and application of international law but as a deliberate endeavour by China to assert control over the strait. Conversely, China's position on the Taiwan Strait should be seen as a reaction to the US emphasis on FON. China's utilization of the classifications within UNCLOS governing various maritime areas appears aimed at securing control over the coastal states in the region. These opposing perspectives reveal a complex interplay of geopolitical interests and legal interpretations surrounding the Taiwan Strait issue.

[41] See UNCLOS, arts 25, 38, 87.

[42] Robert D Blackwill and Philip Zelikow, *The United States, China, and Taiwan: A Strategy to Prevent War* (Council on Foreign Relations 2021).

[43] US Navy, US Marine Corps, and US Coast Guard, *The Commander's Handbook on the Law of Naval Operations* (March 2022).

[44] ibid 2–8.

In the event of an armed conflict over Taiwan, adherence to international laws necessitates the preservation of the FON of third-party states, regardless of whether such conflict occurs during peacetime or wartime.[45] However, for straits that are composed solely of territorial waters, whether international laws grant coastal states the power to close the strait and prohibit third-party passage is up for debate. However, the question of whether coastal states possess the authority to close and deny passage through straits solely composed of territorial waters remains a subject of contention within the realm of international law. This matter holds significant implications for the Korean Strait, situated between Korea and Japan, which shares striking similarities with the Taiwan Strait as an international strait, allowing unrestricted navigation for foreign vessels.[46] Although the international legal status of the Taiwan Strait is an important issue, Korea must carefully consider when and whether it is necessary to actively criticize China's unilateral obstruction of navigation and to assert navigational freedom in the Taiwan Strait.

The security of the Korean Peninsula is intricately linked to the prospective roles that Korea and the USFK might undertake in the event of China resorting to force against Taiwan and subsequent US intervention. Despite the USFK's primary mandate of defending against North Korean threats, its strategic adaptability implies potential shifts in responsibilities contingent upon developments in Northeast Asia. Such adaptability could involve the deployment of the USFK beyond the Korean Peninsula should disputes arise in the region.

In May 2022, through a joint statement at the summit in Seoul, President Yoon and President Biden emphasized the importance of preserving peace and stability in the Taiwan Strait for the security and prosperity of the Indo-Pacific region. Later, the Republic of Korea–United States Security Council Meeting also included, for the first time, the issue of Taiwan in its joint statement.[47] Although the basic response to China's use of force against Taiwan has been established, neither the general nor the specific roles of Korea and the USFK in Korea have been reported.[48]

[45] Tran Đinh Hoanh, 'PacNet #33—China Cannot Hinder International Navigation Through Taiwan Strait' (Pacific Forum, 22 June 2022) <https://pacforum.org/publication/pacnet-33-china-cannot-hinder-international-navigation-through-taiwan-strait> accessed 30 July 2023.

[46] Chi Young Pak, *The Korean Straits* (Martinus Nijhoff, 1988).

[47] White House, 'United States-Republic of Korea Leaders' Joint Statement' (21 May 2022) <www.whitehouse.gov/briefing-room/statements-releases/2022/05/21/united-states-republic-of-korea-leaders-joint-statement/> accessed 30 July 2023.

[48] US Department of Defense, '54th Security Consultative Meeting Joint Communique' (3 November 2022) <www.defense.gov/News/Releases/Release/Article/3209105/54th-security-consultative-meeting-joint-communique/> accessed 30 July 2023.

In formulating the general and specific roles that Korea and the USFK are to assume, Korea must first establish its position on this matter. In this context, two key points warrant emphasis. First, a firm opposition exists to the USFK's participation in military actions alongside the US military in the Taiwan Strait in the event of conflict. Consequently, it becomes imperative to re-evaluate the South Korean military's plans concerning the USFK's strategic flexibility, in addition to devising response measures in anticipation of any potential USFK deployment to the Taiwan Strait. Second, the FON that some countries—including the United States, Australia, and the United Kingdom—are employing in the South China Sea is based on the countries' interpretation and application of the existing international ocean laws and do not necessarily reflect their military position. However, it is crucial to recognize that in times of emergency or armed conflict, the deployment of force renders the application of FON inapplicable, as it is inherently associated with peacetime operations. An awareness of these disparities in international legal perspectives becomes indispensable in navigating the complexities of this issue.

The US–China conflict over the international legal status of the Taiwan Strait stems from fundamentally opposing perspectives.[49] China prioritizes the rights of coastal nations and adherence to coastal laws, while the United States places paramount importance on upholding the principles of a free navigation system. As the legal framework governing navigation and international straits underpins the stability of maritime order, China's justification for denying the navigational rights of other countries in the Taiwan Strait remains dubious. China's endeavour to assert control over all activities in the strait, as part of its pursuit of Taiwan under the 'One China' policy, raises concerns. However, it may not be in Korea's best interest to proactively challenge the intentions behind China's actions at this stage. Caution and a thorough understanding of the complexities surrounding the Taiwan Strait issue are imperative in navigating the dynamics of this conflict.

Korea's approach to the USFK's strategic flexibility as a US ally should be decoupled from involvement in the Taiwan conflict. Upholding peace and security in the Taiwan Strait demands Korea's adherence to the fundamental One China policy, which holds pivotal significance for East Asia's security landscape and China's diplomatic ties with the global community. Given the delicate intricacies surrounding the Taiwan Strait, exercising diplomatic security,

[49] Stephen J Hartnett, *A World of Turmoil: The United States, China, and Taiwan in the Long Cold War* (Michigan State University Press 2021); Kerry Brown and Kalley Wu Tzu-hui, *The Trouble with Taiwan: History, the United States and a Rising China* (Zed Books 2019).

practising restraint, and adopting strategic ambiguity emerge as indispensable elements in preserving the existing status quo. By embracing such an approach, Korea can navigate the complexities of the Taiwan issue while contributing to regional stability and avoiding potential entanglements that may disrupt the fragile balance in the region.

5.7 Does 'Asian international law' exist? Or, no Asian approach to international law?

Does 'Asian international law' exist? If it does exist, how does it manifest itself? The scholarly enquiry into the existence and nature of Asian international law has yielded negative outcomes when analysed through the lens of domestic legislation processes and state practices. It is easy to point out and identify the essential issues of the international law practices of Asian states. While identifying crucial issues in the international law practices of Asian nations is straightforward, a comprehensive understanding demands the conceptualization, materialization, and practical application of these issues. Until concrete results emerge from this ongoing discourse, the true essence and implications of Asian international law, distinct from Eurocentric international law, will remain unanswered.

The question remains open as to whether a distinct Asian approach to international law truly exists. Alternatively, one could contend that there exists a nuanced and subtle concept of an Asian approach within the continent. The diversity of approaches in Asia makes it challenging to delineate a singular, definitive, and overarching Asian approach to international law.

The East Asian approach to the law of the sea is shaped by a combination of national interests, political constraints, and cultural influences. Economic, security, and territorial concerns drive national interests, while domestic and international political factors play a significant role. Additionally, the region's historical cultural interactions contribute to its distinct maritime practices. Understanding these multifaceted dynamics is crucial to grasping the East Asian perspective on the law of the sea.

The notion that Asia is predominantly a 'norm-taker', rather than a 'norm-maker', has been ingrained within the region's collective consciousness. This perspective is influenced by historical and geopolitical factors that have shaped Asia's interactions with the global order. While it is true that there exists a considerable number of international lawyers in Asia, their overall presence and impact on the international legal landscape are not as extensive as in other regions. Promoting closer cooperation among international lawyers in Asia is of paramount importance in challenging the prevailing perception of Asia as a mere norm-taker. By fostering collaboration and dialogue among legal experts in the region, a deeper understanding of the diverse legal traditions, perspectives, and contributions of Asian states can be cultivated. This collaborative effort can unveil the potential for Asia to emerge as a norm-maker rather than a passive recipient of established norms.

One avenue for achieving this objective is to encourage research and scholarly engagement that explore the unique legal viewpoints and approaches adopted by Asian states. By delving into the historical and cultural underpinnings of Asian legal systems, international lawyers can identify instances where Asia has played an active role in shaping global norms and legal principles. Moreover, multilateral forums and institutions in Asia offer opportune platforms for fostering cooperation among international lawyers. By facilitating exchanges of ideas and expertise, these forums can facilitate a re-evaluation of Asia's role in international law and enhance the region's collective voice in shaping the future of global legal norms.

Emphasizing Asia's potential as a norm-maker also underscores the significance of diversity in the international legal landscape. Recognizing and embracing the varied perspectives and experiences of Asian states can enrich the global discourse on legal matters and contribute to more inclusive and equitable legal frameworks. The promotion of closer cooperation among international lawyers in Asia is vital to challenge the perception of Asia as a norm-taker. By fostering collaboration, recognizing Asia's diverse legal traditions, and exploring the region's contributions to international law, a more accurate and comprehensive understanding of Asia's role as a potential norm-maker can emerge. This re-evaluation will not only enrich the global legal discourse but also empower Asian states to shape and influence actively the development of international legal norms.

5.8 Conclusion

The question of whether Asian international law exists or whether there is a distinct Asian approach to international law remains a subject of ongoing debate and exploration. The diverse cultures, histories, and geopolitical contexts within Asia have undoubtedly shaped the attitudes and practices of Asian states in the realm of international law. The dynamic and multifaceted nature of the Asian region, with its diverse cultures, histories, and geopolitical interests, makes it challenging to paint a monolithic picture of the attitudes and practices of Asian states in international law. While some scholars argue for the presence of a unique and coherent Asian approach, others emphasize the heterogeneity of perspectives and practices across the region. The evolving role of Asian states in global affairs, along with their increasing engagement with international organizations and treaties, suggests a growing importance of international law in shaping their interactions. However, it is crucial to recognize that any 'Asian' approach to international law must be approached with caution, given the region's diversity and complexities. As Asian states continue to navigate their interests, engage in dispute settlements, and participate in international fora, further scholarly enquiry will be essential in discerning and understanding any distinct characteristics or commonalities that may define Asian international law. This necessitates a nuanced analysis that takes into account the interplay between domestic interests, regional dynamics, and global ambitions. Unravelling the intricacies of Asian international law demands rigorous academic enquiry that delves into the cultural, historical, and geopolitical intricacies shaping the region's engagement with the international legal order.

6
South Asia

Aniruddha Rajput

6.1 Introduction

Although it is a complex concept comprising several elements, culture can, broadly speaking, be described as a 'way of life'. Culture comprises a set of values based on the experiences of a community that constitutes its characteristics and distinguishes it from others.[1] Culture has an undeniable and indelible influence on all laws. International law, being a 'law of nations', is an outcome of the synthesis of cultural influences. Such a synthesis is most visible in the case of the law of the sea, which is one of the oldest and most highly developed branches of contemporary international law. From time immemorial and much before the Westphalian model of international law, which laid the foundations of contemporary international law, different cultures around the world interacted with one another through the seas and influenced the creation of legal norms that constituted the law of the sea. It would be a mistake to think that the law of the sea commenced with Hugo Grotius, often dubbed the 'father of international law', primarily based on his celebrated contribution to the law of the sea: *mare liberum*. There was a long-lasting tradition, far more peaceful and durable, in other parts of the world and particularly in what we today call South Asia.[2]

The centre of maritime culture and the influence of the South Asian states on the law of the sea has been the Indian Ocean. While the Indian Ocean is not the only sea that the South Asian states abut,[3] it is an appropriate paradigm due to

[1] See generally Robert A Nisbet and Liah Greenfeld, 'History of the Separate Disciplines: Cultural Anthropology', *Britannica* <http://www.britannica.com/topic/social-science/History-of-the-separate-disciplines> accessed 2 August 2022; Pradeep Jeganathan and Suzanne L Hanchett, 'The Major Branches of Anthropology: Cultural Anthropology', *Britannica* <www.britannica.com/science/anthropology/The-major-branches-of-anthropology> accessed 2 August 2022; 'culture', *Cambridge Dictionary*, <https://dictionary.cambridge.org/fr/dictionnaire/anglais/culture> accessed 2 August 2022; 'Définition de culture', *Le Robert* <https://dictionnaire.lerobert.com/definition/culture> accessed 2 August 2022; Serge Guimond, *Psychologie Sociale, Perspective Multiculturelle* (Pierre Mardaga Editeur 2013) 2–3.

[2] The modern South Asia comprises Afghanistan, Bangladesh, Bhutan, India, the Maldives, Nepal, Pakistan, and Sri Lanka.

[3] Other seas being the Arabian Sea, Bay of Bengal, and Andaman Sea.

Aniruddha Rajput, *South Asia* In: *Cultural Influences on the Law of the Sea*. Edited by: James Kraska and Hayoun Ryou-Ellison, Oxford University Press. © Aniruddha Rajput 2025. DOI: 10.1093/9780198944140.003.0006

the sheer amount of activity and exchange that took place through it between the South Asian states and between the South Asian states and the outside world. Through the Indian Ocean, the South Asian states spread their social, cultural, and religious imprint in the East, and trade and commerce with the West, during ancient and medieval times. With the emergence of European powers, the Indian Ocean became the theatre of conflict from the sixteenth century, resulting in the eventual loss of sovereignty of the South Asian states. Thus, the history of the Indian Ocean is linked to that of the South Asian states and the rest of the world.[4] It is this history that can help trace the influence of the South Asian states on the law of the sea. And it is this history that can help us understand the way the culture of South Asian states was deeply impacted, radically transforming the outlook of those states towards the world, international law, and the law of the sea.

The cultural influence of South Asia on the law of the sea encompasses a two-way process whereby the South Asian states influenced the law of the sea and, in turn, their culture was influenced by the law of the sea. This chapter elaborates on that bidirectional process based on four broad timescales since the culture of the region and its influence can best be understood through the prism of history.

The first phase extended from around 3000 BCE to 1600 CE. The South Asian states influenced the law of the sea through extensive maritime trade and the policy of freedom of navigation. This was the longest period of peace, prosperity, and stability on the sea. In contrast, the second phase extended from around 1600 to the mid-1800s, during which time European powers emerged on the scene. First, the Portuguese appeared, followed by the Dutch, French, and British. They brought state-sponsored monopolistic practices, used force to suppress freedom of navigation, and established exclusive rights over maritime trade. This relatively short timescale not only radically transformed the culture of the law of the sea in South Asia but also led to colonization and the loss of sovereignty of South Asian states. The third phase, which stretched into the middle of the twentieth century, saw the consolidation of colonization, wanton exploitation, and looting—led by the British, who established themselves as the unchallenged masters of the Indian Ocean, and backed by other

[4] Michael Pearson, *The Indian Ocean* (Routledge 2003); Philippe Beaujard, *The Worlds of the Indian Ocean: A Global History* (Tamara Loring, Frances Meadows, and Andromeda Tait tr, CUP 2019); Kirti N Chaudhuri, *Trade and Civilization in the Indian Ocean* (CUP 1985); Smriti Srinivas, Bettina Ng'weno, and Neelima Jeychandran, *Reimagining Indian Ocean Worlds* (Routledge 2020); Kousar J Azam, *Indian Ocean: The New Frontier* (Routledge 2019); Shanti Moorthy and Ashraf Jamal (eds), *Indian Ocean Studies: Cultural, Social, and Political Perspectives* (Routledge 2010).

European states that had failed in the competition. Freedom of navigation re-emerged, since it suited colonial interests, and the foundations of the modern law of the sea were laid. In the fourth phase, after throwing off the bondage of foreign subjugation, the South Asian states cooperated with each other and with the rest of the Global South to shape and form the 'new' law of the sea at the Third UN Conference on the Law of the Sea, which resulted in the UN Convention on the Law of the Sea (UNCLOS).[5] Over the years, South Asian states actively participated in maritime affairs and especially in the suppression of piracy at the global level. Finally, with changing 'interests' and a divided Global South, the South Asian states yet again seek to influence the future of the law of the sea with the ongoing negotiations at the Intergovernmental Conference on Marine Biodiversity of Areas Beyond National Jurisdiction.

6.2 First phase: peace, stability, and freedom of navigation

The first phase was the longest, stretching from around 3000 BCE to 1600 CE, characterized by maritime trade and the establishment of relations with South Asia and between the South Asian states and the East and the West based on the principle of freedom of the seas.

6.2.1 Earliest evidence of maritime trade and freedom of navigation

The earliest evidence of international maritime trade originating in South Asia is from the Indus Valley Civilization dating back to 3000 BCE, also known as the Harappan times. Archaeological evidence suggests the use of large-sized seafaring vessels, the presence of large docks in which to park those ships, and deep-sea fishing of large fish.[6] Around this time, maritime trade between India and Babylon took place through middlemen located in what are now Bahrain and the Persian Gulf.[7] Maritime trade at that time was globalized, inclusive, and based on the freedom of navigation.

[5] UN Convention on the Law of the Sea, 10 December 1982, 1833 UNTS 397 (UNCLOS).

[6] Amit Kumar, 'Maritime History of India: An Overview' (2012) 8 Maritime Affairs 93, 96; K Sridharan, *A Maritime History of India* (Publications Division, Ministry of Information and Broadcasting 1965) 8.

[7] SR Rao, 'Shipping and Maritime Trade of the Indus People' (1965) 7(3) Expedition 30, 30.

Ancient Hindu texts—in particular, *Rig Veda*, *Yajur Veda*, *Ramayana*, *Mahabharata*, and *Purana*—have extensive references to ocean voyages for trade. They speak about various aspects of navigation and the profitability of maritime trade.[8] *Rig Veda* is one of the oldest systematically written and compiled texts known to humanity. Dating from around 1500–1000 BCE, it contains around 100 references to the ocean (*Samudra*). Varuna is the titular deity who is said to govern the oceans and to be the knower of all sea routes.[9] There is a description of the maritime trade as it existed at that time, as well as the conduct of naval expeditions to distant lands.[10] *Yajur Veda*, believed to have been compiled around 1200–800 BCE, contains descriptions of large, well-constructed ocean-faring vessels with comfortable cabins used for transporting passengers and for trade.[11] *Yukti-kalpataru*, which dates from between the eleventh and fourteenth centuries, focuses on navigation and the art of shipbuilding. It describes ships of different shapes, sizes, categories, and components and the best ways of decorating them.[12]

Additionally, the knowledge of shipbuilding, routes of navigation, and combat at sea is corroborated by archaeological excavations of coins, commemorative stones, fishing equipment, and paintings—including the oldest surviving paintings in the Ajanta and Ellora caves—as well as literary works in Sanskrit and Pali, and various Roman and Greek sources.[13]

The shipbuilding industry flourished in India around 325 BCE. India was a major source of shipbuilding timber known as Malabar teak, along with materials such as flax and cotton for sails, coconut fibre for ropes, and metals.[14] Alexander the Great returned to Macedonia with his forces in a huge fleet of approximately 800 vessels, all manufactured in India.[15] This was a period that saw the emergence of systemic regulations and institutions that could be seen as the origins of the 'law' of the sea in South Asia. *Arthashastra* and *Manusmriti*, composed around 300 BCE, are two important texts in this regard.

[8] Sridharan (n 6) 22, 24.
[9] *Rig Veda* (N Trubner and Co 1866) I.25.7.
[10] ibid I.48.3, I.56.2, I.116.3.
[11] ibid I.24.35, I.24.36; *Yajur Veda* (BR Publishing Corporation 2011) 10.19.
[12] Pandit Iswar Chandra Sastri (ed), *Yukti-kalpataru of Bhoja* (Siddheshwar Machine Press 1917) 223–30. See also B Mahadevan, Vinayak Rajat Bhat, and Nagendra Pavana, *Introduction to Indian Knowledge System—Concepts and Applications* (PHI Learning 2022) 299–302.
[13] Radha K Mookerji, *Indian Shipping: A History of the Sea-Borne Trade and Maritime Activity of the Indians From the Earliest Times* (Longmans, Green and Co 1912) 4–8, 32–52, 137.
[14] Alan Villiers, *The Indian Ocean* (Museum Press 1952) 93.
[15] Mookerji (n 13) 73.

6.2.2 Law of the seas in ancient India

Arthashastra, the prominent treatise dedicated to statecraft and public policy, was written during the reign of Chandragupta Maurya (321–291 BCE). It created the institution of the Superintendent of Shipping (*navadhyaksha*), responsible for the coasts, seas, and navigation, with control over seagoing ships within his jurisdiction. The jurisdiction of the Superintendent of Shipping also included the harbour and maritime zones beyond inland waters.[16] The jurisdiction over the sea extended to fisheries and pearls found at a considerable distance from land.[17]

Roads and waterways were recognized as important modes of traffic that were to be maintained in good condition, regulated, and taxed as a source of fiscal income for the state.[18] The Superintendent of Shipping was responsible for demanding tolls from ships passing through his jurisdiction.[19] The coastal villages were to pay a fixed amount of tax[20] and the toll levied on the merchants was also fixed.[21] No distinction was made between national and foreign merchants for fiscal purposes, thus following what we understand in contemporary international law as 'most favoured nation' and 'national treatment'.

The Superintendent of Shipping had the duty of enforcing the regulations. If a weather-beaten ship arrived at the port, he was required to 'show fatherly kindness to it'.[22] At the same time, vessels carrying merchandise spoiled by water 'may either be exempted from toll or may have their toll reduced to half and let to sail when the time for setting sail approaches'.[23] Moreover, no fees were to be charged to Brahmanas, ascetics, children, the aged, the afflicted, royal messengers, and pregnant women.[24] The Superintendent of Shipping was directed to 'strictly observe the customs prevalent in commercial towns as well as the orders of the superintendent of towns (*Pattanadhyaksha*)'[25]—an

[16] *Arthashastra*, Verses 2.45.11, 2.45.12; Patrick Olivelle, *King, Governance, and Law in Ancient India: Kautilya's Arthashastra* (OUP 2013) 160.

[17] CH Alexandrowicz, *An Introduction to the History of the Law of Nations in the East Indies (16th, 17th and 18th Centuries)* (Clarendon Press 1967) 62.

[18] *Arthashastra*, Verses 2.45.3–2.45.5, 2.45.11, 2.45.24, 2.45.25, 2.54.3; Olivelle (n 16) 160–61, 172; R Shamasastry (tr), *Kautilya's Arthashastra* (Government Press 1915) 79.

[19] *Arthashastra*, Verse 2.45.11; Shamasastry (n 18) 180.

[20] *Arthashastra*, Verses 2.45.2, 2.45.24; Olivelle (n 16) 161.

[21] *Arthashastra*, Verses 2.45.4–2.45.5, 2.45.21–2.4524; Shamasastry (n 18) 179.

[22] *Arthashastra*, Verse 2.45.8; Shamasastry (n 18) 180.

[23] *Arthashastra*, Verses 2.45.9–2.45.10; Shamasastry (n 18) 180.

[24] *Arthashastra*, Verse 2.45.18; Shamasastry (n 18) 181; *Manusmriti*, Verse 8.406 (Gujarati Printing Press 1969).

[25] *Arthashastra*, Verses 2.45.7, 2.45.12; Shamasastry (n 18) 180.

instance of the application of the *lex specialis* rule. The regulations were aimed at creating a conducive environment for marine trade, the freedom of navigation, and maritime security.

Law and order were to be established on the seas by keeping an eye on weapons, explosives, and suspicious persons moving through sea routes, as well as the smuggling of goods and persons.[26] Security was strictly enforced by ensuring that crossings of the seas occurred only during permitted times and that any violations would attract a heavy penalty.[27] However, there would be no penalty for fishermen and persons carrying vegetables and flowers.[28]

The Superintendent of Shipping was responsible for overseeing maritime routes and the operations of seafaring vessels. That oversight included suppressing piracy and maintaining law and order.[29] Pirate ships, ships bound for the enemy, and those violating the customs and rules in force in port were to be destroyed.[30] Matters of marine warfare were under the control of one of the six departments dedicated to military affairs.[31]

The system was based on accountability and responsiveness to the users of the sea. The Superintendent of Shipping was personally responsible for the failure to enforce the regulations and ensure healthy trading. If a vessel capsized due to a lack of the requisite crew or bad repair, the Superintendent of Shipping would be responsible for anything lost or destroyed.[32]

Fishing was a regulated activity requiring a licence, the fee for which was one-sixth portion of the catch.[33] To protect certain species of fish, another institution, the Superintendent of Abattoirs (*soonadhyaksha*), was responsible for declaring 'sea fish which have strange or unusual forms' as protected species.[34]

Manusmriti also refers to marine insurance arrangements. A sailor was responsible for the damage caused by his fault to the goods of passengers, but was absolved of responsibility for an accident beyond human control.[35] For the losses caused due to their fault, boatmen were to pay the compensation

[26] *Arthashastra*, Verses 2.45.14–2.45.16, 2.45.20; Shamasastry (n 18) 181–82.

[27] *Arthashastra*, Verses 2.45.15–2.45.16; Olivelle (n 16) 161.

[28] *Arthashastra*, Verse 2.45.17; Olivelle (n 16) 161.

[29] *Arthashastra*, Verses 2.45.7, 2.45.12–2.45.16, 2.45.19–2.45.20; Olivelle (n 16) 160–61.

[30] *Arthashastra*, Verse 2.45.12; Shamasastry (n 18) 181.

[31] JW McCrindle, *Ancient India as Described by Megasthenês and Arrian; Being a Translation of the Fragments of the Indika of Megasthenês Collected by Dr. Schwanbeck and of the First Part of the Indika of Arrian* (Trübner & Co 1877) 88–89.

[32] *Arthashastra*, Verse 2.45.26; Olivelle (n 16) 162.

[33] *Arthashastra*, Verse 2.45.3; Shamasastry (n 18) 179.

[34] *Arthashastra*, Verse 2.43.5; Olivelle (n 16) 157; LN Rangarajan (ed, tr), *Kautilya: The Arthashastra* (Penguin Books 2000) 320.

[35] *Manusmriti* (n 24) Verse 409.9.

collectively.[36] People in maritime trade were advised to learn the dialects and languages of other countries to facilitate trade.[37]

A general practice of asylum for refugees fleeing religious persecution in their states was followed. Refugees were provided with shelter and allowed the freedom to practise their religion. In 68 CE, several Jews fleeing Roman persecution took refuge in the kingdom of South India during the reign of the Andhras and settled in Malabar.[38] Zoroastrians came from Persia to India around the seventh century and settled in Sanjan, Gujarat.[39] The followers of those faiths and the descendants of those immigrants have prospered and integrated. They continue to follow their faith and religious practices even today, most of them in India.

There was a flourishing maritime trade and freedom of navigation without any hindrance for all ships in the Indian Ocean. Traders from all nations peacefully transacted under the protection of local laws.[40] This was the age of globalization, free trade, and freedom of navigation, supported by convivial legal regulation.

6.2.3 Globalization and the culture of freedom of navigation

After the Roman conquest of Egypt in 30 BCE, trade relations with the West were enhanced, including several embassies being sent regularly by different states to Rome.[41] These developments were an outcome of maritime trade and, in particular, a growing trade seeking Indian spices and providing gold and silver in return. The trade with India was undertaken in the form of a Roman–Arab partnership. Diplomatic relations with Arab ports were established, leading to the creation of prominent ports in the region.[42]

A small book, *Periplus of the Erythraean Sea*, was prepared by an unknown Roman author as a merchant's handbook for trade with India.[43] The book 'shows how well the routes were known, and how business-like and amicable were the relations between' traders of different countries.[44] Greek merchants,

[36] ibid Verse 8.407.
[37] Mookerji (n 13) 62.
[38] ibid 82.
[39] John R Hinnells and Alan Williams, *Parsis in India and the Diaspora* (Routledge 2007) 1, 6.
[40] J Innes Miller, *The Spice Trade of the Roman Empire: 29 B.C. to A.D. 641* (Clarendon Press 1969) 18–19.
[41] EH Warmington, *The Commerce Between the Roman Empire and India* (Curzon Press 1974) 35–37.
[42] Miller (n 40) 14.
[43] GWB Huntingford, *The Periplus of the Erythraean Sea, by an Unknown Author* (Hakluyt Society 2010) 42–45.
[44] Miller (n 40) 19.

called *Yavanas*, would normally spend three months along the coastal areas of South India.

Since a liberal immigration policy was followed, it became habitual for Roman subjects to settle in southern India. Several Roman colonies sprang up during the first and second centuries. Romans even took jobs—including important ones, such as bodyguards to Indian kings.[45] There are instances of traders from different jurisdictions freely settling in the trading towns of the South Asian states without any obstruction.[46] *Periplus* also describes how the ports were divided into 'designated', 'lawful', and 'authorized' categories, but does not provide further elaboration. There was always guaranteed supervision in these ports by government officials, who levied duties.[47]

Luxury items from India—such as muslin, diamonds and other jewels, and spices—were in great demand during the relative peace of the Roman Empire. Contemporary observers lamented that there was 'no year in which India did not drain the Roman Empire of a hundred million sesterces', sending in return goods sold for 100 times their original value.[48] This created a trade deficit for Romans since they had little to offer for sale in return that would attract the market of the Indian subcontinent.[49] With Rome's gold supply being rapidly depleted due to a trade deficit, Emperor Vespasian prohibited the further export of bullion. The Roman trade declined during the third and fourth centuries, replaced by Sassanids and Persians, and later dominated by Arabs.[50]

Over the centuries, there was a rise and fall in trade with the West until, after a lull in direct relations, the Portuguese emerged on the scene (see Section 6.3.3). On the other hand, trade and cultural exchange with the East continued and expanded. The contact of South Asian states with the East was constantly enriching—economically, culturally, and spiritually.

The prominent chronicle *Mahavansa* notes that Prince Vijaya (543–505 BCE) from Kalinga, present-day Odisha in India, disgruntled over succession, undertook a journey through the sea to Ceylon and founded the great Sinhala Kingdom in what is now Sri Lanka.[51] Ceylon was centrally placed and trade

[45] Warmington (n 41) 68–69.

[46] From several instances, the prominent story is of a Jewish trader from Tunisia who was a resident of Mangalore in the southern part of India: SD Goitein and MA Friedman, *Indian Traders of the Middle Ages* (Brill 2008) 57.

[47] Miller (n 40) 19–20.

[48] Quoted by Mookerji (n 13) 86.

[49] Auguste Toussaint, *History of the Indian Ocean* (tr June Guicharnaud, Routledge and Kegan Paul 1966) 18.

[50] John R Cady, *Southeast Asia: Its Historical Development* (McGraw-Hill 1964) 27.

[51] John M Senaveratna, *The Story of the Sinhalese From the Most Ancient Times Up to the End of 'the Mahavansa' or Great Dynasty: Vijaya to Maha Sena (BC 543 to AD 302)* (Asian Educational Series 1997) 11; Sandagomi Coperahewa, 'Origin of Sinhala and Kalinga–Lanka Linguistic Affinities' (paper

from all sides converged in its ports.[52] Ceylon soon became a flourishing island state with commercial relations through sea routes with India, other countries in the East, the Malay Peninsula, and China. Traders from Southern Arabia also established settlements in Ceylon from the beginning of the first century.[53]

The Maldives has had cultural and economic ties with its neighbours in South Asia for centuries.[54] As early as 2000 BCE, the Maldives lay on the maritime trading routes of early Egyptian, Mesopotamian, and Indus Valley civilizations.[55] In addition, the Maldivians traded with Aceh and many other kingdoms in what are today Indonesia and Malaysia.[56] The first settlers in the Maldives who came by sea were people known as Dheyvis from Kalibanga in India, who arrived around 269–232 BCE, and thus began the nautical culture of the Maldives.[57] Prince Sri Soorudasaruna Adeettiya, son of King Brahmaadittiya, the ruler of Kalinga, established a kingdom of the Adeetta Dynasty in the Maldives.[58] Buddhism was brought to the Maldives at around the same time, when Emperor Ashoka sent missionaries to countries of South Asia during the third century BCE.[59]

Around 75 CE, navigators from Kalinga[60] arrived in Java, perhaps in search of gold, and settled there.[61] Over the next three to four centuries, more Indians travelled in the East, spreading Hinduism and Buddhism. This led to the establishment of organized political kingdoms influenced by the religion and culture of South Asian states in Thailand, Cambodia, Java, Sumatra, and other areas of Indonesia.[62] Thereafter, around 600 CE, Shaka kings of Gujrat undertook large-scale voyages to Java and settled there, forming 'cultural' rather than 'political' empires.[63] They integrated with the locals and the political systems

prepared for seminar on Kalinga–Lanka: Reviving Old Linkages and Exploring New Opportunities, Bhubaneswar, India, 2015); Mookerji (n 13) 28–31.

[52] Friedrich Hirth and WW Rockhill, *Chau Ju-Kua: His Work on the Chinese and Arab Trade in the Twelfth and Thirteenth Centuries, Entitled Chu-fan-chi* (Literature House 1965) 8–9.

[53] Wang Gungwu, 'The Nanhai Trade: A Study of the Early History of Chinese Trade in the South China Sea' (1959) 31(182) Journal of Malaysian Branch of the Royal Asiatic Society 1, 3, 37–41.

[54] Karl E Ryavec, 'Maldives' in Helen Chapin Metz (ed), *Indian Ocean: Five Island Countries* (Headquarters, Department of the Army 1995) 294–307.

[55] ibid 258.

[56] ibid 257.

[57] Naseema Mohamed, 'Note on the Early History of the Maldives' (2005) 70 Archipel 7, 7.

[58] ibid 7, 9.

[59] ibid.

[60] Benudhar Patra, *Early Maritime Contacts Between Kalinga and Bali: A Historical Perspective* (2016) 73 *Odisha Review* 34, 34.

[61] Mookerji (n 13) 103, 148; Mountstuart Elphinstone, *The History of India* (2nd edn, John Murray 1841) 327.

[62] RP Anand, *Origin and Development of the Law of the Sea: History of International Law Revisited* (Martinus Nijhoff 1983) 17.

[63] Sridharan (n 6) 35.

evolved.[64] Thereafter, for around 700 years or more—from the fifth to the thirteenth centuries—until the emergence of Islam in the Eastern regions, close relations were maintained between Hindu–Buddhist Southeast Asian states and Indian states, based on 'uninterrupted sea traffic' with regular 'shipping services'.[65] Trade with China and Japan expanded during this period.[66]

The South Asian states also established diplomatic relations with states further East. There was constant interaction between the Guptas and China.[67] From 350 until 400 CE, the Gupta kings maintained diplomatic relations with China.[68] There are accounts of Chinese visitor Fa-Hien in 399 CE describing maritime trade in India.[69] Another Chinese visitor, Huang Tsang, visited India during the period of Harsha (627–643 CE) through the Silk Route. In his journal, later known as the Hsi-yü Chi or *The Great Tang Dynasty Records on the Western Regions*, he wrote that India had a brisk trade with foreign countries, there were prosperous city ports on its sea coast both in the East and in the West, and the inhabitants procured profit through sea trade and commerce.[70]

The culture of freedom of navigation, respect for freedom of trade, concord, and co-existence allowed extensive use of the seas in a proportion much larger than that of the then population. Trade was a major activity, followed by the spread of religion and pilgrimage. Some important navigation centres were also important religious sites for the prominent faiths of that time, including Hinduism, Jainism, Islam, and Christianity.[71]

The freedom of the seas was a reason for the flourishing of Buddhism and the creation of prominent centres in Southeast Asia.[72] There are several accounts of Buddhist pilgrims traversing the seas to visit the places inhabited by Buddha, and of monks travelling by sea to spread Buddhism.[73] Around 350–380 CE, Śrī Meghavarman, the King of Ceylon, requested permission from Samudragupta and thereafter constructed a Buddhist monastery in Bodha Gaya, the place where Buddha achieved *Nirvana*.[74] During the eleventh and

[64] KK Pillay, 'Early Indian "Imperialism" in the Far East' (1954) 3 Indian Year Book of International Affairs 114, 117–19.
[65] KM Panikkar, *India and the Indian Ocean* (Macmillan 1945) 31.
[66] Mookerji (n 13) 120.
[67] Sridharan (n 6) 33–35.
[68] SR Goyal, *History of the Imperial Guptas* (Central Book Depot: Allahabad 1967) 181.
[69] Sridharan (n 6) 33–34.
[70] Huang Tsang, *The Great Tang Dynasty Record of the Western Regions* (tr Li Rongxi, BDK America 1996) 303.
[71] Himanshu P Ray, 'Writings on the Maritime History of Ancient India' in Sabyasachi Bhattacharya (ed), *Approaches to History: Essays in Indian Historiography* (Primus Books 2011) 27–54.
[72] Cady (n 50) 35, 62, 70–71.
[73] Hirth and Rockhill (n 52) 3.
[74] Bimala Churn Law, 'Contemporaneity of the Kings of India and Ceylon' (1939) 3 Proceedings of the Indian History Congress 280, 281.

twelfth centuries, Islam spread over land and through the sea in different parts of India. Gujrathi shipping fell largely into Muslim hands, but Hindus continued to trade. Later, Muslims from Gujarat and Bengal took Islam to Sumatra through the sea route.[75]

6.2.4 Development of trade centres with favourable regulations

Most parts of the first phase saw globalization based on sustaining long-distance connections and establishing economic and social relations.[76] The period saw the emergence of trade centres along coastal states, bringing profits and fiscal benefits to the rulers. These trade centres were fortified markets, professionally managed and called emporiums. As early as the second century, Roman geographer Ptolemy described them as 'an authorized sea coast (not inland) mart in the Orient where non-Roman dues were levied by non-Roman authorities'.[77] The tasks of persons engaged in maritime trade and at emporiums were divided. The trader would look at the business side and not go aboard a ship, which was under the control of a shipper. The trader would trade by himself or based on finance. These marine finance arrangements would involve detailed provisions for credit facilitation, the consequences of default, and dispute resolution in local courts.[78] Local rulers exercised control over their ports and lands but not the sea, which was accepted as free for all for peaceful navigation. Most states welcomed foreigners since they brought prosperity to their kingdoms—in fact, some kingdoms depended on it. The port rules and regulations were well publicized and the port charges were peacefully applied. There was a certainty of trade. In civil matters, traders were allowed to apply their own laws. Local state authorities rarely interfered in their affairs and left the traders to settle their disputes, unless their actions affected the peace and order of the state.[79]

During the fifteenth century, Bengal, Pegu, Pulicat, Goa, Calicut, and Cochin became thriving centres, with merchants from various places, speaking different languages, and trading under general rules of conduct. Satgaon

[75] MAP Mellink-Roelofsz, *Asian Trade and European Influence in the Indonesian Archipelago Between 1500 and About 1630* (Springer 1962) 21.
[76] Matthew Adam Cobb, 'Introduction' in Matthew Adam Cobb (ed), *The Indian Ocean Trade in Antiquity: Political, Cultural and Economic Impacts* (Routledge 2019) 6–7.
[77] Warmington (n 41) 113–14.
[78] Ray (n 71) 27–54.
[79] Alexandrowicz, *An Introduction* (n 17) 97.

in Bengal was the 'chief emporium of trade in the western part of Bengal.'[80] Moreover, the Pegu River was also the cradle of an emporium, Rangoon.[81] Pulicat appears to have been described as a 'flourishing emporium' as well.[82] In the first part of the fifteenth century, Calicut was becoming an emporium.[83] These coasts competed with one another in attracting traders. For instance, there was a strange practice whereby, in the event of a shipwreck, the coastal state considered it a right to take the wrecked ship and its cargo as a prize—except in the state of Malabar on the Calicut coast, where ownership was not forfeited. Thus, Calicut became a prominent and bustling port attracting a large number of merchants.[84] However, through the sixteenth century, the role of Calicut as a major trade centre declined as other coasts, such as Cochin, flourished.[85]

Freedom of navigation, non-interference in trade, and a cosmopolitan culture were dominant among the South Asian states until the sixteenth century.[86] The knowledge of regular winds and monsoons helped safe navigation, and the threat of pirates was addressed by rules and, on the high seas, by carrying soldiers on ships.[87] This free for all continued until the Portuguese arrived.[88]

6.2.5 Military uses of the sea

Instances of conflict on the sea involving the use of force beyond the maintenance of law and order for the suppression of piracy were rare. The rulers of flourishing coastal towns understood the importance of maintaining peace and order on the sea for the prosperity of their kingdoms. In their relations with each state, they followed the tributary system whereby smaller kingdoms would acknowledge the overlordship of larger kingdoms, and the

[80] Rajnish Kumar, 'Satgaon Port of Hugli from Its Rise to Decline' (2019) 6 International Journal of Research and Analytical Reviews 713, 714.

[81] Hugh Murray, *The Encyclopaedia of Geography, Complete Description of Earth* (Blanchard and Lea 1855) 398.

[82] Jacob Pandian, 'The Hindu Caste System and Muslim Ethnicity: The Labbai of a Tamil Village in South India' (1978) 25(2) Ethnohistory 141, 149.

[83] KS Mathew, 'Calicut, the International Emporium of Maritime Trade and the Portuguese During the Sixteenth Century' (2007) 67 Proceedings of the Indian History Congress 251, 252.

[84] Ibn Battuta, *Travels in Asia and Africa 1325–1354* (tr HAE Gibb, Routledge & Kegan Paul 2013) 189.

[85] ibid 265.

[86] John N Miksic, 'Archeology, Trade and Society in North East Sumatra' (PhD thesis, Cornell University 1979) 8–9.

[87] Anand (n 62) 34.

[88] ibid.

larger kingdoms would not annihilate the ruler and his traditions or colonize. However, there are three noteworthy instances of the sea being used as a theatre for warfare.

First was the conflict between Cholas and Srivijaya. Chola was a Tamilian dynasty from South India that was engaged in a constant struggle for supremacy with the Srivijaya Empire based in Java.[89] The fruitless naval war was fought on the sea between the two powers for around a 100 years until the end of the thirteenth century, weakening both kingdoms and paving the way for Muslim supremacy in the Indian Ocean.[90] Thus, until the thirteenth century, Hindu kingdoms dominated the sea, after which Islamic dominance began. Arab traders dominated the Indian Ocean. They did not seek to have naval control of the oceans, since Arab navigation was developed by merchant adventurers and not as a result of state policy.[91] While this political transition was taking place, freedom of navigation and freedom of trade continued unhindered. The contemporary record of the celebrated traveller Marco Polo, who visited India during 1288–92, shows that, despite the political upheaval, peaceful trade continued at entrepôts by merchants from all parts of the known world.[92] In later years, with the establishment of their empire in the sixteenth century, the Mughals regulated naval activity. An Admiralty Board was created, responsible for the supply of ships for navigation; the supply of mariners, with details of officials and personnel on the ships provided in detail; and the imposition, realization, and remission of duties, never exceeding 2.5 per cent.[93] There are references to minor naval conflicts occurring during the Mughal time.[94]

Second, Kublai Khan sought to expand his control in the region by replacing tributes with dominance over the sea, seeking to monopolize the seas during the thirteenth century. This was met with strong resistance, resulting in defeat and limited short-lived success. Even while Kublai Khan made efforts to monopolize trade through the use of force, free trade mostly continued and was not much hampered.[95]

Third, between 1405 and 1431, the Ming Dynasty sent seven large expeditions to dominate the trade route in the Indian Ocean and establish their

[89] Pierre-Yves Manguin, 'Srivijaya: Trade and Connectivity in the Pre-Modern Malay World' (2021) 3 Journal of Urban Archaeology 87, 87.

[90] OK Nambiar, *Our Seafaring in the Indian Ocean* (Jeevan Publications 1975) 19.

[91] Panikkar, *India and the Indian Ocean* (n 65) 35–36.

[92] Marco Polo, *The Travels of Marco Polo, the Venetian* (ed William Marsden, AMS Press 1968) 251.

[93] Mookerji (n 13) 205–08.

[94] ibid 214–18.

[95] Cady (n 50) 134–35.

presence in the ports. In naval combat, the Chinese forces defeated prominent states in Ceylon, India, the Maldives, and the port of Hormuz on the Persian Gulf, establishing themselves in the ports in the region.[96] In the preceding two centuries, Chinese traders had proven formidable in the region. Fifteen years after Marco Polo, Ibn Battuta, a Moroccan Muslim traveller, recorded the influence of Chinese traders. Chinese ships were the largest vessels, and Chinese traders settled at all the prominent ports in South Asia, including Ceylon and Calicut.[97] Due to the use of force on the sea, this period saw an increase in the number of pirate attacks.[98]

Until the sixteenth century, the seas were used for commercial purposes, religious expansion, cultural intercourse, and international comity. This first phase was the longest period of stability and peace at sea. The fulcrum of this state of affairs was a principles-based system, instead of petty temporary interests. The coastal states in South Asia preferred the function of oversight and ensuring peace and security for the users of the sea. Although they had the resources to do so, they never entered into or urged others to compete in the trade for more profits. They played the role of umpire and played by the rules, allowing them to maintain their credibility and the confidence of the market. This culture did not convert the oceans into a centre-stage of power struggle and domination. The culture changed only with the coming into the picture of the European nations.[99] This led to the second phase, full of conflict and confrontation, which ended the period of freedom of trade and freedom of navigation in the Indian Ocean. This was replaced with state-sponsored monopoly, conflict, the use of force, the disruption of maritime trade, and the eventual colonization of the South Asian states, first by European state-backed corporations and later by the European states.

6.3 Second phase: troubled waters—monopoly and conflict

6.3.1 Fascination for spice

Direct trade between India and Europe died down during the Dark Ages due to the trade-restrictive measures adopted by successive rulers. There was no

[96] Nambiar (n 90) 35.
[97] Battuta (n 84) 187–88; Toussaint (n 49) 77.
[98] Toussaint (n 49) 86.
[99] Sridharan (n 6) 83.

direct contact between Europe and South Asia, except through intermediate traders who took a huge share of profits. Additionally, the rise of Islam proved to be a bulwark further cemented by the taking over of Constantinople by the Turks.[100]

The absence of direct contact, however, did not efface the memories and impressions of the Indian subcontinent from the Western mind. The subcontinent remained a land of riches, 'a magnet, drawing to it mariner and explorer, soldier, and adventurer'.[101] The lure was such that a prominent Roman geographer—who himself never visited India—described the Indian subcontinent as 'the greatest of all nations and the happiest in its lot', and 'the dream of every age and land since the days of Solomon and Semiraimis'.[102] The stories of travellers such as Marco Polo, Friar Odoric, and Monte Carvino in the thirteenth century rekindled the interest in and fascination about India and the South Asian states in the European mind.[103]

On the practical side was the desire for Indian spices, with pepper being a precious commodity at the time. Edward Gibbon noted: 'Pepper may not mean much to us, but in that age, it ranked with precious stones. Men risked the perils of the deep and fought and died for pepper.'[104] Pepper was important to the extent that, in 408 CE, a ransom of 3,000 pounds of pepper was demanded by Alaric to return Rome to the Romans.[105]

The urgent need to access Indian spices was summarized by another eminent historian, Geoffrey F Hudson:[106]

> Spices which became more and more an essential for European cookery could not be obtained except from India and Indonesia and must come through Persia or Egypt; this indispensable and naturally monopolist trade came to be the chief bone of contention in the politics of the Levant and was the most powerful single factor in stimulating European expansion in the fifteenth century. . . . Europeans knew where spices were produced and at what cost, so that when they were again cut off from the Indian market by a hostile

[100] Kate Fleet, 'The Rise of the Ottomans' in Maribel Fierro (ed), *The New Cambridge History of Islam* (CUP 2011) 319.

[101] Miller (n 40) 12.

[102] William S Lindsay, *History of Merchant Shipping and Ancient Commerce*, vol 2 (AMS Press 1965) 21; Villiers (n 14) 144; KM Panikkar, *Asia and Western Dominance: A Survey of the Vasco da Gama Epoch of Asian History 1498–1945* (George Allen & Unwin 1953) 23–24.

[103] GA Ballard, *Rulers of the Indian Ocean* (Duckworth 1927) 146–47.

[104] ibid 127.

[105] Edward Gibbon, *The History of the Decline and Fall of the Roman Empire*, vol 3 (first published 1781, Penguin Classics 1996) 272.

[106] Quoted in Panikkar, *India and the Indian Ocean* (n 65) 25; Geoffrey F Hudson, *Europe and China: A Survey of Their Relations From the Earliest Times to 1800* (Beacon Press 1961) 160.

Islam and by incessant wars in the Levant, they were well aware of the opportunities awaiting any Power that could find a route to the 'Indies where the spices grow'.

6.3.2 Scramble to win the spice trade

During the fourteenth and fifteenth centuries, Arabs were the prominent intermediaries, with few Gujrathi Muslim traders. On the Western side, Venetians controlled the Mediterranean and carried goods to the West. The monopolistic practices of Arabs and Venetians made their ports prosperous and a great emporium of Eastern trade. The supply of Indian spices, particularly pepper, to the West was never sufficient and the prices charged by the Arab and Venetian middlemen were exorbitant.[107]

Genoa, which was competing with Venice, secured limited monopoly rights to trade from the Byzantine emperors.[108] To surpass their Venetian competitors, Genoese traders approached the two Iberian nations of Spain and Portugal, which had led the crusades against the Muslims (or Moors, as they were called by the Europeans) since the tenth century.

Portugal's Prince Henry the Navigator made it his mission to find a sea route to India and turn the tide of Islam.[109] While religion was more important than trade, gold and trafficking in humans had equal lure. Thus, there was a combination of 'greed and godliness' that drove Portugal and Spain. For the Europeans who followed—the British, French, and Dutch—it was mostly greed rather than godliness.[110]

Until the fifteenth century, European navigation was confined to inland seas such as the Mediterranean, the North Sea, the Baltic Sea, and the coast of Europe. Only the Asians and the Arabs had skills in oceanic navigation. All efforts, including technical skills, were brought to bear to foster Prince Henry's mission.[111] To maintain exclusive control and monopoly, the charts, maps, and information of the lands visited were among the most secret national data held by the Portuguese. This practice was followed by other European kingdoms.[112]

[107] Anand (n 62) 41.

[108] Panikkar, *India and the Indian Ocean* (n 65) 26.

[109] Richard S Whiteway, *The Rise of Portuguese Power in India, 1497–1550* (Santiago de Compostela 1967) 2–3.

[110] Charles R Boxer, *The Portuguese Seaborne Empire 1415–1825* (ed JH Plumb, Hutchinson 1969) xxii.

[111] Ballard (n 103) 14; Panikkar, *India and the Indian Ocean* (n 65) 37.

[112] Anand (n 62) 45.

The network of spies made reports of open shops and businesses in diamonds, sapphires, rubies, and pearls from Ceylon and Burma, as well as pepper from Calicut. Above all, the spies were quite surprised to find that there were already some Indian Christians inhabiting the Malabar coast. The records contain an account of the user-friendly administration for navigation and trade.[113] A contemporary Portuguese traveller and writer, Duarte Barbosa, noted:[114]

> As soon as any of these Merchants reached the city, the King assigned him a *Nayre*, to protect and serve him, and a *Chatim* clerk to keep his accounts and looks after his affairs, and a broker to arrange for him to obtain such goods as he had need of, for which three persons they paid good salaries every month.

A series of bulls was issued by Pope Nicholas V in 1454, Pope Calixtus II in 1456, and Pope Alexander VI in 1493, recognizing the claims of the Portuguese and the Spanish to occupy parts of the world. On 4 May 1493, Alexander VI divided the world into two halves and declared Spain the overlord of the West and Portugal the overlord of the East. This was fortified through the Treaty of Tordesillas, signed on 7 June 1494 and blessed and confirmed by Alexander VI.[115] Both the Spanish and the Portuguese set sail to find a sea route to India. Columbus, representing the Spanish emperor, sailed to the West in search of India. He reached America in 1492, believing it to be India—a conviction he did not change until his death.[116]

The papal bull issued by Pope Nicolas V in favour of Henry the Navigator stated that 'never within the memory of man had anyone been known to have navigated the sea to the distant shores of the Orient' and that 'if by his effort the Ocean can be made navigable as for as India . . . he enters into relations with these people, he will induce them to come to the help of the Christians of the West against the enemies of the faith'. Further, 'he was to bring under submission, the pagans of the countries not yet inflicted with the plague of Islam and give them knowledge of the name of Christ'.[117]

[113] Henry H Hart, *Sea Road to the Indies: An Account of the Voyages and Exploits of the Portuguese Navigators, Together With the Life and Times of Dom Vasco da Gama, Capitão-Mór, Viceroy of India, and Count of Vidigueira* (Macmillan 1950) 63–65.

[114] Duarte Barbosa, *The Book of Duarte Barbosa: An Account of the Countries Bordering on the Indian Ocean and Their Inhabitants*, vol 2 (tr and ed Mansel Longworth Dames, Hakluyt Society 1921) 77.

[115] Anand (n 62) 43–44.

[116] Ballard (n 103) 18.

[117] Anand (n 62) 44; Leften S Stavrianos, *The World Since 1500: A Global History* (Prentice-Hall 1966) 100–01.

The papal bull also created a monopoly in favour of the Portuguese by declaring:[118]

> King Affonso, the Prince [Henry the Navigator], and all their successors, occupy and possess in exclusive rights the said islands, ports and the seas undermentioned, and all faithful Christians are prohibited without the permission of the said Affonso and his successors to encroach on their sovereignty. Of the conquests already made, or to be made, . . . all the Orient is perpetually and for the future the sovereignty of King Affonso.

This was the first occasion of seeking to establish a monopoly in the Indian Ocean and the involvement of a state, blessed by the Pope, in monopolizing the trade.

6.3.3 Emergence of the Portuguese

Calicut was an important port, ruled by the Zamorins, and became the first target of the Portuguese. Until their intervention and control, Calicut under the Zamorins was a prominent port for international maritime trade and commerce. Despite some conflicts on the land, the prominent trading ports were safe. Recording the absolute security at the port and beyond in the famous Calicut port, Muslim writer Abd-er-Razzak noted:[119]

> Calicut is a perfectly secure harbour, which . . . brings together merchants from every city and from every country; in it are to be found an abundance of precious articles brought thither from maritime countries. . . . Security and justice are so firmly established in this city, that the most wealthy merchants bring tither from maritime countries considerable cargoes, which they unloaded, and unhesitatingly send into the markets and the bazaars, without thinking in the meantime of any necessity of checking the account or of keeping watch over the goods. The officers of the custom-house take upon themselves the charge of looking after the merchandise, over which they keep watch, day and night. When a sale is effected, they levy a duty on the

[118] Quoted in Stavrianos (n 117) 100–01; Panikkar, *Asia and Western Dominance* (n 102) 31.

[119] Abd-er-Razzak, 'Narrative of the Journey of Abd-Er-Razzak' in RH Major (ed), *India in the Fifteenth Century* (Hakluyt Society 1985) 13–14.

goods of one-fortieth part; if they are not sold, they make no charge on them whatsoever.

The efficiency of administration and the probity of traders were praised by Vatherman, an Italian who visited Calicut in 1505.[120]

Based on the intelligence reports prepared by spies, Vasco da Gama, a nobleman of the king's household, set out for India. When da Gama reached the shores of Calicut on 12 May 1498, he was received with courtesy and honour. Two messengers were sent by the Zamorin with fine clothes and a welcome message. It was in the interests of the town to have as many trade links as possible for commerce and prosperity, and direct trade with Europe was considered advantageous. Upon receiving the letter of Don Mauel requesting commercial facilities, Zamorin graciously replied and asked da Gama to communicate to the Treasurer what commodities he wanted.[121]

Zamorin was a prominent kingdom surviving on maritime trade. People from all religions lived in the kingdom with mutual tolerance. The wealthiest residents were the Arab traders, who had their own laws and judges (*kadis*).[122] The worldview of da Gama and his companions was quite typical of the Dark Ages. They believed that Calicut was a Christian territory and worshipped at the temple, thinking of it as a Church.[123]

It was a practice to present fine gifts, but the gifts brought by da Gama were so poor that the king's officer laughed and decided not to forward them to him. The king continued to be gracious, allowing da Gama's goods to be transported free of charge. After a stay of a few months, da Gama's arrogance and haughtiness caused concern. However, King Zamorin continued to be courteous and respectful. Eventually, da Gama refused to pay the customs due and sailed away with five hostages after quarrels with local authorities and traders.[124]

After leaving Calicut, da Gama went to Cannanore. The port city was ruled by Kolathiri Raja, who was already in conflict with Zamorin and keen to win Portuguese friendship. After meeting Kolathiri Raja and establishing relations with his kingdom, da Gama returned to Lisbon on 20 August 1499.[125] Although the journey was undertaken purportedly for trade, it soon took on the nature of interference in domestic politics.

120 Whiteway (n 109) 26–27.

121 For interesting details of the meeting, see Hart (n 113) 177–79; Panikkar, *India and the Indian Ocean* (n 65) 35–36.

122 Panikkar, *India and the Indian Ocean* (n 65) 24–25.

123 Hart (n 113) 176–77.

124 ibid 182–88; Villiers (n 14) 127–30.

125 Panikkar, *Asia and Western Dominance* (n 102) 38.

The trip was a great success because de Gama found a new route, but it invoked jealousy among the Venetians, who were trading through Arabs in the Indian Ocean and, above all, cutting the revenue source for the Turks.[126] Da Gama suffered many losses on the way, yet the goods he brought fetched 60 times the cost of the expedition.[127] King Manuel assumed for himself the title 'Lord of Guinea and the Conquests, Navigation and Commerce of Ethiopia, Arabia, Persia, and India.'[128]

The following year, da Gama's successor, Admiral Cabral, reached Calicut. He was unable to purchase goods since the Arabs were offering a better price. Despite a patient and respectful reception from Zamorin, Cabral forced himself onto the market by capturing a Moorish ship loaded with spices for the Red Sea route to Europe. This unwarranted aggression created shock in the port, which was otherwise always peaceful. Traders and others became anguished and a riot broke out against the Portuguese. Zamorin controlled the mob and contained the damage to the Portuguese warehouse, but Cabral held him responsible and retaliated brutally by burning Arab vessels, massacring their crews, and bombarding the city.[129] This was just the beginning of an age in which the sound of canons replaced the sounds of traders from all nationalities bidding for goods in a free market.

6.3.4 Monopolies and conflicts

On the next visit, the Portuguese king sent an armada to enforce its sovereignty and retaliate against Zamorin. Da Gama led the mission, along the way committing several acts of piracy and armed robbery at sea. All advances by Zamorin for peace were contemptuously rejected by da Gama, finally leading to the bombardment of the city, the taking of hostages, plundering, and the destruction of trading ships and goods. The modus operandi of the Portuguese, followed by other European colonizers, was to take control of the ports and monopolize trade. This would allow them to trade exclusively with maximum profits to the exclusion of all others. To enforce the monopoly, important ports and entrepôts were taken over, and fortified garrisons were built to control the sea trade. The Portuguese began forcing ships to move towards Goa,

[126] Hart (n 113) 196–201.
[127] Lindsay (n 102) 23.
[128] Hart (n 113) 201.
[129] ibid 211–12; KM Panikkar, *Malabar and the Portuguese* (DB Taraporevala Sons & Co 1929) 40–42.

where they had established themselves, and to use it as a port and pay taxes. Portuguese middlemen worked at Goa, thus adding to the Lisbon treasury. Indian rulers tried to equip themselves with a navy to respond, but they were too late to enter the arms race at sea and they were unable to respond to state-sponsored monopolistic practices. Normally, ships sailing in the Indian Ocean did not use iron; instead, they relied on less sturdy material to allow speed. The sole purpose of vessels was for trade rather than military use.[130] As per Anand, the 'arrival of Portuguese ships with heavy cannons, therefore introduced a new and revolutionary factor in the Indian Ocean . . . which gave them a decisive advantage'.[131] By now, the culture of free navigation and trade had been decapitated by the Portuguese in the Indian Ocean.

Soon, a viceroy was created for India to retain exclusive control over the trade in the Indian Ocean that had been won through brute force. The holders of the office continued the practice of plunder, arson, violence, bombardment, and the burning down of cities along the coast that did not acknowledge the monopoly of the Portuguese. The wealth of the East was intoxicating. Portuguese viceroys brought back huge personal wealth, as did other officers.[132] Despite the first-mover advantage, the Portuguese—lacking the territorial size and human resources necessary to sustain a large empire—could not hold onto their possessions. Their European competitors soon emerged to share in the intoxicating wealth of the markets surrounding the Indian Ocean.[133] The increasingly corrupt Portuguese Empire could not maintain its monopoly of trade in the Indian Ocean.

The Portuguese managed to destroy the freedom of the seas in a short period, ushering in a culture of competition and mistrust. Along with the culture came Portugal's European competitors.

Other European countries were jealous of the benefits drawn by Portugal's monopoly in the spice trade and by the bullions flowing into Spain from the American continent: the 'New World'. Europeans had to pay heavy prices for the spices brought from the Indian Ocean. The Dutch, French, and English wished to break into that monopoly.

The Dutch were the first to challenge the Portuguese monopoly. They were heavily taxed and their commercial interests were severely affected by the monopolies of both the Portuguese and the Spanish.[134] They had some experience

[130] Anand (n 62) 54–60.
[131] ibid 52.
[132] Hart (n 113) 256–58.
[133] Anand (n 62) 64–67.
[134] ibid 72–74.

with the spice trade in the East as financiers supplying money for the purchase of pepper and other spices, and they played a large part in distributing the products brought by the Portuguese to the rest of Europe.[135]

While the sea routes and other details of the trade were zealously guarded by the Portuguese, one adventurous Dutchman, Jan Huyghen von Linschoten, managed to travel with the Portuguese. He published their trading secrets, ushering the Dutch into the game. Soon, expeditions were undertaken. The Dutch East India Company was established in 1602 with a complete monopoly of trade in the East, including the right to establish colonies, make peace or war, raise whatever funds were necessary, and construct military establishments. To prevent confrontation, the first expedition avoided the Indian Ocean and landed in Java, expanding the Dutch share in the market. The Dutch soon began increasing their presence in the Indian Ocean, gaining control over Ceylon. They also began inducing local rulers to enter into exclusive agreements with them, excluding the Portuguese. The local rulers relented, being tired of the Portuguese monopoly and seeing the Dutch as saviours, but they were soon to realize that the Dutch were no different.[136]

The Dutch East India Company entered into an agreement with Zamorin to expel the Portuguese.[137] In 1612, the kingdom of Kandy in Ceylon granted the Dutch exclusive rights to trade in cinnamon and permission to build a fort.[138] In 1766, the Dutch forced Kandy to grant an exclusive right of trade in all goods; in addition, foreigners entering the land would be handed over to the Dutch.[139] Several such treaties were concluded with rulers in Asia.[140] These treaties steadily eliminated all international relations among the Asian states, which very soon lost their sovereignty and independence too. The treaties were contrary to international law as it then existed, heralding an era of power politics in the region.[141] The rulers were reluctant but were forced to enter into the treaties, including with regard to smuggling and illegal trafficking undertaken in their ports by the European powers.[142]

135 Toussaint (n 49) 118–19.

136 Anand (n 62) 76–77.

137 Charles H Alexandrowicz, 'The Discriminatory Clause in South Asian Treaties in the Seventeenth and Eighteenth Centuries' (1957) 6 Indian Year Book of International Affairs 126, 129.

138 William Milburn, *Oriental Commerce; Containing a Geographical Description of the Principal Places in the East Indies, China, and Japan*, vol 1 (Black, Parry, & Co 1813) 369.

139 Alexandrowicz, 'The Discriminatory Clause' (n 137) 132–39.

140 See Alexandrowicz, *An Introduction* (n 17) 43.

141 Charles H Alexandrowicz, 'A Treatise by J. H. G. Justi on Asian Government' (1961) 9–10 Indian Year Book of International Affairs 136–42, 137.

142 GJ Resink, *Indonesia's History Between the Myths: Essays in Legal History and Historical Theory* (W van Hoeve 1968) 46–47.

By 1663, within 16 years of entry into the Indian Ocean, the Dutch had gained control over important ports. They would indulge in burning plantations to artificially inflate prices and increase their profits.[143] The Dutch East India Company maintained its dominance from 1639 to 1693, excluding the British from Java. To avoid any direct confrontation with the Dutch, the British focused their attention on India, which turned out to be a good bet after all.

The Dutch expanded rapidly, but that pace of territorial conquest based on military expeditions weakened them financially, making them unable to hold onto their possessions—like the Portuguese, from whom they had snatched control. The French established a company in 1604 but did not seriously engage in trade until 1664, with their first trading post opened in Surat in 1668, another in Pondicherry in 1672, and one in the small town of Chandernagore in 1673. The Danish reached Coromandel in 1616 and established a factory with the permission of the King of Tanjore. After making initial profits, they withdrew due to ongoing battles in Europe. Their situation was observed as 'poor whites' living by their wits and even by piracy.[144] The British, although late entrants to the race, were making advents in technology and the shipping industry.[145]

The Maldives is a textbook case of the chain of succession of colonization among the dominant European powers. In 1558, the Portuguese had established themselves in the Maldives, which they administered from Goa on India's west coast. However, a few years later, a revolt by the people of the Maldives drove the Portuguese away.[146] In the mid-seventeenth century, the Dutch replaced the Portuguese as the dominant power in Ceylon and established hegemony over the Maldives without involving themselves directly in local matters.[147] The British expelled the Dutch from Ceylon in 1796 and included the Maldives as a British-protected area.[148]

England's quest for the spice trade began in 1527 with the extensive piratical activities of Sir Francis Drake, who would make profits by capturing Portuguese ships laden with spices.[149] Later, in 1615, Sir Thomas Roe sought permission from the Mughals to do 'quiet trade'.[150] After winning the Napoleonic Wars in Europe, and armed with the products of the Industrial Revolution, Britain

143 Anand (n 62) 91–92.
144 Toussaint (n 49) 124–25.
145 ibid 136–37.
146 Ryavec (n 54) 258.
147 ibid 259.
148 ibid.
149 Anand (n 62) 94–95.
150 Villiers (n 14) 158.

was a force in the Indian Ocean that no European competitor could match.[151] Soon, the British outmanoeuvred other Europeans and with brute force ultimately won India, the 'jewel' of the British Crown.

Until the arrival of Europeans, the Indian Ocean was never a theatre of serious naval conflicts except for the three instances discussed above. But this period saw unprecedented naval conflicts, first between the Europeans and the local rulers and then between the Europeans themselves to establish their supremacy over the waters of the Indian Ocean and all the important trading posts. In the process, they destroyed freedom in trade and navigation in the Indian Ocean. Before the Europeans arrived, even if there were naval conflicts, they never interfered with freedom of navigation, disturbed traders, or created monopolies—either state-sponsored or otherwise. Naval warfare was not acknowledged as a science, since the seas were to be used primarily for peaceful purposes.[152] For example, the Gujrathis were dominant traders and well known for their peace-loving character. According to Tomé Pires, they 'held that they must never kill anyone, nor must they have an armed man in their company. If they were captured and [their captors] wanted to kill them all, they did not resist'. But, over time, they began to 'have many men-at-arms to defend their ships'.[153]

There was all-round confusion and anarchy in the Indian Ocean, just like in Europe. There was 'only one rule of law at the sea in those days, to destroy one's rivals and make as much money as possible in the shortest possible time'.[154] From the sixteenth to the early nineteenth centuries was a free-for-all of lawless anarchy, with piracy as the norm in the Indian Ocean and no order.[155] Several acts of piracy were conducted by persons of one European nation against another, dubbed privateering: as explained by McFee, 'privateering was merely licensed piracy'.[156]

The Europeans benefited from the liberal traditions of freedom of navigation and trade, with foreign merchants permitted to establish themselves—including the freedom to decide the laws by which they wished to regulate themselves. When the Europeans entered the stage in Asia, the relations 'took place on a footing of equality and the ensuing commercial and political

[151] Anand (n 62) 115–16.
[152] ibid 51.
[153] Tomé Pires, *The Suma Oriental of Tomé Pires: An Account of the East, from the Red Sea to Japan, Written in Malacca and India in 1512–1515*, vol 1 (tr and ed Armando Cortesão, Hakluyt Society 1944) 45.
[154] William McFee, *The Law of the Sea* (JB Lippincott 1950) 13.
[155] Anand (n 62) 111–15.
[156] McFee (n 154) 88.

transactions, far from being in a legal vacuum, were governed by the law of nations as adjusted to local inter-State custom'.[157]

6.3.5 Battle of the books

The appearance of the Portuguese—followed by the Dutch, French, and British—in the Indian Ocean led to the emergence of the discourses on the law of the sea that formed the basis of the contemporary law of the sea. The discourse in Europe was a scramble to gain or retain access to the South Asian market. The South Asian states and the Indian Ocean had a critical impact on the foundations of the law of the sea as developed in Europe. Europeans writing on these issues were aware of the rules and practices in relation to the seas existing in Asia, particularly in South Asia.[158] Franciscus Seraphin de Freitas, for example, relied upon the Indian practice of fishing and security enforcement to argue an exclusive title over the territorial sea. He described this practice as the 'customary law of the Indian Ocean'.[159] These writings did not translate into European law for almost two centuries, since they 'were not immediately accepted or acceptable to the European states who were too busy vying with each other to grab as much of the Asian spice trade as they could to the exclusion of others'.[160] It was only in the late eighteenth century, with the convergence of European interests, that they all geared to propound some of the ideas that formed the basis of the contemporary law of the sea (discussed in Section 6.4). The activities in the Indian Ocean were the reason for the evolution of the law among Europeans. But these ideas developed through conflict—rightly described as the 'battle of the books'.[161]

While naval and political action was taking place in the Indian Ocean and changing the culture and legal regime regulating the law of the sea in South Asia, the claims of the European countries were being strengthened by scholars as hired guns—of which Grotius's *Mare Liberum* was an outcome.[162] To challenge the Portuguese claim to a monopoly on trade in the Indian Ocean, Grotius argued that the Portuguese had obtained the right to trade from the states in the Indian Ocean, since those territories were not *res nullius* and the

[157] Alexandrowicz, *An Introduction* (n 17) 224.
[158] Anand (n 62) 5.
[159] Alexandrowicz, *An Introduction* (n 17) 67–71.
[160] Anand (n 62) 5–6.
[161] ibid 102–04.
[162] ibid 77–89.

people there were not 'chattels of the Portuguese, but are free men'.[163] He relied upon the Roman law and the fact that the Romans had extensive trade with India. This trade was happening under the laws then existing in the Indian Ocean, emanating from the *Arthashastra* and local customs and practices.[164] Ridiculing the Portuguese claims to a monopoly as false, Grotius referred to the freedom of navigation practised for time immemorial by the Roman Empire in the Indian Ocean and the Asian states. He relied on the practice of Indian states and of Ceylon to support his contentions.[165] He also referred to the unobstructed fishing and navigation conducted by the Asian states.[166] Any exclusivity obtained by Portugal through coercion of the Asian and other states was illegal, since 'coercion is contrary to the law of nature and obnoxious to all mankind, it cannot establish a right'.[167]

After establishing themselves in the Indian Ocean, the Dutch, including Grotius as a practitioner, began arguing for a monopoly and rejecting *mare liberum*.[168] Support for monopolistic rights over the seas was found in the idea of *mare clausum*. The battle of the books that went on in Europe was between *Mare Liberum* by Grotius and *Mare Clausum* by the British jurist John Selden (who was specifically commissioned by King Charles, to whom the book was dedicated), an outcome of the ultimate objective of controlling the trade in the Indian Ocean.[169] States pleading for *mare liberum* in Europe were arguing for *mare clausum* in the Indian Ocean, and vice versa.[170] The Dutch used the argument of *mare liberum* to break the Portuguese monopoly in the Indian Ocean. But soon after establishing themselves, they started arguing *mare clausum* to exclude other Europeans. Those who followed the Dutch—the English and the French—used the same pattern to suit their own self-interests. To enforce a monopoly, each of these European powers began entering into treaties providing exclusive rights to rulers in the Indian subcontinent. These were obtained through force or deceit. Thus, the Indian subcontinent was 'covered by a network of monopolies and discriminatory arrangements, a situation which remained in a state of flux until it resulted in a more rigid distribution of possessions'.[171]

[163] Hugo Grotius, *The Freedom of the Seas or The Right Which Belongs to the Dutch to Take Part in the East Indian Trade* (tr Ralph van Deman Magoffin, OUP 1916) 20.
[164] Anand (n 62) 82–83.
[165] Grotius (n 163) 40–41.
[166] ibid 60.
[167] ibid 68.
[168] Anand (n 62) 89–92, 95–99.
[169] ibid 102–07.
[170] ibid 110.
[171] Alexandrowicz, 'The Discriminatory Clause' (n 137) 126, 127.

The second phase lasted for only a few centuries, but it destroyed the culture of freedom of navigation, fair competition, and peace among the Indians that had existed for several centuries. It also shaped the view of Asian states towards the international legal order created essentially to protect European self-interests. But, as the control over the Indian Ocean consolidated with the British to the exclusion of other Europeans, there was a sudden shift in the approach of the Europeans aimed at consolidating colonization and taking as large a share as possible of the booty by standing behind the British.

6.4 Third phase: colonization and the consolidation of the law of the sea

The third phase saw the firm establishment and consolidation of the colonial power in South Asia. By the first half of the nineteenth century, the British had suppressed the whole of India, and India was not merely its possession but 'a country "owned" by the British people and governed primarily in their interests'.[172] The British used India as a base to consolidate and expand their power in the region to the exclusion of all other European states—red-faced they were, but they had no alternative in light of the British supremacy in the region.[173]

The British conquest of India was a unique event in the history of both Europe and India. It led to remarkable economic growth in Europe and particularly in England. The winner in the race was evident and the rest of the European states decided to draw benefits from the situation rather than continuing to squabble. And, considering that the British Empire strongly defended India with its naval power, other states were keen to draw as much benefit as they could by standing behind and acknowledging British supremacy.

From being sources of finished products, the South Asian states were systematically converted into sources of raw material and then into markets for European finished products, produced in excess due to the industrial revolution. In the process, the domestic industries and commerce in the colonies were systematically destroyed by the British to secure two-way profits.[174]

Once England had established itself as the foremost power, most of its practices translated into those of Europe to form the basis of the modern law of

[172] Panikkar, *Asia and Western Dominance* (n 102) 144.
[173] Anand (n 62) 125.
[174] ibid 124–29.

the sea. While the European states had originally rejected the practices of the Asian states, they soon started turning to some of those principles—albeit for proffering their collective interests, essentially aimed at protecting their colonies abroad and their own commercial interests.[175]

This period saw the resurgence of *mare liberum* and the consolidation of the modern law of the sea, geared largely to consolidating the colonial possessions—the most prominent of which were in South Asia. Although it had argued for *mare clausum* for 200 years, England realized that it could make more profits through free trade since it controlled the important ports. There was a turn to freedom of the seas, with Grotius—the 'villain' who for 200 years had been much abused by the British—becoming a great hero and a 'father' of international law for his self-disowned *mare liberum*. As commented by Christian Meurer, Grotius was welcomed as a 'knight whose kiss awakened' the freedom of the seas, which until modern times 'slumbered the sleep of the Sleeping Beauty'.[176] Of course, Selden was discarded by his own compatriots, since his ideas were not useful for the expanding empire in South Asia.[177] Suddenly, it became a divine right to trade freely and unnatural for a government to restrain free trade.[178]

It was on this basis that the modern law of the sea was developed, and freedom of navigation was proposed as a novel creation based exclusively on the practice of European states to the complete exclusion of South Asian states. The South Asian states were characterized as not 'civilized enough' to be a part of the international society.[179] By becoming masters, the British excluded the South Asian states from the process of making international law for the ensuing century, dubbing 'uncivilized' those whose very practice was used by European scholars to create the law of the sea. The non-recognition of Asian states during this period was used as a tool to treat South Asian states and their people as chattel. They were to be converted to the word of God and trained to be good subservient slaves so that they could be treated as civilized.[180] For centuries, foreign merchants had been allowed to be regulated by their own domestic laws, even during trading, but all were forced to follow colonial laws.[181]

[175] ibid 159.
[176] Christian Meurer, *The Program of the Freedom of the Sea: A Political Study in International Law* (tr Leo J Frachtenberg, Government Printing Office 1919) 7.
[177] Anand (n 62) 130–31.
[178] Panikkar, *Asia and Western Dominance* (n 102) 123.
[179] Alexandrowicz, *An Introduction* (n 17) 2.
[180] Anand (n 62) 135–36.
[181] Alexandrowicz, *An Introduction* (n 17) 99.

The law at this time continued to be dominated by the interests of the maritime powers of Europe, with little or no say for the Asian states. Freedom of the seas was seen as a laissez-faire state of the law, where fishing was possible even close to the shores of other states—especially since Europe and the United States had the technology, especially large trawlers, to do so.[182] The practice of specially affected states became an important factor in determining the existence of customary international law and continues to be so today.[183] All States other then European states and the United States were excluded from having and representing maritime interests had the obvious implication that the practice of the powerful Western States became the basis of the modern law of the sea.

As the modern law of the sea developed, it continued to be bedevilled by the conflicting interests of the Western states. The goal of the law, to the extent agreed to by those states, was geared towards the protection of their economic, political, strategic, and military interests.[184] The South Asian states traditionally exercised jurisdiction for security and other interests over parts of the sea but did not claim title over it. However, in Europe, due to incessant wars, the practice of claiming territorial seas emerged. There continued to be disagreement over the distance of the territorial sea, depending on the interests involved. States with strong navies insisted on a narrower belt and other states on a broader region. Likewise, there was the question of the extent of the exercise of jurisdiction over the exclusive economic zone, the exclusive fisheries zone, and the right of innocent passage through the territorial sea. Some of these controversial issues were settled later, as discussed below.[185]

The South Asian states had no influence on the law of the sea at all during this phase, since they had lost whatever little control they had over the sea in

[182] Anand (n 62) 152–53.

[183] The concept of 'specially affected' states, as developed as part of the law of the sea by colonial powers, continues to be considered. See International Law Commission, *Draft Conclusions on Identification of Customary International Law, With Commentaries*, UN Doc A/73/10 (2018) 136–37; International Law Commission, *Second Report on Identification of Customary International Law, by Sir Michael Wood, Special Rapporteur*, UN Doc A/CN.4/672 (22 May 2014) 186–88; International Law Commission, *Third Report on Identification of Customary International Law, by Sir Michael Wood, Special Rapporteur*, UN Doc A/CN.4/682 (27 March 2015) 112; International Law Commission, *Fifth Report on Identification of Customary International Law, by Sir Michael Wood, Special Rapporteur*, UN Doc A/CN.4/717 (14 March 2018) 28, 31–32, 34; *North Sea Continental Shelf (Federal Republic of Germany v Denmark) (Judgment)* [1969] ICJ Rep 3, 43, 74; Kevin J Heller, 'Specially-Affected States and the Formation of Custom' (2018) 112 American Journal of International Law 191; Shelly Aviv Yeini, 'The Specially-Affecting States Doctrine' (2018) 112 American Journal of International Law 244; *Fisheries Jurisdiction (United Kingdom v Iceland)* [1974] ICJ Rep 90 (Judge De Castro); Michael Wood, 'The Evolution and Identification of the Customary International Law of Armed Conflict' (2021) 51 Vanderbilt Law Review 727.

[184] Anand (n 62) 135–53.

[185] ibid 141–51.

the second phase, discussed above, and had even lost their sovereignty and freedom as a constituent of the international community.

6.5 Fourth phase: decolonization and the foundations of the 'new' law of the sea

The world that emerged after 1945 was entirely different, not just in terms of the number of states but also in terms of its culture and priorities. The newly independent states wished to improve their lot and undo historic wrongs and sufferings.[186] This was the age of Global South and Third World solidarity, where interests converged and there was a readiness to accommodate each other's concerns to address the injustices and inequality caused by colonization. The Asian and African states collaborated with the disgruntled Latin American states to form the Third World.[187] The South Asian states, with India predominant due to its size and political power, collaborated with other Asian, African, and Latin American states and played an active role in the development and formulation of modern maritime law.[188]

Protecting sovereignty by warding off future colonization in both direct and indirect forms was a priority. Maritime borders and areas were to be kept secure from the potential use of force by the militarily advanced Western states. Another important concern was the threat posed by scientific advancements in the West. The South Asian states and the Third World generally were left behind in scientific progress, due to colonization and the resulting rampant drain on their resources to benefit the Western states. With large fishing vessels capable of undertaking long-range sea voyages, there was a threat of losing the essential marine resources that fed coastal populations in the South Asian states that were impoverished by colonization. In addition, the hydrocarbons near their shores could be taken away by the Western states with advanced marine technology. All these resources were indispensable for much-needed growth and development.[189]

The law of the sea based on unrestricted exploitation of the sea and its resources, as developed and practised by European states in their own interests, was threatening to the Third World. Therefore, the law of the sea made in the

[186] ibid 161.
[187] ibid 161–62.
[188] ibid 6.
[189] ibid 162–63.

third phase was outdated and needed to be replaced with a 'new' law of the sea.[190]

At the first UN Conference on the Law of the Sea, 54 of the 86 participating states were newly independent. While all supported freedom of navigation, they were sceptical towards the expansive activities sought to be undertaken as part of freedom of navigation in its abstract form. Such an interpretation of freedom of the seas preserved the privileged position of the developed states.[191] They 'alone . . . benefitted from the freedom of the high seas; they were laying claim to hegemony of the high seas'.[192]

The major area of contention was the width of the territorial sea. The Western states insisted on a narrow belt of territorial sea, while the South Asian states sought larger areas to ward off potential security and economic threats. The Western states were reluctant to agree to anything more than 3 nautical miles. The representative of the United States argued that a territorial sea greater than 6 nautical miles would profoundly affect US acceptance of an agreement since that would 'threaten the security of the United States by reducing the efficiency of its naval and air power, and by subjecting it to the increased risk of surprise attack'.[193] The proposal for a 6-nautical-mile limit was defeated with the support of Asian, African, and Latin American states.[194] Despite a numerical majority, the powerful nations could not reach an agreement on the breadth of the territorial sea and the unhindered right to fish on the high seas at the first conference.[195]

The Second Conference on the Law of the Sea failed due to the increased number of developing states and their unwillingness to forgo their security concerns and resources due to the limits sought to be placed on the territorial sea by the Western maritime powers. The Western states continued to insist on their privileges. This was all to change at the Third Conference, where the law of the sea underwent major transformations.[196]

The Third UN Conference on the Law of the Sea was a major success for the solidarity of the Third World. Those states succeeded in achieving most of their demands and largely moulded the law of the sea in light of their desires and

[190] ibid 6.

[191] See statement of the Representative of Mexico: UN Conference on the Law of the Sea (UNCLOS I), 20th plen mtg, UN Doc A/CONF.13/C.1/SR.16-20 (19 March 1958) 64.

[192] See statement of the Representative of Iran: UNCLOS I, 20th plen mtg, UN Doc A/CONF.13/C.1/SR.16-20 (19 March 1958) 65.

[193] See statement of the Representative of the United States: UNCLOS I, 10th plen mtg, UN Doc A/CONF.13/C.1/SR.61-66 (11 March 1958) 25.

[194] Anand (n 62) 176–80.

[195] ibid 184–85.

[196] ibid 185–88.

expectations, which were reflected in UNCLOS. The Third World—despite its political, cultural, social, religious, and historic differences—came together to form the Group of 77 (G-77). South Asian states urged the need to change the legal regime established by the 1958 Conventions[197] and, through UNCLOS, aimed to create the 'new law of the sea'.[198]

The most important issue that had remained unresolved until settled by UNCLOS was the breadth of the territorial sea. Former colonizing Western powers continued to insist on a narrow belt of 3 nautical miles as the territorial sea. The South Asian states and other newly independent states were not happy with that proposal. Afghanistan, despite being a landlocked state, insisted on the importance of determining the extent of the territorial sea.[199] The South Asian states argued that it was important to maintain a balance between freedom of navigation and the need for coastal states to exercise sovereignty to take measures for security and well-being.[200] The 3-nautical-mile territorial sea was not the rule and, even if it had been followed in the practice of the colonizing Western states, it was a relic of the past and had to be changed. Upon achieving their independence, newly independent states had already renounced it, assuming that it was a rule. There were economic grounds for an area stretching anywhere between 3 and 12 nautical miles.[201] Many smaller states considered 12 nautical miles necessary for protecting their essential interests, including security interests. Thus, many states did not favour the 3-nautical-mile territorial sea.[202] The South Asian states joined the Mexican proposal to extend the territorial sea to 12 nautical miles. It was time to achieve what the League of Nations Codification Conference held at the Hague in 1930 and the first and second Law of the Sea Conferences had failed to achieve.[203] The South Asian and G-77 states succeeded in stretching the territorial sea to 12 nautical miles,[204] with an additional contiguous zone of 12 nautical miles.[205]

[197] See statements by Mr Cheema (Pakistan) and Mr Fraser (India): Third UN Conference on the Law of the Sea (UNCLOS III), 18th plen mtg, UN Doc A/CONF.62/C.2/SR.18 (29 July 1974) 153 para 66; UNCLOS III, 14th plen mtg, UN Doc A/CONF.62/C.2/SR.14 (23 July 1974) 141 para 91.

[198] See statement by Mr Jagota (India): UNCLOS III, 4th Sess, 59th plen mtg, UN Doc A/CONF.62/SR.59 (5 April 1976) 17–18 paras 42–45.

[199] See statement by Mr Tabibi (Afghanistan): UNCLOS I, 8th plen mtg, UN Doc A/CONF.62/C.1/SR.8 (7 March 1958) 18 para 14.

[200] See statement by Mr Bhutto (Pakistan): UNCLOS I, 17th plen mtg, UN Doc A/CONF.62/C.1/SR.17 (17 March 1958) 50 para 3.

[201] ibid 50 para 9.

[202] See statement by Mr Sen (India): UNCLOS I, 39th plen mtg, UN Doc A/CONF.62/C.1/SR.39 (9 April 1958) 118 para 3.

[203] See statement by Mr Shaha (Nepal): UNCLOS I, 59th plen mtg, UN Doc A/CONF.62/C.1/SR.59 (21 April 1958) 186 para 57.

[204] UNCLOS art 3.

[205] UNCLOS art 33.

They also joined the proposal for exclusive sovereignty over the seabed under and the airspace above the territorial sea.[206] The coastal states were to have exclusive control over the territorial sea subject to an innocent passage,[207] and the innocent passage would not be arbitrarily suspended.[208] The unlimited right of suspension of freedom of navigation in the territorial sea by the United Kingdom was objected. It was proposed and accepted that there had to be an objective criterion, based on which the suspension could take place. The coastal states could not act arbitrarily and with impunity.[209] International straits should be free to use but without compromising the security of the coastal state, based on a distinction between merchant vessels and warships.[210]

Concerns about the nature of the right of freedom of fishing were raised by the South Asian states due to the fear of Western states fishing off their coasts. The South Asian states supported the proposal that coastal states should have the right to protect and conserve fisheries adjacent to their coasts[211] without any restrictions on fishing.[212] As part of conservation, Nepal invoked its tradition of Buddha, peace, and compassion to conduct activities in the sea without causing harm to marine life, especially the cruelty involved in the killing of whales and the need to stop it. India also supported this suggestion.[213]

It was insisted that the definition of the continental shelf be based on geographical criteria.[214] The mere exploitability test, contained in Article 1 of the 1958 Convention on the Continental Shelf,[215] was inappropriate and there had to be a limit on the extent of claims or else there would be disputes between states with potentially overlapping claims.[216] The right to exploit the

[206] See statement by Mr Sikri (India): UNCLOS I, 50th plen mtg, UN Doc A/CONF.62/C.1/SR.50 (16 April 1958) 143 para 15; UNCLOS art 2.

[207] See statements by Mr Jagota (India) and Mr Rashid (Bangladesh): UNCLOS III, 2nd plen mtg, UN Doc A/CONF.62/C.2/SR.2 (9 July 1974) 98 para 6; UNCLOS III, 5th plen mtg, UN Doc A/CONF.62/C.2/SR.5 (16 July 1974) 109 para 9; UNCLOS art 17.

[208] See statement by Mr Kharas (Pakistan): UNCLOS III, 4th plen mtg, UN Doc A/CONF.62/C.2/SR.4 (16 July 1974) 105 para 21; UNCLOS art 25.

[209] See statement by Mr Sikri (India): UNCLOS I, 33rd plen mtg, UN Doc A/CONF.62/C.1/SR.33 (1 April 1958) 95 para 2.

[210] See statements by Mr De Alwis (Sri Lanka) and Mr Fraser (India): UNCLOS III, 11th plen mtg, UN Doc A/CONF.62/C.2/SR.11 (22 July 1975) 126 para 27; UNCLOS III, 14th plen mtg, UN Doc A/CONF.62/C.2/SR.14 (23 July 1974) 141 para 91.

[211] See statement by Mr Panikkar (India): UNCLOS I, 5th plen mtg, UN Doc A/CONF.62/C.3/SR.5 (10 March 1958) 4 para 12.

[212] See statement by Mr Qureshi (Pakistan): UNCLOS I, 11th plen mtg, UN Doc A/CONF.62/C.3/SR.11 (19 March 1958) 26 para 1.

[213] See statements by Mr Shaha (Nepal) and Mr Narayanan (India): UNCLOS I, 35th plen mtg, UN Doc A/CONF.62/C.3/SR.35 (16 April 1958) 99 paras 4, 5.

[214] See statement by Mr Chowdhary (Bangladesh): UNCLOS III, 16th plen mtg, UN Doc A/CONF.62/C.2/SR.16 (26 July 1974) 144 para 13.

[215] Convention on the Continental Shelf, 29 April 1958, 499 UNTS 311.

[216] See statement by Mr Samad (Pakistan): UNCLOS I, 10th plen mtg, UN Doc A/CONF.62/C.4/SR.10 (14 March 1958) 19 para 1.

continental shelf should not be based on effective occupation and control.[217] Also, the resources in the exclusive economic zone of 200 nautical miles were necessary for economic progress.[218]

Emphasis was laid on the need for the use of marine resources to satisfy developmental needs.[219] The South Asian states, except the landlocked states, insisted on a distance criterion for the continental shelf. Major states, including India, agreed to share their resources in those areas with their less advantaged landlocked neighbours, such as Afghanistan, Bhutan, and Nepal, to find a 'fair and durable framework'.[220]

The extension of the continental margin beyond 200 nautical miles and the sharing of the gains with the International Seabed Authority in the communal interest was an idea supported by the South Asian states.[221] The use of resources in what now constitutes an 'Area' under UNCLOS was to be reserved as a 'common heritage of mankind'.[222] It was elaborated that 'common heritage' meant equitable distribution of the benefits derived from the resources, and not just for the benefit of a select few states.[223] The Area had to be used on a fair and equitable basis. The G-77 proposed a mechanism to administer the Area and was supported by the South Asian states.[224] Thus, an international regime was created for administering the seabed to ensure fair and equitable use for all.[225] Fears were expressed that exploitation of polymetallic nodules may be used by the Western states to bring down the prices of land minerals, which were a major source of livelihood and development for the newly independent developing states. It was thought necessary for the seabed authority to control prices.[226]

[217] See statement by Mr Jhirad (India): UNCLOS I, 8th plen mtg, UN Doc A/CONF.62/C.4/SR.8 (12 March 1958) 12 para 5.

[218] See statement by Mr Rashid (Bangladesh): UNCLOS III, 2nd Sess, 27th plen mtg, UN Doc A/CONF.62/SR.27 (3 July 1974) 101–02 paras 47–62.

[219] See statement by Mr Gokhale (India): UNCLOS III, 2nd Sess, 27th plen mtg, UN Doc A/CONF.62/SR.27 (3 July 1974) 95–97 paras 2–10.

[220] ibid.

[221] ibid.

[222] See statement by Mr Rana (Nepal): UNCLOS III, 6th plen mtg, UN Doc A/CONF.62/C.1/SR.6 (16 July 1974) 24 para 2.

[223] See statement by Mr Kharas (Pakistan): UNCLOS III, 5th plen mtg, UN Doc A/CONF.62/C.3/SR.5 (17 July 1974) 324 para 15.

[224] See statement by Mr Pinto (Sri Lanka): UNCLOS III, 9th plen mtg, UN Doc A/CONF.62/C.1/SR.9 (30 July 1974) 44 para 2.

[225] See statements by Mr Gokhale (India), Mr Malikyar (Afghanistan), Mr Jagota (India), and Mr Rahman (Bangladesh): UNCLOS III, 2nd Sess, 27th plen mtg, UN Doc A/CONF.62/SR.27 (3 July 1974) 95–97 paras 2–10; UNCLOS III, 2nd Sess, 33rd plen mtg, UN Doc A/CONF.62/SR.33 (9 July 1974) 113 paras 1–12; UNCLOS III, 4th Sess, 59th plen mtg, UN Doc A/CONF.62/SR.59 (5 April 1976) 17–18 paras 42–45; UNCLOS III, 11th Sess, 162nd plen mtg, UN Doc A/CONF.62/SR.162 (31 March 1982) 44–45 paras 21–28; UNCLOS arts 136–155, annex III.

[226] See statement by Mr Vardhan (India): UNCLOS III, 6th plen mtg, UN Doc A/CONF.62/C.1/SR.6 (16 July 1974) 334 para 88.

Protection of the maritime environment was equally important for the South Asian states, due to their limited resources and the fear that their coasts would be polluted by vessels from more advanced seafaring states.[227]

The South Asian states strongly supported the conduct of marine scientific research on the high seas without arbitrary restrictions.[228] The outcome of the research was not to be restricted to industrial use but shared broadly, accompanied by the transfer of technology.[229] However, in areas within the jurisdiction of coastal states, research had to be conducted with prior authorization and, wherever possible, the participation of the coastal state.[230] The coastal state may restrict the dissemination of the outcome of the scientific research in the national interest and in the public interest.[231]

Regarding the peaceful use of the seas, India proposed an amendment regarding the right of the coastal states to prevent the continental shelf from being used to build military bases or installations.[232] The construction of military bases or installations on the continental shelf was illegal. In addition to interfering with the recognized right of the coastal state to explore and exploit the natural resources of its continental shelf, such construction constituted a violation of the freedom of the high seas and Article 2(4) of the UN Charter.[233] Sri Lanka supported this proposal.[234] India regarded the passage of warships through the territorial sea as a courtesy and not a right: it had a right to refuse such passage.[235] There should be external signs distinguishing state-owned

[227] See statement by Mr Kharas (Pakistan): UNCLOS III, 2nd Sess, 35th plen mtg, UN Doc A/CONF.62/SR.35 (10 July 1974) 146 para 46.

[228] See statements by Mr Rashid (Bangladesh), Mr Kharas (Pakistan), Mr Kakodkar (India), Mr Vandergert (Sri Lanka), and Mr Vandergert (Sri Lanka): UNCLOS, 3rd plen mtg, UN Doc A/CONF.62/C.3/SR.3 (17 July 1974) 315 para 52; UNCLOS III, 16th plen mtg, UN Doc A/CONF.62/C.3/SR.16 (23 August 1974) 377 para 15; UNCLOS III, 9th plen mtg, UN Doc A/CONF.62/C.3/SR.9 (19 July 1974) 352 para 61; UNCLOS III, 7th plen mtg, UN Doc A/CONF.62/C.3/SR.7 (18 July 1974) 336 para 8.

[229] See statement by Mr Vandergert (Sri Lanka): UNCLOS III, 7th plen mtg, UN Doc A/CONF.62/C.3/SR.7 (18 July 1974) 336 para 11.

[230] See statements by Mr Rashid (Bangladesh), Mr Kakodkar (India), and Mr Vandergert (Sri Lanka): UNCLOS III, 3rd plen mtg, UN Doc A/CONF.62/C.3/SR.3 (17 July 1974) 315 para 52; UNCLOS III, 9th plen mtg, UN Doc A/CONF.62/C.3/SR.9 (19 July 1974) 352 para 61; UNCLOS III, 7th plen mtg, UN Doc A/CONF.62/C.3/SR.7 (18 July 1974) 336 para 8.

[231] See statements by Mr Rashid (Bangladesh), Mr Kakodkar (India), and Mr Vandergert (Sri Lanka): UNCLOS III, 4th plen mtg, UN Doc A/CONF.62/C.2/SR.4 (15 July 1974) 315 para 50; UNCLOS III, 6th plen mtg, UN Doc A/CONF.62/C.2/SR.6 (17 July 1974) 334 para 88; UNCLOS III, 7th plen mtg, UN Doc A/CONF.62/C.2/SR.7 (18 July 1974) 336 para 8.

[232] See statement by Mr Jhirad (India): UNCLOS I, 28th plen mtg, UN Doc A/CONF.62/C.4/SR.28 (2 April 1958) 83 para 29.

[233] See statement by Mr Jhirad (India): UNCLOS I, 29th plen mtg, UN Doc A/CONF.62/C.4/SR.29 (2 April 1958) 85 para 12.

[234] See statement by Mr Kanakaratne (Ceylon): UNCLOS I, 13th plen mtg, UN Doc A/CONF.62/C.4/SR.13 (3 April 1958) 89 para 23.

[235] See statement by Mr Sikri (India): UNCLOS I, 20th plen mtg, UN Doc A/CONF.13/38 (27 April 1958) 67 para 34.

commercial ships so that they would not be liable to inspection by warships.[236] A distinction should be made between the passage of merchant vessels and that of warships. Sri Lanka was in support of including new regime provisions for warships: (i) warships must observe laws and regulations of the coastal state; (ii) prior notification would be required for the passage of any warship (iii); failure to comply with laws and regulations would necessitate leaving the straits immediately along the designated route; and (iv) where more than one state is involved, those states should cooperate for joint administration.[237]

According to India, it was necessary to lay down provisions prohibiting warships from engaging in any exercises or manoeuvres, using weapons, launching or taking on board any aircraft, and carrying out scientific research.[238]

Since UNCLOS came into force, South Asian states have—both within and outside the Convention framework—lived up to their position in the suppression of piracy through the activities of their defence forces. India took measures through its navy and supported international cooperation to tackle piracy off the Somalian coast, especially after the activities of pirates began taking place further seawards.[239] At the regional level, Sri Lanka, India, and the Maldives signed a trilateral maritime security agreement to strengthen their Maritime Domain Awareness.[240] The Indian Navy has engaged both the Maldives Coast Guard and the Sri Lanka Navy through bilateral naval exercises, regular ship visits, training, the transfer of naval hardware, and the sharing of intelligence.[241] The Pakistan Navy has deployed ships to Combined Task Force 151 to battle the pirates and has been regularly participating in the UN Contact Group on Piracy, which was established following UN Security Council Resolution 1851[242] to coordinate more effectively the response to Somali piracy.[243] For some South Asian states, such as India, it was the long-standing historic ties with Somalia that formed the basis for their willingness to

[236] UNCLOS I, 4th plen mtg, UN Doc A/CONF.13/40 (11 March 1958) 12 para 9.

[237] Statement by Mr De Alwis (Sri Lanka), UNCLOS III, 11th plen mtg, UN Doc A/CONF.62/C.2/SR.11 (16 July 1974) 126 paras 27–30.

[238] See statement by Mr Fraser (India): UNCLOS III, 14th plen mtg, UN Doc A/CONF.62/C.2/SR.14 (23 July 1974) 141 para 94.

[239] UN Security Council, 6473rd mtg, UN Doc S/PV.6473 (25 January 2011) 19–20.

[240] Ministry of External Affairs (India), 'NSA Level Meeting on Trilateral Maritime Security Cooperation Between India, Sri Lanka and Maldives' (6 March 2014) <www.mea.gov.in/outoging-visit-detail.htm?23037/NSA+level+meeting+on+trilateral+Maritime+Security+Cooperation+between+India+Sri+Lanka+and+Maldives> accessed 3 August 2022.

[241] EU-Asia Dialogue, *Maritime Security and Piracy: Common Challenges and Responses from Europe and Asia* (Konrad-Adenauer Stiftung and European Union 2014) 121.

[242] UN Security Council, Resolution 1851, UN Doc S/RES/1851 (16 December 2008).

[243] 'Pakistan Navy Takes Over Command of Multinational Combined Task Force-151' *Navy News* (Pakistan, May 2022) 2.

support and re-establish security in Somalia[244]—including providing humanitarian assistance to alleviate famine and drought, as well as capacity-building to tackle piracy.[245]

6.6 Fifth phase: insight into the future—learning the game of 'interests'

The approach of South Asian states towards the law of the sea and their influence in the creation of UNCLOS was influenced by their experiences in the first three phases. The South Asian states seem to have learnt, more or less, the game of 'interests' that lies at the core of modern international relations. Additionally, as generations pass and direct experiences of colonization start to wither, the approach of South Asian states to the law of the sea seems to be on the brink of another transformation. This change in approach would thus influence the law of the sea as we see it now and the shape it may take in the future. It may be too early to draw any concrete conclusions, but some trends could be traced, especially in light of the negotiations for a treaty on Marine and Biological Resources Beyond National Jurisdiction. Those negotiations are ongoing at the time of writing.

An unmissable trend is the emergence of early signs of fissures in Global South solidarity. While, in theory, all states align themselves with the position of the G-77, in their statements they do not seem to agree.[246] This gives the impression of artificiality in the so-called alignment and solidarity. The record of the meetings of the four sessions of the Intergovernmental Conference on Marine Biodiversity of Areas Beyond National Jurisdiction that have taken place reflects that several South Asian states, including major states such as India, are either not present or, even if present, do not appear to be engaging actively. Bangladesh, Nepal, Sri Lanka, and the Maldives are the only South Asian states that seem to have attended all four sessions, with Sri Lanka appearing to be most active during the negotiations.[247] This is very much in

[244] UN Security Council, 6494th mtg, UN Doc S/PV.6494 (10 March 2011) 18–19.

[245] UN Security Council, 6641th mtg, UN Doc S/PV.6641 (14 September 2011) 15–16.

[246] See, for example, China's position on benefit-sharing and the prioritization of non-monetary benefit: IISD Reporting Services, 'Summary of the First Session of the Intergovernmental Conference on an International Legally Binding Instrument under the UN Convention on the Law of the Sea on the Conservation and Sustainable Use of Marine Biodiversity of Areas Beyond National Jurisdiction: 4–17 September 2018' (2018) 25(179) Earth Negotiations Bulletin 1, 5.

[247] UN General Assembly, 'List of Participants', UN Doc A/CONF.232/2018/INF.3 (28 September 2018); UN General Assembly, 'Final List of Participants', UN Doc A/CONF.232/2019/INF.3/Rev.2 (26 April 2019); UN General Assembly, 'Final List of Participants', UN Doc A/CONF.232/2019/INF/5/

contrast to participation in the Conferences on the Law of the Sea and in activities relating to the suppression of piracy over the years.

An element that stands out in the positions of some South Asian states is the importance of sharing the resources and the benefits from those resources, as the high seas are part of the 'common heritage of mankind'.[248] For example, the representative of Sri Lanka stated, at the fourth session, that 'we need to underscore the principle that the equitable sharing of the resources on the basis of an intelligible rationale for any differentia is a sine qua non'.[249] Bangladesh, on the other hand, appears to be more flexible, seeking to find common ground and pointing out the difficulty, if not the practical impossibility, of the principle of the common heritage of mankind and the principle of the freedom of the high seas, thus 'calling for a hybrid solution'.[250] The landlocked states—such as Afghanistan, Bhutan, and Nepal—may find themselves closer to the position of the Group of Landlocked Developing Countries, maintaining that the benefits and outcomes of these resources should be shared with the landlocked states as well.[251]

There are divergent views about the nature of resources found in the water column above the continental shelf, since those resources straddle into areas beyond national jurisdiction and it is not clear how to categorize them. For example, Bangladesh raised a practical difficulty with nationality claims over marine and biological resources. Under UNCLOS, the consent of the coastal state would be required to use resources in that water column. However, Bangladesh underlined that many organisms living in water float and thus move around, making it difficult—if not impossible—to request the consent of the coastal state.[252] It nevertheless argued that the Marine and Biological Resources Beyond National Jurisdiction instrument should apply to the water column.[253] Mauritius did not take a particular stance on what that water

Rev.1 (23 October 2019); UN General Assembly, 'Final List of Participants', UN Doc A/CONF.232/2022/INF.3 (1 April 2022).

[248] Statement of Sri Lanka on Agenda Item 6: 5.5 Content of Environmental Impact Assessment Reports (1 April 2019) <www.un.org/bbnj/sites/www.un.org.bbnj/files/sri-lanka2-04-01_1202pm.pdf> accessed 3 August 2022; Closing Statement on Behalf of the Group of 77 and China by Pakistan (18 March 2022) <www.un.org/bbnj/sites/www.un.org.bbnj/files/hxbpxickm8rf_en.pdf> accessed 3 August 2022.

[249] Statement of Sri Lanka (n 248) 2; Closing Statement (n 248).

[250] IISD Reporting Services, 'Summary of the First Session' (n 246) 1, 3.

[251] Closing Statement (n 248).

[252] Intervention of Bangladesh on Paragraph 2.1 (4 April 2019) <www.un.org/bbnj/sites/www.un.org.bbnj/files/bangladesh2-4-april-pm.pdf> accessed 3 August 2022.

[253] IISD Reporting Services, 'Summary of the Second Session of the Intergovernmental Conference on an International Legally Binding Instrument under the UN Convention on the Law of the Sea on the Conservation and Sustainable Use of Marine Biodiversity of Areas Beyond National Jurisdiction: 25 March–5 April 2019' (2019) 25(195) Earth Negotiations Bulletin 1, 15.

column should or should not entail, but enquired about the legal status of the area, implicitly stressing the certain importance of those waters for it.[254] India does not seem to have expressed any position on this issue.

Overall, the South Asian states—like many other developing states—do not want to be left aside in the negotiations. They hope to see an outcome of the legally binding instrument that does not solely benefit developed states, with an important research and development capacity, as well as financial, administrative, and technical resources. In its general statement at the first session, India emphasized the importance of respecting existing rights under UNCLOS, as well as the significance of environmental impact assessments for the protection of the marine environment.[255] Moreover, India highlighted the importance of the traceability of samples.[256] With regard to benefit-sharing, India argued that a phased approach is the preferable option for an equitable benefit-sharing. The rights of states under UNCLOS should be protected, including the rights of coastal states.[257] Indeed, 'India called for due regard to the rights and legitimate interests of coastal states'.[258] Bangladesh, Nepal, Pakistan, and Sri Lanka aligned with the least developed countries, insisting that any exploitation of the resources should happen with the consent of the coastal state[259] and the sharing of benefits.[260]

6.7 Conclusion

As I write, the negotiations for a treaty on Marine and Biological Resources Beyond National Jurisdiction continue. The situation will evolve and interests will align. But it certainly does not appear to be the same as during the

254 ibid 3.

255 Statement of India on Environmental Impact Assessment (EIA) (September 2018) <www.un.org/bbnj/sites/www.un.org.bbnj/files/india.pdf> accessed 3 August 2022.

256 IISD Reporting Services, 'Summary of the First Session' (n 246) 4.

257 IISD Reporting Services, 'Summary of the Second Session' (n 253) 5.

258 ibid 6.

259 IISD Reporting Services, 'Summary of the First Session' (n 246) 9; IISD Reporting Services, 'Summary of the Third Session of the Intergovernmental Conference (IGC) on the Conservation and Sustainable Use of Marine Biodiversity of Areas Beyond National Jurisdiction: 19–30 August 2019' (2019) 25(218) Earth Negotiations Bulletin 1, 10, 13 <https://enb.iisd.org/events/3rd-session-intergovernmental-conference-igc-conservation-and-sustainable-use-marine/summary>; Intervention of Bangladesh (n 252).

260 IISD Reporting Services, 'Summary of the Second Session' (n 253) 4; IISD Reporting Services, 'Summary of the Fourth Session of the Intergovernmental Conference on an International Legally Binding Instrument under the UN Convention on the Law of the Sea on the Conservation and Sustainable Use of Marine Biodiversity of Areas Beyond National Jurisdiction: 7–18 March 2022' (2022) 25(225) Earth Negotiations Bulletin 1, 18, 19 <https://enb.iisd.org/marine-biodiversity-beyond-national-jurisdiction-bbnj-igc4-summary>.

negotiations for UNCLOS. Leadership from the states of South Asia, as traditionally provided, is not visible; nor does there appear to be a discernible coherent policy. Or the incoherence may be aimed at protecting self-interests. In any event, the geopolitical alignments may result in several South Asian states, if not all of them, continuing to stick together. It is, therefore, to be seen whether, as a divided force, they will be able to influence the law of the sea with their culture and experience or will themselves come under its influence. If the latter happens, there will be consequences for international law and international relations. It will be worth observing how things evolve at these and other negotiations and whether the South Asian states succeed in consolidating and developing the law of the sea in furtherance of the achievements at the Third UN Conference on the Law of the Sea, or whether those achievements will be undone.

The author thanks Nithin Ramkrishnan, Akshita Saxena, Adhira Menon, Bhavnish Kaur, Margot Donze, and Abeer Tiwari for their excellent research assistance.

7
Africa

Tafadzwa Pasipanodya

7.1 Introduction

It bears emphasis that Africa comprises 54 sovereign states, each with its individual character shaped by its geographic, ethnic, socio-economic, and political particularities. Yet this chapter attempts to identify Africa's cultural influences on the law of the sea. This is not intended to minimize the diversity and fluidity of the continent's culture. It is a recognition that, despite this, many African states do share certain philosophies and experiences that appear to have influenced, and to continue to influence, the law of the sea. As discussed below, these African perspectives have manifested themselves in the declarations, treaties, and votes of African states acting through the Organization of African Unity (OAU), the African Union (AU), and other multilateral entities. They have also been expressed by individual African states and their representatives in a variety of contexts. The analysis of Africa's cultural influences on the law of the sea is an opportunity to understand and celebrate the continent's considerable contributions to the law of the sea.

Following the introduction, this chapter discusses two African philosophies and experiences that are reflected in the practice of African states concerning the law of the sea. The first is the philosophy of ubuntu, or 'moral worth through community', which is evident in traditions across the continent. The second is the colonial experience, which left an indelible imprint on African states and their outlook on international law.

These two facets of African shared culture and experience help explain the position and practice of African states concerning certain aspects of the law of the sea in which African influence is particularly palpable. Four of the most significant of these are addressed in this chapter: deep seabed mining and the common heritage of mankind, the exclusive economic zone (EEZ), the maritime rights of landlocked states, and biodiversity beyond national jurisdiction.

Tafadzwa Pasipanodya, *Africa* In: *Cultural Influences on the Law of the Sea*. Edited by: James Kraska and Hayoun Ryou-Ellison, Oxford University Press. © Tafadzwa Pasipanodya 2025. DOI: 10.1093/9780198944140.003.0007

7.2 Salient philosophy and experience reflected in African positions on the law of the sea

7.2.1 Ubuntu or moral worth through community

In the Southern African languages of Zulu, Xhosa, and Ndebele, 'ubuntu' refers to the concept that an individual's humanity is inextricably connected to the group to which they belong.[1] The philosophy is encapsulated in the saying '*umuntu ngumuntu ngabantu*'—literally, 'a person is a person through other persons' or, more loosely, 'I am what I am because of who we all are'.[2] The philosophy considers that the duty to relate humanely with others is a prerequisite to one's own personhood,[3] placing our connections with other people at the centre of human life.

Ubuntu is referred to as *hunhu* in Shona and as *botha* in Sotho and Tswana. It appears in several other African languages as well.[4] The term became known popularly through two South African Nobel laureates, President Nelson Mandela and Archbishop Desmond Tutu,[5] but concepts similar to ubuntu have significance throughout the continent.[6]

[1] Dorine Eva van Norren, 'The Nexus Between Ubuntu and Global Public Goods: Its Relevance for the Post 2015 Development Agenda' (2014) 1(1) Development Studies Research 255, 256; John S Mbiti, *African Religions and Philosophy* (Doubleday 1970) 141; Steve Paulson, '"I Am Because We Are": The African Philosophy of Ubuntu' (interview with James Ogude, *To the Best of Our Knowledge*, 22 June 2019) <www.ttbook.org/interview/i-am-because-we-are-african-philosophy-ubuntu> accessed 30 October 2022 (further explaining that ubuntu is 'a relational form of personhood': 'As a person, you have a responsibility to the people around you, the plants around you, the animals around you, the ancestors, and by extension to the supreme being.').

[2] Van Norren, 'The Nexus' (n 1) 256, citing JS Mbiti, *African Religions and Philosophy* (2nd edn, Heinemann 1990) 106.

[3] Cristian van Eijk and Timiebi Aganaba, 'Inspired by Africa: A New Approach to Global Space Governance' (2021) 9(1) New Space 2, citing Edwin Etieyibo, 'Ubuntu, Cosmopolitanism, and Distribution of Natural Resources' (2017) 46(1) Philosophical Papers 142, 146; Mogobe B Ramose, *African Philosophy Through Ubuntu* (Mond Books 1999) 75.

[4] Van Norren, 'The Nexus' (n 1) 256.

[5] See, for example, Mandela's preface in Richard Stengel, *Mandela's Way: Fifteen Lessons on Life, Love, and Courage* (Crown 2009), calling ubuntu an African concept that means 'the profound sense that we are human only through the humanity of others; that if we are to accomplish anything in this world, it will in equal measure be due to the work and achievements of others'.

[6] Rowland Cole, 'Africa's Approach to International Law: Aspects of the Political and Economic Denominators' (2012) 18(1) *African Yearbook of International Law Online/Annuaire Africain de droit international* 287, 308; Van Norren, 'The Nexus' (n 1) 257; A Wingo, 'Akan Philosophy of the Person' *Stanford Encyclopedia of Philosophy* (Fall edn, 2008) <http://plato.stanford.edu/archives/ fall2008/entries/akan-person> accessed 30 October 2022; Souleymane Bachir Diagne, 'Individual, Community and Human Rights: A Lesson from Kwasi Wiredu's Philosophy of Personhood' (2009) 101 Transition 8; Josiah AM Cobbah, 'African Values and the Human Rights Debate: An African Perspective' (1987) 9 Human Rights Quarterly 309, 321.

For the Akan people of West Africa, personhood 'is the reward for contributing to the community' and an individual's moral worth stems from common humanity.[7] According to Kwasi Wiredu, in traditional Akan society, the concept of moral worth through common humanity was so important that the Akans came to think of life as mutual aid: *obra ye nnoboa*.[8]

Relatedly, former Ghanaian President Kwame Nkrumah noted that '[t]he traditional face of Africa includes an attitude towards man which can only be described, in its social manifestation, as socialist' and that '[i]n the traditional African society, no sectional interest could be regarded as supreme. . . . The welfare of the people was supreme'.[9]

Former Senegalese President Leopold Sedar Senghor also recalled the concept of moral worth through common humanity in a speech he delivered at the opening of the meeting of African experts to develop the first draft of the African Charter on Human and Peoples' Rights in Dakar, Senegal:[10]

> In Europe, human rights are considered as a body of principles and rules placed in the hands of the individual, as a weapon, thus enabling him to defend himself against the group or entity representing it.
>
> In Africa, the individual and his rights are wrapped in the protection the family and other communities ensure everyone. . . . To live in Africa is to give up being an individual . . . man is to live with others, in peace, in harmony, with the dead and living, with the natural environment and the spirits inhabiting or livening it up.

As Dorine van Norren summarizes, ubuntu, in its various formulations across the continent, is a 'collective ontology stressing intra-community relations. Ancestors and future generations are part of this community, and by extension nature is too (ancestors are identified within the Earth)'.[11]

[7] Van Norren, 'The Nexus' (n 1) 257.

[8] ibid; Kwasi Wiredu, 'The Moral Foundations of an African Culture' in PH Coetzee and APJ Roux (eds), *The African Philosophy Reader* (2nd edn, Routledge 2003) 345; Mogobe B Ramose, *African Philosophy Through Ubuntu* (rev edn, Mond Books 2007) 350. See also Dismas A Masolo, 'Communitarianism: An African Perspective' in Stephen Dawson and Tomoko Iwasawa (eds), *Intercultural Philosophy*, vol 12 of *The Proceedings of the Twentieth World Congress of Philosophy* (Philosophy Documentation Center, Bowling Green State University 2001) 209 ('communitarian theory indigenous to African culture').

[9] Kwame Nkrumah, *Consciencism: Philosophy and Ideology for De-Colonization and Development with Particular Reference to the African Revolution* (NYU Press 2009) 68–69.

[10] Address delivered by Leopold Sedar Senghor, President of the Republic of Senegal (1979) in CH Heyns (ed), *Human Rights Law in Africa* (Martinus Nijhoff 1996).

[11] Dorine E van Norren, 'African Ubuntu and Sustainable Development Goals: Seeking Human Mutual Relations and Service in Development' (2022) 43(12) Third World Quarterly 2791, 2793.

As discussed in Section 7.3, the philosophy of ubuntu is evident in the contributions of African states to the law of the sea.

7.2.2 Colonial experience

For the African states emerging from liberation wars in the 1960s, colonialism was evil.[12] It was a flagrant act of aggression that had resulted in the oppression of African peoples and the pillage of the continent's resources.[13] Not only did international law fail to proscribe the acquisition of African territories, it prescribed the rules and legal norms that supported colonization and legitimized it as a permissible means of establishing military and geopolitical influence.[14] Following the Berlin Conference of 1884 and the resultant Act of 1885 that sanctioned the partition and colonization of Africa, international law allowed European industrial powers to exploit their claimed portions of Africa, according myriad preferential benefits and protections to European states and nationals in their dealings in Africa.

Nasila Rembe explains:[15]

> Traditional international law created a legal framework which made it difficult for the newly independent States to exercize sovereignty over their natural resources. . . . The dominant economic doctrine of laissez faire and the notion of sanctity of property, placed economic activities largely in private hands, with the blessing of both municipal and international law. For example, under common law, inadequate consideration does not render a contract void. International law offered additional safeguards by capitulation agreements, recognition of vested rights and of certain vaguely stated

[12] Nasila S Rembe, *Africa and the International Law of the Sea* (Sijthoff & Noordhoff 1980) 24, 27; Ram Prakash Anand, *New States and International Law* (Vikas Publishing House 1972) 53.

[13] UN Commission on Permanent Sovereignty Over Natural Resources, Third Session, Summary Record of the Thirty-Third Meeting, UN Doc A/AC.97/SR.33 (14 June 2961) 7 (and quoted in Rembe (n 12) 24); Cole (n 6) 291.

[14] Tayo Akintoba, *African States and Contemporary International Law: A Case Study of the 1982 Law of the Sea Convention and the Exclusive Economic Zone* (Martinus Nijhoff 1996) 24.

[15] Rembe (n 12) 13. See also Edwin Egede, *Africa and the Deep Seabed Regime* (Springer 2011) 8; UO Umozurike, 'International Law and Colonialism in Africa: A Critique' (1970) 3(1) Eastern Africa Law Review 47, 81 ('international law developed by Western powers before the 20th century served as a buttress for the colonization of African peoples. It connived at the subordination of African dignity to Western economic interests. It was essentially racialist and therefore contrary to the basic norms of law applicable to all mankind.'); Akintoba (n 14) 28 ('For African states, traditional international law became synonymous with the past world order—imperialism, colonialism, repression, and domination.').

principles of 'minimum' or 'universal' treatment as an internationally accepted standard of justice for the treatment of aliens and their property.

Consequently, African states found that the political independence they had won had not necessarily resulted in economic independence. Foreigners controlled the major means of production, while the extensive economic and political concessions, privileges, and facilities that had been acquired by colonial governments or their charted companies remained in place.[16]

However flawed the international legal order that confronted them might have been, African states chose at independence to adapt it, rather than reject it.[17] Collectively and actively, they participated in the United Nations and other international organizations, advocating for an international law that would redress some of the most debilitating socio-economic effects of colonialism, help them regain control over their natural resources, and prevent similar aggression and exploitation from taking place in the future.[18] As discussed below, this experience also influenced the position of African states concerning the law of the sea.

7.3 Primary African contributions and influences on the law of the sea

Consistent with the prevailing international legal order, the law of the sea in place at the time when most African states gained independence in the 1960s was based on the customs and usages of industrial European states and served their interests.[19] In particular, the prevailing doctrine of *mare liberum*, or freedom of the seas, granted the naval and fishing fleets of the great maritime powers unrestricted access to the sea at the expense of less technologically advanced coastal states.

Much of the existing law of the sea was codified in the four 1958 Geneva Conventions on the Territorial Sea and the Contiguous Zone,[20] the High Seas,[21] the Continental Shelf,[22] and the fishing and conservation of the living

[16] Rembe (n 12) 14–15.
[17] ibid 12.
[18] ibid 11. See Egede (n 15) 2–3, 9.
[19] Rembe (n 12) 8.
[20] Convention on the Territorial Sea and the Contiguous Zone, 29 April 1958, 516 UNTS 205.
[21] Convention on the High Seas, 29 April 1958, 450 UNTS 11.
[22] Convention on the Continental Shelf, 29 April 1958, 499 UNTS 311.

resources of the high seas,[23] products of the first UN Conference on the Law of the Sea (UNCLOS I). The extent to which these international treaties incorporated African perspectives is reflected in the fact that only 6 of the 86 states that participated in UNCLOS I were African.[24]

African concerns with the existing law of the sea became more vocal as additional African states became independent. The Tanzanian delegate to the Third Conference on the Law of the Sea (UNCLOS III), for example, asserted that the doctrine of freedom of the seas had[25]

> ceased to serve the interests of international justice. It had become a catchword and an excuse for a few countries to exploit ruthlessly the resources of the sea, to terrorize the world and to destroy the marine environment. That type of freedom belonged to the old order and had outlived its time.

Senegal went as far as to denounce formally the Convention on the Territorial Sea and the Contiguous Zone and the Convention on Fishing and Conservation of the Living Resources of the High Seas. In a communication to the Secretary General of the United Nations on 9 June 1971, President Senghor sharply criticized a legal regime that reduced the territorial sea to a minimum and thereby permitted wealthy industrialized states with technologically advanced vessels and equipment to exploit, almost exclusively, the resources off the coast of Senegal and other West African states:[26]

> The situation of the coastal States of West Africa is inextricable, because today they do not yet have the vessels and equipment necessary to carry out large-scale catches, as do the fishermen of the industrialized countries, and tomorrow, when they have these vessels and equipment, the fishing zones will have been exhausted by the activities of the industrialized countries. . . . The rich, industrialized States still espouse theses which restrict the extent of the territorial sea and make the high seas an area where the superiority of

[23] Convention on Fishing and Conservation of the Living Resources of the High Seas, 29 April 1958, 559 UNTS 285.

[24] The African states in attendance were Ghana, Liberia, Libya, Morocco, South Africa, and Tunisia. See United Conference on the Law of the Sea, *Official Records*, vol 2, UN Doc A/CONF.13/38 (1958) xvii–xxiv.

[25] Third UN Conference on the Law of the Sea, 26th plen mtg, UN Doc A./CONF.62/SR.26 (1974) para 67.

[26] Excerpts from the letter of President Senghor are reproduced in Daniel Bardonnet, 'La dénonciation par le Gouvernement sénégalais de la Convention sur la mer territoriale et la zone contiguë et de la Convention sur la pêche et la conservation des ressources biologiques de la haute mer, en date du 29 avril 1958 à Genève' (1972) 18 Annuaire français de droit international 123, 128, 133 (translated here from the original French).

> their financial and technical means allows them to enjoy, in an almost exclusive manner, the riches of the waters off the coast of Senegal. The regime of freedom benefits the richest and the best equipped, rather than the underdeveloped and the poorest.

Other developing states around the world agreed that *mare liberum* benefited 'the richest and the best equipped, rather than the underdeveloped and the poorest'.[27] As more and more of them joined the United Nations, *mare liberum* was increasingly challenged by certain coastal states that sought to make extensive claims to territorial seas in order to assert sovereignty over as much of the waters that lay adjacent to their coasts as possible (*mare clausum*).[28]

As Thomas Brantley observed, 'most of the impetus for dramatic departures from the law as expressed in the Geneva Conventions has come from developing countries, and in particular, developing coastal countries, who had no part in the formulation of the existing codified law' and 'regard the customs on which it was based as closely identified with the colonial regime, and feel that its legal arrangements often work to their economic disadvantage'.[29]

By their sheer number, these developing states were able to ensure not only that a third Conference on the Law of the Sea would be convened in 1973 but also that the Conference would lead to a wholescale review and modification of the law of the sea. By 1973, forty more African states had won their independence, as compared to the situation in 1958. They had organized themselves into the OAU in order to promote unity and solidarity among African states, to defend the sovereignty of their members, and to amplify the voice of African states in the international community.[30] In a resolution issued shortly before the onset of UNCLOS III, the Council of Ministers of the OAU recalled that the 'Law of the Seas at present in force does not take into account the interests of the African countries'[31] and emphasized the 'imperative need for OAU member states to act in concert on all the points and to harmonise their positions in order to present a common front on the occasion of any confrontation on the Law of the Sea'.[32]

[27] ibid.
[28] Egede (n 15) 5.
[29] Thomas Brantley, 'Law of the Sea' (1973) 14 Harvard International Law Journal 555, 556.
[30] V Nmehielle and T Pasipanodya, 'African Union' in Patrick Vrancken and Martin Tsamenyi (eds), *The Law of the Sea: The African Union and Its Member States* (Juta 2017) 37–38, 41–44.
[31] OAU Council of Ministers, Resolution on the Law of the Sea, OAU Doc CM/Res 289 (XIX) (5 June 1972) preamble.
[32] ibid.

As evident from the discussion that follows, African states did ultimately ensure that the new law of the sea better served the interests of African peoples.[33]

7.3.1 Use of the deep seabed for the common heritage of mankind

The very first resolution of the OAU on the law of the sea addressed the seabed and subsoil beyond the limits of national jurisdiction (the deep seabed or the 'Area'). Entitled 'Problems of the Sea-Bed', it began by noting the urgent need for African states to 'participate profitably and effectively in the exploitation of the sea-bed'.[34] In the first of its two operative clauses, the resolution recommended that the OAU member states 'issue the necessary directives on the vital and urgent problem of international regulation of the exploration, exploitation and utilisation of the natural resources of the sea and its sub-soil, having particular regard to the legitimate interests of the African countries'.[35] In the second, it requested that the OAU Secretariat[36]

> study all aspects of the problem of the exploration, exploitation and utilisation of the natural resources of the sea and its sub-soil, and to prepare for Member States as soon as possible a memorandum designed to facilitate the harmonising of their positions in regard to this problem, with a view to presenting a united front at international meetings on the subject.

Other developing states shared the concern of African states with the development of the seabed area. As is well documented, the nine-year-long UNCLOS III negotiations that resulted in the 1982 UN Convention on the Law of the Sea (UNCLOS)[37] were triggered by a Maltese proposal concerning the seabed. Specifically, Ambassador Arvid Pardo inserted in the agenda of the Twenty-Second Session of the UN General Assembly the following item:[38]

> Examination of the question of the reservation exclusively for peaceful purposes, of the sea-bed and ocean floor, and the subsoil thereof, underlying the

[33] Rembe (n 12) 201.

[34] OAU Council of Ministers, Resolution on the Problems of the Sea-Bed, OAU Doc CM/Res 238 (XVI) (11 June 1971) preamble.

[35] ibid para 1.

[36] ibid para 2. The results of the study are not known, but, as evidenced below, the OAU did seek to harmonize the position of its member states during the negotiations at UNCLOS III.

[37] UN Convention on the Law of the Sea, 10 December 1982, 1833 UNTS 397 (UNCLOS).

[38] Note verbale dated 17 August 1967 from the Permanent Mission of Malta to the United Nations addressed to the Secretary-General, UN Doc A/6695 (18 August 1967).

> high seas beyond the limits of present national jurisdiction and the use of their resources in the interest of mankind.

Pardo's proposal to use the deep seabed for peaceful purposes only and 'in the interest of mankind' sounded a clarion call that resonated with African states concerned that the unilateral mining of the deep seabed by technologically advanced states would lead to a partition of the deep seabed in favour of developed states reminiscent of the scramble and partition of Africa during colonization.[39]

Rembe notes that, at the time, states around the world were increasingly conscious of the wealth to be exploited from the Area because of the 'scientific and technological data which featured the sea as an El Dorado' with the potential to grant a state that acquired part of the Area or its resources 'considerable economic and political power'.[40] Indeed, certain developed states had begun threatening to exploit the seabed unilaterally, pursuant to the doctrine of the freedom of the seas.[41]

Not only did African states lack the technological resources to mine the seabed, but the mining of seabed minerals that would otherwise have been purchased in African territories would negatively affect the economies of the relevant African states.[42]

As the Ghanaian delegation to UNCLOS III recalled, the colonial experience had a profound impact on the position of African states concerning the regulation of the Area:[43]

> His delegation supported the establishment of an autonomous regime with legal bodies of its own and in effective control of all activities in the area of the seabed and ocean floor beyond the limits of national jurisdiction. That position stemmed from memories of the 18th and 19th centuries when, in the scramble for overseas territories, the colonialists had parcelled out African lands which it had taken over a century to recover from them.

The notion of the development of the seabed in the interest of the common heritage of mankind expressed by Pardo also echoed the philosophy of ubuntu.

[39] Egede (n 15) 11.
[40] Rembe (n 12) 44.
[41] ibid 49.
[42] ibid 45.
[43] Third UN Conference on the Law of the Sea, 25th plen mtg, 2 July 1974, *Official Records*, vol 2, UN Doc A/CONF.62/SR.25 (1974) 87 para 92.

Rather than a few states exploiting and ultimately depleting the Area for their own individual benefit, all peoples—including future generations—would benefit, both individually and collectively, from the use and management of the Area in a communal manner that served the interests of all.

The concept of the common heritage of mankind also appealed to the basic problems and needs of developing states because of its support for peace and for the equal treatment of all states.[44] As Rembe explains, 'African and other developing countries became united for fear that the developed technologically advanced countries, if not forestalled by a regime embodying this concept, would parcel out the seabed and its resources, to the exclusion of many and particularly the deprived part of mankind'.[45] Thus, during the Twenty-third Session of the General Assembly, the one that followed Pardo's speech, Liberia cosponsored a draft resolution that later culminated in the moratorium resolution, declaring that states should refrain from exploiting the resources of the Area pending the establishment of a seabed regime.[46]

On the basis of a draft resolution sponsored by 10 African states, the General Assembly also established an ad hoc committee to study the peaceful uses of the seabed and ocean floor.[47] The General Assembly subsequently reconstituted the committee as a standing committee on 'the Peaceful Uses of the Seabed beyond the Limits of National Jurisdiction'.[48] African states were key to the committee, constituting between 20 and 30 per cent of its membership in the years that followed.[49]

Moreover, a working paper on the draft declaration of general principles—prepared by 15 developing countries and cosponsored by Kenya, Liberia, Egypt, and Tanzania—contributed significantly to the formulation of the Declaration of Principles, which was unanimously adopted by the General Assembly in 1970.[50] This declaration established important principles governing the Area. In particular, in its first paragraph, it declared that '[t]he

[44] Rembe (n 12) 52.
[45] ibid.
[46] UN General Assembly, Resolution 2574 (XXIV), UN Doc A/RES/2574 (XXIV) (15 December 1969); Rembe (n 12) 52.
[47] See UN General Assembly, Resolution 2340 (XXII), UN Doc A/RES/2340 (XXII) (18 December 1967); Rembe (n 12) 40–41.
[48] Rembe (n 12) 40.
[49] ibid 40–41.
[50] ibid 52. Working paper on the draft Declaration of General Principles proposed by Argentina, Brazil, Ceylon, Chile, Ecuador, El Salvador, India, Kenya, Liberia, Libya, Pakistan, Peru, Thailand, United Arab Republic, and United Republic of Tanzania concerning the item 'Examination of the question of the reservation exclusively for peaceful purposes of the sea-bed and the ocean floor, and the subsoil thereof, underlying the high seas beyond the limits of present national jurisdiction, and the use of their resources in the interests of mankind', UN Doc A/AC.135/36 (28 August 1968); Organization of African Unity, 'The Lusaka Manifesto' (1970) 58(343) Current History 173.

seabed and ocean floor and the subsoil thereof, beyond the limits of national jurisdiction . . . as well as the resources of the area, are the common heritage of mankind'.[51]

For René-Jean Dupuy, the adoption of the principle of developing the Area in the interest of the common heritage of mankind represented a 'movement towards implicit recognition of mankind as a subject of international law, for the interest of mankind is not simply that of the concertation of all states; it is a notion integrating the state, the collectivities and the individual'.[52]

Bernard Röling also emphasized how the emerging international law addressed itself to humanity and the community of states:[53]

> [T]he emphasis is no longer on the concept of liberty or equality, but on that fraternity, the idea of humanity, which implies responsibility for and duty of caring for the welfare of the whole. . . . Traditional international law, taking as starting point the individual States, was a law of liberty, the thought of mutual assistance as a legal duty was foreign to it. The new international law now coming to the fore, necessarily will have as its starting point the community of States.

As the Norwegian representative to UNCLOS III noted following the issuance of the Moratorium and the Declaration of Principles: 'It is now settled . . . in solemn words and in a most authoritative way that the riches on and under the seabed are the common heritage of mankind. This is a new item in international law and met with opposition from many quarters.'[54]

The first comprehensive statement of the views of the developing countries on the seabed was articulated in the draft statute for the International Seabed Authority (ISA) tabled by Tanzania before the Seabed Committee.[55] The Tanzanian proposal provided in Article 8 that 'all activities regarding exploration and exploitation of the resources of the International Seabed Area, and other related activities, shall be subject to regulation by the International Seabed Authority'.[56] For Tanzania and for African states as a whole, it was important to have an effective international regime and machinery that would be

[51] UN General Assembly, Resolution 2749 (XXV), UN Doc A/RES/25/2749 (17 December 1970).
[52] René-Jean Dupuy, *The Law of the Sea: Current Legal Problems* (AW Sijthoff 1974) 52.
[53] BVA Röling, *International Law in an Expanded World* (Djambatan 1960) 85–86.
[54] Quoted in Andres Aguilar, 'How Will the Future Seabed Regime Be Organized?' in John King Gamble and Giulio Pontecorvo (eds), *Law of the Sea: The Emerging Regime of the Oceans* (Balinger Publishing Company 1974) 45–46.
[55] Rembe (n 12) 58–59.
[56] ibid 62.

'democratic, representative, and free of control from the control of any State or group of States'.[57]

Whereas the developed countries envisaged a weak regime under which the role of the ISA would 'almost be reduced to a licensing and registry office', providing 'incentives and prospects for an early exploitation of the seaboard resources and development of technology', African states feared that such a regime would 'reinstate a *laissez-faire* situation conducive to a common heritage of the multinational companies and a few States, rather than a common heritage of mankind'.[58]

These matters were negotiated for numerous years throughout UNCLOS III. The specific committee designated to address the seabed area, the First Committee, was chaired by an African, PB Engo of Cameroon.[59] African states maintained a cohesive negotiating group position in the First Committee throughout the negotiations.[60] Their position was well articulated by the Chair of the African Group within the First Committee: 'The African countries advocate an instrument covering the whole international zone, which should not establish the right of the strongest or of the first comers but ensure that the general interest prevailed.'[61] They sought a system that 'enshrined the supremacy of the International Seabed Authority which is vested with title to the Area and its resources'.[62]

Their position was ultimately reflected in UNCLOS. In a significant departure from the tradition of open access and freedom of the high seas, the Convention declared the seabed area beyond natural jurisdiction and its resources the 'common heritage of mankind'.[63] All rights in the resources of the Area were 'vested in mankind as a whole' and only the ISA is able to act on behalf of mankind.[64] Moreover, all mineral exploration and exploitation activities were subjected to the approval of the Authority.[65] Significantly, UNCLOS

[57] ibid 58–59. See also Third UN Conference on the Law of the Sea, 'Organization of Work', UN Doc A/CONF.62/63 (18 April 1978); draft proposals tabled by Group of 77 and at the nonaligned conferences.

[58] Rembe (n 12) 60, citing Mr Njenga in a panel discussion at the Ninth Annual Conference of the Law of the Sea Institute, 6–9 January 1975, in Francis T Christy (ed), *Law of the Sea: Caracas and Beyond* (Ballinger 1975) 382.

[59] Egede (n 15) 15.

[60] Rembe (n 12) 58.

[61] Statement by Delegate of Zaire, Third UN Conference on the Law of the Sea, *Official Records*, 13th mtg, UN Doc A/CONF.62/C.1/SR.13 (8 August 1974) 65 para 18.

[62] Rembe (n 12) 62.

[63] MIDAS: Managing Impacts of Deep Sea Resources Exploitation, 'The International Legal Framework for Deep Sea Mining: A Primer' <http://eu-midas.net/legal_framework> accessed 27 January 2017.

[64] UNCLOS, art 137(2).

[65] UNCLOS, art 153.

also required that special regard be given to developing states in the use of the Area.[66]

While African and other developing states also managed to achieve the inclusion in UNCLOS of provisions for the transfer of technology to developing states,[67] limitations to the production of minerals from the seabed,[68] and payments by state parties into a compensation fund intended to assist developing states that suffer adverse effects caused by activities in the Area,[69] these provisions were later modified upon the threat of certain industrialized states to boycott UNCLOS. The US Reagan administration, for example, viewed Part XI of the Convention as 'international socialism'.[70] It rejected the central planning principles envisioned for the Authority, the mandatory transfer of technology, the production limitations, the review conference (at which the interests of industrialized states could have been overridden), the compensation fund for land-based producers, the high fees for miners, and the disbursement of royalties received from mining operations in the Area.[71] These aspects of UNCLOS were modified by the 1994 Agreement Relating to the Implementation of Part XI of UNCLOS.[72] Although the changes persuaded most of the industrialized states to become party to UNCLOS, the United States is yet to do so.

While the industrialized states were able to claw back some of the gains that African and other developing states had successfully negotiated, many of the significant changes to the existing legal norms on the seabed that the OAU and others had helped instigate remained. Deep-sea mining is no longer a freedom of the high seas that is open to all states and available to be enjoyed by anyone who can afford to do so. All exploration and exploitation of the mineral resources of the Area is controlled by the ISA. The 1994 Agreement itself reaffirmed that the Area and its resources are the common heritage of mankind.[73] Moreover, the provisions on the protection of the marine environment and the protection of human life, as well as the obligations that activities in the Area be undertaken with 'special regard for developing countries' and only for peaceful purposes, also survived.

[66] UNCLOS, art 140(1).
[67] UNCLOS, art 144.
[68] UNCLOS, art 151(4).
[69] UNCLOS, art 151(10).
[70] Edwin Egede and Peter Sutch, *The Politics of International Law and International Justice* (Edinburgh UP 2013) 311.
[71] ibid.
[72] Agreement Relating to the Implementation of Part XI of the United Nations Convention on the Law of the Sea of 10 December 1982, 28 July 1994, 1836 UNTS 3.
[73] See the preamble to the Agreement.

7.3.2 The exclusive economic zone

By 1970, sonar and satellites to locate fish, automatic fish-gutting machines, and other advances in fishing technology had resulted in the factory ship fleets of only a few states usurping half of the total world catch of fish.[74] The existing law permitted distant water fishing states to fish as close to the shores of coastal states as they wished, 'frequently destroying one area and then proceeding to another'.[75]

Chile, Ecuador, and Peru had begun trying to redress this situation by claiming that they possess exclusive sovereignty and jurisdiction over the sea, seabed, and subsoil along their coasts to a minimum of 200 nautical miles—the 'patrimonial sea'—in 1952,[76] and then through the 1972 Santo Domingo Declaration.[77]

As they became independent, African states coalesced around the need to craft new international legal norms that would enable coastal states to benefit from and conserve the fishery resources off their coasts more effectively. In Tayo Akintoba's words, without this, the 'close and natural relationship between the sea, the land, and the men who dwell on it' would be disrupted to the detriment of coastal states, which had the most to lose from the failure to manage adjacent stocks effectively.[78] As Senegal had indicated in its denouncement of the 1958 Geneva Conventions, it was imperative that a new legal order prevent wealthy industrialized states from using their superior financial means and technology to enjoy the riches along African coasts in 'a near exclusive manner'.[79]

At a session of the Asian-African Legal Consultative Committee (AALCC) in Colombo in January 1971, Kenya's representative, Ambassador Frank Njenga, suggested extending coastal state jurisdiction as a possible solution.[80] In response, a working group comprised of Kenya, Ceylon, India, Indonesia,

[74] Akintoba (n 14) 68.

[75] Icelandic Ministry of Foreign Affairs, Memorandum on Fisheries Jurisdiction in Iceland (February 1972) in ICJ, *Fisheries Jurisdiction Cases: Pleadings, Oral Arguments and Documents*, vol 1 (1972) 28. See also Akintoba (n 14) 69.

[76] The Santiago Declaration by Chile, Ecuador, and Peru was the first international instrument to proclaim a 200-mile zone whereby those countries 'each possess exclusive sovereignty and jurisdiction over the sea along the coasts of their respective countries' (Article II): Declaration on the Maritime Zone, 18 August 1952, 1006 UNTS 326 (Santiago Declaration). See also Declaration of Santo Domingo, 9 June 1972, Doc CCM/RC/5 (1972), reprinted in (1972) 66 American Journal of International Law 918.

[77] Declaration of Santo Domingo (n 76).

[78] Akintoba (n 14) 69–70.

[79] See Section 7.2.

[80] Akintoba (n 14) 72.

Japan, and the Maldives was tasked with considering coastal state rights within this zone, as well as other law of the sea matters. At the next session of the AALCC in Lagos, Njenga presented a working paper on the concept of an exclusive zone. He proposed a 200-nautical-mile zone beyond the state in order to 'safeguard the coastal state's economic interests without interfering unduly with another state's movement and communication in the zone'.[81] As Njenga explained, the concept of the EEZ was an attempt to create 'a framework to resolve the conflict of interests between the developed and developing countries in the utilization of the sea. It [was] an attempt to formulate a new jurisdictional basis which will ensure a fair balance between the coastal states and other users of the neighbouring waters'.[82] The AALCC endorsed his proposals.

African states did the same. In June 1971, the Council of Ministers issued a resolution urging African states to 'take all necessary steps to proceed rapidly to extend their sovereignty over the resource of the high seas adjacent to their territorial waters and up to the limits of their continental shelf'.[83] Later that year, the OAU's Scientific Council of Africa recommended that African states extend their territorial seas to a maximum limit of 200 nautical miles.[84]

The African position was further refined in June 1972 in the context of the African States Regional Seminar on the Law of the Sea in Yaoundé, Cameroon. The Yaoundé Conclusions adopted there declared the right of African states to 'establish beyond the Territorial Sea an Economic Zone over which they will have an exclusive jurisdiction for their purpose of control regulation and national exploitation of the living resources of the Sea and their reservation for the primary benefit of their peoples and their respective economies, and for the purpose of the prevention and control of pollution'.[85] The Conclusions noted that the establishment of the zone was without prejudice to the freedoms of navigation, of overflight, and to lay marine cables and pipelines. With regard to landlocked and near landlocked states, the Conclusions indicated that the exploitation of the living resources within the economic zone 'should be open to all African states, both land-locked and near land-locked'.[86] The Yaoundé

[81] ibid 72; Kenya, 'The Exclusive Zone Concept' (working paper) in AALCC, *Report of the Thirteenth Session Held in Lagos* (1972) 241.

[82] Akintoba (n 14) 72; Kenya, 'The Exclusive Zone Concept' (n 81) 24.

[83] OAU Council of Ministers, Resolution on the Permanent Sovereignty of African Countries Over Their Fishery Resources Off the Shores of Africa, OAU Doc CM/Res 250 (XVII) (15 June 1971) preamble para 2; Penelope Simoes Ferreira, 'The Role of African States in the Development of the Law of the Sea at the Third United Nations Conference' (1979) 7 Ocean Development & International Law 89, 101.

[84] Rembe (n 12) 120.

[85] Report of the African States Regional Seminar on the Law of the Sea, UN Doc A/AC.138/79 (21 July 1972), reprinted in (1973) 12 International Legal Materials 210.

[86] ibid.

Conclusions were unanimously adopted by all African states participating in the Conference and were shared with all African states, the OAU, and the UN Committee on the Peaceful Uses of the Sea-Bed.[87]

Later that year, at the 1972 Geneva Session of the UN Sea-Bed Committee, Kenya, joined by 13 other African states, presented its Draft Articles on the EEZ Concept.[88] Consistent with the Yaoundé Conclusions, the Draft Articles provided that all states have the right to establish an economic zone of no more than 200 nautical miles in which sovereign rights would be exercised over natural resources for the purpose of exploration and exploitation.[89] The Draft Articles also guaranteed the freedoms of navigation, overflight, and communication within the zone.[90] They further indicated that a coastal state 'shall permit' the exploitation of the living resources within its EEZ to the neighbouring developing landlocked and near landlocked states, and that such rights, together with the rights of access to the sea and to transit, 'shall be embodied in multilateral or regional or bilateral agreements'.[91] In addition, the Draft Articles noted the ability of coastal states to establish special regulations concerning the exploitation of marine resources; the protection and conservation of renewable resources; the control, prevention, and elimination of pollution in the marine environment; and scientific research.[92]

The EEZ concept as posited in the Kenya Draft Articles was adopted unanimously by the OAU Council of Ministers at its meeting in May 1973. The OAU Declaration on the Issues of the Law of the Sea further formalized the OAU's adoption of the Kenyan position.[93]

The only group of African states that voiced disagreement with the EEZ concept as proposed by the OAU at this point comprised the landlocked and near landlocked states, which continued to reject coastal state exclusive jurisdiction and exploitation rights in any area beyond the territorial sea. But, ultimately, they too supported the EEZ concept promoted by African coastal states in exchange for assurances of bilateral or regional arrangements that would grant nationals of those states rights of access that were equal to those granted to nationals of the coastal state.[94]

[87] Akintoba (n 14) 73.

[88] ibid; Kenya, Draft Articles on Exclusive Economic Zone Concept, UN Doc A/AC.138/SC.II/L.10 (1972), reprinted in (1973) 12 International Legal Materials 33.

[89] Kenya, Draft Articles (n 88) art II.

[90] Akintoba (n 14) 73; Kenya, Draft Articles (n 88) art III.

[91] Akintoba (n 14) 73; Kenya, Draft Articles (n 88) art VII.

[92] Akintoba (n 14) 73; Kenya, Draft Articles (n 88) art V.

[93] Akintoba (n 14) 73; OAU Declaration on the Issues of the Law of the Sea—CM/Res 289 (XIX), OAU Doc CM/St.11 (XXI) (2 July 1973), reprinted in (1975) 12 International Legal Materials 1200.

[94] Akintoba (n 14) 74.

Other states joined the African coastal states. By the time of the Caracas Session of UNCLOS III in 1974, '[o]ver 100 countries spoke in support of an economic zone extending to a limit of 200 nautical miles as part of an overall treaty settlement'.[95]

The rapid acceptance of the recognition of sovereign rights for the coastal state over the exploration, exploitation, conservation, and management of living resources within the 200-nautical-mile EEZ has been described as 'almost revolutionary'.[96] Indeed, the International Court of Justice recognized the EEZ as customary international law even before the entry into force of UNCLOS.[97]

7.3.3 Landlocked state rights

Africa is the continent with the largest number of landlocked states. At the commencement of UNCLOS III, landlocked states numbered 14 and represented one-third of the states on the continent.[98] The OAU helped amplify the voices of those states during the Conference.[99]

The 1973 OAU Declaration, for example, advocated various rights for landlocked states. As indicated above, the Declaration stated that landlocked states were entitled to share in the exploitation of living resources of the neighbouring EEZs.[100] It also endorsed the right of landlocked states to access the sea.[101] Subsequently, in June 1976, the OAU affirmed the rights of landlocked states related to the seabed beyond national jurisdiction when it argued that '[i]n sharing the benefits resulting from the exploitation of the resources of the international zone consideration should be given to the needs of developing countries, in particular land-locked countries and the least developed among the developing countries'.[102]

[95] John R Stevenson and Bernard H Oxman, 'The Third United Nations Conference on the Law of the Sea: The 1974 Caracas Session' (1975) 69 American Journal of International Law 1, 16.

[96] Akintoba (n 14) 91, citing Carolyn Hudson, 'Fishery and Economic Zones as Customary International Law' (1980) 17(3) San Diego Law Review 661.

[97] See *Continental Shelf (Libyan Arab Jamahiriya/Malta) (Merits)* [1985] ICJ Rep 13 para 33.

[98] Rembe (n 12) 143.

[99] See, for example, OAU Council of Ministers, Resolution on the Law of the Sea, OAU Doc CM/Res 514 (XXVII) (24 June 1976); OAU Council of Ministers, Resolution on the Law of the Sea, OAU Doc CM/Res 539 (XXVIII) (21 February 1977).

[100] OAU Doc CM/St.11 (XXI) (n 93) para B(10).

[101] ibid para A(3).

[102] OAU Council of Ministers, Resolution on the International Zone Extending Beyond National Jurisdiction, UN Doc A/CONF.62/50 (14 September 1976) para 5.

Through the collective efforts of the OAU, the landlocked states, the Group of 77, and other collaborators, UNCLOS established, for the first time, rights of landlocked states beyond the traditional high seas freedoms.[103] The preamble to UNCLOS makes special note of landlocked states by noting that it aimed to 'contribute to the realisation of a just and equitable international economic order which takes into account the interests and needs of mankind as a whole and, in particular, the special interests and needs of developing countries, whether coastal or land-locked'.[104] Even though many of the rights accorded landlocked states depend on the cooperation of neighbouring coastal states, UNCLOS represented major progress in the advancement of the interests of those states.[105]

7.4 Biodiversity beyond national jurisdiction

The influence of African states in the law of the sea is increasing. In UNCLOS, African states were referenced only once, in Part XI on the composition of the Council of the ISA to ensure an equitable geographical distribution of seats. In the representative voting chambers for the ISA Council, 18 members are elected, provided that each geographical region shall have 'at least one member' elected from 'Africa, Asia, Eastern European (Socialist), Latin America and Western European and Others'.[106]

African states had a greater influence on the 2023 High Seas Biodiversity Treaty.[107] The agreement has four main sections: marine genetic resources (Part II); area-based management tools (Part III); environmental impact assessments (Part IV); and capacity-building and technology transfer (Part V). African states are mentioned six times in the agreement. The objective of Part II is to increase the technical capacity of state parties, 'particularly developing States Parties, in particular the least developed countries, landlocked developing countries, geographically disadvantaged States, small island developing States, coastal African States, archipelagic States and developing middle-income countries'.[108] There are also special provisions to support area-based

[103] See Martin Tsamenyi and Kamal Deen Ali, 'African States and the Law of the Sea Convention: Have the Benefits Been Realized?' (2012) 26 Ocean Yearbook 113, 123.

[104] UNCLOS, preamble.

[105] See Tsamenyi and Ali (n 103) 153–54.

[106] UNCLOS, art 161(1)(e).

[107] Agreement Under the United Nations Convention on the Law of the Sea on the Conservation and Sustainable Use of Marine Biological Diversity of Areas Beyond National Jurisdiction, UN Doc A/CONF.232/2023/4* (19 June 2023).

[108] ibid art 9.

management tools and conduct environmental impact assessments for coastal African states.[109] African states were leaders in seeking to access and share the benefits arising from marine genetic resources beyond national jurisdiction and in the development of marine technology.[110]

7.5 Conclusion

This chapter identifies and celebrates the African influence on the law of the sea in several respects: the governance of the deep seabed for the common heritage of mankind, the EEZ, the rights of landlocked states, and biodiversity beyond national jurisdiction. Having been excluded from the articulation of the law of the sea during colonization, African states seized the opportunity to be heard throughout UNCLOS III, despite the challenging nation-building exercises and economic crises that occupied them domestically following independence. Indeed, the subjugation of African peoples and the pillage of their resources during colonization galvanized African states to prioritize the negotiation of a fair law of the sea and influenced their position on the governance of the Area and the need for an EEZ.

The chapter further posits that, in addition to the colonial experience, the philosophy of ubuntu, or moral worth and personhood through community, shared across many African cultures, is also reflected in the positions of African states on the common heritage of mankind, the recognition of the rights of landlocked states under the law of the sea regime, and biodiversity beyond national jurisdiction.

In the aftermath of UNCLOS III, African states have sought to implement UNCLOS domestically while furthering their collective action through regional organizations.[111] In particular, African states, acting under the auspices of the AU, have addressed fisheries, the continental shelf, climate change, maritime security, maritime transport, and the creation of wealth from Africa's oceans and seas through the pursuit of a blue economy.[112] It is expected that

[109] ibid arts 17(c), 27(f).

[110] ibid arts 40(c), 41(3), 52(12).

[111] Patrick Vrancken and Martin Tsamenyi (eds), *The Law of the Sea: The African Union and Its Member States* (Juta 2017).

[112] See, for example, OAU Council of Ministers, Resolution on the Declaration of the African Year of the Environment 1991, OAU Doc CM/Res 1299 (LII) (8 July 1990); African Maritime Transport Charter (11 June 1974); Decision on African Process for the Development and Protection of the Marine and Coastal Environment in Africa, OAU Doc AHG/Dec 181 (XXXVIII) (8 July 2002); Decision on the Extension of the African Continental Shelf and Climate Change, Doc Ex.CL/391 (XII), AU Doc Assembly/AU/Dec.179 (X) (2 February 2008); Decision on the Report of the First Conference of

African states will continue to seek ways to ensure that the law of the sea develops in a manner that supports their sustainable economic development and preserves Africa's inland waters, oceans, and seas and their resources for the fair use of all peoples and future generations.

African Ministers of Fisheries and Aquaculture (CAMFA), Doc EX.CL/627 (XVIII), AU Doc EX.CL/Dec.614 (XVIII) (28 January 2011); African Union, *2050: Africa's Integrated Maritime Strategy (2050 AIM Strategy)* (6 December 2012); African Charter on Maritime Security, Safety and Development in Africa, 15 October 2016 (Lomé Charter). That the Lomé Charter attempts to address security concerns, economic development opportunities, and environmental protection conjointly in a single instrument is commendable. The Charter also adopts a blue-economy approach to marine development that values sustainability and social well-being.

8
South America

María Teresa Infante

8.1 Introduction

In his seminal book titled *Principles of International Law*,[1] Andrés Bello, one of the founding fathers of international and civil law in Latin America, called attention to the nature of state dominion over the sea and its implications for the freedom of navigation and the preservation of living marine natural resources in common spaces. The book critically analysed the exclusivity on the territorial sea enjoyed by each coastal state and the move towards the appropriation of portions of the ocean. Time has passed and the law of the sea has been modelled to respond to those challenges.

In the years before the era of great changes to the law of the sea in Latin America, marine affairs exhibited characteristics of a state-centred debate dominated by the neat distinction between the territorial sea and the high seas. The situation was, then, not different from the prevailing practices and doctrines of the time. Moreover, a number of nineteenth-century civil codes of Latin American states asserted territorial seas of 1 nautical league and a contiguous zone of up to 4 nautical leagues from the shore for fiscal, customs, migration, and sanitary purposes.[2] Mexico, in 1935, seems to have been the first state to enlarge its territorial sea from 3 to 12 nautical miles.[3]

The scene was also characterized by the process of boundary definitions and of territorial disputes with maritime connotations. In that context, the issue of straits would also appear. Chile and Argentina included a clause in the 1881 Treaty of Limits in respect of the Strait of Magellan,[4] making the Strait of Magellan subject to the sole sovereignty of Chile. The clause would be tested

[1] Andrés Bello, *Principios de derecho internacional* (3rd edn, Imprenta de la Patria 1864) 36–39.
[2] Those of Chile, Argentina, El Salvador, and Ecuador: C John Colombos, *International Law of the Sea* (6th edn, Longmans, Green and Co 1967) 100.
[3] Alfonso García Robles, *La anchura del mar territorial* (El Colegio de México 1966).
[4] The English text of the Boundary Treaty of 1881 is reproduced in *Case Concerning the Beagle Channel Region (Argentina v Chile)* (1977) 21 RIAA 53, 84–88.

María Teresa Infante, *South America* In: *Cultural Influences on the Law of the Sea*. Edited by: James Kraska and Hayoun Ryou-Ellison, Oxford University Press. © María Teresa Infante 2025. DOI: 10.1093/9780198944140.003.0008

in the First World War.[5] Also, in a different setting, the Beagle Channel south of Tierra del Fuego was also part of the legal landscape of the post-1881 period between Argentina and Chile. In addition, the concept of historic bays or historic waters would appear in the region, such as in the cases of the Gulf of Fonseca[6] and the Gulf of Guayaquil, which was finally delimited in 1971 by Ecuador with a line stretching up to the existing limit with Peru.[7] The view of the jurist Luis María Drago, acting as arbitrator, would also be relevant in this respect.[8]

While it seems that the law of the sea was not particularly subject to systematic collective discussions in the regional domain, the teaching of international law paid special attention to the distinction between sovereign and non-sovereign maritime spaces and, remarkably, the application of customary law in the maritime war and its ramifications, such as blockade, prize law, and the use of flags.[9] Besides, when the Seventh American International Conference analysed the issue of the territorial sea in 1933, no treaty could be agreed upon by the states. In an academic setting, such as the American Institute of International Law, a draft Agreement on the Territorial Sea had been prepared by the Cuban jurist Antonio Sánchez de Bustamante y Sirvén in 1931.[10] No action resulted from this initiative. Among the discrepancies related to the territorial sea measurement, the issue of its bearings on the exterior limit of the Rio de la Plata (Argentina and Uruguay) and the characterization as waters appertaining to the river, as the riparian states asserted, are to be noted.[11]

In respect of marine resources, although not successful in terms of reaching an agreement, it is worth mentioning the initiative to adopt regulations to protect the marine fauna (characterized as valuable resources for humanity), which was the object of a report submitted by the Argentine jurist José León

[5] Chilean Decree 1896 of 1914, *Memoria del Ministerio de Relaciones Exteriores de Chile* (1914–15) 88–89.

[6] *El Salvador v Nicaragua (Judgment)*, Central American Court of Justice, 9 March 1917, para 383, in (1917) 11 *American Journal of International Law* 693. See also Historic Bays: Memorandum by the Secretariat of the United Nations, in United Conference on the Law of the Sea, *Official Records*, vol 1, UN Doc. A/CONF.13/1 (30 September 1957) 9.

[7] Supreme Decree No 959-A of 28 June 1971. The term 'historic bay' is used in the Ecuador-Peru Joint Declaration on the International Recognition of the Gulf of Guayaquil as a Historic Bay, 23 November 2012: US Department of State, Bureau of Oceans and International Environmental and Scientific Affairs, *Ecuador Maritime Claims and Boundaries* (Limits in the Seas No 147, 23 July 2020) 28–29.

[8] See *North Atlantic Coast Fisheries Case*, Grounds for the Dissent to the Award on Question V by Dr Luis M Drago (1910) 11 RIAA 206.

[9] Ernesto Barros Jarpa, *Derecho internacional público* (2nd edn, Editorial Jurídica de Chile 1938) 157–66.

[10] See (1932) 21 *Revista de derecho internacional* 84.

[11] Lilian del Castillo Laborde, 'Legal Regime of the Río de La Plata' (1996) 36(2) Natural Resources Journal 251.

Suárez in 1925 before a group of experts of the League of Nations. The reaction from states was not unanimous and ultimately led to a process of setting up a draft agreement on cetaceans by the Economic Committee of the organization.[12]

On a different matter, Latin American and Caribbean states actively participated in the 1907 Second Peace Conference, held at The Hague, where a series of maritime conventions were adopted.[13] Only few of those conventions were ratified by the states.[14]

In the imagery of Latin America, the law of the sea appears as an area of innovation and creative cooperation. In fact, the second half of the twentieth century was a scenario of progressive changes enhancing the role of the law of the sea, in terms of both spatial conceptualization and the promotion of scientific and technical advancements regarding marine resources and the environment.

The question whether significant developments in Latin America have also influenced the global delineation of the law of the sea has consistently been answered affirmatively. This chapter will cover some areas in which the law of the sea has been the object of concerted efforts by the Latin American countries aimed at developing its institutions and foundations, as well as providing legal responses on selected topics. From a contemporary perspective, Ximena Hinrichs Oyarce postulates that, in line with concern about global ocean governance, there is vivid regional interest in participating in current deliberations about matters such as marine genetic resources beyond national jurisdiction and the creation of marine protected areas.[15] In turn, Hugo Caminos would posit that harmonization of domestic Latin American legislation with the UN Convention on the Law of the Sea (UNCLOS)[16] has been a sign of convergence with the main institutions of the law of the sea—most noticeably, between territorial and exclusive economic zone (EEZ) approaches.[17] These are two complementary views on salient practices in Latin America.

[12] Gilbert Gidel, *Le droit international public de la mer: le temps de paix*, vol 1 (Librairie Edouard Duchemin 1981) 464–67.

[13] UN Institute for Disarmament Research, *The Role and Importance of the Hague Conferences: A Historical Perspective* (UNIDIR Resources 2017) 3.

[14] Manley O Hudson, 'Present Status of the Hague Conventions of 1899 and 1907' (1931) 25 American Journal of International Law 114, 116.

[15] Ximena Hinrichs Oyarce, 'The Latin American Perspective on Global Ocean Governance' in David Joseph Attard and others (eds), *The IMLI Treatise on Global Ocean Governance*, vol 1: *UN and Global Ocean Governance* (OUP 2018) 279–80.

[16] UN Convention on the Law of the Sea, 10 December 1982, 1833 UNTS 397 (UNCLOS).

[17] Hugo Caminos, 'Harmonization of Pre-Existing 200-Mile Claims in the Latin American Region With the United Nations Convention on the Law of the Sea and Its Exclusive Economic Zone' (1998) 30 University of Miami Inter-American Law Review 9.

On the road to the Third UN Conference on the Law of the Sea (UNCLOS III) (1973–82), the advancement of new ideas was part of a process whereby regional perspectives would nurture broader debates. Those initiatives renovated the dialogues about the equation between sovereign maritime spaces, sovereign rights, jurisdictional issues, and rising concerns on the applicable principles and standards on common spaces. It also became apparent that there were states in Latin America that did not enjoy naturally prolonged continental shelves as a mere natural prolongation of the land territory,[18] and those states adhered to positions based on the entitlement to declare a maritime zone that compensated the lack of the aforesaid space.[19]

This survey intends not to duplicate what has thoughtfully been exposed, but rather to go through selected subjects where a Latin American character appears with force in the law of the sea. History has not been static and whereas Latin American nations have initiated certain international processes, they have also been recipients of global tendencies and have projected ambitions through the integration of positions in broader concerted efforts with other states and regions. Thus, on certain matters, Latin American states have joined efforts with non-regional countries, enhancing their respective capacities to influence a negotiating agenda. The post-UNCLOS agenda on high seas fisheries shows this attribute.[20]

In its *Outlook for Oceans, Seas and Marine Resources in Latin America and the Caribbean*, the UN Economic Commission for Latin America and the Caribbean[21] envisions these interactions from an updated phase. It addresses the implementation of the law of the sea through a combination of measures spanning from the ratification of UNCLOS to the enforcement of agreements necessary to comply with Goal 14 of the Sustainable Development Goals, which addresses the conservation and sustainable use of the oceans, seas, and marine resources.[22] Among other measures, the *Outlook* recommends the implementation of the law of the sea via the Land Based Sources

[18] *North Sea Continental Shelf (Germany v Denmark; Germany v Netherlands) (Judgment)* [1969] ICJ Rep 3, paras 19, 39.

[19] JM Yepes, 'Les nouvelles tendances en droit international de la mer et le droit international américain' (1956) Revue générale de droit international public 10, 40; H Caminos and V Marotta Rangel, 'Les sources du droit de la mer' in René-Jean Dupuy and Daniel Vignes (eds), *Traité du nouveau droit de la mer* (Economica 1985).

[20] Andrés Couve, 'Negociaciones sobre el régimen pesquero en Alta Mar en el Marco de la Conferencia de Naciones Unidas' (1994) 21 Pacífico Sur 137, 140–42; Francisco Orrego Vicuña, *The Changing International Law of High Seas Fisheries* (CUP 1999) 118–24.

[21] Marcia Tambutti and José Javier Gómez (eds), *The Outlook for Oceans, Seas and Marine Resources in Latin America and the Caribbean* (ECLAC and Norwegian Ministry of Foreign Affairs 2020) 63.

[22] Goal 14 in United Nations, *Transforming Our World: The 2030 Agenda for Sustainable Development* (2015).

Protocol of the Cartagena Convention;[23] the international framework for addressing illegal, unreported, and unregulated fisheries; and Annex VI of the International Convention for the Prevention of Marine Pollution from Ships, known as MARPOL, which provides for the prevention of air pollution from ships.[24] This is a more target-oriented document than one focused on theoretical elucubrations. Together with considerations connected with climate change and its impact on sea level rise, the approach responds to a vision that prioritizes the implementation of instruments over a conceptual analysis of the general law of the sea.

This is the scenario where the law of the sea operates amid general and regional interactions.

8.2 In search of certainties and the role of the territorial sea as a point of departure in the expansion of coastal state powers

Historically, various measures and claims issued by the Latin American countries after the Truman Fisheries Proclamation[25] and the Proclamation on the Continental Shelf[26] in 1945, including concepts of exclusive jurisdiction, and the right to utilize and exploit natural resources, jointly with the status of the superjacent waters covering the continental shelf, among other issues, were recalled in national proclamations and legislation. Regarding the continental shelf, although with a limited scope, the treaty of 1942 between Venezuela and the United Kingdom on the delimitation of their respective interests in the submarine areas of the Gulf of Paria[27] was an initial agreement over rights of sovereignty and control on areas that accrued to each party.

Mexico would claim, in a 1945 Presidential Declaration, the continental platform or shelf adjoining its coastline as defined by the 200-metre isobath,

[23] Protocol Concerning Pollution from Land-Based Sources and Activities to the Convention for the Protection and Development of the Marine Environment of the Wider Caribbean Region, 6 October 1999 (Cartagena Convention).

[24] International Convention for the Prevention of Marine Pollution from Ships, 2 November 1973, 1340 UNTS 184 (MARPOL).

[25] US Presidential Proclamation 2668, Policy of the United States with Respect to Coastal Fisheries in Certain Areas of the High Seas, 10 Fed Reg 12304 (28 September 1945).

[26] US Presidential Proclamation 2667, Policy of the United States With Respect to the Natural Resources of the Subsoil and Sea Bed of the Continental Shelf, 10 Fed Reg 12303 (28 September 1945).

[27] Treaty Relating to the Submarine Areas of the Gulf of Paria, 26 February 1942, 205 LNTS 122. By a new Treaty on the Delimitation of Marine and Submarine Areas, 18 April 1990, between Venezuela and Trinidad and Tobago, the Gulf of Paria Treaty and an Agreement on the Delimitation of Marine and Submarine Areas (First Phase), 4 August 1989, should cease to have effect between the parties on their becoming bound by the 1990 Treaty.

and each and all of the natural resources existing there, known or still to be discovered, and to supervise, utilize, and control the zones of fishing protection necessary for the conservation of this source of well-being.[28] Argentina, in 1944, decreed a continental shelf and an epicontinental sea, declaring them as transitory zones of mineral reserves,[29] and, in 1946, announced that those spaces were subject to its sovereign power, without affecting the character of the waters for purposes of free navigation.

The sequence of claims and proclamations over the continental shelf would continue with Brazil, Guatemala, Nicaragua, the Dominican Republic, and other countries. With slight differences, Argentina, Panama, and Honduras, among others, referred to both the continental shelf and the superjacent waters. Francisco García Amador has depicted this prospect as an unprecedented contribution to innovation in the existing law of the sea.[30]

The proclamation of a 200-nautical-mile maritime zone from the continental coasts and contiguous to islands, made by Chile in 1947,[31] was a breakthrough from the legal, scientific, and political perspectives in respect of the maritime zones. The idea of a perimeter, and the concept of national sovereignty, would anticipate a movement towards a comprehensive reform of the law of maritime spaces. The Chilean proclamation concluded with a statement that '[t]he present declaration of sovereignty does not disregard the similar legitimate rights of other States on a basis of reciprocity, nor does it affect the rights of free navigation on the high seas'.

Two months later, Peru issued Presidential Decree No 781,[32] based on the premises of national sovereignty and jurisdiction over the submarine continental or insular areas, and proclaiming the right to reserve, protect, maintain, and utilize natural resources and wealth of any kind that may be found in or below those waters. Rights over the sea adjacent to the coasts would be exercised 'in a zone lying between those coasts and an imaginary line parallel to them, drawn on the sea at a distance of two hundred (200) marine miles, measured by following the line of the geographical parallels'.

[28] United Mexican States, Presidential Declaration, 29 October 1945 (*El Universal*, Mexico City, 30 October 1945, 1, 17) in (1948–49) 46 *International Law Studies* 185.

[29] Argentine Republic, Presidential Decree, 11 October 1946 (Decree 14.708/46, *Boletín Oficial*, 5 December 1946), in (1947) 41 *American Journal of International Law* Supplement 11–12.

[30] FV García Amador, *América Latina y el derecho del mar* (Editorial Universitaria 1976) 13–20; FV García Amador, 'The Latin American Contribution to the Development of the Law of the Sea' (1974) 68 American Journal of International Law 33.

[31] *El Mercurio*, 29 June 1947, 27.

[32] Presidential Decree No 781 Concerning Submerged Continental or Insular Shelf of 1 August 1947; *El Peruano*, 11 August 1947, 1.

Both proclamations employed the term 'sovereignty' and marked a difference from previous documents. They set out a claim over a comprehensive 200-marine-mile zone from the coasts; such distance could be changed at any time, according to the needs of each nation.[33] Contemporary with these declarations, Costa Rica, El Salvador, and Honduras proclaimed either national sovereignty, rights, and interests, or the right to protect and exercise control over the adjacent seas, and to exploit the natural resources existing therein. The freedom of navigation was to be respected.[34]

The Declaration on the Maritime Zone (Santiago Declaration), signed in 1952[35] and ratified as a treaty by the three original participating countries (Chile, Ecuador, and Peru), favoured an extended maritime zone up to 200 nautical miles.[36] The Declaration was seen as a foundational claim concerning the entitlement and regulation over each national maritime zone of sovereignty and jurisdiction. The three states proclaimed 'as a norm of their international maritime policy that they each possess exclusive sovereignty and jurisdiction over the sea along the coasts of their respective countries to a minimum distance of 200 nautical miles from these coasts', and that the 'exclusive jurisdiction and sovereignty over this maritime zone shall also encompass exclusive sovereignty and jurisdiction over the seabed and the subsoil thereof'.[37] In 1967, Panama endorsed the principles and purposes of the Santiago Declaration,[38] and in 1979 Colombia became party to the Permanent Commission for the South Pacific (CPPS).[39] The CPPS was created simultaneously with the Declaration, aiming to ensure that the fishing and hunting quotas established by each party annually in the exercise of its exclusive rights do not threaten the conservation of the marine resources of the South Pacific.[40]

In the 1950s, with the persistent voice of the states that set forth the Santiago Declaration and of others that adhered to its principles (the 200-nautical-mile group), a common position was sought out at the regional level. This path was recalled by a declaration of the parties submitted in 1982 to UNCLOS III,

[33] (1950) 2 *Yearbook of the International Law Commission* 86–87.

[34] García Amador, *América Latina* (n 30) 18–19.

[35] Declaration on the Maritime Zone, 18 August 1952, 1006 UNTS 326 (Santiago Declaration).

[36] Frida M Armas Pfirter, 'Argentina y el Derecho del Mar' (1973) 5 Revista del Colegio de Abogados, Rosario 19.

[37] Declaration on the Maritime Zone (n 35) paras II, III.

[38] Act No 31 of 2 February 1967, in United Nations, *National Legislation and Treaties Relating to the Territorial Sea, The Contiguous Zone, The Continental Shelf, The High Seas and to Fishing and Conservation of the Living Resources of the Sea*, United Nations Legislative Series, Book 15 (UN Sales No E/F.70.V.9, 1970).

[39] Permanent Commission for the South Pacific, 'History and Work of the CPPS' (1979) <https://cpps-int.org/index.php/home/cpps-historia> accessed 25 November 2024.

[40] Santiago Declaration (n 35) para 3.

where it was stated that 'the universal recognition of the rights of sovereignty and jurisdiction of the coastal state within the 200-mile limit provided for in the draft Convention is a fundamental achievement of the countries members of the CPPS, in accordance with its basic objectives stated in the Santiago Declaration of 1952'.[41]

Latin American states actively participated in the UN Conferences on the Law of the Sea in 1958 and 1960. In the 1958 Conference, Latin American voices would raise the issue of the insufficiency of the rules governing fisheries in the high seas to protect the special interests of coastal states, asserting that new approaches towards the question of the breadth of the territorial sea, or the emerging extended maritime zones, were needed.[42] This position was reiterated in 1960.[43] In the *Fisheries* case of 1951, Judge Álvarez of the International Court of Justice (ICJ) had advocated reasonableness behind the determination of the extent of the territorial sea.[44]

At the hemispheric level, the evolution of the subject showed that some of the unilateral or subregional legal stances were not fully reconcilable with each other, given the disparities over either an extended maritime zone of exclusive authority and control of the marine natural resources or an extended sovereign territorial sea. On the other hand, while a loose agreement was embedded in the Principles of Mexico on the Juridical Regime of the Sea,[45] adopted by the Council of Jurisconsults of the Organization of American States in 1956, the subsequent Resolution of Ciudad Trujillo on the Preservation of the Natural Resources of the Continental Shelf and Marine Waters[46] showed discrepancies among states concerning the status of the special interests of coastal states over the area adjacent to the territorial sea.

The diplomatic background to these developments combined an array of national interests and legal policy definitions emerging among states sustaining analogous views, motivating decisions to participate in a reform of the

[41] Letter from the Representatives of Colombia, Chile, Ecuador, and Peru to the President of the Conference, dated 18 April 1982, UN Doc A/CONF.62/L.143 (1984).

[42] See Declaration by the Chairmen of the Delegations of Chile, Ecuador, and Peru, UN Doc A/CONF.13/L.50 (27 April 1958). See also Enrique García Sayán, 'La doctrina de las 200 millas y el derecho del mar' (1974) 32 Revista de la Facultad de Derecho 12, 17–18.

[43] Declaration by the Head of the Peruvian Delegation, Second United Nations Conference on the Law of the Sea, UN Doc A/CONF.19/L.16 (27 April 1960).

[44] *Fisheries (United Kingdom v Norway) (Judgment)* [1951] ICJ Rep 116, 150 (Judge Álvarez).

[45] Principios de México sobre Régimen Jurídico del Mar, Resolución XIII, III Reunión del Consejo Interamericano de Jurisconsultos. México, 1956, in Edmundo Vargas Carreño, *América Latina y los problemas bontemporáneos del derecho del mar* (Andrés Bello 1973) 119–21.

[46] Resolution of Ciudad Trujillo of 1956, in Vargas Carreño, *América Latina* (n 45) 123–24, also in Shigeru Oda, *The International Law of the Ocean Development: Basic Documents*, vol 1 (AW Sijthoff 1976) 346–47.

law of the sea. This would take place through agreements and customary law. While fisheries and non-living resources were at the heart of the approach, those matters did not exhaust queries regarding the nature of the coastal jurisdictional titles and their relationship with the ensuing competences.

In 1958, matters in Latin America had evolved significantly. The early proclamations of sovereignty or jurisdiction on larger areas beyond the baseline that served to measure the territorial sea had become a regular public policy. It is worth recalling that negotiations at the 1958 Geneva Conference would have the extension of the territorial sea as a central discussion.[47] The Conference also paved the way for the recognition of the special interests of coastal states in the maintenance of the productivity of the living resources in areas of the high seas adjacent to their territorial seas. The resulting 1958 Convention on Fishing and Conservation of the Living Resources of the High Seas[48] did not obtain many ratifications, although some Latin American and Caribbean states did ratify it.[49] In this context, the Southeast Pacific countries did not abandon their maritime zone proclamations of 200 nautical miles and continued enjoying increasing degrees of support in the region.[50]

Regarding the continental shelf, Latin American states were satisfied that this space extended 'to where the depth of the superjacent waters admits of the exploitation of the natural resources of the said areas', as set out in Article 1 of the Convention on the Continental Shelf of 1958.[51] In 1972, the insufficiency of these criteria was made clear by a List of Subjects and Questions related to the Law of the Sea, submitted jointly to the UN Seabed Committee by Latin American (Argentina, Brazil, Colombia, Costa Rica, Chile, El Salvador, Guatemala, Jamaica, Mexico, Trinidad and Tobago, Uruguay, and Venezuela) and some African and Asian states.[52] Among other goals, the plan aimed to establish the precise outer limits of the continental shelf.[53]

[47] García Robles (n 3) 68–100.

[48] Convention on Fishing and Conservation of the Living Resources of the High Seas, 29 April 1958, 559 UNTS 285.

[49] Colombia, Dominican Republic, Haiti, Jamaica, Mexico, and Venezuela. There were 39 parties in total: 'Status of Treaties: Convention on Fishing and Conservation of the Living Resources of the High Seas' (UN Treaty Collection) <https://treaties.un.org/Pages/ViewDetails.aspx?src=TREATY&mtdsg_no=XXI-3&chapter=21&clang=_en> accessed 4 February 2023.

[50] See Statement by Chile, Second UN Conference on the Law of the Sea, 14th mtg, 4 April 1960, UN Doc A/CONF.19/C.1/SR.14 (1960) 94–95.

[51] Convention on the Continental Shelf, 29 April 1958, 499 UNTS 311. See Luis Melo Lecaros, 'El Derecho del Mar' (1959) 27(110) Revista de Derecho (Universidad de Concepción) 415, 453–55; Jorge A Vargas, 'Latin America and Its Contribution to the Law of the Sea' in Finn Laursen (ed), *Towards a New International Marine Order* (Martinus Nijhoff 1982) 64–66.

[52] United Nations, Seabed Committee List of Subjects and Issues to Be Discussed at Law of the Sea Conference, 16 August 1972, in (1972) 11 *International Legal Materials* 1174.

[53] Vargas (n 51) 65–66.

In sum, Latin America merits to be studied as a contributor to the creation of new institutions in the law of the sea and the development of capacities to influence global maritime agendas. Over the years, a slightly different approach would be taken by Panama (1967), Ecuador (1970), and Brazil (1970) when employing the term 'territorial sea' to denominate the extended maritime zone of 200 nautical miles. In its turn, Uruguay showed an analogous pattern to that of Argentina[54] when, in 1969, it asserted that sovereignty reached up to a 200-nautical-mile zone of territorial sea, extending to the air space over the territorial sea and to the soil and subsoil, qualified with innocent passage through the 12 nautical miles of the territorial sea and of freedom of navigation and overflight beyond that distance. This was a national practice enshrining a plurality of territorial sea regimes. All in all, when Chile[55] and Uruguay[56] signed UNCLOS, both asserted the sui generis legal nature of the EEZ as a sign of harmonization of their respective conceptions as to the non-territorial character of the zone. Julio César Lupinacci would remark that the national jurisdictional nature of the EEZ accommodated this depiction.[57]

The footprints of the early positions of Chile and Peru re-emerged in *Maritime Dispute (Peru v Chile)* (2008–14), where the central issue of delimitation served as a basis to consider the status and effect of the 1952 Santiago Declaration, along with subsequent agreements and policies.[58] The ICJ emphasized the question as to the delimitation effect of those instruments. From the Santiago Declaration and the 1954 Agreement Relating to a Special Maritime Frontier Zone,[59] the Court deduced the pre-existence of a tacit agreement. The ICJ decided between two divergent positions regarding the validity and scope of the Santiago Declaration and subsequent treaties, emerging with the thesis that it was the 1954 Agreement that cemented a tacit agreement.[60] Then, the Court affirmed the existence of a boundary up to 80 nautical miles from the coast following the parallel of latitude. Beyond that, an equidistance line was drawn from the endpoint of an 80-nautical-mile segment (point A) with an 80-nautical-mile radius.[61] Although both parties had pledged to the validity of the

[54] García Amador, *América Latina* (n 30) 25.

[55] 'The exclusive economic zone has a sui generis legal character distinct from that of the territorial sea and the high seas.' *Law of the Sea Bulletin* No 5, 1985, 9.

[56] ibid 24. Uruguay's approach is ratified in Act 17.033 of 20 November 1998, establishing the boundaries of the territorial sea, the adjacent zone, the EEZ, and the continental shelf.

[57] Julio César Lupinacci, 'The Legal Status of the Exclusive Economic Zone in the 1982 Convention on the Law of the Sea' in Francisco Orrego Vicuña (ed), *The Exclusive Economic Zone: A Latin American Perspective* (Westview 1984) 112–13.

[58] *Maritime Dispute (Peru v Chile) (Judgment)* [2014] ICJ Rep 4.

[59] Agreement Relating to a Special Maritime Frontier Zone, 4 December 1954, 2274 UNTS 527.

[60] *Maritime Dispute* (n 58) para 91.

[61] Natalie Klein, 'Chile-Peru [Report Number 3-5(2)]' in Coalter Lathrop (ed), *International Maritime Boundaries* (Brill 2016).

Santiago Declaration and the subsequent instruments up to 200 nautical miles, to which Ecuador also was party, and that their effective implementation was central to avoiding maritime frontier incidents, this idea was not followed as a prime argument by the ICJ in this case.

In these proceedings, the ICJ took note of the approaches by each state regarding the 200-nautical-mile maritime zone. While Chile had become party to UNCLOS and applied its terms, Peru maintained a position based on a single maritime dominion extending to a distance of 200 nautical miles.[62] In paragraph 178 of its 2014 judgment, the Court stated:[63]

> Both Parties claim 200-nautical-mile maritime entitlements. Neither Party claims an extended continental shelf in the area with which this case is concerned. Chile's claim consists of a 12-nautical-mile territorial sea and an exclusive economic zone and continental shelf extending to 200 nautical miles from the coast. Peru claims a 200-nautical-mile 'maritime domain'.

The Court also noted that Peru's agent formally declared on behalf of his government that '[t]he term "maritime domain" used in [Peru's] Constitution is applied in a manner consistent with the maritime zones set out in the 1982 Convention'. The Court then affirmed that this was a formal undertaking by Peru.[64]

8.3 The patrimonial sea and the search for universalization of the 200-mile economic zone

In the years preceding the opening of UNCLOS III in 1973—in tune with the extension of the special competences of coastal states and their relationship with sovereignty issues, the development of legislation, and even the conclusion of international agreements—Latin America showed both creativity and restraint. In that regard, Winston Conrad Extavour has advanced the thesis that the Latin American claims may be regarded 'as the ultimate expression of the functional approach to maritime jurisdiction'.[65]

[62] Article 54 of Peru's 1993 Constitution also makes reference to the law and treaties ratified by the state for the exercise of sovereignty and jurisdiction.

[63] *Maritime Dispute* (n 58) para 178.

[64] ibid.

[65] Winston Conrad Extavour, *The Exclusive Economic Zone: A Study of the Evolution and Progressive Development of the International Law of the Sea* (Sijthoff 1979) 140.

The 'patrimonial sea' concept introduced clarifications to the approach of an extended maritime zone as a territorial sea with different components. It was a direct outcome of initiatives taken by the Interamerican Juridical Committee and the perception that the mere extension of the territorial sea, although it could be characterized by a plurality of regimes, was not endorsable. The underlying economic factors were to be prevalent in a transition between the previous burgeoning of exclusive maritime zones and the territorial sea. This meant differentiating the territorial sea with a zone of exclusive sovereign rights over natural resources and jurisdictional powers regarding scientific research, the environment, and other activities.

In this respect, the construction of the EEZ owes central elements to the Santiago Declaration. A few decades later, in 1972, the Declaration of Santo Domingo[66] marked the singularization of a patrimonial sea as a direct precedent to the EEZ. The prior work of the Interamerican Juridical Committee, although not using the term 'patrimonial sea', postulated that powers entrusted to coastal states with respect to the zone differentiated themselves according to the territorial sea status of the first 12 nautical miles, and the area measured from there up to 200 nautical miles.[67] Before adopting the Declaration of Santo Domingo, Latin American states gathered in Montevideo[68] and Lima[69] to design a set of principles governing the law of the sea in Latin America, based on an assumption of the 'geographical, economic and social link between the sea, the land, and man who inhabits it, which confers on coastal populations a legitimate priority right to utilize the natural resources of their maritime environment'.[70]

This concept adheres to the proposal made by Edmundo Vargas Carreño to the Interamerican Juridical Committee, which was later reflected in a resolution of 1971.[71] In 1973, another resolution of that Committee endorsed the distinction between a territorial sea and the adjacent zone up to 200 nautical miles, elaborating on the sovereignty over the continental shelf to explore and exploit the natural resources up to the edge of the continental margin. The idea

[66] Declaration of Santo Domingo, 9 June 1972, Doc CCM/RC/5 (1972), in (1972) 66 *American Journal of International Law* 918. The Declaration was signed by Colombia, Costa Rica, Guatemala, Haiti, Honduras, Mexico, Nicaragua, the Dominican Republic, Trinidad and Tobago, and Venezuela. It was not signed by Barbados, El Salvador, Guyana, Jamaica, or Panama.

[67] Interamerican Juridical Committee of the Organization of American States, Resolution of 1973 on the Law of the Sea, OAS/SER.G, CP/Doc.262/73/Rev.1 (13 February 1973), in Oda (n 46) vol 2, 38–40.

[68] Declaration of Montevideo on Law of the Sea, 8 May 1970, in (1970) 9 *International Legal Materials* 1081.

[69] Declaration of the Latin American States on the Law of the Sea, 8 August 1970.

[70] ibid preamble.

[71] Inter-American Juridical Committee, Resolution on the Law of the Sea, 10 September 1971, in (1972) 11 *International Legal Materials* 11894.

of a compromise was captured by LDM Nelson in the article 'The Patrimonial Sea'.[72]

The notion was based on the distinction of a zone where innocent passage was applicable, and a second zone up to 200 nautical miles where free navigation and overflight were the rule. There was also a reference to the soil and subsoil up to 200 nautical miles, over which sovereignty and jurisdiction of the coastal state were the norm, and another section of continental shelf up to the outer edge of the continental margin. Beyond this, there was the oceanic seabed and its resources, already declared a common heritage of mankind.[73]

Vargas Carreño would explain that the Latin American positions were mainly inspired by socio-economic ideas and that the prevalence of specialized competences was the common thread of a regional position.[74] Accordingly, the 1973 Interamerican Juridical Committee resolution on the Law of the Sea[75] would form a consolidated basis for a regional legal approach. The power to regulate by the coastal state was reiterated accordingly.

On the other hand, the relationship between this agenda and the other chapters of an imminent global negotiation was the subject of a paper introduced to the Seabed Committee by Latin American and Caribbean states in 1971.[76] In this paper, regional members highlighted the role of the seabed regime, defined along the principles of the common heritage of mankind, as a matter of key importance. In 1972, Latin American and Caribbean states expressed support for including in the agenda the international regime for the seabed and the ocean floor beyond national jurisdiction.[77] This subject, together with the concept of an (exclusive) economic zone, became the basis of the future regime of the oceans embedded in UNCLOS.

[72] LDM Nelson, 'The Patrimonial Sea' (1973) 22 International and Comparative Law Quarterly 668.

[73] UN General Assembly, Resolution 2749 (XXV), Declaration of Principles Governing the Sea-Bed and the Ocean Floor, and the Subsoil Thereof, Beyond the Limits of National Jurisdiction, UN Doc A/RES/25/2749 (12 December 1970).

[74] Vargas Carreño, *América Latina* (n 45) 49–51.

[75] OAS Inter-American Juridical Committee Resolution on the Law of the Sea, 9 February 1973, in (1973) 12 *International Legal Materials* 711.

[76] United Nations, Seabed Committee List (n 52).

[77] They proposed that the following six issues be taken up by the Conference: the nature and characteristics; the structure, functions, and powers of the international machinery; the economic implications; the equitable sharing of benefits, bearing in mind the special interests and needs of the developing countries, whether coastal or landlocked; the definition and limits of the area; and the use of the area exclusively for peaceful purposes. See Working Paper on the Régime for the Sea-Bed and Ocean Floor, and the Subsoil Thereof Beyond the Limits of National Jurisdiction submitted by Chile, Colombia, Ecuador, El Salvador, Guatemala, Guyana, Jamaica, Mexico, Panama, Peru, Trinidad and Tobago, Uruguay, and Venezuela, in *Report of the Committee on the Peaceful Uses of the Sea-Bed and the Ocean Floor Beyond the Limits of National Jurisdiction*, UN GAOR, 26th Session, Supp No 21, UN Doc A/8421 (1971) 93–101, cited in John R Stevenson and Bernard H Oxman, 'The Preparations for the Law of the Sea Conference' (1974) 68 American Journal of International Law 1, 4n10.

From the outset of UNCLOS III, maritime countries conveyed views such as that of Chile:[78]

> It was a source of great satisfaction to Chile that the 200-mile limit, which it had been the first country to declare 27 years before and which, together with Ecuador and Peru, it had long defended, had been made the central pillar of the international negotiations. Those three countries, with modest investments and simply-equipped coastal fishing fleets, had increased their catch twentyfold because of the maritime zone, and had now joined the great fishing nations of the world.

Moreover, 'the primary relationship between land, man and the sea and the link between a nation and the resources of its adjacent sea' constituted the core of this political and legal narrative.[79] And, in the immediate time frame, it was acknowledged that this central element would be part of a negotiation together with the seabed international regime. From the Atlantic coast, Uruguay sustained a similar idea.[80]

In the Seabed Committee framework, as Bernardo Zuleta[81] would recall, propositions submitted on 3 April 1973, first by Kenya and secondly by Mexico, Venezuela, and Colombia,[82] would be crucial in the advance towards a patrimonial sea as an antecedent of the economic zone. Other proposals followed this tendency.[83] The Interamerican Juridical Committee, through its representative, would state in 1974 before the plenary of UNCLOS III:[84]

> All believed that the 200-mile limit, a concept which had originated on that continent, was the best means whereby the developing coastal States—and all the coastal States of Latin America were developing countries—could derive

[78] Statement by Fernando Zegers, Third United Nations Conference on the Law of the Sea, 30th plen mtg, 4 July 1974, UN Doc A/CONF.62.SR.30 (4 July 1974) 117.

[79] ibid.

[80] ibid 118–30.

[81] Bernardo Zuleta, 'Le tiers monde et la Convention' in *Perspectives du droit de la mer à l'issue de la 3e Conférence des Nations Unies* (Société Française pour le Droit International 1983) 63.

[82] UN Doc A/AC.138/SC.II/L.21 (1973).

[83] A joint informal working paper submitted by Canada, Chile, Iceland, India, Mauritius, Mexico, New Zealand, and Norway proposed a framework for discussions that included a section on the economic zone, with sovereign rights and other rights and duties: Third United Nations Conference on the Law of the Sea, UN Doc A/CONF.62/L.4 (26 July 1974) 81–83.

[84] Edmundo Vargas Carreño on behalf of the Interamerican Juridical Committee, Third United Nations Conference on the Law of the Sea, 48th plen mtg, 7 August 1974, *Official Records*, vol 1, UN Doc A/CONF.62/SR.48 (1982) 208.

rational benefit from the marine resources in the areas adjacent to their coasts and thus serve the interests of their peoples.

In this line of thought, the extended maritime zones that emerged in the Southeast Pacific in the 1940s and the proclamation of continental shelf entitlements were oriented towards a twofold goal: on the one hand, reserving for the exclusive benefit of the coastal state the natural resources of such a zone subject to its competences; and, on the other hand, bolstering legal and political cooperation aimed at developing an agreed framework to deal with third-state interests. These latter issues would then be addressed whenever the core elements of the EEZ had been agreed.

The advancement of those positions was further channelled by meetings and exchanges of ideas between Latin America and African and Asian countries (in the Asian-African Legal Consultative Committee). The contribution of African states, through a Regional Seminar (in Yaoundé, 1972)[85] and through the Organization of African Unity (in Addis Ababa, 1973),[86] would be characterized by a position whereby the precursory patrimonial sea evolved into an economic zone. A fine line between the maritime spaces was set up. In Yaoundé, the African states declared that they have[87]

> the right to establish beyond the Territorial Sea an Economic Zone over which they will have an exclusive jurisdiction for the purpose of control regulation and national exploitation of the living resources of the Sea and their reservation for the primary benefit of their peoples and their respective economies, and for the purpose of the prevention and control of pollution.

This was supplemented by a reference to the continental shelf and the seabed, making it explicit that the 'Economic Zone embodies all economic resources comprising both living and non-living resources'.[88] References to landlocked states were also introduced in this declaration. There was also the backdrop question of reconciling the right of a coastal state to take regulatory measures and the freedom of navigation and flight of ships and aircraft in transit, without distinguishing as to their flags. Santo Domingo and Yaoundé

[85] African States Regional Seminar on the Law of the Sea, General Report of 1972, in Oda (n 46) vol 2, 23–25.

[86] Declaration of the Organization of African Unity on the Issues of the Law of the Sea, 1974, in Third United Nations Conference on the Law of the Sea, *Official Records*, vol 3, UN Doc A/CONF.62/33 (19 July 1974).

[87] African States Regional Seminar (n 85) 23.

[88] ibid 24.

enshrine inspirational elements to forge a compromise between the existing notions in the law of the sea and the new dimensions of coastal sovereign rights and interests as projected beyond the territorial sea.[89]

These declarations and resolutions contributed to a complex set of accommodations during UNCLOS III, including matters such as the situation of landlocked states and disadvantaged countries. At a very early stage, on 4 December 1975, Mexico set out its EEZ, recalling the terms of the sovereign rights of exploration and of exploitation, conservation, and management, as well as exclusive rights and jurisdiction in the zone.[90]

The EEZ contained in Part V of UNCLOS would be the outcome of this trend. Among other effects, the Convention had a real impact on the status of the extended maritime zone for those states that had adhered to a territorial sea theory. This was the case not only for some Latin American states (Ecuador, Panama, and Nicaragua) but also for other regions.

On the other hand, two Latin American non-parties to UNCLOS (Colombia and Venezuela) would enact legislation based on the distinction between a territorial sea and the EEZ. This is the harmonization process praised by Hugo Caminos.[91] During the negotiation of UNCLOS, members of the 'territorialist' group—such as Brazil,[92] Argentina,[93] and Uruguay[94]—showed a clear inclination to balance their positions with the Convention, even amending legislation in line with the distinction between the territorial sea and the EEZ. In Uruguay, the scope of the residual rights according to Article 58 of the Convention, as well as the status of artificial islands, installations, and structures (Article 60), would be spelled out in stricter terms than in the conventional texts themselves.[95] Declarations made by those states upon signature or ratification of the Convention have further revealed that UNCLOS created a scenario of adaptation and renewal. Something of the sort appears in Peru's

[89] See Venezuela's proposals, UN Doc A/AC.138/SR.64; Declaration of Santo Domingo (n 66); S Houston Lay, Robin Churchill, and Myron Nordquist (eds), *New Directions in the Law of the Sea: Documents*, vol 1 (British Institute of International and Comparative Law 1973) 247; Kenya, Draft Articles on the Concept of an Exclusive Economic Zone Beyond the Territorial Sea, UN Doc A/8721 (7 August 1972); Colombia-Mexico-Venezuela, Draft Articles for a Treaty of the Territorial Sea, UN Doc A/AC.138/SC.II/L.21 (2 April 1973).

[90] Mexico, Law on Exclusive Economic Zone, in (1976) 15 *International Legal Materials* 382.

[91] Hugo Caminos, 'Some Consideration on Harmonization of Pre-Existing 200 Mile Territorial Sea Claims in Latin America with Part V of the United Nations Convention on the Law of the Sea' in Verena Soltau (ed), *Liber amicorum Günther Jaenicke—Zum 85. Geburstag* (Springer 1998) 481.

[92] Law No 8.617 of 4 January 1993.

[93] Act No 23.968 of 14 August 1991.

[94] Act 17.033 of 20 November 1998.

[95] United Nations, *The Law of the Sea: Practice of States at the Time of Entry into Force of the United Nations Convention on the Law of the Sea* (1994) 176–82.

Constitution of 1993, which refers to a maritime domain with no distinction of maritime spaces, but the language used can be read as a harmonization stance with regard to UNCLOS: 'The State exercises sovereignty and jurisdiction on the airspace over its territory and its adjacent sea up to the limit of two hundred miles, without prejudice to the freedoms of international communication, in conformity with the law and the treaties ratified by the State.'[96]

In general, the declarations made by states upon ratification of UNCLOS show that they are motivated by their domestic legislation and that they remain conscious of the need to reconcile national laws with the new law of the sea. Those definitions, although phrased with different words and emphases, serve to appraise the general acceptance of the EEZ and the continental shelf provisions by Latin American state parties to the Convention, as Felipe H Paolillo has underscored.[97] This formulation can be found in the Declaration by Ecuador upon adhering to UNCLOS in 2012, which states:[98]

> The Ecuadorian State, in accordance with the provisions of the Convention, exercises sovereignty and jurisdiction over the 200 nautical miles that comprise the following maritime spaces:
> 1. Internal waters, which are the waters on the landward side of the baselines;
> 2. The territorial sea, which extends from the baselines to a limit not exceeding 12 nautical miles;
> 3. The exclusive economic zone, which is an area that extends for 188 nautical miles from the outer limits of the territorial sea; and,
> 4. The continental shelf...

8.4 Looking forward in Latin America post-UNCLOS: the Convention is not the end of the story

Since the adoption of UNCLOS, participation has followed a pattern of active ratification—except for some countries that have not joined the Convention

[96] Constitution of Peru, 1993, art 54.

[97] Felipe H Paolillo, 'The Exclusive Economic Zone in Latin American Practice and Legislation' (1995) 26 Ocean Development & International Law 105, 120–21.

[98] United Nations, 'Status of Treaties: United Nations Convention on the Law of the Sea' (UN Treaty Collection) <https://treaties.un.org/pages/ViewDetailsIII.aspx?src=TREATY&mtdsg_no=XXI-6&chapter=21&Temp=mtdsg3&clang=_en#EndDec> accessed 4 February 2023.

as parties. This is the case with El Salvador, Venezuela, Colombia, and Peru. There seems to be no common ground in their decisions but rather a range of reasons for nonparticipation, such as delimitation issues, the regime of islands, the historic bay concept, and dispute settlement methods.

As Jean-François Pulvenis remarks,[99] the evolution of the legal regime of fisheries that has characterized the law of the sea finds its historic origins in the concept of the territorial sea as a security and sovereign strip along coastal states; the emergence of the maritime zone of 200 nautical miles, which later became the EEZ, in South American countries (such as Chile, Peru, Costa Rica, and El Salvador, and the 1952 Santiago Declaration); and the emergence of the continental shelf as a legal concept.

On the other hand, the organization created in 1952—prior to the adoption of UNCLOS—jointly with the Santiago Declaration, the CPPS (comprising Colombia, Ecuador, Peru, and Chile), would continue to evolve along a diversified agenda, notwithstanding that some participating states were not parties to the Convention. Cooperation among member states has accrued on matters such as the Southeast Pacific Action Plan (1981),[100] which the CPPS administers, and the elaboration of a set of related instruments. The Agreement on the Protection of the Marine Environment and the Coastal Area of the South-East Pacific (1981)[101] has been a catalyst for this purpose. It applies to the 'maritime area and the coastal area of the South-East Pacific within the maritime zone of sovereignty and jurisdiction of the High Contracting Parties up to the 200-mile limit and, beyond that zone, the high seas up to a distance within which pollution of the high seas may affect that area'. Related instruments, such as the Protocol for the Conservation and Management of Protected Marine and Coastal Areas of the Southeast Pacific (1989),[102] illustrate the interrelationship between the region and the global agenda. On the governance approach, it could be asserted that the CPPS has been a successful technical regional organization.[103]

[99] Jean-François Pulvenis de Séligny, 'The Marine Living Resources and the Evolving Law of the Sea' (2009) 1 Aegean Review of the Law of the Sea 61, 80–81.

[100] Comisión Permanente del Pacifico Sur, 'Plan de Acción Regional' <http://cpps-int.org/index.php/principal> accessed 4 February 2023.

[101] Agreement on the Protection of the Marine Environment and the Coastal Area of the South-East Pacific, 12 November 1981, 1648 UNTS 3.

[102] Protocol for the Conservation and Management of Protected Marine and Coastal Areas of the Southeast Pacific, 21 September 1989.

[103] Eduardo Ferrero Costa, 'Latin America and the Law of the Sea' in Harry N Scheiber and Jin-Hyun Paik (eds), *Regions, Institutions, and Law of the Sea: Studies in Ocean Governance* (Martinus Nijhoff 2013) 400–02.

The work plan of the CPPS is indicative of the incorporation of issues of general concern, such as the management of marine litter, the conservation of marine mammals, and the Regional Study Program of El Niño Phenomenon in the Southeast Pacific (ERFEN). The Regional Study Program has produced a crucial set of biological oceanographic reports about climate change factors and variabilities.[104] In turn, the Wider Caribbean region also has an Action Plan for the Environment, along the lines of the Regional Seas Programs of the UN Environment Programme, encompassing—among other issues—land-based sources of contamination, the over-exploitation of resources, increased urbanization, and coastal development.[105]

In 1982, the Latin American Organization for Fisheries Development (OLDEPESCA)[106] was created as an instrument for cooperation within the Latin American Economic System. OLDEPESCA boasts ample geographical representation, including North, Central, and South American countries.[107] It has mainly contributed to studies on aquaculture, the assessment of biomasses, and the protection of turtles.

8.5 Evolution of the legal process and the definition of legal interests beyond national jurisdiction zones

Some forward-looking topics have featured prominently since UNCLOS entered into force in 1994, marking the direction in the law of the sea as it applies in Latin America. These include the role of fisheries in an interlinked scenario with comprehensive environmental agendas; delimitation and related problems; and the delineation of the outer continental shelf.

In other areas—such as the implementation of the seabed regime along the lines of Part XI of UNCLOS and its annexes—the scenario is currently quite dynamic, although not merely regional, due to the ongoing studies regarding the completion of a Mining Code. So far, the International Seabed Authority

[104] Comisión Permanente del Pacifico Sur, *Plan Estratégico del Programa Estudio Regional del Fenómeno El Niño (ERFEN) 2020–2024* (CPPS 2020).

[105] UN Environment Programme, 'Wider Caribbean' <www.unep.org/explore-topics/oceans-seas/what-we-do/working-regional-seas/regional-seas-programmes/wider> accessed 4 February 2023.

[106] Agreement Instituting the Latin American Organization for Fisheries Development (with amendments of 2 November 1984), 29 October 1982, 1427 UNTS 115.

[107] Belize, Bolivia, Cuba, Costa Rica, Ecuador, El Salvador, Guyana, Honduras, Mexico, Nicaragua, Panama, Peru, and Venezuela.

has agreed on 31 contracts for deep-sea mineral exploration in the Area, two of them from Latin American countries: Brazil and Jamaica.[108]

Other issues on the current agenda—namely, the sea level rise and biodiversity beyond the national jurisdictions—have shown great potential to facilitate associations between Latin American countries and other regions. There are efforts towards coordination on specific issues, such as the cross-cutting initiative by the International Law Commission to address sea level rise and the role of international law. Given the level of involvement of the Caribbean countries in the Small Island Developing States group, which aligns them with small island developing states in the Pacific,[109] sea level rise is a crucial topic in the region.

8.5.1 Fisheries

The post-UNCLOS debate over fisheries—including those that are illegal, unreported, and unregulated—would mark the agenda in Latin America, in parallel with the adoption of a series of instruments at the global level. Latin American states, either unilaterally or multilaterally, have participated in debates about illegal, unreported, and unregulated fisheries, joining initiatives to regulate the ensuing problems based on the premises of UNCLOS.

The contributing factors fostering the debate stem from the sustainable development agenda, together with the real interests and rights present in the situations covered by Article 63 of UNCLOS, on '[s]tocks occurring within the exclusive economic zones of two or more coastal States or both within the exclusive economic zone and in an area beyond and adjacent to it'. The progression in the law of fisheries enunciated in UNCLOS would serve to connect the high seas regime with the EEZs. In Latin America, there have been noticeable attempts by some states (Chile and Argentina) to establish rules and governance schemes in this respect.

Frida María Armas Pfirter[110] has shown that in the 1990s, several Latin American states (including Chile, Argentina, Venezuela, and Mexico) adopted stances implementing Article 63, by referring either to the special interests over

[108] International Seabed Authority, 'Exploration Contracts' <www.isa.org.jm/es/deep-seabed-minerals-contractors> accessed 4 February 2023.

[109] Bogdan Aurescu and Nilüfer Oral, *Sea-Level Rise in Relation to International Law*, UN Doc A/CN.4/740 (20 February 2020).

[110] Frida María Armas Pfirter, 'Straddling Stocks and Highly Migratory Stocks in Latin American Practice and Legislation: New Perspectives in Light of Current International Negotiations' (1995) 26 Ocean Development & International Law 127, 136–37.

the associated or migratory species occurring in the waters adjacent to the EEZ, or to the right to adopt conservation measures and monitor transshipments and landing operations, among other formulas.

In those circumstances, the idea of a 'presential sea' proposed by Chile in 1990 was an audacious step in highlighting the importance of conservation measures in fishing practices in the high seas and their relationship with the rights and interests of coastal state in the adjacent EEZ.[111] The notion could have matched with a restricted high seas model of coastal state intervention related to Articles 116–119 of UNCLOS, as Francisco Orrego Vicuña commented.[112] It was predicated by the Chilean Law of Fisheries[113] as part of the high seas, existing for the international community, in a defined area where special interests of coastal states on fisheries and other activities were present, from the perspective of a seaward-looking nation. Comments about this concept would raise a range of queries, mostly oriented towards the elucidation of the content and implications in terms of competences, rights, and obligations.[114]

Finally, a policy-oriented doctrine, rather than a legal concept, was enunciated in 2010 by the Book of the Defence of Chile, where, among other issues, the high seas nature of the area of projection of special responsibilities regarding the safeguarding of life at sea, according to existing international legal instruments, was clearly reassessed.[115] Argentina would advance another model of unilateral action in 1991, targeting the interactions following migratory patterns or associations with the trophic chain of species found in its EEZ,[116] which implied a sort of extension of the national jurisdiction beyond this zone.

[111] Jorge Martínez Busch, 'El Mar Presencial: actualidad, desafíos y futuro' (1991) 3 Revista de Marina 231–38.

[112] Orrego Vicuña, *The Changing International Law* (n 20) 107–11. See also Francisco Orrego Vicuña, 'Toward an Effective Management of High Seas Fisheries and the Settlement of the Pending Issues of the Law of the Sea' (1993) 24(1) Ocean Development & International Law 81, 87–89.

[113] Decree No 430 of 1991, systematizing the General Law of Fisheries and Aquaculture and updates. There is also a reference in Law No 19,300 of 1994 on General Bases of the Environment, art 33.

[114] Thomas A Clingan Jr, 'Mar Presencial (The Presential Sea): Déjà-Vu All Over Again?—A Response to Francisco Orrego Vicuña' (1993) 24 Ocean Development & International Law 93; JG Dalton, 'The Chilean Mar Presencial: A Harmless Concept or a Dangerous Precedent?' (1993) 8 International Journal of Marine & Coastal Law 397; Erik J Molenaar, 'Port State Jurisdiction' *Max Planck Encyclopedia of International Law* <https://opil.ouplaw.com/home/mpil> accessed 4 February 2023.

[115] Ministerio de Defensa Nacional, *Libro de la Defensa, Ministerio de Defensa Nacional de Chile* (2010) 39–40.

[116] Alberto Luis Daverede, 'Medidas unilaterales a la luz del derecho internacional del mar' (1994) 21 Pacífico Sur 68.

The negotiations on the Agreement Relating to the Conservation and Management of Straddling Fish Stocks and Highly Migratory Fish Stocks (1995 Fish Stocks Agreement)[117] took a different direction, as it was seen as a complementary instrument to UNCLOS. In this scenario, Latin American countries would refresh positions and project new profiles regarding marine policies. Before the 1992 Conference on Environment and Development in Rio de Janeiro, which provided political groundwork on the subject, several steps undertaken by Southeast Pacific countries in the framework of the CPPS[118] were supplemented by initiatives adopted by Chile jointly with Canada, New Zealand, and Argentina. Those steps would elaborate on the principles applicable to the management of marine living resources in the high seas and the coherence with the measures on the EEZ of riparian states, based on the premise of 'responsible fishing'.[119]

In the interaction between regional and third-country interests, Latin American countries, including CPPS members, were instrumental in achieving consensus on advanced principles. As Hugo Llanos Mansilla remarks,[120] a 1991 Declaration, adopted in Santiago in a CPPS meeting, enlarged the concepts embodied in the 1990 St John's principles.[121] On the other hand, in preparation for the forthcoming Rio Conference on Environment and Development, four Latin American states (Argentina, Barbados, Chile, and Peru) joined nine other states in submitting draft principles and measures regarding an effective regime for fisheries in the high seas,[122] based on sustainable and ecologically sound practices effectively monitored and enforced. In the same process, the core group of Argentina, Canada, Chile, Iceland, and New Zealand was joined by other states.[123] Ecuador also presented a working paper during the Conference.[124]

All in all, Latin American states would keep the subject under active review, both on principles and on mechanisms. It was conducted via meetings, as in

[117] Agreement for the Implementation of the Provisions of the United Nations Convention on the Law of the Sea of 10 December 1982 Relating to the Conservation and Management of Straddling Fish Stocks and Highly Migratory Fish Stocks, 4 August 1995, 2167 UNTS 3 (Fish Stocks Agreement).

[118] Working paper submitted by Chile, Colombia, Ecuador and Peru, UN Doc A/CONF.164/L.14 (16 July 1993), and Corrigendum, UN Doc A/CONF.164/L.14 (23 July 1993).

[119] Couve, 'Negociaciones sobre el régimen pesquero' (n 20) 140–41.

[120] Hugo Llanos Mansilla, 'Conservación y ordenación de recursos pesqueros en la alta mar' (1996) 23 Pacífico Sur 122, 128–29.

[121] UN Conference on the Conservation and Management of the Living Resources of the High Seas, St John's, Newfoundland, 5–7 September 1990.

[122] UN Doc A/CONF.151/PC/WG.II/L.16 (15 August1991). A continuation of the proposal was submitted seven months later: UN Doc A/CONF.151/PC/WG.II/L.16//Rev.1 (16 March 1992).

[123] Andrés Couve, 'Negociaciones sobre la pesca en alta mar' (1996) 69 Revista Diplomacia 124.

[124] UN Doc A/CONF.164/L.44 (23 June 1994).

1992, when Canada, the United States, Mexico, Colombia, Ecuador, Peru, Argentina, and Chile gathered in Santiago to exchange views on future multilateral negotiations,[125] or later by coordinated efforts during the Conference itself.[126] The perception that a possible weakening of the EEZ concept could be attempted by distant water fishing nations, and uncertainties related to the future functioning of notions such as the precautionary approach and the biological unit, together with the question of the compatibility of conservation and management measures on the high seas with those adopted for areas under national jurisdiction, explain the wide assessment process by states before adhering to this Agreement. It was noticeable that participation in the Agreement would also entail an enhanced cooperation between coastal states and other parties. The issue of preserving the integrity of the EEZ was crucial in that debate. In its turn, Uruguay submitted a proposal to enhance coordination between adjacent countries in the EEZ.[127]

In 2000, before the entry into force of the 1995 Fish Stocks Agreement, four Southeast Pacific countries adopted, in Santiago, a Framework Agreement for the Conservation of the Living Marine Resources of the High Seas of the South Pacific (Galápagos Agreement).[128] The contracting parties were Colombia, Ecuador, Peru, and Chile. After several attempts to facilitate the entry into force, including the negotiation of a Protocol, the Framework Agreement did not get ratified by all the signatories. Among its characteristics, it provided for the initial participation of the four coastal states and, once the Agreement had entered into force, other interested states could become parties. Conservation measures adopted by a Commission were to be applied in the high sea's zones of the Southeast Pacific, 'with special references to straddling and highly migratory fish populations' (Article 2).[129]

[125] Couve, 'Negociaciones sobre el régimen pesquero' (n 20) 142.

[126] In 1993, a core group composed of Argentina, Canada, Chile, Iceland, and New Zealand, joined by Peru and Norway, advanced a Draft Convention on the Conservation and Management of Straddling Fish Stocks and Highly Migratory Fish Stocks on the High Seas: UN Doc A/CONF.164/L.11 (14 July 1993).

[127] UN Doc A/CONF.164/L.34 (29 July 1993).

[128] Framework Agreement for the Conservation of the Living Marine Resources of the High Seas of the South Pacific, 14 August 2000 (Galápagos Agreement).

[129] The decision-making process on substantive matters would have to allow for the participation of states with different positions, whether coastal or distant water fishing countries, and in cases where two-thirds of votes were attained, a majority of coastal states had to be present (Article 12(1)). For measures whose application might affect the conservation of fish stocks within the national jurisdiction zone of a coastal state, such measures should require that state's affirmative vote. Access to ports followed the logic of prevention of disembarkation and ship-to-ship transfers 'when reasonable grounds exist to believe that captures of fish in the Agreement's area of application have been carried out in the contravention of the rules and conservation measures adopted by the States Parties, or, in the absence of such measures, when such captures have served to undermine the effectiveness of the measures in force with respect to the same fish populations in the coastal States' national jurisdiction zones' (Article 9(b)).

In the very same year, a dispute aroused between Chile and the European Union in connection with the conservation and sustainable exploitation of swordfish stocks in the south-eastern Pacific Ocean.[130] The controversy was submitted, by an agreement (exchange of letters), to the International Tribunal for the Law of the Sea in December 2000.[131] Whereas Chile asserted that the dispute referred to the obligations under UNCLOS, especially in Articles 116–119, to ensure the conservation of swordfish activities by vessels flying the flag of a member of the European Union in the high seas adjacent to Chile's EEZ, the European Union contended that the problem was about the purported application of unilateral conservation measures by Chile on the high seas, in breach of those UNCLOS articles.

In April 2000, another complaint had been submitted by the European Union to the World Trade Organization invoking Articles V and XI of the General Agreement on Tariffs and Trade[132] in respect of an alleged prohibition on the unloading of swordfish in Chilean ports based on the Chilean legislation, or transshipping it onto other vessels.[133] Eventually, in 2009 and 2010, both proceedings were discontinued by agreement communicated to the competent bodies pursuant to the applicable rules in each institutional framework.[134] The agreement envisaged a 'more structured framework of fisheries cooperation to replace and transform the 2001 bilateral Provisional Arrangement into a definitive commitment to cooperate for the long-term conservation and management of the swordfish stocks in the South Eastern Pacific'.[135]

On a regional scale, participation in Food and Agriculture Organization (FAO) agreements of 1993 (on compliance)[136] and 2009 (on port state measures),[137] as well as in the 1995 Fish Stocks Agreement, has served as a

[130] Astrid Espaliat, 'Conflictos pesqueros contemporáneos: el caso del pez espada' in Angela del Vecchio (ed), *La gestión de los recursos marinos y la cooperación internacional* (Universidad LUISS Guido Carli di Roma e Instituto Italo-Latino Americano 2006) 111–52.

[131] *Conservation and Sustainable Exploitation of Swordfish Stocks in the South-Eastern Pacific Ocean (Chile/European Union)*, Notification of Special Agreement, ITLOS Case No 7.

[132] Marrakesh Agreement Establishing the World Trade Organization, 15 April 1994, 1867 UNTS 3, annex 1A (General Agreement on Tariffs and Trade (GATT) 1994).

[133] *Chile—Measures affecting the Transit and Importing of Swordfish*, WTO Doc WT/DS193 (19 April 2000).

[134] The Joint Communiqué of 28 May 2010 sets out that 'Chile and the European Union hereby notify the Dispute Settlement Body and the Council for Trade in Goods that they have unconditionally agreed that neither party shall further exercise any procedural right accruing to it under the *DSU* in case DS193 *Chile-Measures Affecting the Transit and Importation of Swordfish*': WTO Doc WT/DS 193/4 (3 June 2010).

[135] *Conservation and Sustainable Exploitation of Swordfish Stocks in the South-Eastern Pacific Ocean*, Order 2009/1 (16 December 2009) para 12. The case was removed from the Tribunal's list in 2009.

[136] Agreement to Promote Compliance with International Conservation and Management Measures by Fishing Vessels on the High Seas, 24 November 1993, 2221 UNTS 91.

[137] Agreement on Port State Measures to Prevent, Deter, and Eliminate Illegal, Unreported, and Unregulated Fishing, 22 November 2009.

benchmark to test the influence of the global agenda on fisheries matters and to overcome differences related to participation in UNCLOS. Although not all Latin American states are partners in the same agreements, some countries do have the status of parties in all of them. This is the case for Brazil, Chile, and Uruguay. The impact of the Fish Stocks Agreement has slowly been felt in the region, to the extent that 10 Latin American states have become parties to it. Declarations made by states upon adhering to or ratifying the Agreement are also relevant in assessing the positions adopted in the region regarding extra-territorial port states competences.

Uruguay (in 1999) and Chile (in 2016)[138] would refer to this issue—although not exactly in the same terms. For Uruguay, if a port state conducts an inspection on a fishing vessel that is voluntarily present in one of its ports and the inspection reveals that there are evident grounds for believing that the vessel has been involved in an activity contrary to the subregional or regional conservation and management measures on the high seas, then, 'in exercise of its right and duty to cooperate in conformity with article 23 of the Agreement, the port State should so inform the flag State and request that it take over responsibility for the vessel for the purpose of ensuring compliance with the said measures'. Chile stated that Article 23 of the Agreement does not prevent the taking of stricter measures than those provided for in the Agreement, in accordance with international law.[139] It then reaffirmed this legal policy when ratifying, in 2012, the 2009 Agreement on Port State Measures to Prevent, Deter, and Eliminate Illegal, Unreported, and Unregulated Fishing.[140] When acceding to that Agreement, the Bahamas also reaffirmed sovereignty over the ports in accordance with international law, 'including the right to deny entry thereto'.[141]

There have also been initiatives in the field of highly migratory species, including with regard to tuna fishing, revealing the difficulties in accommodating positions and strategies.[142] That has been the case with a 1983 Agreement on

[138] United Nations, 'Chronological Lists of Ratifications of, Accessions and Successions to the Convention and the Related Agreements' (Oceans & Law of the Sea, 25 October 2023) <www.un.org/depts/los/reference_files/chronological_lists_of_ratifications.htm> accessed 4 February 2023.

[139] United Nations, 'Status of Treaties: Agreement for the Implementation of the Provisions of the United Nations Convention on the Law of the Sea of 10 December 1982 relating to the Conservation and Management of Straddling Fish Stocks and Highly Migratory Fish Stocks' (UN Treaty Collection) <https://treaties.un.org/Pages/ViewDetails.aspx?src=TREATY&mtdsg_no=XXI-7&chapter=21&clang=_en#EndDec> accessed 4 February 2023.

[140] Agreement on Port State Measures (n 137).

[141] Agreement on Port State Measures: Accession by the Bahamas, FAO Ref. LE-78 (22 December 2016).

[142] United Nations, *The Law of the Sea: Practice of States* (n 95) 186–87.

tuna fishing between Costa Rica, Panama, and the United States[143] and its Protocol,[144] as well as a 1989 Agreement between five Latin American states establishing the Eastern Pacific Tuna Fishing Organization.[145] Both instruments, which have not come into force, have shown imbalances with the relevant provisions of UNCLOS. As Jean-François Pulvenis highlights, they appeared not to meet the conditions required to ensure an ample participation of interested states.[146] A methodology regarding the authority for the issuance of licences (for states or organizations) was set up by each Agreement, but both lacked focus on the rights of coastal states.

Regarding this historically contentious subject, Latin American countries have also engaged in normative processes based on the legal principles embedded in UNCLOS and other instruments regarding compliance, as well as the principles and standards for responsible fisheries in the FAO framework. The Antigua Convention (2003), which replaced the old 1949 treaty establishing the Interamerican Tropical Tuna Commission, closely follows those definitions.[147] For the conservation of Atlantic tunas, there is also an International Convention signed in 1966, with revisions,[148] to which several Latin American and Caribbean states are parties.

Ulterior developments are present in the establishment of regional organizations for fisheries administration, such as the South Pacific Regional Fisheries Management Organization, due to the initiative of Chile, New Zealand, and Australia, which entails a new model of cooperation.[149] Peru and Ecuador are also parties to the Organization, which was formed in 2009. There is a conceptual line, relating this structure to the 1995 Fish Stocks Agreement, that is tested in at least two scenarios: the conservation and sustainability of the covered natural resources, and the prevention of illegal, unreported, and unregulated fisheries.

[143] Eastern Pacific Ocean Tuna Fishing Agreement, 14 March 1983.

[144] Protocol to Eastern Pacific Ocean Tuna Fishing Agreement, 15 March 1983.

[145] Agreement Creating the Eastern Pacific Tuna Fishing Organization, 21 July 1989.

[146] Jean-François Pulvenis, 'Vers une emprise des états riverains sur la haute mer au titre des grands migrateurs? Le régime international de la pêche au thon dans le Pacifique Oriental' (1989) 35 Annuaire français de droit international 784. See also Orrego Vicuña, 'Toward an Effective Management' (n 112) 85.

[147] Convention for the Strengthening of the Inter-American Tropical Tuna Commission Established by the 1949 Convention between the United States of America and the Republic of Costa Rica, 27 June 2003 (Antigua Convention).

[148] International Convention for the Conservation of Atlantic Tunas, 14 May 1966, 673 UNTS 63.

[149] South Pacific Regional Fisheries Management Organization, Convention on the Conservation and Management of High Seas Fishery Resources in the South Pacific Ocean, 14 November 2009.

8.5.2 The continental shelf

One of the subjects that shows Latin American imprints is the continental shelf, which has been a privileged scenario in claiming inherent rights to the natural soil and seabed resources from the coastline of Latin American countries up to a certain distance. The continental shelf would first appear in the Mexican Declaration of 1945[150] and in the Argentine Epicontinental Sea (and over the 'zocalo continental').[151] Other countries—such as Brazil, Guatemala, El Salvador, Nicaragua, the Dominican Republic, Honduras, Panamá, and Venezuela—followed this trend.

According to Vicente Marotta Rangel, it is thanks to the role of revendicating regionalism (Latin American and Afro-Asian) that UNCLOS could reflect this concept from a double perspective, functional and geographical:[152] functional in targeting species and uses; and geographical in including states present in the same geographical setting. The issue of the extension and the need to set up criteria for its outer limit was anticipated in the Latin American debates, as previously exposed.

The unity or autonomy of the notions of the continental shelf and the EEZ are insinuated to a certain extent by very early propositions lodged by some Latin American states, such as Nicaragua.[153] From a more unified approach, Colombia, Mexico, and Venezuela proposed, in the Seabed Committee in 1973, a formula based on the close relationship between the novel concept of a patrimonial sea and the continental shelf. The unifying element was the connection with the sovereign status of the rights over renewable and non-renewable resources in the waters and in the soil and subsoil of this zone. Moreover, the regime of the continental shelf should extend over the seabed and subsoil beyond the patrimonial sea up to the outer limits of the continental rise bordering on the ocean basin or abyssal floor.[154] The coexistence and

[150] United Mexican States, Presidential Declaration, 29 October 1945.

[151] García Amador, *América Latina* (n 30) 14–16.

[152] Vicente Marotta Rangel, 'Le plateau continental dans la Convention de 1982 sur le droit de la mer' (1985) 194 Recueil des cours 269, 305.

[153] Nicaragua, Working Paper on Characteristics of the National Zone, in Third United Nations Conference on the Law of the Sea, *Official Records*, UN Doc A/CONF.62/C.2/L.17 (23 July 1974) 195.

[154] Articles 13 and 15 of the proposal by the three states: UN Doc A/AC.138/SC.II/L.21 (n 89). United Nations, *Report of the Committee on the Peaceful Uses of the Sea-Bed and the Ocean Floor Beyond the Limits of National Jurisdiction*, vol 3, UN GAOR, 28th sess, Supp No 21 (A/9021) (1973) 19–22.

complementarity of the regimes of the EEZ and the continental shelf was finally enshrined in UNCLOS.[155] This was the intention of a working paper submitted to UNCLOS III by Canada, Chile, Iceland, India, Indonesia, Mauritius, Mexico, New Zealand, and Norway in 1974.[156]

In 1985, after the adoption of UNCLOS, two Southeast Pacific countries (Chile and Ecuador) declared extended continental shelves around their respective Pacific islands and archipelagos.[157] After intense work, their proclamations were refined by submissions to the Commission on the Limits of the Continental Shelf, in 2020 and 2022 respectively, following the criteria and guidelines adopted therein.[158] In addition, in 2020, Ecuador and Costa Rica made a Joint Partial Submission on the limits of the continental shelf beyond 200 nautical miles from the baselines in the Panama Basin.[159] So far, Argentina, the Bahamas, Nicaragua, Mexico (two areas), Guyana, Cuba, Chile, Ecuador, Costa Rica (jointly with Ecuador), Uruguay, Trinidad and Tobago, Barbados, and Brazil (various regions) have submitted partial or full submissions to the Commission.

At present, a dispute between Nicaragua and Colombia is pending before the ICJ. The case concerns the continental shelf delimitation, recalling the question of the regime's unity or differentiation with the EEZ. In 2013, Nicaragua requested the delimitation of the continental shelf between the two countries beyond 200 nautical miles from the Nicaraguan Coast.[160] Colombia is a non-party to UNCLOS.

[155] Caminos and Marotta Rangel (n 19) 48–49.

[156] UN Doc A/CONF.62/L.4 (n 83).

[157] Declaration by the Ministry of Foreign Affairs of 14 September 1985 (on Easter Island and Isla Salas y Gómez, Extension of Undersea Sovereignty); Declaration on the Continental Shelf, 19 September 1985.

[158] Chile's submission applies to Easter Island and Isla Salas y Gómez: Continental Shelf National Committee Chile, 'Eastern Continental Shelf of Easter Island Province: Executive Summary' (2020). Ecuador's submission applies to the Southern Region of the Carnegie Ridge: Ecuador, 'Partial Submission to the Commission on the Limits of the Continental Shelf Through the Secretary-General of the United Nations' (March 2022).

[159] Ecuador had already submitted preliminary information to the Commission in 2021: Ecuador, 'Información preliminar relativa al límite exterior de la plataforma continental ecuatoriana, más allá de las 200 millas marinas, y el estatus de preparación y fecha estimada de presentación final de información y datos a la Comisión de Límites de la Plataforma Continental' (20 September 2021).

[160] The proceedings were instituted by Nicaragua requesting that the Court adjudge and declare the 'precise course of the maritime boundary . . . in the areas of the continental shelf which appertain to each of them beyond the boundaries determined by the Court in its Judgment of 19 November 2012': *Question of the Delimitation of the Continental Shelf between Nicaragua and Colombia beyond 200 Nautical Miles from the Nicaraguan Coast (Nicaragua v Colombia)*, Application Instituting Proceedings, 16 September 2013.

8.5.3 Delimitations

This theme has never ceased to be present in the region, either as a top priority when an application to a court or tribunal is lodged by a state or when there is a joint submission. The process of maritime delimitations in the region, through either negotiations or adjudicative proceedings, has generally been characterized by concepts combining territorial entitlements and geostrategic elements. From a macrogeographical perspective, it is difficult to assume that the region is a single methodological unit or that it is accurate to generalize about common features in maritime delimitations. While authors have underscored that the delimitation landscape of the South American coast over the Pacific Ocean would, in general, follow a system based on the parallel of latitude from a basepoint,[161] with variations according to the ICJ judgment in *Peru v Chile* (2014),[162] maritime delimitations over the South American Atlantic coast follow an equidistance method approximately.

The issue of the point at which the maritime boundary commences, or the extension of the seashore and its bearing on that point, has also been discussed. The maritime and territorial elements of a case such as that in the Gulf of Fonseca,[163] where three coastal states enjoy historical entitlements, as well as the maritime zone definitions between Chile and Argentina in the Mar de la Zona Austral (Sea of the Southern Zone),[164] the *Costa Rica v Nicaragua* case (in a short section of the coast),[165] or the *Nicaragua v Colombia* case,[166] are indicative of the frequent presence of territorial elements in maritime delimitation disputes. In *Guyana v Venezuela*,[167] not phrased as a maritime delimitation, this subject may appear in connection with the central issue of the territorial entitlement. The *Guatemala/Belize* case submitted to the ICJ also

[161] Eduardo Jiménez de Aréchaga, 'Region III: South American Maritime Boundaries' in Jonathan I Charney and Lewis M Alexander (eds), *International Maritime Boundaries*, vol 1 (Martinus Nijhoff 1993) 286; Prosper Weil, 'Geographic Considerations in Maritime Delimitation' in Jonathan I Charney and Lewis M Alexander (eds), *International Maritime Boundaries*, vol 1 (Martinus Nijhoff 1993) 127.

[162] *Maritime Dispute* (n 58).

[163] *Land, Island and Maritime Frontier Dispute (El Salvador/Honduras: Nicaragua intervening) (Judgment)* [1992] ICJ Rep 558.

[164] Treaty of Peace and Friendship, 29 November 1984, 1399 UNTS 89.

[165] *Maritime Delimitation in the Caribbean Sea and the Pacific Ocean (Costa Rica v Nicaragua)* and *Land Boundary in the Northern Part of Isla Portillos (Costa Rica v Nicaragua) (Judgment)* [2018] ICJ Rep 139.

[166] *Territorial and Maritime Dispute (Nicaragua v Colombia) (Judgment)* [2012] ICJ Rep 624. This case was followed by a submission to the ICJ from Nicaragua in 2013, regarding the continental shelf: *Question of the Delimitation of the Continental Shelf between Nicaragua and Colombia beyond 200 Nautical Miles from the Nicaraguan Coast (Nicaragua v Colombia) (Judgment)* (13 July 2023).

[167] *Arbitral Award of 3 October 1899 (Guyana v Venezuela) (Jurisdiction of the Court)* [2020] ICJ Rep 455.

entails land and insular territories and their maritime areas.[168] These cases are part of a larger number of arrangements and solutions that shape the Latin American and Caribbean legal and political maritime delimitation landscape.

During UNCLOS III, discussions about preferred provisions displayed political and legal dynamics regarding principles, rules, and criteria, together with the consolidation of the rights and jurisdictions appurtenant to coastal states. The criteria finally set forth in Articles 74 and 83 of UNCLOS, regarding maritime delimitation of adjacent or opposite coasts between neighbouring states, were not indifferent to the existing disputes and difficulties encountered in diplomatic negotiations at the time. The situation between Venezuela and Colombia, along with other cases, has been part of the picture, as has the debate between the equity and equidistance groups of states.[169] Additionally, Latin American countries would be involved in this regard in discussions conducive to the provisions on dispute settlement mechanisms and the role of adjudication and exceptions.

On delimitation, it is worth noticing the place of adjudication and its diverse experiences. Colonial and postcolonial effectivities and *uti possidetis juris* have been invoked in this domain. The *uti possidetis* doctrine relates to the assumption adopted in Latin America that there was no terra nullius in the continent at the end of the colonial era.[170] From this, the right to succeed to the motherland in all its rights and territorial claims was inferred. The determination of boundaries between states was a consequence of the doctrine and not the origin itself. The transposition of the *uti possidetis juris* to the Latin American scenario and its bearing on the establishment of zones and in maritime delimitations cannot be overlooked. The real impact of doctrine would relate to the alleged succession of states to already settled boundaries or the interplay between boundaries and possessions. Influential cases include the frontier disputes between Colombia and Venezuela in 1922[171] and between Burkina Faso and the Republic of Mali in 1986,[172] where the ICJ admitted that the principle was applicable by the deliberate choice of the parties.

[168] *Guatemala's Territorial, Insular and Maritime Claim (Guatemala/Belize)*, ICJ Case No 177; International Court of Justice, 'The Court Seised of a Dispute Between Guatemala and Belize' (Press Release No 2019/25, 12 June 2019) <www.icj-cij.org/public/files/case-related/177/177-20190612-PRE-01-00-EN.pdf> accessed 4 February 2023.

[169] SP Jagota, 'Maritime Boundary' (1981) 171 Recueil des cours 165.

[170] Giuseppe Nesi, 'Uti possidetis Doctrine' *Max Planck Encyclopedia of Public International Law* (updated February 2018).

[171] *Affaire des frontières Colombo-vénézuéliennes (Colombie contre Vénézuéla)* (1948) 1 RIAA 223, 228.

[172] The ICJ stated that there is 'no doubt that the obligation to respect pre-existing international frontiers in the event of a State succession derives from a general rule of international law, whether or not the rule is expressed in the formula uti possidetis': *Frontier Dispute (Burkina Faso/Republic of Mali) (Judgment)* [1986] ICJ Rep 554, para 24. The respect of borders existing on the achievement of

It is not evident that the jurisprudence has validated the doctrine as a prior principle in maritime delimitation cases between Latin American countries. Tribunals have based their decisions either on the non-existence of an established maritime delimitation line before the independence of the concerned states, or on the different legal nature of the maritime spaces to be delimited as compared with those governed by the existing maritime delimitation treaty agreed by the predecessor state. Other views could value the evidence of pre-independence exploitation actions on seabed areas as a sign of an acquiesced de facto delimitation, or that it traditionally could have served as a maritime boundary.[173]

In the *Territorial and Maritime Dispute between Nicaragua and Honduras* (1999–2007),[174] Honduras maintained that the *uti possidetis juris* principle referred to in the Gámez-Bonilla Treaty[175] and the 1906 Arbitral Award that the King of Spain applied to the maritime area off its coasts and Nicaragua. The existence of a traditional maritime boundary resulting from the said principle would be an emanation of that status. Moreover, Honduras asserted that the 15th parallel constituted the line of maritime delimitation resulting from that principle, and that both countries have succeeded in a maritime area extending up to 6 nautical miles. The ICJ decided that the principle was not applicable to the maritime delimitation in this case, recalling that the 1906 Arbitral Award imposed on Nicaragua and Honduras, 'which indeed was based on the *uti possidetis juris* principle', did not deal with the maritime delimitation. The Court said that the Award fixed 'the extreme boundary points on the coast of the Atlantic', which, among other things, determined the point of commencement of the territorial boundary westwards.[176]

In addition, the ICJ found no indication in the Award that the 15th parallel was perceived as the boundary line.[177] The Court also did not uphold the contention that the *uti possidetis juris* principle provided grounds for an alleged 'traditional' maritime boundary along that parallel.[178] Regarding a de facto boundary based on a tacit agreement, the Court stated that there may be

independence had also been discussed in *Frontier Dispute (Benin/Niger) (Judgment)* [2005] ICJ Rep 4, para 140, and in *Frontier Dispute (Burkina Faso/Niger) (Judgment)* [2013] ICJ Rep 45, para 63.

[173] *Continental Shelf (Tunisia/Libyan Arab Jamahiriya) (Judgment)* [1982] ICJ Rep 18, para 102 (Judge Jiménez de Aréchaga); see also para 5 (Judge Ago).

[174] *Territorial and Maritime Dispute between Nicaragua and Honduras in the Caribbean Sea (Nicaragua v Honduras) (Judgment)* [2007] ICJ Rep 659.

[175] Gámez-Bonilla Treaty, 7 October 1894.

[176] *Nicaragua v Honduras* (n 174) para 235.

[177] ibid paras 235–36.

[178] ibid para 229.

de facto lines, but a distinction should be drawn between 'a provisional line found convenient for a period of time' and an international boundary.[179] The requirement that '[e]vidence of a tacit legal agreement must be compelling'[180] was then enunciated by the ICJ.

The judgment in *Nicaragua v Honduras* can be referred to as a source of a single line to delimit maritime spaces. It is also a reference case for the equitable principles or relevant circumstances method suited to achieving an equitable result. Thus, the judgment made an assertion in the sense that the equidistance method does not automatically have priority over other methods of delimitation and, according to the circumstances, 'there may be factors which make the application of the equidistance method inappropriate'.[181] In the Caribbean Sea, as David Freestone and Clive Schofield point out, equidistance lines are present with some innovations in terms of cooperative arrangements (joint regime or joint scientific research and fishing zone). These unique formulas are found between Colombia and the Dominican Republic (1978) and between Colombia and Jamaica (1993).[182]

8.5.4 Expectations around marine protected areas and biodiversity beyond national jurisdictions

Concurring in time and, to an extent, in location, but with differences in legal and factual terms, the current agenda comprises subjects such as marine protected areas to protect vulnerable marine ecosystems and biodiversity beyond national jurisdiction. The Convention on Biological Diversity[183] and the Aichi Biodiversity Targets, 2011–20,[184] interacting with UNCLOS, are qualified parameters for further studies aimed at illustrating how much legal instruments can influence the promotion of sustainable uses and improve the status of biodiversity by safeguarding ecosystems, species, and genetic diversity.

In this regard, Latin America and the Caribbean score as a region with 'an extraordinary biological and cultural diversity'[185] that has made great progress

[179] ibid para 253.
[180] ibid para 253.
[181] ibid para 272.
[182] David Freestone and Clive Schofield, 'The Caribbean Sea and Gulf of Mexico' in Donald R Rothwell and others (eds), *The Oxford Handbook of the Law of the Sea* (OUP 2016).
[183] Convention on Biological Diversity, 5 June 1992, 1760 UNTS 79.
[184] 'Aichi Biodiversity Targets' (Convention on Biological Diversity, 18 September 2020) <www.cbd.int/sp/targets/> accessed 4 February 2023.
[185] Protected Planet, *Protected Planet Report 2020* (updated May 2021) ch 11 <https://livereport.protectedplanet.net/chapter-11> accessed 4 February 2023.

in terms of protected and conserved areas, with 18 per cent of its marine area enjoying that status.[186] The 1990 Protocol Concerning Specially Protected Areas and Wildlife[187] to the Cartagena Convention has introduced primary tools for planning and managing protected areas. Among the political tools for addressing higher levels of protection for marine areas in view of biodiversity targets, Latin American and Caribbean countries are actively participating in broader collective initiatives. This is the case with, for example, the Global Ocean Alliance 30by30 target,[188] the High-Level Panel for a Sustainable Ocean Economy,[189] and the Our Ocean initiative[190] to confront the ocean climate crisis.

A final theme relates to the Latin American positions on the law of the sea as reflected in the negotiations for a legally binding instrument, under UNCLOS, on the biodiversity beyond national jurisdiction. The scenario is about the conservation and sustainable use of marine biological diversity of those areas, together with, and as a whole, marine genetic resources.[191] Coordination within the Core Latin American Group has been essential in fostering Latin American participation, creating a dynamic of exchanges regarding the main themes of the agenda for a future international legally binding instrument.

The legal status of the resources and related activities, in the sense of a legal vacuum, or subject to the freedom of scientific research, or to the common heritage of mankind,[192] were a starting point of the discussion. Latin America has been participating along the lines of an agreed package of themes. In fact, states have supported the setting of four core elements in the negotiations: marine genetic resources, including the sharing of benefits; measures such as area-based management tools, including marine protected areas; environmental impact assessments; and capacity-building and the transfer of marine technology. On some of these subjects, the density of regulatory schemes applicable

[186] ibid.

[187] Protocol Concerning Specially Protected Areas and Wildlife to the Convention for the Protection and Development of the Marine Environment of the Wider Caribbean Region, 18 January 1990, in (1990) 1 *Yearbook of International Environmental Law* 441.

[188] UK Government, 'Global Ocean Alliance (Archived)' <www.gov.uk/government/topical-events/global-ocean-alliance-30by30-initiative> accessed 4 February 2023.

[189] The Ocean Panel <www.oceanpanel.org> accessed 4 February 2023.

[190] Our Ocean, 'Commitments' <https://ourocean2022.pw/commitments/> accessed 4 February 2023.

[191] UN General Assembly, Resolution 72/249, UN Doc A/RES/72/249 (19 January 2018).

[192] Charlotte Salpin, 'Marine Genetic Resources of Areas Beyond National Jurisdiction: Soul Searching and the Art of Balance' in Elisa Morgera and Kati Kulovesi (eds), *Research Handbook on International Law and Natural Resources* (Edward Elgar 2016); Fernanda Millicay, 'A Legal Regime for the Biodiversity of the Area' in Myron H Nordquist and others (eds), *Law, Science and Ocean Management* (Brill 2007).

in each subregion of Latin America and the Caribbean may vary according to the states, which renders critical the whole negotiating exercise.[193]

Coincidences around the elements of area-based management tools and marine genetic resources seem to be fundamental questions, as Dire Tladi highlights.[194] There is also the nature of the regime of access to the resources, as well as institutional arrangements and the relationships with UNCLOS and with other instruments and frameworks and relevant global, regional, and sectoral bodies. Among the relationships with other regimes, the intellectual property issue should not be an obstacle to building a response to a fair and equitable sharing of benefits.[195]

Within Latin America, there are also voices of concern regarding the applicability of provisions of UNCLOS to which states are not parties, including dispute settlement mechanisms and the possible drafting of clauses in that regard. The content and scope of a clause such as a text drawn on the basis of the 1995 Fish Stocks Agreement (Article 4) poses several questions in this respect: 'Nothing in this Agreement shall prejudice the rights, jurisdiction and duties of States under the Convention. This Agreement shall be interpreted and applied in the context of and in a manner consistent with the Convention.'[196]

Regarding existing instruments and frameworks and relevant global, regional, and sectoral bodies, Ted L McDorman postulates that the issue is that relevant treaty-based instruments and frameworks, alongside relevant global, regional, and sectoral bodies that also contain 'treaty-based obligations and rights', would be unaffected by the future convention on biodiversity beyond national jurisdiction.[197]

Being a regime in development, the supplementary agreements to be negotiated will remain essential. To conclude these reflections, the concept of

[193] For the Caribbean and Atlantic subregions, see Marta Chantal Ribeiro, 'South Atlantic Perspectives on the Future International Legally Binding Instrument Under the LOSC on Conservation and Sustainable Use of BBNJ' (2017) 32 International Journal of Marine and Coastal Law 733.

[194] Dire Tladi, 'An Institutional Framework for Addressing Marine Genetic Resources Under the Proposed Treaty for Marine Biodiversity in Areas Beyond National Jurisdiction' (2019) 19(4–5) International Environmental Agreements: Politics, Law and Economics 485, 486.

[195] Fernanda Millicay, 'Marine Genetic Resources of Areas Beyond National Jurisdiction and Intellectual Property Rights' in Tomas Heidar (ed), *New Knowledge and Changing Circumstances in the Law of the Sea* (Brill Nijhoff 2020).

[196] Further revised draft text of an agreement under the UN Convention on the Law of the Sea on the Conservation and Sustainable Use of Marine Biological Diversity of Areas Beyond National Jurisdiction (30 May 2022) annex, art 4(1).

[197] Ted L McDorman, 'A Few Words on the "Cross-Cutting Issue"—The Relationship Between a BBNJ Convention and Existing, Relevant Instruments and Frameworks and Relevant Global, Regional and Sectoral Bodies' in Myron H Nordquist and Ronán Long (eds), *Marine Biodiversity of Areas Beyond Jurisdiction* (Brill Nijhoff 2021) 283.

freedom of scientific research and technology transfer will clearly bring more material to this debate.

8.6 Conclusion

Significant law of the sea concepts and regimes have been inspired or driven by Latin American and Caribbean initiatives and agreements. This has been the case not only with the EEZ and the continental shelf but also with the need to consider the interlinkages between the EEZ and the high seas on matters of marine living resources and the inspiration provided by environmental principles and the building of a regime for straddling stocks and highly migratory species.

Two elements seem to assert the role of UNCLOS in shaping these marine policies. The first is the overall restructuring of the spatial distribution of competences among states, including their customary value, where the status of the EEZ enjoys general acceptance—even when some domestic norms may not always reflect it. The second element stems from the delimitation processes, the status of islands (including rocks), and the role of residual rights in the EEZ, among other subjects.

Experiences characterized by the search for a common position in the lead-up to UNCLOS III have been abundantly studied. Additional initiatives in the sphere of fisheries that reflect the capacity of Latin American countries to create alliances and to work on a political agenda aiming to set forth a general accord with innovative core principles have provided fertile areas for research. While the EEZ and the continental shelf marked the practice in Latin America and the Caribbean in the coming years, the ability to establish new connections on strategic issues regarding marine living resources and the environment has also been noticeable.

There are also robust examples of the harmonization of national policies and local regulations with general international law, including through agreements and regional plans of action. Without assuming that a set of agreed principles and rules with general value necessarily emerges from the regional agreements, their influence may occasionally transcend national marine policies and be part of wider international agendas. This could be the case with the area-based management tools and marine protected areas as mechanisms to design for the future international legally binding instrument on biodiversity beyond national jurisdiction, as well as with an assessment of the practice around marine scientific research activities.

It is also worth studying the scenario of interactions between the Caribbean and Latin America on environmental issues, biodiversity, migratory species, and even the implementation of the seabed regime. Further developments resulting from such studies should be able to address the singularities of the various agendas and their interlinkages at the regional basis.

9
North America

James Kraska

9.1 Introduction

As former colonies of the British Empire, the United States and Canada share an English cultural heritage, which has been dispositive in their liberal approach to law and the role of the international law of the sea. Their position in North America has had a dispositive effect on their place in the world and has led to a separate and broadly more liberal approach to international law that belies their continental European roots. From the colonial era, the similarities of these two states, overlapping with the Dutch seafaring tradition, gave way to geographic and political imperatives that have influenced how each has approached the law of the sea. Canada, as an offshoot of the British Empire, shares in these experiences. As cultural and geographic neighbours, Canada and the United States occupy a continent and share an inheritance that John F Kennedy described as a familial connection. The cultural perspectives of the two states have been largely aligned.[1]

The cultural heritages of the United States and Canada are intermingled. Since the establishment of the Dominion of Canada in 1867, the two states have shared a perspective shaped by classical liberalism. Given the disparity in size, power, and influence in world affairs between them and their overlapping perspectives, this chapter focuses only on American cultural norms and how they have shaped the law of the sea. As the largest state in North America and a leading global maritime power, the United States embodies numerous cultural streams rooted in the English and European traditions that have affected its approach to law generally and to the international law of the sea more specifically. Traditionally, the US culture was based on liberalism but with increasing elements of state control beginning in the early 1900s. The latter tendency has grown more powerful over the past 100 years and may be expressed today

[1] 'The Hemisphere is a family into which we were born—and we cannot turn our backs on it in time of trouble': John F Kennedy, 'Address Before the Canadian Parliament in Ottawa' *The American Presidency Project* (17 May 1961) <www.presidency.ucsb.edu/node/234997> accessed 4 July 2024.

James Kraska, *North America* In: *Cultural Influences on the Law of the Sea*. Edited by: James Kraska and Hayoun Ryou-Ellison, Oxford University Press. © James Kraska 2025. DOI: 10.1093/9780198944140.003.0009

through the authority of the administrative state and oceans legislation, such as the Coastal Zone Management Act.[2]

This chapter first assesses the early US cultural influences on the law of the sea. In the colonial era, the United States advanced the doctrine of freedom of the seas as a natural expression of the liberal political philosophy of the Founding Fathers and as a strategic economic imperative for the freedom to trade.

9.2 Early liberal culture

A large and culturally diverse country, the United States has varied social and civilizational influences, which include anchor traditions from English constitutionalism and Dutch liberalism and Puritanism. Other defining cultural elements include a very large German and Polish influence, as well as Mediterranean, African, Mexican, Nordic, and Native American populations and practices. Each of these large populations may also be subdivided according to regional and local heritage. There are, for example, more than 500 Native American tribes that contributed to the formation of the US cultural identity.[3] Most Americans can trace their cultural identity from these European and non-European groups, which settled in different parts of the country. The English settled along the Atlantic Coast, the Dutch in New England, the Spanish in Florida and the Southwest (and, more recently, in the Mexican and Spanish-speaking diaspora throughout Texas, New York, and California), and Nordic and French settlers made their way to the upper Midwest. The Western populations contained a balance of Catholic and Protestant traditions that aligned somewhat with continental and British influences.

Intrepid, mostly Catholic explorers dispatched from Portugal and Spain began to creep down the coast of Africa and out into the Atlantic Ocean in the early 1400s. After forays by Vikings in late antiquity and the early Middle Ages, the earliest persistent Western encounter with North America was by Italian Christopher Columbus in 1492. The next year, Pope Alexander VI issued a papal bull or decree, 'Inter Caetera', authorizing Spain and Portugal to colonize the Americas. The division of this authority was refined in 1494 with

[2] 16 USC 1451 et seq.

[3] Statement of William 'Pat' Ragsdale, Acting Assistant Secretary for Indian Affairs, Department of the Interior, Federal Government's Relationship with American Indians: Hearings Before the Special Committee on Investigations of the Select Committee on Indian Affairs, United States Senate, 101st Congress, 1st Session, 21, 22, 23, 27 February 1989, Part 3 at 188, 190.

the Treaty of Tordesillas, assigning the Western Atlantic Ocean to Spain and the Eastern Atlantic Ocean (and, presumably, the Indian Ocean) to Portugal.[4] The line of division stretched from the North Pole to the South Pole, located 370 marine leagues west of Cape Verde Islands.[5] Meanwhile, Spanish explorers in the New World moved north and west into Central and North America. Juan Rodríguez Cabrillo reached San Diego Bay on 28 September 1542, becoming the first European to visit California. In 1625, New Amsterdam was founded as a provincial capital of the Dutch provinces in the New World. The exploration into the New World followed the Dutch rejection of Portuguese and Spanish maritime claims. The English eliminated Dutch rule from North America in 1665 and, by the early 1700s, controlled most of the Atlantic coast. France also forfeited most of its holdings there after the Seven Years' War from 1756 to 1763. The US colonial government declared its independence from the British Crown in 1776, and this act was recognized by Britain in 1783, ending the American Revolutionary War.

Ironically, while the American political tradition was liberal and derivative of England, it formed the basis for American independence from the mother country. The leaders of this American movement were born in the United States (or, in the case of Alexander Hamilton, in nearby Haiti) but were English in their outlook on culture, governance, and law. Among the wealthy plantation owners and businessmen were George Washington, Hamilton, John Adams and Samuel Adams, Thomas Jefferson, Benjamin Franklin, James Madison, and John Jay. These influential figures led the rebellion against King George III over a list of colonial grievances seeking freedom and equality, albeit imperfect, through self-government.

John Locke was the most prominent European political theorist to inform American conceptions of governance. His ideas on human rights and liberties are reflected in the Declaration of Independence, which proclaims, 'all men are created equal and are endowed by their creator with certain inalienable rights, among them, life, liberty and the pursuit of happiness'. The American founders held that just governments derive their power and authority from the people, endowed with natural rights. All people have a natural right to life, liberty, and property. Locke believed that humans exist in a benign environment—unlike Thomas Hobbes, who regarded people as living in a state of nature that was unpredictable and violent, marked by peril and continuous crisis. This condition

[4] Henry Harrisse, *The Diplomatic History of America: Its First* Chapter 1452–1493–1494 (BF Stevens 1897) 74–79.

[5] ibid 78.

requires a strong government, but Locke argued that it would inevitably become tyrannical. In Locke's view, while the natural order is imperfect, it is not fraught with omnipresent danger, as Hobbes believed. Locke thought that an effective social contract built on institutions and law could be negotiated among reasonable men. People are free only when they are subject to political authority to which they have freely consented. Liberty exists, but the rule of law requires respect for the lives and welfare of others. Political power is despotic when it is exercised arbitrarily, inconsistent with the rule of law. The Founding Fathers were informed by the idea of the pursuit of liberty and considered deviations from the rule of law illegitimate.

The Articles of Confederation fashioned a loose-knit country that empowered the individual states at the expense of national identity. The experience of living under the British Crown also fostered a liberal tradition of diffuse power and local control. For example, the Continental Congress, which was established on 29 November 1775, held both executive and legislative powers. The Congress conducted foreign affairs by a team, the Committee of Secret Correspondence, which proved unworkable.[6] The following year, with the adoption of the Constitution, the Committee of Secret Correspondence was superseded by the Department of Foreign Affairs, which was renamed on 15 September 1789 as the Department of State.

The strong desire to protect the sovereignty of the states and limit federal control over their economies and the lives of their citizens reflected the cultural sense of independence, local autonomy, and rejection of control embodied in political liberalism. US leaders negotiated a new Constitution when it became evident that the Articles of Confederation were not suited for protecting or advancing a coherent and unified nation. The Constitution balances power between larger and smaller states through federalism. The goal of federalism is to preserve personal liberty by separating the powers of the government so that one government or group cannot dominate all other centres of power. American leaders cherished the idea of divided or disaggregated power to prevent its concentration and thereby ensure personal liberty and local governance. Through the concept of checks and balances, the federal power within the US government is distributed among three complementary and sometimes competing branches: the executive, the legislature, and the judiciary.

During this early period, the greatest threat faced by the American colonies was being locked out of the European system of trade monopoly, with France and England using their colonies only as a source of raw materials. Having

[6] John Bassett Moore, *American Diplomacy: Its Spirit and Achievements* (Harper & Bros 1905) ix.

escaped from the position of a British colony, the United States still needed to export raw materials to Europe in exchange for finished goods and to access commodities from the Caribbean colonies of France and England. But London and Paris prohibited foreign ships from trading with their colonies directly, under the principle of exclusion. Historian John Bassett Moore observed: 'When our ancestors embarked on the sea of independence, they were hemmed in by a system of monopolies. It was to the effects of this system that the American revolt against British authority was primarily due; and of the monopolies under which they chafed; the most galling was the commercial.'[7]

In the oceans, American liberalism was reflected in the doctrine of freedom of the seas. The US concept of freedom of the seas reflected the basic freedom of American citizens to exercise individual liberty and autonomy, to engage with and trade with merchants in other states anywhere in the world, and to be free from the depredation of piracy and foreign rulers. Freedom of the seas was the single point on which American interests at sea have collided with those of other nations.[8] From the founding of the country, the cultural impetus and legal doctrine of freedom of the seas were shared by American leaders across the political spectrum. President Hamilton was driven by political realism, advocating a vision of America grounded in economic development and prosperity. He risked war with European great powers to protect American commercial interests. Likewise, Thomas Jefferson, who was an agrarian pacifist, conducted naval campaigns to safeguard American shipping against the Barbary pirates. In thinking about freedom of the seas, Walter Russell Mead concluded that '[n]o other principle has played such a major role in [American] diplomatic history'.[9]

The idea of a free trading system was initially promoted by the Dutch and then by the American colonialists, who were cut out of the powerful mercantilist systems of England and France. These views emerged from a position of weakness and a desire for rules that would bind more powerful European maritime powers. In the mid-1700s, the world trading system was rooted in mercantilism. In this system, Great Britain and France were dominant. The 13 American colonies were dependent on manufactured goods, textiles, furniture, and luxuries from Great Britain. In exchange, they provided lumber, furs, dried fish, whale oil, iron, gunpowder, rice, tobacco, and indigo to the home country. Similarly, the West Indies provided sugar, molasses, and fruit to

[7] ibid 2.
[8] Walter Russell Meade, *Special Providence: American Foreign Policy and How It Changed the World* (Routledge 2001) 106.
[9] ibid 107.

the mother country. Within North America, the West Indies provided enslaved persons, molasses, and sugar to the 13 colonies, which, in return, exported flour, fish, and meat to the Caribbean colonies. This closed mercantilist system was based on the theory that there was some fixed quantum of wealth in the form of land, gold, and property, and that one state or area could be enriched only by taking from another country. The major European powers dominated the carrying trade in which they controlled and taxed a closed system to protect their wealth and prevent it from leaking to the colonies. Colonies could only trade through the mother country in this closed trade system. The idea was to make the colonies work for the mother country rather than being a burden to it. This system was underscored in the Seven Years' War.

The British viewed the colonies as a drain on their budget. Wealth was going the wrong way: the Crown was spending money in North America and North America was not paying its way. In response, Britain strengthened the Navigation Acts and France adopted similar statutes. British naval superiority stopped France from supplying and trading with its West Indian colonies. France, in response, relaxed its state monopoly on colonial trade and officially opened French ports to foreign ships, including Dutch, Spanish, and colonial American vessels. To counter this new strategy, Britain adopted the rule of 1756. The rule stated that if a neutral nation were prohibited from a particular type of trade during peacetime, such as under the closed mercantilist system, it would also be prohibited from the same variety of trade during a period of armed conflict. The rationale was that the neutral nation was aiding the enemy by entering into a new trade relationship. This strict approach was rejected by the United States and other neutral nations as a violation of neutral rights and an attempt to circumvent international law. Nonetheless, English doctrine legitimized the seizure of neutral vessels trading with French possessions. The British rationale was that any trade prohibited by municipal law in peacetime should also be prohibited by international law in wartime. In 1758, the British tightened the rule with the doctrine of continuous voyage. Traders became adept at landing goods in a mercantilist port to comply with the law, only to immediately reship them to a foreign destination. This doctrine focused on the ultimate port of destination of the goods rather than at the initial port where the goods were landed. This was because it had become obvious to the British that even this strict rule was being continuously evaded by vessels transferring contraband from one ship to another. For example, during the Napoleonic Wars, American merchant ships attempted to evade the British blockade against France by carrying trade with the West Indies into an American port, offloading the goods into the colonies, and reloading the same goods onto a ship bound for France, often in the same vessel that had carried them into the colonies.

The American colonies had chafed under the British Navigation Acts since 1651. This series of laws limited trade by Britain's colonies to the mother country, impeding colonial commercial maritime navigation so that all the wealth extracted from the colonies flowed through London. The first Navigation Act was designed to eliminate Dutch competition. Finished goods bound for the colonies had to travel in English hulls crewed by English sailors and through English ports. Likewise, exports from the colonies had to travel through Britain. The Navigation Act was followed by the Sugar Act in 1764, the Stamp Act in 1765, and the Tea Act in 1773. The Sugar Act, which imposed a duty on sugarcane and molasses, was designed to recover the costs of protecting the American colonies during the French and Indian War, fought from 1754 to 1763. The Stamp Act imposed a duty on printing newspapers, magazines, cards, and legal documents. Colonial printers and their customers, including Benjamin Franklin, opposed the new law. The Tea Act of 1773 applied to tea imported from Britain and precipitated the Boston Tea Party. Dressed as Native Americans, the Sons of Liberty boarded a ship and dumped imported tea into Boston Harbor. The Tea Act was followed by the Intolerable Acts in 1774 to punish the colony of Massachusetts Bay for the Boston Tea Party. The Intolerable Acts consisted of four separate pieces of English legislation—including the Boston Port Act, which permitted the Royal Navy to blockade Boston Harbor because 'the commerce of his Majesty's subjects cannot be safely carried on there'.[10] These laws brought the American colonies into a closed maritime trading system tightly controlled by and for the benefit of the mother country. They provided the basis for the war between the colonies and Britain, which commenced in April 1775. From the colonial era, the United States fought for the reality and the ideal of freedom of the seas.

The US Revolutionary War inflated transportation prices. In Europe, neutral states could harvest windfall profits earned in the wartime environment if they could access the American market. Britain claimed the right to search for enemy property on any neutral flagged vessel. The 'armed neutrality' of Russia and the Nordic states resisted the Royal Navy's efforts to search their ships. France was a beneficiary of neutral attempts to break the British blockade, and it championed the cause of neutrals. The American colonies began negotiating with France and Spain to circumvent the British mercantilist system, and the

[10] The Boston Port Act, 31 March 1774, Avalon Project, Yale Law School, Lilian Goldman Law Library <http://avalon.law.yale.edu/18th_century/boston_port_act.asp> accessed 4 July 2024.

talks evolved into political and military strategy discussions. In return for aid, the United States recognized French possessions in the West Indies and Spanish subjugation of Pensacola. The colonial victory in the battle of Saratoga in December 1777 convinced France to throw its lot in with the Americans and emboldened the colonialists to propose a Treaty of Alliance. Thereafter, France recognized the independence of the United States and the two allies signed a Treaty of Commerce and a Treaty of Alliance. The Treaty of Commerce was the first step towards the opening of colonial trade and the abolition of discriminating duties. The Treaty of Alliance brought France into the war on the American side to 'maintain effectually the liberty, sovereignty and independence, absolute and unlimited, of the United States'.[11] The agreements with France were the most consequential treaties of the American Revolutionary War. They also were imbued with French and American notions of liberalism and idealism against the old, closed order. The peace terms were remarkably transparent and liberal as well. Negotiating for the United States, John Adams sought and obtained fisheries rights off Newfoundland while conceding the right of British creditors to bring suit for property seized by the individual states, declaring in the presence of British plenipotentiaries that he had 'no notion of cheating anybody'.[12] In this phase of American independence and sovereignty, the political philosophy of liberalism and transparent or open governance is reflected in both French and American legal cultures. While power politics underlay the French–American relationship, the two shared ideals of the freedom and equality of citizens in relation to their government, as well as the rights of independent states in the international system in relation to each other as sovereign equals.

The conflict ended with the Treaty of Paris in 1783, but unresolved issues persisted until the completion of Jay's Treaty, negotiated by Supreme Court Chief Justice John Jay and signed by the United States and Great Britain on 19 November 1794.[13] Jay's Treaty addressed three lingering irritants to normalization. First, British exports flooded American markets, while British tariffs blocked US exports to Britain. The Americans sought a more equitable relationship. Second, Britain had failed to vacate forts in the American Midwest, such as Detroit. Third, the Americans accused Britain of inciting Native American attacks on US frontier settlements. Moreover, the diplomacy

[11] Moore (n 6) 13.
[12] ibid 28.
[13] Treaty of Amity Commerce and Navigation, Between His Britannick Majesty; and The United States of America, 19 November 1794, Avalon Project, Yale Law School, Lilian Goldman Law Library <https://avalon.law.yale.edu/18th_century/jay.asp> accessed 4 July 2024.

unfolded within the context of the British and French antagonism of the French Revolution and the Napoleonic Wars. France desperately needed to trade with the United States, which threatened to join the armed neutrality. Jay conceded that the United Kingdom could seize US goods bound for France if the property owners were reimbursed. The Royal Navy also could confiscate French goods far from shores without payment.

Jay's Treaty underscores that the Revolutionary War and the construction of the peace that followed were largely about freedom to trade—the colonial right to trade freely and not be taxed by a distant sovereign. While Jay's Treaty resolved outstanding issues that had been percolating since the end of the Revolutionary War, it sacrificed the US relationship with France. When France learned of the US negotiations, it felt betrayed that its interests had been sacrificed—to which Benjamin Franklin admitted that the American negotiators had 'been guilty of neglecting a point of bienséance'.[14] Franklin pleaded with France not to have the relationship with the United States 'ruined by a single indiscretion'.[15] He assured Paris: 'The English, I just now learn, flatter themselves they have already divided us. I hope this little misunderstanding will therefore be kept a secret, and that they will find themselves totally mistaken.'[16]

9.3 Freedom of the seas

The Quasi-War of 1798–1800 was an undeclared naval conflict between the United States and France that arose after the federalists in the United States—including George Washington, Alexander Hamilton, John Jay, and John Adams—sought to normalize relations with Great Britain through Jay's Treaty of 1794. France, which was embroiled in conflict with Great Britain, viewed the American policy as incompatible with the French–American 1778 Treaty of Alliance and Treaty of Commerce. When diplomatic negotiations failed to resolve the disagreement, French privateers began attacking US merchant ships and foreign ships in American waters to prevent the shipment of raw materials to Great Britain. Seeking to disrupt the British trade, France unleashed privateers against American commercial shipping in the Caribbean. France objected to US trade as a neutral state with Britain, while at the same time it

[14] Moore (n 6) 33.
[15] ibid.
[16] ibid.

was outraged that US ships would submit to visit and search and hand over French goods to the Royal Navy. Consequently, the peace treaty with Britain that sought to liberalize trade with the former mother country directly led to the Quasi-War with France, the first conflict that the United States fought as an independent country. Trade between the United States and Britain nearly tripled in value between 1794 and 1801.[17] The conflict ended with the signing of the Convention of 1800, which affirmed the rights of US neutral shipping to trade with Britain.[18]

The second war that the United States fought as an independent country was also over the issue of freedom of navigation, once again reflecting the American culture of liberalism and independence. Algiers, Tunis, Tripoli, and Morocco deployed marauders and privateers into the Mediterranean Sea and the Atlantic Ocean to seize US and European ships and extract tribute for their protection. Although the Barbary principalities of the Ottoman Empire had captured and enslaved Europeans for some 200 years, the first American vessel, the *Betsy*, was not seized until 1784. The crews and passengers were enslaved, and the goods were seized as booty of war. The Democratic-Republicans, under President Thomas Jefferson, refused to pay tribute to protect American flagged vessels and raised a force to protect them. Lacking the ability to purchase safe conduct, the United States launched naval campaigns in 1801–05 against Tripoli and in 1815 against Algiers to protect American shipping. In 1815, the US Navy, joined by forces from the Netherlands and the United Kingdom, put an end to the Ottoman threat to shipping.

Between 850,000 and 1,200,000 Europeans were captured by the Muslim city-states and reduced to slavery. After numerous incidents, the United States launched the First Barbary War in 1801. While the United States opposed impediments to maritime trade, becoming enmeshed in international campaigns was anathema to the cultural identity of independence.

The United States was so committed to a liberal order of the oceans that, like France, it rejected joining the British campaign against the maritime slave trade in 1807. The Act Prohibiting Importation of Slaves in 1807 was adopted the same year that the United Kingdom adopted the Slave Trade Act. The US law was designed to shut down the transatlantic slave trade. Thomas Jefferson promoted the Slave Trade Act of 1794 as the first US statute to fight against the

[17] Jerald A Combs, *The Jay Treaty: Political Battleground of the Founding Fathers* (University of California Press 1992) 23–24.

[18] Convention between the French Republic, and the United States of America, 30 September 1800, Avalon Project, Yale Law School, Lilian Goldman Law Library <https://avalon.law.yale.edu/19th_century/fr1800.asp> accessed 4 July 2024.

odious institution of slave trafficking. That law made it illegal for American ships to participate in the trade or export of slaves from the United States. The 1807 law supplemented the 1794 Act by making all importation of slaves a crime. These laws reflected the general trend towards abolishing the international slave trade, which Virginia, followed by all other states, had already restricted. South Carolina, however, had reopened its trade, providing impetus for the 1807 federal law.

At the same time, the British Slave Trade Act authorized the Royal Navy to establish the West Africa squadron to suppress the slave trade. The squadron patrolled the mid-Atlantic and asserted authority over vessels of all nations under a theory of universal jurisdiction, like maritime piracy. Great Britain proposed wartime-like measures of visit and search of merchant ships to ensure that no vessels were engaged in human trafficking. Although the United States and France had similarly outlawed slave trafficking, neither would join the British effort to permit shipboarding of its merchant vessels by the Royal Navy. The British wanted to expand universal jurisdiction at sea from piracy to also encompass slave trafficking, arguing that slave traffickers, like pirates, were the enemy of all mankind.

Britain declared war on France in 1803. As the French Revolutionary War evolved into the Napoleonic Wars, the United States again challenged the right of Britain to board US flagged ships to search for French goods and contraband. Conflicts between the United States and Great Britain festered following American independence. After 1807, the Royal Navy began to disrupt US trade with France and began boarding US ships to impress into service Royal Navy deserters and subjects crewing American warships and merchant vessels—even those with newly granted American citizenship. To provide large numbers of sailors to the Royal Navy, Britain seized British-born naturalized US citizens from American merchant ships and even warships. In 1806, France prohibited all neutral trade with Great Britain and the following year, Great Britain banned trade between France, her allies, and the Americas. The impressment of American seamen by the Royal Navy accelerated and became a matter of national sovereignty, leading to the War of 1812.

The Royal Navy imposed a blockade on US maritime trade between 1812 and 1814. President James Madison declared war on Great Britain on 1 June 1812. After Napoleon's disastrous Russian campaign of 1812, the British concentrated their effort on the American continent by imposing a crippling blockade of the East Coast. British forces landed in Chesapeake Bay and marched to Washington, DC, where they burned the White House and other buildings. With the abdication of Napoleon in 1814, however, the British requirement for sailors for the Royal Navy became less acute and the need to disrupt US shipping to France abated. Yet the United States had important victories on Lake Champlain and at Detroit and Baltimore, and the two sides fought to a draw. Since the conflict was a sideshow to the Napoleonic conflicts and the two sides had fought to a standstill, the British and Americans reached a treaty of peace. Mediated by Russia, Britain and the United States signed the Treaty of Ghent on 24 December 1814, restoring the political boundaries and status quo antebellum. Much like the previous conflicts, the United States was motivated by preserving the right to sail commercial ships or warships unhampered by another power, underpinned by the liberal doctrine of freedom of the seas. Soon afterwards, the Barbary states once again began to target US and European flagged ships.

When the United States moved against the British Navigation Acts, mercantilism had dominated Europe and confined the New World. By the end of the Napoleonic era, the United States proved to be the exponent and defender of neutral rights and commercial liberalism and freedom of the seas. This shift was driven by the US political culture of an open society composed of free individuals—the same liberal theory that was reflected in its diplomacy. The American effort ultimately vanquished the closed political system and vindicated a political and legal culture grounded in liberty.[19] These early conflicts show the willingness of the United States as a weak power willing to stand up to Great Britain and France, the two superpowers of the era. The US disposition towards freedom of the seas only grew during the nineteenth century, as there was a natural alignment between the concept of liberty as a central theme of the American social and political fabric and an open and liberal order of the oceans freely accessible to all states.

9.4 Paris Declaration

America's perspective on maritime governance during the mid-nineteenth century was illustrated by its unwillingness to join the 1856 Paris Declaration Respecting Maritime Law.[20] The Declaration emerged from the Congress of Paris following the Crimean War, which was fought from 1853 to 1856 over Russia's efforts to accelerate the collapse and dismantlement of the Ottoman Empire. In 1854, the Crimean War found the two allied powers, Great

[19] Moore (n 6) 32.
[20] Paris Declaration Respecting Maritime Law, 16 April 1856, 115 CTS 1.

Britain and France, with different principles as to the maritime law of capture. Historically, Britain had claimed the right to seize enemy goods at sea that were not contraband as a method of economic warfare. For example, this classic view was reflected in Jay's Treaty of 1794. The traditionally neutral Scandinavian powers asserted their right to trade freely so long as they abstained from participation in the war. In order to prosecute the war against Russia more efficiently, the United Kingdom agreed to permit enemy goods on neutral ships to go free from capture, and neutral goods on enemy ships also to be exempt from capture. Following the declaration of war against Russia, on 28 March 1854, the United Kingdom released another declaration, stating: 'Her Majesty is willing, for the present, to waive a part of the belligerent rights appertaining to her by the Law of Nations. . . . But Her Majesty will waive the right of seizing enemy's property laden on board a neutral vessel unless it be contraband of war.'[21] During the Crimean War, Britain adhered to the rule of the *Consolato del Mare*, which rendered enemy property, ships, or cargo subject to capture during the war, while neutral property, ships, or cargo would be released. France was more restrictive and acted on the maxim *robe d'ennemi confisque robe d'ami*, by which neutral goods on board enemy ships and neutral ships carrying enemy goods were liable to capture.

The Paris Declaration reconciled and liberalized these two approaches and protected neutral rights by ensuring that enemy goods on neutral ships would not be seized nor would neutral goods on enemy ships. The allied powers further intimated that they would not issue Letters of Marque to license privateers. The British proposed the text as the first modern multilateral ocean treaty. It has just four provisions:[22]

1. Privateering is, and remains, abolished;
2. The neutral flag covers enemy's goods, with the exception of contraband of war;
3. Neutral goods, with the exception of contraband of war, are not liable to capture under enemy's flag;
4. Blockades, in order to be binding, must be effective.

[21] Charles H Stockton, 'The Declaration of Paris' (1920) 14 American Journal of International Law 356, 359–60.

[22] The verbatim statement of the fourth provision is: 'Blockades, in order to be binding, must be effective, that is to say, maintained by a force sufficient to prevent access to the coasts of the enemy.' Stockton (n 21) 356.

These practices, which at first were intended to apply only to the war in progress, were embodied in the Paris Declaration and gradually crystallized into customary international law. The United States, however, continued to object to the provisions because they did not go far enough to ensure neutral rights to trade during armed conflict. In the spring of 1854, Secretary of State William L Marcy set forth to John F Crampton, his British counterpart, the US objective: that the United States sought to settle permanently the principles of 'free ships make free goods', except contraband of war in order 'to prevent it [the principle] from being called in question from any quarter or from any circumstances'.[23]

In offering the proposal, Marcy stated:[24]

> Those who may have at any time a control on the ocean will be strongly tempted to regulate its use in a manner to subserve their own interests and ambitious projects. The ocean is the common property of all nations, and instead of yielding to a measure which will be likely to secure to a few—possibly to one—an ascendancy over it, each should pertinaciously retain all the means it possesses to defend the common heritage. A predominant Power upon the ocean is more menacing to the well-being of others than such a Power on land, and all are alike interested in resisting a measure calculated to facilitate the permanent establishment of such domination, whether to be wielded by one Power or shared among a few others.
>
> The injuries likely to result from surrendering the dominion of the seas to one or a few nations which have powerful navies arise mainly from the practice of subjecting private property on the ocean to seizure by belligerents. Justice and humanity demand that this practice should be abandoned, and that the rule in relation to such property on land should be extended to it when found upon the high seas.

Privateering had been considered a lawful business and a traditional feature of naval warfare. Secretary of State Marcy called it 'as incontestable as any other right appertaining to belligerents'.[25] Marcy reiterated the American ideal that '[t]he ocean is the common property of all nations' and insisted that, accordingly, each nation, whether through privateers or a standing navy,

[23] Mr Marcy to Mr Crampton, 28 April 1854, in United States Senate, 34th Congress, 1st Session, Doc 35, 27 February 1856, 5–6.
[24] Mr Marcy to Count Sartiges, 28 July 1856, reprinted in (1870) 55 British and Foreign State Papers 589, 597.
[25] ibid 591.

'should pertinaciously retain all the means it possesses to defend the common heritage'.[26] The United States was attracted to the provisions of the Paris Declaration supporting neutral rights, but ultimately the Americans rejected the agreement because it abolished privateers. Having a small standing Navy, the United States depended on privateers to fight at sea. Furthermore, although neutral rights were protected, implicit in the agreement was that belligerents could exercise the right of visit and search to determine the enemy character of the ship or its cargo, which could be misused to impede freedom of navigation during armed conflict.

Even the United States during the Civil War and Spain and the United States during the War of 1898 adhered to the provisions of the Paris Declaration. By 1894, only a handful of Latin American states—including Mexico, Venezuela, Bolivia, and Uruguay—together with Spain and the United States, declined to join the Paris Declaration. Finally, at the Seventh Plenary Meeting of the Hague Conference on 27 September 1907, the delegates of Spain and Mexico, in voting on the Hague Convention (VII) on the conversion of merchant ships into warships,[27] declared their acceptance of the Paris Declaration. The Congress of Paris never adopted the Marcy amendment, but it remained US policy until 1907. Thus, even into the early twentieth century, the United States cherished a radically open view of freedom of the seas as a neutral state, demanding that all private property be protected during wartime, even while sailing on vessels under the flag of a belligerent state.

At the same time, the closing of the American frontier by 1890 brought an end to the American ideal of unlimited potential and energy fuelled by unlimited natural resources. Frederick Jackson Turner explained the significance of the frontier in shaping the American cultural psyche. Most nations have experienced development in a defined area, but the United States experienced in the West conditions of a primitive society marked by perennial rebirth as the frontier advanced towards the Pacific Ocean, physically and metaphorically away from European influence.[28] This vast ungoverned or self-governed arena between 'savagery and civilization' dominated the American character into the early twentieth century.

[26] ibid 597.

[27] Convention (VII) Relating to the Conversion of Merchant Ships into War-Ships, 18 October 1907, 205 CTS 319.

[28] Frederick J Turner, *The Significance of the Frontier in American History* (1893), reprinted in American Historical Association, *Annual Report of the American Historical Association for the Year 1893* (1894) 197.

9.5 Twentieth century

Distinguished American historian Samuel Flagg Bemis called the doctrine of freedom of the seas the 'ancient birthright' of the American Republic.[29] While the doctrine rose to vindicate neutral rights during armed conflict, by the First World War, it had evolved into a peacetime doctrine.[30] President Woodrow Wilson led the expansion of the concept. Before American entry into the war, the president used the term to promote US neutral rights that were being undermined by the German campaign of unrestricted submarine warfare, even as the decidedly unneutral conduct of the United States favoured Britain and the Allies. After the attack on a series of US flagged vessels by German submarines, Wilson accused Germany of violating international law and conducting a war of aggression 'against all nations'. In his 'peace without victory' speech on 22 January 1917, Wilson insisted that the 'paths of the sea must alike in law and in fact be free'.[31] Similarly, he called for 'openness' (transparency) in all diplomacy and trade and an emphasis on free trade.

On 2 April 1917, the president asked a joint session of Congress for a declaration of war against Germany over Berlin's resumption of unrestricted U-boat warfare. As Congress was debating the measure, the *Aztec*, a US armed merchant vessel, was sunk by a U-boat.[32] Two days later, a German submarine torpedoed and shelled the American steamship *The Missourian* without warning. That same day, the Senate voted 82 to 6 in favour of a declaration of war. The House also supported a declaration of war by a vote of 373 to 50 on 6 April. Wilson set forth the war aims of the United States in intervening in the European conflict. In a speech reduced to Fourteen Points, he called in Point II for 'freedom of navigation upon the seas, alike in peace and war'.[33] The Fourteen Points provided the principles that would serve as a basis for peace after the war. The American ideal of freedom of the seas had become ensconced as a cornerstone of the League of Nations.[34] However, with the slow-motion collapse of naval arms control and advancements in submarines during the interwar period, the concept of the free sea was again threatened in the Second

[29] Samuel Flagg Bemis, *A Diplomatic History of the United States* (4th edn, Holt, Rinehart & Winston 1955) 875.

[30] James Kraska and Raul Pedrozo, *The Free Sea: The American Fight for Freedom of Navigation* (Naval Institute Press 2018) 77.

[31] Woodrow Wilson, Address on the Essentials of Permanent Peace (United States Senate, 22 January 1917) in James Brown Scott (ed), *President Wilson's Foreign Policy: Messages, Address, Papers* (OUP 1918) 359–62.

[32] 'Armed American Steamship Sunk; 11 Men Missing' *New York Times* (2 April 1917) 1.

[33] Woodrow Wilson, Address on the Conditions of Peace (8 January 1918) in Scott (n 31).

[34] Julian Corbett, *The League of Nations and Freedom of the Seas* (OUP 1918) 3.

World War. Like his predecessor, President Franklin Roosevelt rejected a coastal defence strategy and used freedom of the seas as a basis of American grand strategy. Roosevelt met with Prime Minister Winston Churchill on 14 August 1941 at a secret conference at the newly established US Naval Station Argentia, Newfoundland, where they fashioned the war aims of the nations united against fascism. The Atlantic Charter was a statement on British and American war aims to construct global governance after the war. The seventh of eight principles declared that all nations have the right to travel the high seas and oceans without hindrance.[35] As the Atlantic Charter gained traction throughout the war, it was fashioned into the Declaration by the United Nations on 1 January 1942.[36] This pronouncement was signed by 26 states (and by an additional 21 states before the end of the Second World War) and referenced in the Charter of the United Nations.[37]

While Wilson and Roosevelt were championing a liberal world order, they were moving towards less liberal political positions at home. During the First World War, Wilson suppressed free speech and opposition to the war. He jailed political rivals, including socialist Eugene Debs, who urged resistance to the war and the military draft. Roosevelt expanded the federal government's role in American society and economy, with the New Deal concentrating power in Washington, DC, signalling a dramatic turn in American political culture away from liberalism and laissez-faire governance. The reaction to the New Deal was advanced by political philosopher and economist Friedrich Hayek, who promoted a vision of a free society that pushed back against statism. Hayek was the principal critic of socialism, arguing in his seminal work, *The Road to Serfdom*, that planned economies are unworkable.[38] Economist John Maynard Keynes had bitter disputes with Hayek during the 1930s. Keynes observed that Hayek himself favoured some government action and that he did not support a strict laissez-faire approach. By doing so, Keynes suggested that Hayek was also walking on the 'road to serfdom'. To navigate this quandary, Hayek stressed in his later writings that the rule of law meant that rules should be general in character and accessible to everyone. The rule of law means that the

[35] Douglas Brinkley and David R Facey-Crowther (eds), *The Atlantic Charter* (Palgrave Macmillan 1994) 40–41.

[36] A Joint Declaration by the United States, the United Kingdom, the Union of Soviet Socialist Republics, China, Australia, Belgium, Canada, Costa Rica, Cuba, Czechoslovakia, Dominican Republic, El Salvador, Greece, Guatemala, Haiti, Honduras, India, Luxembourg, Netherlands, New Zealand, Nicaragua, Norway, Panama, Poland, South Africa, Yugoslavia, 1 January 1942, Avalon Project, Yale Law School, Lilian Goldman Law Library <https://avalon.law.yale.edu/20th_century/decade03.asp> accessed 4 July 2024.

[37] UN Charter, art 3.

[38] FA Hayek, *The Road to Serfdom* (Routledge 1944) 177–78.

law is equally applicable among citizens in society regardless of class, wealth, or social standing, and, importantly, that it is also binding on the government. This latter point meant that the rule of law could serve as a criterion for when the government exceeded its authority. Law forms the institutional basis for protecting individual freedom and the individual from an overreaching government. The laws apply equally to all citizens—if a person is singled out, there is neither freedom nor the rule of law.

Hayek's study about economics is generalized to states operating within the international system and to US notions of universal norms in the oceans. Like individual citizens, ships may engage freely in commerce and transit the seas unimpeded. The *Lotus* case reflects this liberal approach that flag states (and, indeed, states more generally) may take any action that is not explicitly prohibited by a rule of international law.[39]

9.6 Coastal state approach

Freedom of the seas and the liberal order of the oceans were the first and dominant cultural streams in American thought on oceans governance. The burgeoning oversight and control of the administrative state brought about by the Great Depression created the second cultural trend in US oceans governance, which is still unfolding. This trend, which has continued unabated since the 1930s, infused American society with a dimension of management and technocratic control that is at odds with the classical liberal notions of liberty and individualism. President Franklin Roosevelt was elected in 1932 to lead the country through the economic calamity of the Great Depression, changing forever the relationship between the citizen and the state. Roosevelt offered a 'New Deal' that was based on a massive expansion in state control to solve problems and affect the lives of ordinary citizens. This was the greatest expansion in federal power since the end of the Civil War in 1865, as the government assumed vast new powers over industry and the economy. In 1935, for example, unions were granted the right to organize and bargain collectively. Price supports and development programmes aided agriculture, while fiscal policy adopted a Keynesian approach that sought to accelerate economic growth through government deficit spending. By the end of the decade, the large federal administrative and bureaucratic apparatus was positioned to harness US economic power to win the Second World War. At the same time, there

[39] *SS Lotus (France v Turkey) (Judgment)* [1927] PCIJ (ser A) No 10, 31.

was growing awareness that economic commodities and materials—inputs into the economy—were in scarce supply and required greater administration at the national level. The government intervened to regulate the economic and eventually political and social spheres of the United States, first to escape the Great Depression and win the war, and then as a functional governance model. These changes had a symbiotic relationship with American culture, as planning, governance by metrics, and a closer association with the state were introduced into everyday life, eroding the individualism of the past. The government became a central part of daily life, taxation increased greatly, and deference to experts, commissions, and the administrative state multiplied. The consequences of these changes have transformed national views on international maritime law.

The economic and military insecurity of the Great Depression and the Second World War led to a new coastal state orientation that augmented and sometimes sat uncomfortably alongside the US historical interest in freedom of the seas. From the outset of the conflict, the United States sought to use the oceans as a vast moat to keep fascism at bay. In 1939, for example, the United States led the Organization of American States to declare a large zone surrounding North and South America off-limits to belligerent operations. The Declaration of Panama asserted:[40]

> As a measure of continental self-protection, the American Republics, so long as they maintain their neutrality, are as of inherent right entitled to have those waters adjacent to the American continent, which they regard as of primary concern and direct utility in their relations, free from the commission of any hostile act by any non-American belligerent nation, whether such hostile act be attempted or made from land, sea or air.

The Declaration of Panama encompassed all water surrounding the continents and extending 200 to 300 miles from shore.[41] The zone blatantly violated belligerent rights on the high seas.[42] Using the Organization of American States, members endeavoured to prohibit belligerent operations in the Atlantic

[40] William E Masterson, 'The Hemisphere Zone of Security and the Law' (1940) 26 American Bar Association Journal 860; Neutrality (Declaration of Panama), Declaration adopted by the Meeting of the Foreign Ministers of the American Republics at Panama, 3 October 1939.

[41] Masterson (n 40); Neutrality (Declaration of Panama) (n 40).

[42] Quincy Wright, 'Rights and Duties Under International Law as Affected by the United States Neutrality Act and the Resolutions of Panama' (1940) 34 American Journal of International Law 238, 246.

and Pacific Oceans surrounding the American continents, and to consult together to determine appropriate enforcement measures.

The new coastal orientation was even more evident in the Truman Proclamation on the continental shelf.[43] The continental shelf was discussed during the 1930 Hague conference on the law of the sea, where participants considered whether the 'whole extent of the ocean bed' was regarded as 'forming part of the continental shelf . . . along the coasts where the depth does not exceed 200 meters'.[44] The individual states of the United States were already active in developing offshore oil and gas, principally to obtain tax revenue from the resources. In 1938, for example, the state of Louisiana claimed jurisdiction over an area extending 24 marine miles from a 3-mile marginal sea. The federal government moved to check this assertion of authority by Louisiana to ensure that offshore oil and associated tax revenues were under federal control.

On 1 July 1939, Roosevelt, who always sought ways to maximize federal power, wrote in an interagency memo that to make a claim to the offshore resources of the United States, 'new principles of international law might have to be asserted, but such principles would not in effect be wholly new, because they would be based on the consideration that inventive genius has moved jurisdiction out to sea to the limit of inventive genius'.[45] In effect, Roosevelt was signalling that the continental shelf claim might extend hundreds of miles beyond the coast. During the election of 1940, however, the president nudged away from this position for domestic political purposes when the Republican nominee, Wendell Willkie, adopted the politically popular position of supporting states' rights.[46]

In this way, the push for the continental shelf was shaped by the republican form of the US government and American federalism, and the evolving relationship between the states and the federal government shifted power to Washington, DC, during the Great Depression and the Second World War. Secretary of the Interior Harold Ickes was a leading figure in this effort. During the war, he solidified federal authority over offshore energy policy. In June 1943, Ickes proposed 'to evolve new concepts of maritime territorial limits beyond

[43] US Presidential Proclamation 2667, Policy of the United States With Respect to the Natural Resources of the Subsoil and Sea Bed of the Continental Shelf, 10 Fed Reg 12303 (28 September 1945).

[44] Questionnaire No 7: Exploitation of the Products of the Sea, Annex (1926) 20 *American Journal of International Law* 230, 231–32.

[45] Daniel Margolies, 'Jurisdiction in Offshore Submerged Lands and the Significance of the Truman Proclamation in Postwar U.S. Foreign Policy' (2020) 44 Diplomatic History 447, 452.

[46] Ann L Hollick, *U.S. Foreign Policy and the Law of the Sea* (Princeton UP 1981) 30; John Briscoe, 'Federal-State Offshore Boundary Disputes: The State Practice' in Robert B Krueger and Stefan A Riesenfeld (eds), *Developing Order of the Oceans* (Law of the Sea Institute, University of Hawaii 1985) 380.

three miles, and of rights to occupy and exploit the surface and subsoil of the open sea'.[47] Ickes also urged the president to claim the riches of the seabed as far as 100 or 150 miles from shore.[48] The legal innovation of the continental shelf was validated by an interdepartmental committee composed of officials from the departments of State, Interior, and Justice, with Ickes shepherding the issue through the US government. On 7 December 1944, the ever-assertive Ickes recommended that the United States make unilateral proclamations. Before the announcement, however, Ickes recommended socializing the US claim with neighbouring states and allies.[49]

By 1945, Ickes had served three secretaries of state and two presidents and was representative of a certain type of government official who had amassed a great deal of power. On 12 April 1945, Harry S Truman was sworn in as president. The war ended on 2 August. Less than two months later, on 28 September, the president issued the continental shelf proclamation. The United States claimed to extend jurisdiction over the 'submerged lands and subsoil' of the outer continental shelf.[50] The proclamation converted the geophysical term of the continental margin into a legal term imbued with coastal state sovereign rights in which 'the government of the United States regards the natural resources of the subsoil and seabed of the continental shelf beneath the high seas but contiguous to the coasts of the United States as appertaining to the United States, subject to its jurisdiction and control'.[51] The United States claimed exclusive rights to the resources of the seabed to a depth of 200 metres. The proclamation also assured other states that 'the character of the high seas of the waters above the continental shelf and the right to their free and unimpeded navigation are in no way thus affected'.[52]

The US government was motivated by an insatiable need for petroleum to feed the American war machine, setting up a clash between the federal government and the states for offshore control over resources. On 19 October 1945, the federal government filed suit against the state of California, claiming that

[47] The Secretary of the Interior (Ickes) to President Roosevelt, Washington, 5 June 1943, Document 760, Foreign Relations of the United States: Diplomatic Papers, 1945, General: Political and Economic Matters, vol II, 811.0145/11–2844 <https://history.state.gov/historicaldocuments/frus1945v02/d760> accessed 4 July 2024.

[48] ibid.

[49] The Secretary of State to the Secretary of the Interior (Ickes), Washington, 19 December 1944, Document 769, Foreign Relations of the United States: Diplomatic Papers, 1945, General: Political and Economic Matters, vol II, 811.0145/11–2844 <https://history.state.gov/historicaldocuments/frus1945v02/d769> accessed 4 July 2024.

[50] US Presidential Proclamation 2667 (n 43).

[51] ibid.

[52] ibid.

it and not the state held 'paramount rights in the submerged lands within the three-mile belt':[53]

> The ocean, even its three-mile belt, is thus of vital consequence to the nation in its desire to engage in commerce and live in peace in the world; it also become of crucial importance should it ever again become impossible to preserve that peace. And as peace and world commerce are the paramount responsibilities of the nation, rather than an individual state, so if wars come, they must be fought by the nation.

On the same day as the continental shelf proclamation was released, Truman also issued a proclamation on fisheries. The proclamation stated that it was imperative to conserve and protect fisheries resources from overfishing, especially from foreign vessels. For example, the USSR and Japan were fishing off the coast of Alaska and rapidly depleting fish stocks. The United States issued the proclamation as the basis of authority to establish conservation zones 'in those areas of the high seas contiguous to the coasts of the United States wherein fishing activities have been or in the future may be developed and maintained on a substantial scale'.[54] The proclamation provided the basis for regulating US fishers and a mechanism for bilateral arrangements with other states to regulate foreign flagged fishing vessels. Somewhat ambiguously, the proclamation claimed authority to regulate all fishing activities in such zones, subject to agreement.[55]

Even more so than the proclamation on the continental shelf, the fisheries proclamation was widely interpreted as a decisive abandonment of freedom of the seas, since freedom of fishing is a key component of the doctrine.[56] The document declared an intention to unilaterally, or jointly in conjunction with other states, create 'fishery conservation zones' contiguous to the coastline of the United States but beyond the 3-mile territorial sea. The fisheries proclamation was never operationalized because the United States reached agreement with distant water fishing nations.[57] The United States, Canada, and Japan

[53] *United States v California* 332 US 19, 35 (1947).

[54] US Presidential Proclamation 2668, Policy of the United States with Respect to Coastal Fisheries in Certain Areas of the High Seas, 10 Fed Reg 12304 (28 September 1945). See also William T Burke, *The New International Law of Fisheries: UNCLOS 1982 and Beyond* (OUP 1994).

[55] Presidential Proclamation 2668 (n 54) Burke (n 54).

[56] Harry N Scheiber, *Inter-Allied Conflicts and Ocean Law, 1945–53: The Occupation Command's Revival of Japanese Whaling and Marine Fisheries* (Institute of European and American Studies 2001) 9.

[57] Harry N Scheiber, 'The 1953 International North Pacific Fisheries Convention: Half-Century Anniversary of a New Departure in Ocean Law' (2004) 6 San Diego International Law Journal 5.

negotiated the International North Pacific Fisheries Convention in Tokyo in November and December 1951. The treaty established the tripartite North Pacific Fisheries Commission, which protected salmon, halibut, and other designated fish stocks in the eastern North Pacific Ocean area. The Commission was empowered to establish allocation levels for the catch in high seas waters. The agreement was the first international engagement undertaken by the government of Japan beyond the 1945 Peace Treaty and defence pact that ended the post-war occupation (1945–52), restoring Japan to full sovereign status in the global community of nations.

American officials understood that the proclamations for the continental shelf and fisheries had served as precedent that other states could follow, but it was hoped that the preservation of navigational rights would be respected and that states would not use the continental shelf or fisheries proclamation to expand their territorial sea. In one sense, the US proclamations sprang from the notion that the United States was a regional rather than global power intent on protecting its marine resources from outside poaching. In another sense, however, the proclamations were globally oriented, establishing a new distribution of power between the coastal state and the flag state in littoral waters by recognizing heightened coastal state control over the resources while respecting navigational freedoms.

The US proclamations on the continental shelf and fisheries captured the zeitgeist of post-war America's engagement with the world. In 1945, America stood at the ramparts of global governance, creating institutions and rules for the world to live by. New institutions included the United Nations, the World Bank, the International Monetary Fund, the General Agreement on Tariffs and Trade, and the North Atlantic Treaty Organization (NATO). New rules included war crimes tribunals at Nuremburg and Tokyo, new limitations on the use of force and self-defence reflected in the UN Charter, and new rules on the conduct of armed conflict set forth in the 1949 Geneva Conventions.

The shift from a liberal order of the oceans towards integrated ocean management and coastal state enclosure coincided with the rise of the administrative state at home and international governance abroad, including regional institutions such as NATO, the Warsaw Pact, and the European Community system that followed from the proposal of French Foreign Minister Robert Schuman on 9 May 1950. Progressive thinking was not new, having emerged in the early twentieth century in reaction to the excesses of the Gilded Age of the 1890s. One element of this approach focused on improving the condition of the 'common man', elevating the agrarian and urban poor through government intervention: universal education. The natural environment was associated with the masses and their need for (or right to) fresh air, clean water, liveable conditions, and space, as well as the expansion of national parks to provide access for everyday citizens. Another element involved applying scientific or rational methods to governance to make government processes and operations more efficient and to make the administration of public services more effective and less corrupt. The idea that educated elites and technocrats could design and construct a better society percolated through American culture from the progressive era beginning in the 1910s to through the New Deal of the 1930s, setting the stage for the contemporary American approach to oceans governance. While elements of both ocean enclosure and freedom of the seas persisted, the continental shelf and fisheries proclamations signalled a new coastal state awareness that reflected a change in the philosophical culture in the relationship between the individual and the state, towards collectivism, social obligations, and social justice.

9.7 Conclusion

The coastal state orientation that emerged in the twentieth century sprang from shifts in American political culture and social philosophy. The influence of these characteristics on America's approach to international law and oceans law and governance has been dispositive. In the decades since the Second World War, the US policies of freedom of navigation, on the one hand, and a maximalist view of coastal state rights and jurisdiction, on the other hand, have frequently been in tension. The US adoption of a 200-mile fishery zone in 1976 akin to an exclusive economic zone, for example, undercut Washington's negotiating position on freedom of navigation at the Third UN Conference on the Law of the Sea. The tension persists today as bureaucratic effort is expended to strengthen coastal state governance while at the same promoting a liberal view to ensure unimpeded global freedom of navigation.

American oceans law and policy have increasingly adhered to a coastal state orientation over the past half century, even as the United States champions an open order of the oceans through initiatives such as the 1979 Freedom of Navigation Program. Since the Truman proclamations, even as the United States attempted to promote its historic interest in freedom of the seas, it has been even more active in strengthening coastal state control over offshore areas. The positions of freedom of the seas and coastal state control reflect the past and the future of American oceans law and policy and can be traced to the cultural shift from an individualistic approach in political culture to a collectivist approach. Just as American culture still reflects both strands, so too does American oceans law and policy.

Beginning in the 1990s, the classical liberal perspective of the oceans gave way to a coastal state orientation dedicated to marine spatial planning. This tool is used to deconflict ocean activities and ensure that a coherent and integrated approach minimizes impacts on the marine environment. The liberal idea that states could freely operate without restriction receded. By the early 2000s, freedom of navigation had fallen into desuetude. During the Bush administration, the number of freedom of navigation operations plummeted from more than 30 per year during the Clinton era to just a handful per year by 2005. Just a few years later, China was challenging the established order at sea. In 2009, it popularized its dashed line claim over most of the South China Sea, purporting to extinguish high seas freedoms while at the same time encroaching on the maritime rights of regional states. On 22 January 2013, the Philippines brought a case against China at an international arbitral tribunal under Annex VII of the United Nations Convention on the Law of the Sea over China's interference with Philippine offshore rights under the treaty. China responded by constructing massive artificial islands in the Philippine Exclusive Economic Zone. The United States was not publicly supportive of the litigation until the Philippines won key arguments in an award on jurisdiction in 2015. In subsequent years, China has converted the islands into military outposts capable of projecting power over the South China Sea. Meanwhile, China also accelerated harassment of US and other foreign naval operations in the region.

At home, the United States has continued to advance a coastal state view of oceans governance while attempting to restrain excessive coastal state claims abroad. For example, just as the United States was reinvigorating the Freedom of Navigation Program in 2015 to counter China's expansive maritime claims, it was engaging in the preparatory committee for a new treaty to strengthen rules to protect biodiversity beyond national jurisdiction—including new area-based management tools that could restrict freedom of navigation.[58] The High Seas Treaty on biodiversity was adopted in 2023 with a mandate to expand area-based management tools that could include measures to diminish navigational freedoms.

[58] Views Expressed by the United States Delegation Related to Certain Key Issues Under Discussion at the Second Session of the Preparatory Committee on the Development of an International Legally Binding Instrument Under the United Nations Convention on the Law of the Sea on the Conservation and Sustainable Use of Marine Biological Diversity (9 September 2016) <www.un.org/depts/los/biodiversity/prepcom_files/USA_Submission_of_Views_Expressed.pdf> accessed 4 July 2024.

How will the two impulses of coastal control and liberal freedom of the seas be reconciled in American law and policy? The United States has been at the forefront of building out the legal and policy architecture for coastal state jurisdiction and control offshore through the promotion of vast marine protection areas, often in combination with the precautionary approach and marine spatial planning.[59] This tilt towards a coastal state perspective is evident in the division of labour concerning the development of US oceans policy inside the White House. During the administration of President Bill Clinton, oceans policy development shifted from the National Security Council (NSC) to the Council on Environmental Quality (CEQ). Clinton had attended the Rio Summit in 1992, and the change in presidency from George HW Bush to Clinton that year marked the passing of the Second World War generation and realpolitik to the Boomer generation, which placed a greater emphasis on environmental challenges over traditional military security. While the NSC has a mandate to ensure the vitality and prosperity of the US economy, including global trade and the maintenance of military alliances through the unimpeded movement of US naval forces to Europe and Asia, CEQ is focused on developing and implementing an ever-growing menagerie of regulations and rules for reducing human impact on the natural ecology and pursuing the conservation of marine resources and the protection of the marine environment. The threat of climate change and its impact on ocean acidification, ocean warming, and deoxygenation provide further impetus towards greater regulation of marine activities. While many of the new global rules officially rely on flag states for their principal enforcement, in fact they have clearly tipped the balance towards coastal and port state authority. The shift in American culture away from individualism and towards social and bureaucratic responses was perhaps a natural progression to address increasingly sophisticated problems and shared challenges. It is undoubtable, though, that the evolution in US culture has informed and shaped how Americans have thought about oceans law and policy.

[59] James Kraska, *Maritime Power and Law of the Sea* (OUP 2011) 404.

10

Oceania

Karen N Scott

10.1 Introduction

During the Third UN Conference on the Law of the Sea (UNCLOS III), the 'Oceania Group' was an informal regional cluster of states comprising Australia, the Cook Islands, Fiji, Micronesia, Nauru, New Zealand, Papua New Guinea, Tonga, and Western Samoa.[1] Today, the term is sometimes used to refer specifically to the Pacific Island states and emphasizes their connection by and to the Pacific Ocean.[2] For the purposes of this chapter, 'Oceania' will be used to refer to the geography and culture of the South Pacific, including Australia and Aotearoa New Zealand.[3] Fourteen postcolonial Pacific Island states are located within the South Pacific (the Cook Islands, the Federated States of Micronesia, Fiji, Kiribati, the Marshall Islands, Nauru, Niue, Palau, Papua New Guinea, Samoa, the Solomon Islands, Tonga, Tuvalu, and Vanuatu), in addition to the remaining dependent territories of France (New Caledonia, Wallis and Futuna, and French Polynesia), Britain (Pitcairn Islands), New Zealand (Tokelau), and the United States (American Samoa, Guam, and the Commonwealth of the Northern Mariana Islands).[4] The combined exclusive economic zones (EEZs) of these states cover an area of 30.57 million square kilometres—around 55 times the land area of the island states (approximately 555,000 square kilometres).[5] Australia's maritime zone is the third-largest in the world, with an EEZ of around 6.15 million square kilometres (compared to

[1] Fredrick L Ramp, 'Regional Law of the Sea: A Proposal for the Pacific' (1977) 18 Virginia Journal of International Law 121, 123–24.

[2] Epeli Hau'ofa, 'Our Sea of Islands' in Erik Waddell, Vijay Naidu, and Epeli Hau'ofa (eds), *A New Oceania. Rediscovering Our Sea of Islands* (University of the South Pacific 1993).

[3] It is nevertheless acknowledged that 'Oceania', together with other terms for the Pacific region and its peoples, is not unproblematic. See, particularly, Damon Salesa, *An Indigenous Ocean: Pacific Essays* (Bridget Williams Books 2023) ch 2.

[4] Greg Fry and Sandra Tarte, 'The "New Pacific Diplomacy": An Introduction' in Greg Fry and Sandra Tarte (eds), *The New Pacific Diplomacy* (ANU Press 2015) 3, 4.

[5] Ludwig Scharmann, 'The UN Convention on the Law of the Sea and Its Implications for Third World Countries: The Case of Tuna Fishery in South Pacific Countries' (1991) 15 Ocean and Shoreline Management 309, 312.

Karen N Scott, *Oceania* In: *Cultural Influences on the Law of the Sea*. Edited by: James Kraska and Hayoun Ryou-Ellison, Oxford University Press. © Karen N Scott 2025. DOI: 10.1093/9780198944140.003.0010

a land territory of 5.9 million square kilometres) and an additional 2.5 million square kilometres of continental shelf beyond 200 nautical miles.[6] Aotearoa New Zealand's maritime zone, including its continental shelf beyond 200 nautical miles, comprises 5.7 million square kilometres and is 21 times the area of terrestrial Aotearoa New Zealand. Owing to the fortunate geographical location of various offshore islands, Aotearoa New Zealand has the sixth-largest EEZ of any state. While Oceania is defined in terms of the Pacific, the maritime zone of Australia also reaches west into the Indian Ocean and the jurisdiction of both Australia and Aotearoa New Zealand extends into the Southern Ocean by means of their sub-Antarctic island territories and claims to the continent of Antarctica proper.

This chapter will examine the extent to which the states of Oceania can be said to have exerted a cultural influence on the development of the international law of the sea. Although the states in the region are united, to a greater or lesser extent, by the fact that they are all 'large ocean states' and are dependent upon the oceans for communication, trade, prosperity, and culture, it is nevertheless not possible to speak of a unified Pacific culture—even among Pacific Island states themselves.[7] Moreover, while the Indigenous peoples of all the Pacific states have strong traditions of use and governance of the oceans and, at the domestic level, this is being slowly recognized within legal and policy frameworks, there is little evidence to date that these traditions are influencing the substantive development of the international law of the sea. Rather, the history of the cultural influence of Oceania is a colonial one, a legacy that persists to this day.

This chapter will focus, first, on the role of Oceania as a group of states and as individual states—primarily Australia, Aotearoa New Zealand, and Fiji—during UNCLOS III, a pivotal period in the development of the modern law of the sea and the time during which Pacific regionalism was emerging and having a cultural impact in multilateral processes and through its substantive contributions to global state practice. Specific examples will be highlighted, including the fundamental role played by Oceania in the formation of the EEZ, fisheries management, the continental shelf, and the pollution prevention provisions ultimately incorporated into the 1982 UNCLOS.[8] In the context of UNCLOS

[6] Stuart Kaye, 'Australia' in Seokwoo Lee (ed), *Encyclopedia of Ocean Law and Policy in Asia-Pacific* (Brill Nijhoff 2023) 573. These figures do not include the 2 million square kilometres of maritime zones associated with the Australian Antarctic Territory.

[7] For a recent eloquent, critical, and highly engaging account of the Pacific and Pacific regionalism, see Salesa (n 3).

[8] UN Convention on the Law of the Sea, 10 December 1982, 1833 UNTS 397.

III and beyond, '[n]o one has contributed more to stability and peaceful order in the world's oceans in the last four decades than Satya N. Nandan'[9] from Fiji, who was elected representative of the Asian Regional Group to serve as rapporteur of the Second Committee of the Conference[10] and who played an influential and fundamental role in the drafting of the Convention.[11] The chapter will then turn to developments post-UNCLOS and will examine how a highly collaborative regional approach developed by Pacific Island states in the wake of decolonization has shaped a Pacific culture with respect to fisheries management and, more recently, in fixing maritime boundaries in light of sea level rise. The chapter will conclude with brief remarks on the likely future impact of Oceania on the development of the law of the sea as it faces the challenges and implications of climate change: the law of the sea in the Anthropocene.

10.2 Colonial and Indigenous cultures and the law of the sea in Oceania

The relationship between Australia, Aotearoa New Zealand, and the Pacific Islands region and the international law of the sea has been, until recently, largely a colonial one. Writing in relation to Australia, but arguably equally accurate in respect of the wider Pacific region, SE Jackson asserts that a Western (colonial) approach to geography has led to a neglect of the oceans in favour of land and has largely ignored Indigenous peoples' relationships with marine areas.[12] But the Indigenous peoples of the Pacific region have an ancient and strong relationship with the oceans. In Australia, for Indigenous peoples, 'Sea Country' is fully part of 'Country':[13]

[9] Michael W Lodge and Myron H Nordquist, 'Introduction' in Michael W Lodge and Myron H Nordquist (eds), *Peaceful Order in the World's Oceans: Essays in Honor of Satya N. Nandan* (Brill 2014) 1.

[10] Myron H Nordquist, 'Tribute to Ambassador Satya N Nandan' in James Kraska, Ronan Long, and Myron H Nordquist (eds), *Peaceful Maritime Engagement in East Asia and the Pacific Region* (Brill 2022) 3.

[11] See Gudmundur Eiriksson, 'Satya N. Nandan's Role in Drafting the Informal Single Negotiating Text: Aspects of the Preparatory Work for UNCLOS' in Michael W Lodge and Myron H Nordquist (eds), *Peaceful Order in the World's Oceans: Essays in Honor of Satya N. Nandan* (Brill 2014); Satya N Nandan with Kristine E Daleker, *Reflections on the Making of the Modern Law of the Sea* (NUS Press 2021).

[12] SE Jackson, 'The Water Is Not Empty: Cross-Cultural Issues in Conceptualising Sea Space' (1995) 26 Australian Geographer 87.

[13] Amanda Kearney, Michael O'Leary, and Spencer Platten, 'Sea Country: Plurality and Knowledge of Saltwater Territories in Indigenous Australian Contexts' (2022) Geographical Journal 1, 3.

> Indigenous people's distinctions of Country melt away the 'interstitial' or otherworldliness as conventionally applied to bodies of water. Sea Country has its own spatial ontology of power and operates through hyper relationality. Interstices do not exist, for Sea Country is not in between, it is not a space of emptiness, nor a margin, nor a point of becoming. It is full and complete.

The notion of the oceans as whole and facilitating connection between, as opposed to dividing, peoples is equally strong in Pacific Island culture.[14] All Indigenous peoples within the region characterize themselves as guardians or stewards (to use a Western term) of the oceans and its resources. In Aotearoa New Zealand, for example, Māori regard the ocean as *taonga* (treasures), and the relationship with the oceans and its resources is based on *tikanga Māori* (Māori customary law) founded in *whakapapa* (genealogy), *mana* (authority), and *kaitiakitanga* (guardianship).[15] This ancient connection between Indigenous peoples and the oceans is perhaps no better exemplified than by the oral traditions among Aboriginal Australians of sea level rise between 13,000 and 7,000 years ago and the characterization of landscapes submerged as a consequence of sea level rise as part of Country/Sea Country.[16] The identity of Pacific Island nations is firmly anchored in the oceans. As Epeli Hau'ofa writes, '[t]he sea is our pathway to each other and to everyone else, the sea is our endless saga, the sea is our most powerful metaphor, the ocean is in us'.[17]

Modern relationships with the ocean have undoubtedly been changed and, in most cases, diminished, through the process of colonization of the Pacific. In respect of some Pacific Island nations, such as Vanuatu, for example, the settlement of the coastline was in fact a 'product of the countries' colonial history', with people moving from inland areas to the coast in order to be located close to Christian missions.[18] Throughout the Pacific region, Indigenous customary title and rights were largely disregarded by the colonial settlers—and,

[14] See Hau'ofa, 'Our Sea of Islands' (n 2); Epeli Hau'ofa, 'The Ocean in Us' (1998) 10(2) Contemporary Pacific 392.

[15] Karen N Scott, 'Aotearoa New Zealand' in Seokwoo Lee and Lowell Bautista (eds), *Encyclopedia of Ocean Law and Policy in Asia-Pacific* (Brill 2022) 621–22.

[16] See Patrick D Nunn and Nicholas J Reid, 'Aboriginal Memories of Inundation of the Australian Coast Dating from More Than 7000 Years Ago' (2016) 47(1) Australian Geographer 11; Amy L Roberts and others, 'Marine Transgression, Aboriginal Narratives and the Creation of Yorke Peninsula/Guuranda, South Australia' (2020) 15 Journal of Island and Coastal Archaeology 305; Kearney, O'Leary, and Platten (n 13). From an anthropological perspective, these oral traditions challenge the accepted view that oral histories can survive no longer than 500 to 800 years. See Nunn and Reid (n 16).

[17] Hau'ofa, 'The Ocean in Us' (n 14) 409.

[18] David Gilbert, 'Traditional Village Fishing in Fisheries Development Planning in Vanuatu' in John Morrison, Paul Geraghty, and Linda Crowl (eds), *Science of Pacific Island Peoples: Ocean and Coastal Studies, Volume 1* (Institute of Pacific Studies, University of the South Pacific 1994) 15.

in the case of the Pacific, subsequent independent governments—and it is only in recent years that such rights are undergoing an increasing recognition at the national level.

In Australia, following the seminal *Mabo* case[19] in 1992, several hundred claims to the sea/seabed or rights therein were lodged, largely (but not exclusively) under the Native Title Act 1993.[20] Nevertheless, working within a system of essentially European (postcolonial) law, courts in Australia have struggled to move away from the notion of offshore national sovereignty and marine rights have typically been limited to traditional usufructuary rights.[21] Almost 30 years after *Mabo*, Lee Godden opined that 'Indigenous peoples within Australia remain subject to a postcolonial, economic and legal regime that very reluctantly concedes marine space and resources to Aboriginal Peoples and Torres Strait Islanders'.[22]

This assertion is equally true with respect to Aotearoa New Zealand and Māori. In contrast to Australia, the relationship between the Crown and Māori is underpinned by a treaty (or treaties)—the 1840 Te Tiriti o Waitangi and Treaty of Waitangi[23]—and New Zealand formalized a process to hear grievances from Māori against the Crown in 1975 through the establishment of the Waitangi Tribunal. Moreover, in 1995, the Office of Treaty Settlements was established and a process of negotiation was formally begun between the Crown and iwi (an extended kinship group) to agree and implement the settlement of historical Te Tiriti o Waitangi and Treaty of Waitangi claims.[24] However, a dispute between Māori and the Crown over marine and foreshore rights in the early 2000s was one of the most divisive Indigenous disputes in recent Aotearoa New Zealand history. Following recognition by the New Zealand Court of Appeal in 2003 that Māori customary title to the foreshore and seabed had *not* been extinguished by legislation adopted after 1840,[25] the New Zealand

[19] *Mabo v Queensland (No 2)* (1992) 175 CLR 1.
[20] See Anthony Bergin, 'A Rising Tide of Aboriginal Sea Claims: Implications of the *Mabo* Case in Australia' (1993) 3(3) International Journal of Marine and Coastal Law 359; Lee Godden, 'The Evolving Governance of Aboriginal Peoples and Torres Strait Islanders in Marine Areas in Australia' in Stephen Allen, Nigel Bankes, and Øyvind Ravna (eds), *The Rights of Indigenous Peoples in Marine Areas* (Bloomsbury Publishing 2019); Stuart B Kaye, 'Jurisdictional Patchwork: Law of the Sea and Native Title Issues in the Torres Strait' (2001) 15 Melbourne Journal of International Law 381; Victor Prescott and Stephen Davis, 'Aboriginal Claims to Seas in Australia' (2002) 17(1) International Journal of Marine and Coastal Law 1.
[21] Godden (n 20) 135–38.
[22] ibid 127–28.
[23] Te Tiriti o Waitangi is written in te reo Māori and the Treaty of Waitangi is written in English. While intended to be Māori and English-language versions of the same treaty, there are significant linguistic differences between the two texts and some legal scholars now refer to the two versions separately as distinct treaties.
[24] Scott, 'Aotearoa New Zealand' (n 15) 621–22.
[25] *Attorney-General v Ngati Apa* [2003] 3 NZLR 643.

Parliament, in 2004, passed legislation effectively reversing that decision, vesting ownership of the foreshore and seabed in the Crown and extinguishing any Māori customary rights therein. The 2004 Act was itself subsequently repealed by the Marine and Coastal Area (Takutai Moana) Act 2011, which declared that the foreshore and seabed (referred to as the 'common marine and coastal area') could not be owned by the Crown or by any other person. That Act restored any customary interest in the common marine and coastal area and created three new statutory rights to the marine environment. As a consequence of the Act, a number of customary claims to the foreshore and seabed are currently under consideration by the New Zealand courts or through the treaty settlement negotiation process.[26] Outside of this dispute, the rights of Māori in the marine environment and to marine resources—principally, but not exclusively, fish—have been increasingly embedded in legislation over the last 40 years in Aotearoa New Zealand,[27] to the extent that such rights have in recent times successfully challenged government ocean governance initiatives, such as the proposed and now apparently stalled 620,000-square-kilometre Kermadec Ocean Sanctuary.[28]

The historical approach to customary marine title is not dissimilar with respect to Pacific Island states. While such title was 'traditionally widespread in the South Pacific, except perhaps in Tonga',[29] it was largely unrecognized by colonial and, subsequently, newly independent governments, with '[c]ustomary "ownership" or tenure . . . [being] eroded in most places to become "customary (sometimes exclusive) fishing rights" '.[30] Moreover, attempts to adopt Western models of fisheries management, including marine protected areas, have, in some cases, met resistance—similar to that from Indigenous peoples

[26] The dispute is far from resolved, however. The 2011 Act has itself been challenged as failing to comply with the Crown's commitment under Te Tiriti o Waitangi/Treaty of Waitangi and, in June 2020, in the first of two reports, the Waitangi Tribunal concluded that the Act's procedural and resourcing mechanisms were not sufficient to allow the Crown to meet its obligations under the Treaty. See Waitangi Tribunal, *The Marine and Coastal Area (Takutai Moana) Act 2011 Inquiry: Stage 1 Report* (2020).

[27] See Andrew Eruti, 'New Zealand/Aotearoa and the Rights of Māori to Natural Resources in Marine Areas' in Stephen Allen, Nigel Bankes, and Øyvind Ravna (eds), *The Rights of Indigenous Peoples in Marine Areas* (Bloomsbury Publishing 2019).

[28] On the early development of this proposal, see Karen N Scott, 'Evolving MPA Management in New Zealand: Between Principle and Pragmatism' (2016) 47(3) Ocean Development and International Law 289. For a more recent critical assessment of the proposal and the process from a colonial perspective, see Fiona McCormack, 'The Kermadec Ocean Sanctuary: Terraqueous Territorialization and Māori Marine Environments' (2021) 94(1) Pacific Affairs 77.

[29] Leon Zann and Veikila Vuki, 'Marine Environmental Management and the Status of Customary Marine Tenure in the Pacific Islands' in G Robin South and others (eds), *Traditional Marine Tenure and Sustainable Management of Marine Resources in Asia and the Pacific* (University of the South Pacific 1994) 68–69.

[30] ibid.

in Aotearoa New Zealand (and Australia[31])—from groups reluctant to 'relinquish traditional rights and uses' derived from 'complex communal land and sea tenure systems'.[32]

While, at the national level, the last two decades have witnessed significant advances in the rights of Indigenous peoples over marine resources and their participation in national and local marine governance across the Pacific, this has not necessarily translated into influence on the development of the international law of the sea. Godden has argued that Aboriginal Australians and Torres Strait Islanders have been marginalized from the implementation of the law of the sea in Australia and that the 'growing acceptance of knowledge pluralism has not been matched by enhanced legal pluralism'.[33] Unsurprisingly, how Indigenous peoples view the oceans is not necessarily coterminous with the maritime boundaries and rights and obligations as set out in UNCLOS. In respect of Australian Aboriginal Sea Country, for example, the ocean 'is given its own political distinction through cultural ancestral features which trace their origins to the influences of maritime and salt water lifeworlds'.[34] The same broad conclusion in relation to the marginalization of Indigenous peoples can be reached in respect of Aotearoa New Zealand, although there is increasing formal recognition of the government's obligations under the Te Tiriti o Waitangi and Treaty of Waitangi to Māori in the context of negotiating and implementing international agreements.[35] Nevertheless, the cultural influence of Australia and Aotearoa New Zealand on the international law of the sea is, to date, overwhelmingly derived from the postcolonial settler state.

Part of the cause of the marginalization of Indigenous peoples is that, historically, they have more generally been excluded from the global frameworks that provide the foundation for the modern international law of the sea.[36] For example, neither the 1958 Geneva Conventions on the law of the sea nor the 1982 UNCLOS provide for any express reference to the rights of Indigenous

[31] Godden (n 20) 143.

[32] ibid 69. See also Michelle Lam, 'Consideration of Customary Marine Tenure System in the Establishment of Marine Protected Areas in the South Pacific' (1998) 39 Ocean & Coastal Management 97; Joeli Veitayaki, 'Traditional Marine Resource Management Practices Used in the Pacific Islands: An Agenda for Change' (1997) 37 Ocean & Coastal Management 123.

[33] Godden (n 20) 132.

[34] Kearney, O'Leary and Platten (n 13) 4.

[35] For example, the Aotearoa New Zealand Ministry of Foreign Affairs and Trade (MFAT) signed a Memorandum of Understanding with Te Taumata (a group of recognized leaders in Māori socio-economic and cultural development) to engage more directly on trade policy and Māori priorities. See further MFAT, 'Māori Engagement and Interests in Trade' <www.mfat.govt.nz/en/trade/trade-engagement-with-maori/#bookmark1> accessed 13 August 2023.

[36] See generally Endalew Lijalem Enyew and Nigel Bankes, 'Interaction Between the Law of the Sea and the Rights of Indigenous Peoples' in Nele Matz-Lück, Øystein Jensen, and Elise Johansen (eds), *The Law of the Sea: Normative Context and Interactions With Other Legal Regimes* (Routledge 2022) 151.

peoples.[37] Indigenous peoples have no independent rights to participate in the processes and institutions associated with the International Seabed Authority, the Commission on the Limits of the Continental Shelf,[38] or dispute resolution under the Convention. Developments outside of the law of the sea, such as the adoption of the 2007 UN Declaration on the Rights of Indigenous Peoples (UNDRIP),[39] and under the 1992 Convention on Biological Diversity,[40] are, however, slowly increasing the recognition of Indigenous peoples within the law of the sea. While there is only one reference to Indigenous peoples in the 1995 Fish Stocks Agreement,[41] the 2023 High Seas Agreement,[42] by contrast, expressly acknowledges the rights of Indigenous peoples, as set out in the UNDRIP;[43] requires parties to use relevant traditional knowledge of Indigenous peoples and local communities, where available;[44] and provides for the involvement of Indigenous peoples in the processes for designating and monitoring protected areas beyond national jurisdiction,[45] as well as environmental impact assessment.[46] Whether this greater acknowledgement and recognition of the rights and interests of Indigenous peoples in the law of the sea at the international level will facilitate increased influence over, and participation in, multilateral law-making processes by Indigenous peoples in Australia and Aotearoa New Zealand remains to be seen, but there are certainly positive indications that this is likely to occur.[47]

[37] ibid.

[38] See, for example, Zhannah Voukitchevitch, 'Procedural Barriers to Indigenous Peoples' Participation in International Lawmaking—Extended Continental Shelf Delimitation in *Inuit Nunaat*' in Karen N Scott and others (eds), *Changing Actors in International Law* (Brill Nijhoff 2021) 185.

[39] UN General Assembly, Resolution 61/295: United Nations Declaration on the Rights of Indigenous Peoples, UN Doc A/RES/61/295 (13 September 2007) (UNDRIP). Article 25 of UNDRIP refers to the rights of Indigenous peoples to maintain and strengthen their spiritual relationship with the lands, waters, coastal seas, and other resources.

[40] Convention on Biological Diversity, 5 June 1992, 1760 UNTS 79, art 8(j).

[41] Agreement Relating to the Implementation of Part XI of the United Nations Convention on the Law of the Sea of 10 December 1982 Relating to the Conservation and Management of Straddling Fish Stocks and Highly Migratory Fish Stocks, 4 August 1994, 2167 UNTS 88, art 24(2)(b) (Fish Stocks Agreement).

[42] Agreement Under the United Nations Convention on the Law of the Sea on the Conservation and Sustainable Use of Marine Biological Diversity of Areas Beyond National Jurisdiction, UN Doc A/CONF.232/2023/4* (19 June 2023) (High Seas Agreement).

[43] ibid preamble, art 7(k).

[44] ibid art 7(j). Also, Article 13 requires that parties ensure that traditional knowledge of Indigenous peoples held in relation to marine genetic resources beyond national jurisdiction is accessed only with the free, prior, and informed consent of the relevant Indigenous peoples and local communities.

[45] ibid arts 19(2)–(4), 21, 24(3), 26(5).

[46] ibid arts 31, 32, 35, 37.

[47] For example, the Free Trade Agreement between the European Union and Aotearoa New Zealand, signed on 9 July 2023, includes a chapter on Māori trade and economic cooperation and, in addition to acknowledging the Te Tiriti o Waitangi/Treaty of Waitangi as a foundational document of constitutional importance to Aotearoa New Zealand, expressly recognizes the value of Māori approaches, informed by te ao Māori, mātauranga Māori, and Kaupapa Māori (ch 20). I am grateful to my colleague Professor Chris Riffel for bringing this to my attention.

For Pacific Island states, the absence of a dominant settler population has meant that Indigenous Pacific peoples have participated directly at the international level through the processes of statehood and self-determination from the 1970s onwards.[48] This notwithstanding, the approach of Pacific Island states to the creation, codification, and practice of the law of the sea nevertheless has its origins in, and has been shaped by, colonialism. Arguably, the most significant cultural influence of the Pacific region—or Oceania—on the law of the sea has been one of regional cooperation and collaboration. This is sometimes referred to as 'Pacific diplomacy'[49] or the 'Pacific Way'[50] and was developed by Pacific Island states beginning in the 1960s, while they were emerging from colonial rule, as a means of leveraging their collective resources and rights.[51] As will be discussed below, this strong regional approach was integral to the negotiation of maritime zones within UNCLOS III and to managing the valuable Pacific tuna fishery. More recently, it has been deployed in responding to the impacts of climate change and sea level rise on the stability of maritime zones. It is notable that while this regional approach has been implemented generally in international relations, the greatest degree of Pacific unity has occurred in relation to the oceans and the law of the sea.[52] Nevertheless, as Hau'ofa has argued, Pacific regionalism 'is a direct creation of colonialism' and has its origins in the South Pacific Conference established by Australia, France, the Netherlands, New Zealand, the United Kingdom, and the United States following the Second World War.[53] Hau'ofa is critical of the historical regional Pacific approach:[54]

> In our part of the world, regionalism first emerged as a creation of colonialism to pre-empt the rise of revolutionary or even nonrevolutionary independence movements. This is the root of much of the problem of regionalism in the Pacific. We have not been able to define our world and ourselves without direct and often heavy external influences.

[48] With the notable exception of Tonga, all Pacific Island nations were colonized by the United Kingdom, the United States, Australia, and New Zealand and began attaining independence from the 1960s onwards—for many of them, during the UNCLOS III negotiations. Samoa was the first to obtain independence, in 1962, and Palau, the most recent, in 1994.

[49] Fry and Tarte (n 4) 4.

[50] Hau'ofa, 'The Ocean in Us' (n 14) 394.

[51] Fry and Tarte (n 4) 4.

[52] Hau'ofa, 'The Ocean in Us' (n 14) 400.

[53] ibid 398.

[54] ibid 397.

The roles of Australia and Aotearoa New Zealand in Pacific regionalism have waxed and waned over the last 50 years, with—as will be discussed below—the two states playing a strong leadership role during UNCLOS III in promoting Pacific interests, but with Pacific Island states more recently moving diplomacy away from the Pacific Islands Forum (which includes Australia and New Zealand as members) to other institutions that exclude the former Pacific colonial states.[55] Internally, Pacific regionalism and the Pacific Way suffered as a consequence of regional disunity in the 1980s[56] and, led by Fiji, a so-called new Pacific diplomacy has emerged over the last decade.[57] This more assertive version of Pacific regionalism has been described as 'reminiscent' of the immediate postcolonial, with its 'emphasis on Pacific Island control of the diplomatic agenda, the creation of new institutions, its appeal to regional identity, and its concern with negotiating global agendas that are impacting Pacific societies'.[58] Nevertheless, Australia and Aotearoa New Zealand remain strong regional partners in ocean governance issues and are, for example, playing an important role in supporting the demands of Pacific Island states for fixed maritime boundaries in the context of sea level rise.[59] That said, the geopolitical context of the Pacific has shifted in recent years owing to a much more active China in the region and, latterly, a resurgent interest of the United States in response to China's regional rise.

In summary, the culture of Oceania in the context of the international law of the sea is one that has its origins in, and is shaped by, the colonial history of the region—and it is a culture that persists to this day. As will be discussed below, Australia and Aotearoa New Zealand participated in the twentieth-century codification and practice of the law of the sea as colonial/postcolonial states. Their culture largely reflects Western/European approaches to the law of the sea, rather than the culture of Aboriginal Australians and Torres Strait Islanders and Māori. Nevertheless, united to some extent by the common interests of these large ocean states, a strong regional approach to the law of the sea has emerged in the Pacific, and this regional culture has undoubtedly influenced the development of the law of the sea through multilateral processes, as well as through state practice. The extent to which this regional approach is

[55] Fry and Tarte (n 4) 7–13. For example, led by Fiji (following its suspension from the Pacific Island Forum in 2009, as the result of a coup), the Pacific Small Island Developing States Group was reinvigorated and has become the primary vehicle for representing Pacific Island states at the United Nations: ibid 6–7.

[56] Hau'ofa, 'The Ocean in Us' (n 14) 394.

[57] Fry and Tarte (n 4) 3.

[58] ibid 3.

[59] See the discussion below.

inclusive of Australia and Aotearoa New Zealand has varied both temporally and substantively; at times, the interests of the Pacific Island states are clearly divergent from the interests of the former (some would argue current) colonial powers in the region. Nevertheless, the impact of a strong regional approach within the Pacific can be discerned with respect to the development of the law of the sea in areas such as the creation of the EEZ, fisheries management, and climate change and sea level rise, as will be demonstrated below.

10.3 The cultural influence of Oceania on the law of the sea prior to UNCLOS III

In contrast to other regions—notably, Western Europe—while the oceans were fundamental to the culture, occupation, sustenance, and prosperity of Oceania for hundreds if not thousands of years, it cannot be said that the Pacific region was culturally influential on the development of the international law of the sea prior to the twentieth century. Moreover, during the first half of the twentieth century, most of Oceania remained under colonial rule. Although Australia and Aotearoa New Zealand emerged as fully independent states after the Second World War, their principal maritime interests remain allied with the United Kingdom and the United States. It is notable, for example, that while Australia was represented at the Hague Codification Conference in 1930, 'a distinctive Australian contribution towards the codification and progressive development of the international law of the sea did not emerge, however, until the United Nations first conference on the law of the sea in 1958'.[60]

During the middle part of the twentieth century, including through the negotiations for the 1958 Geneva Conventions at the first Conference on the Law of the Sea (UNCLOS I), both Australia and Aotearoa New Zealand prioritized protecting the freedom of navigation in order to protect lines of communication and trade and the interests of naval vessels.[61] Australia was also keen to protect the freedom of overflight.[62] Thus, neither state supported an

[60] Ivan A Shearer, 'Australia and the International Law of the Sea' (1986) 24 Archiv des Völkerrechts 22, 23.

[61] See Michael Landale and Henry Burmester, 'Australia and the Law of the Sea—Offshore Jurisdiction' in KW Ryan (ed), *International Law in Australia* (2nd edn, Law Book Company 1984) 391; Kenneth Bailey, 'Australia and the Geneva Conventions on the Law of the Sea' in DP O'Connell (ed), *International Law in Australia* (Law Book Company 1965) 231; Malcolm Templeton, 'The Law of the Sea' in Malcolm Templeton (ed), *New Zealand as an International Citizen: Fifty Years of United Nations Membership* (New Zealand Ministry of Foreign Affairs and Trade 1995) 147, 154.

[62] Bailey (n 61) 241.

extension of the territorial sea beyond 3 nautical miles[63] nor the 200-nautical-mile-zone claims emerging from states within South America around that time.[64] Australia was further resistant to the unilateral claims to restrict navigation in archipelagic waters that were being put forward by Indonesia and the Philippines, including the use of straight baselines.[65] Writing in 1965, Sir Kenneth Bailey commented:[66]

> Not as a mere survival from the Colonial period therefore but in the exercise of deliberate national choice, Australia has rated the maximum freedom of communications, by sea and by air, as the highest desideratum whenever the international law of the sea is under consideration. This has brought, and kept, Australia broadly in line with the policy adopted—though in some respects for quite different reasons—by the United Kingdom and the United States.

Interestingly, Bailey chaired the first committee at UNCLOS I, which focused on the territorial sea and contiguous zone, and, while at 'the forefront of negotiations to achieve agreement on the permissible breadth of territorial waters', was unable to broker such an agreement.[67] By the 1960s, Aotearoa New Zealand's position in relation to the extension of maritime zones had begun to change. It supported the proposal for a 6-nautical-mile territorial sea and a 6-nautical-mile fishing zone at the Second Conference on the Law of the Sea (UNCLOS II) in 1960.[68] A decade on, Aotearoa New Zealand's position shifted more fundamentally as the potential advantages of its geographical isolation began to be realized. Aotearoa New Zealand decided that its 'essential interests lay, not with the maritime powers but with other coastal states'[69] and, moreover, that freedom of passage was 'no longer . . . the sole determinant' of New Zealand's maritime policy.[70] Aotearoa New Zealand extended its territorial sea (declared in 1965) to 12 nautical miles in 1977,[71] while at the same

[63] Templeton, 'The Law of the Sea' (n 61) 164; Bailey (n 61) 241.

[64] R Cullen and PA Memon, 'Impact of the Exclusive Economic Zone on the Management and Utilisation of the New Zealand Fishery Resources' (1990) 31 Pacific Viewpoint 44, 45.

[65] Landale and Burmester (n 61) 391–92; Bailey (n 61) 241; Stuart Kaye, 'Australia and the Negotiation of the Law of the Sea' (2015) 7 Australian Journal of Maritime and Ocean Affairs 256, 257.

[66] Bailey (n 61) 242. Sir Kenneth Bailey was the leader of the Australian delegation at UNCLOS I.

[67] Shearer (n 60) 23.

[68] KJ Keith, 'International Law 1960 to 2010: Now and Then' (2012) 43 Victoria University of Wellington Law Review 21, 31.

[69] Bill Mansfield, 'Resource Diplomacy: New Zealand's EEZ and the UNCLOS Treaty Regime' in Brian Lynch (ed), *New Zealand the World: The Major Foreign Policy Issues, 2005–2010* (NZIIA 2006) 149.

[70] Templeton, 'The Law of the Sea' (n 61) 154.

[71] Territorial Sea, Contiguous Zone, and Exclusive Economic Zone Act 1977, s 3.

time claiming a 200-nautical-mile EEZ.[72] By contrast, Australia declared a 12-nautical-mile fishing zone in 1967,[73] but did not extend its territorial sea to 12 nautical miles until the 1990s. It asserted only a 200-nautical-mile fishing zone in the late 1970s,[74] with an EEZ not being declared until 1994.[75]

With respect to the continental shelf, however, Australia led the vanguard in the region in terms of claiming exclusive rights over continental shelf resources and in influencing the terms of the 1958 Geneva Conventions in this respect.[76] While Aotearoa New Zealand did not formally claim a continental shelf until 1964,[77] Australia began the process of claiming rights with the Pearl Fisheries Act 1952, which purported to exercise jurisdiction over foreign nationals in addition to Australian citizens.[78] Its first continental shelf proclamation took place in 1953.[79] This brought Australia into direct dispute with Japan—in respect of Japanese nationals who were taking mother-of-pearl from the continental shelf of northern Australia—and Australia agreed, in principle, that the dispute be submitted to the International Court of Justice.[80] While the dispute was resolved by treaty in 1954,[81] Australia organized a Commonwealth working party at UNCLOS I to develop a definition of the 'natural resources of the continental shelf' to include biological resources.[82] Foreshadowing the debates at UNCLOS III, the issue turned on whether such resources would include only those fixed to the shelf or whether they would extend to species capable of locomotion.[83] The 'Australian-sponsored formula' of 'organisms which, at the harvestable stage, either are immobile on or under the sea bed or are unable to move except in constant physical contact with the sea bed or the subsoil' was incorporated into Article 2(4) of the Geneva Convention on the Continental Shelf[84] (and provides the basis for Article 77(4) of UNCLOS).[85] Following the adoption of the Geneva Conventions, Australia proclaimed a continental shelf in accordance with its provisions in 1967, although[86]

[72] ibid s 9.
[73] Landale and Burmester (n 61) 391.
[74] Kaye, 'Australia' (n 6) 576. While Australia generally has asserted a 12-nautical-mile territorial sea, its territorial sea remains at 3 nautical miles in parts of the Torres Strait.
[75] Proclamation under the Seas and Submerged Lands Act 1973, s 10B (26 July 1994).
[76] Bailey (n 61) 231.
[77] Continental Shelf Act 1964.
[78] Bailey (n 61) 234–35.
[79] Kaye, 'Australia' (n 6) 583.
[80] ibid.
[81] Shearer (n 60) 23.
[82] Bailey (n 61) 235–36.
[83] ibid.
[84] Convention on the Continental Shelf, 29 April 1958, 499 UNTS 311.
[85] Shearer (n 60) 23.
[86] ibid 24.

> [t]echnology had advanced so rapidly after 1958 that the 200 metre isobath was virtually a dead letter, and effectively the definition was interpreted by 1967 as meaning that Australia had sovereign rights to the edge of the continental margin. This interpretation was expressly endorsed by the Australian foreign minister in a statement in parliament on the 30th of October 1970.

Thus, for much of the first half of the twentieth century, the interests of Australia and Aotearoa New Zealand were largely aligned with one another and with their former colonial power, the United Kingdom, and its ally, the United States. Freedom of navigation was the principal priority rather than the expansion of territorial maritime zones. Both states nevertheless supported the creation of the juridical continental shelf, with Australia taking a robust and early leadership role in light of its dispute with Japan over seabed resources off its northern coast. By the end of this period, Aotearoa New Zealand's interests began to shift as the benefits of a large coastal zone began to materialize and the development of the EEZ became a priority for it and for Pacific Island states, which were emerging from colonial rule, during the early stages of UNCLOS III.

10.4 Oceania and UNCLOS III

The Oceania Group was active and influential during UNCLOS III as a group and—particularly in the case of Australia and Aotearoa New Zealand—as individual states. Australia was the first state from the region to become actively involved as a member of the Committee on the Peaceful Uses of the Sea-Bed and the Ocean Floor Beyond the Limits of National Jurisdiction, established by UN General Assembly Resolution 2340 (XXII) of 18 December 1967.[87] Fiji joined when the Committee was enlarged to 91 members.[88] At the onset of UNCLOS III, however, all the states and other territories from the Pacific region recognized the importance of the negotiations to their strategic and economic interests. The Prime Minister of Aotearoa New Zealand, in 1976, asserted that[89]

> [t]here is not the slightest doubt, that, if the Law of the Sea Conference takes the course that is apparent at the moment but not firmly certain, it will be

[87] Keith Brennan, 'Australia and the Law of the Sea—the International Sea-Bed' in KW Ryan (ed), *International Law in Australia* (2nd edn, Law Book Company 1984) 419.

[88] Lodge and Nordquist (n 9) 2.

[89] New Zealand, Parliamentary Debates (*Hansard*), vol 405, 12 August 1976.

> the most important economic event in this country's recent history, and will require from New Zealand, a vast effort to exploit and administer the fourth largest area of sea in the world.

Similarly, the Australian Foreign Minister, in 1981, stated that 'it is self-evident and needs no emphasizing by me that, as an island continent with extensive offshore areas under heavy dependence on international trade, Australia has a vital interest in the issues before the Law of the Sea Conference'.[90] While not all Pacific Island states participated directly in UNCLOS III,[91] as a region, they collectively viewed the negotiations as an opportunity to increase their share of ocean resources, and they regarded an expanded maritime jurisdiction as a means to provide the necessary resources to support their newly acquired self-determination, which had resulted from the process of decolonization in the 1960s and 70s.[92] In 1976, the South Pacific Forum adopted a Declaration on the Law of the Sea Questions, which affirmed 'their common interest in securing the adoption of a new and comprehensive Convention on the Law of the Sea' and that the Convention must confirm 'the sovereign rights of coastal states' in their 200-mile EEZs with respect for navigation and overflight, as well as providing for 'a stable and orderly regime for the exploitation of the deep sea-bed which is the common heritage of mankind'.[93] As Transform Aqorau has written, '[i]n no other region of the world is the confluence between the development of the EEZ and political independence so closely related'.[94]

While there was significant synergy between the members of the Oceania Group on most issues under negotiation, there were nevertheless areas where interests diverged. For example, the question of the continental shelf, which was of special concern to Australia and Aotearoa New Zealand, was not of particular interest to Pacific Island states.[95] Fiji and Papua New Guinea were

[90] Minister for Foreign Affairs, the Hon A Street, Commonwealth of Australia, House of Representatives, Parliamentary Debates (*Hansard*), 26 May 1981, 22524–36, as quoted in Landale and Burmester (n 61) 390.

[91] Roy S Lee, 'The New Law of the Sea and the Pacific Basin' (1983) 12 Ocean Development and International Law 247, 252. For example, Kiribati was represented by the United Kingdom until its independence in 1979 and, while there were 'cursory consultations' between the United Kingdom and Kiribati, 'British interests prevailed'. See Roniti Teiwaki, *Management of Marine Resources in Kiribati* (Atoll Research Unit, Institute of Pacific Studies of the University of the South Pacific 1988) 60.

[92] Transform Aqorau, 'The Role of the Pacific Islands Forum in Ocean Governance' (background paper prepared for the Pacific Islands Oceans Forum University of the South Pacific, Suva, 2–6 February 2004) 3.

[93] 'South Pacific Forum' (1976) 47(10) Australian Foreign Affairs Record 555, 556.

[94] Transform Aqorau, 'The Evolution of International Fisheries Law in the Island Nations of the Pacific: The Quest for Control' in Michael W Lodge and Myron H Nordquist (eds), *Peaceful Order in the World's Oceans: Essays in Honor of Satya N. Nandan* (Brill 2014) 338.

[95] GPM Dabb, 'The Development of the Law of the Sea in the South Pacific' in Igor I Kavass (ed), *Australian and South Pacific Law: Structure and Legal Materials* (WS Hein 1983) 277.

engaged with the question of archipelagic waters,[96] which was not of interest to most other Pacific states or to Aotearoa New Zealand and was in fact a concern for Australia, given its opposition to earlier claims by Indonesia and the Philippines.[97] Neither Aotearoa New Zealand nor the Pacific Island states were especially involved in the negotiations for the deep seabed minerals regime,[98] but Australia was highly engaged in the development of what became Part XI of UNCLOS.[99]

More generally, for all states in the Pacific region, but particularly for Aotearoa New Zealand, UNCLOS III was about more than acquiring a larger share of ocean resources; it was a fundamental process contributing to the creation of the international rules-based order, which Aotearoa New Zealand was (and remains) committed to protect. As Chris Beeby, one of New Zealand's principal negotiators of UNCLOS, articulated in 1975, '[s]elf-interest, as well as a traditional concern for the rule of law, should lead New Zealand to place considerable emphasis on the broad community interest in ensuring that the oceans do not become a battleground in the search for, and exploitation of, scarce resources'.[100] The importance of developing a rules-based law of the sea is also implicitly recognized in Australia's list of seven objectives for UNCLOS III, as set out by Keith Brennan, the leader of the Australian delegation at the outset of the negotiations.[101]

10.4.1 Expanding maritime zones under the jurisdiction of states

One of the most important cultural contributions from Oceania to the international law of the sea during UNCLOS III was the advocation for, and shaping of, an extended maritime zone that ultimately became the EEZ. Aotearoa New Zealand was the leading early advocate for the EEZ and, in 1974—together with Canada, Chile, Iceland, India, Mauritius, Mexico, and Norway—tabled an influential paper supporting its inclusion in UNCLOS.[102] The paper argued for the EEZ on the basis that coastal states were more likely to manage fisheries

[96] ibid 282.
[97] Landale and Burmester (n 61) 391–92.
[98] Dabb (n 95) 91; Malcolm Templeton, 'New Zealand and the Development of International Law' in Bruce Brown (ed), *New Zealand in World Affairs III, 1972–1990* (Victoria UP 1999) 71.
[99] Shearer (n 60) 28.
[100] Chris Beeby, 'The United Nations Conference on the Law of the Sea: A New Zealand View' (1975) 16 Pacific Viewpoint 113, 121.
[101] Landale and Burmester (n 61) 393.
[102] Bill Mansfield, 'UNCLOS: Its Importance and Impact' in Bill Mansfield (ed), *New Zealand and the United Nations: 70th Anniversary* (New Zealand Institute of International Affairs 2016) 72.

in a sustainable manner compared with distant water fishing states[103] and thus the environmental credentials of the EEZ were established early on. Australia was supportive of the creation of the EEZ in 1974, but was keen to preserve navigational and other high seas freedoms therein.[104] It was an early advocate of characterizing the EEZ as a sui generis regime.[105] The 1976 South Pacific Forum Declaration expressed strong support for the EEZ concept and, in the first substantive ocean-focused regional initiative in the Pacific, called upon its members to declare individual EEZs in order to maximize their maritime entitlements.[106]

An issue of particular significance to the Pacific was whether all or only some islands should generate an EEZ and other maritime zones, such as the continental shelf. Opposition to the rights of very small islands to the full panoply of maritime zones emerged from African and communist states, which were concerned that colonial powers would gain benefits from large maritime zones associated with remote territories.[107] Aotearoa New Zealand took the position that *all* islands should generate an EEZ[108]—a position that not only served its own strategic interests but also advocated for the interests of Pacific Island states.[109] Aotearoa New Zealand argued, in a joint submission with Fiji, Tonga, and Western Samoa, that the entitlement of an island to an EEZ should not be based on population or geological structure, but that any island that is a naturally formed area of land surrounded by water and above water at high tide should have an EEZ.[110] Australia supported the proposal[111] and the Pacific Island nations 'adopted a united voice' on the issue,[112] with Western Samoa and Tonga going further, arguing that a restriction on the maritime entitlements of oceanic islands would be a denial of their sovereignty.[113] The text of Article 121(3) of UNCLOS, which brokered a comprise between features that are entitled to an EEZ (islands and rocks capable of sustaining human habitation or economic life of their own) and those that are not (rocks that cannot

[103] Mansfield, 'Resource Diplomacy' (n 69) 150.

[104] Landale and Burmester (n 61) 399.

[105] ibid.

[106] 'South Pacific Forum' (n 93) 556, paras 2, 3. All 22 Pacific Island states declared an EEZ between 1977 and 1986. See Scharmann (n 5) 312, and, more generally, Robert B Krueger and Myron H Nordquist, 'The Evolution of the 200-Mile Exclusive Economic Zone: State Practice in the Pacific Basin' (1979) 19 Virginia Journal of International Law 321.

[107] Teiwaki (n 91) 71.

[108] Templeton, 'The Law of the Sea' (n 61) 154.

[109] Templeton, 'New Zealand and the Development' (n 98) 75.

[110] JC Phillips, 'The Economic Resources Zone and the Southwest Pacific' (1982) 16 International Lawyer 265, 276.

[111] Landale and Burmester (n 61) 413.

[112] Dabb (n 95) 278.

[113] Teiwaki (n 91) 72.

sustain human habitation or economic life of their own), 'originated in a formula developed by [Aotearoa New Zealand negotiators] Tony Small and Chris Beeby with Malcolm Templeton and injected behind the scenes at a critical moment in the Conference'.[114] Fijian Ambassador Satya Nandan played an important role in the drafting of Article 121 of UNCLOS through his role as rapporteur, whereby he was entrusted to prepare a single negotiating text for the Second Committee by its chairman, Ambassador Reynaldo Galindo Pohl, and this text 'proved to be the basis on which all subsequent negotiations on the matters before the Second Committee were based'.[115]

The third matter connected with the EEZ and on which the Oceania Group was influential was the question of whether foreign vessels would be permitted to fish within an EEZ and, of particular significance to the Pacific, whether coastal states were entitled to exercise sovereign rights over highly migratory species (such as tuna) in their maritime zones. In respect of the first issue, Aotearoa New Zealand and Australia submitted a joint paper to the Seabed Committee in 1972, proposing that coastal states be granted exclusive control over EEZ fisheries with third states entitled to access any surplus catch.[116] This proposal was adopted in essential form in Articles 62, 69, and 70 of UNCLOS. The Article 64 compromise in respect of highly migratory species also had its origins in a joint Australian and Aotearoa New Zealand proposal.[117] Nevertheless, while the UNCLOS compromise favoured the interests of the Pacific Island state tuna fishery—from which around 50 per cent of the world catch of tuna is taken[118]—the United States continued to refuse to recognize state sovereignty over migratory species well into the 1980s,[119] precipitating the development of a unique Pacific regional approach to fisheries management, which will be discussed below.

Of equal importance to Australia and to Aotearoa New Zealand (although not to Pacific Island states) during the UNCLOS III negotiations were the rights associated with the continental shelf. Both states played an important role in the group of 14 states, known as 'the margineers' on account of their broad continental shelves.[120] Notably, Australia was 'not always comfortable in this group', owing to its relatively modest coastal claims.[121] Nevertheless, Part

[114] Mansfield, 'UNCLOS' (n 102) 73.
[115] Eiriksson (n 11) 38.
[116] Beeby (n 100) 125–26.
[117] Landale and Burmester (n 61) 402.
[118] Camille Goodman, '"Strength Through Cooperation": A 21st Century Treaty for Multilateral Maritime Enforcement in the Pacific' (2013) 31 Australian Yearbook of International Law 11, 12.
[119] Landale and Burmester (n 61) 402–03.
[120] Don McKay (Director, Legal Division, MFAT), 'Law of the Sea—and the Continental Shelf' (1996) 4(11) New Zealand Foreign Affairs and Trade Record 4, 5; Landale and Burmester (n 61) 393.
[121] Landale and Burmester (n 61) 393.

VI of UNCLOS ultimately produced a compromise that is weighted heavily in favour of the maritime 'haves', such as Australia and Aotearoa New Zealand, over the 'have nots'.[122] While Aotearoa New Zealand made a significant contribution to developing the rights of the 'have nots' in promoting the idea of revenue sharing in respect of mineral resources found on the continental shelf beyond 200 nautical miles,[123] Australia maintained its opposition to Article 82 of UNCLOS during the negotiations, arguing that the formula for revenue sharing was inconsistent with the principle of permanent sovereignty over natural resources and would deter offshore development.[124] Australia was also initially unenthusiastic about the role of the Commission on the Limits of the Continental Shelf, but was unsuccessful in persuading other states to support a form of wording whereby final outer shelf limits need only 'take into account' the recommendations of the Commission.[125]

Finally, for the sake of completion, it is worth noting that, contrary to the position of Aotearoa New Zealand and the Pacific Island states, Australia initially favoured a 3-nautical-mile territorial sea, but recognized early on in the negotiations that this proposal was politically and legally unrealistic.[126] Nevertheless, although supporting a 12-nautical-mile territorial sea during negotiations,[127] Australia advocated strongly for the preservation of innocent passage therein, including that of warships, asserting, in the case of the latter, that notification requirements were unlawful.[128] In an example of occasional disunity within Oceania, Papua New Guinea advocated the opposite view and was in favour of a notification requirement in respect of the passage of warships through the territorial sea.[129] Australia also put forward the compromise wording that formed the basis of Article 21(2) of UNCLOS: that coastal states cannot regulate the design, construction, and manning of ships in their territorial sea unless they are giving effect to generally accepted international rules and standards.[130]

122 McKay (n 120) 5.

123 Templeton, 'The Law of the Sea' (n 61) 155.

124 Landale and Burmester (n 61) 407.

125 ibid 406.

126 Anthony Bergin, 'Australia and UNCLOS III' (1983) 29 Australian Journal of Politics and History 427, 432.

127 While Australia now generally claims a 12-nautical-mile territorial sea, special provision is made in respect of the territorial sea in the Torres Strait, which is limited to 3 nautical miles under the Torres Strait Treaty (Australia-Papua New Guinea) of 18 December 1978.

128 Landale and Burmester (n 61) 396–97.

129 ibid 397.

130 ibid 396–97.

10.4.2 Straits and archipelagos

In light of the extension of the territorial sea to 12 nautical miles, the issue of passage through straits was critical to Australia during the negotiations[131] given that much international trade passes through straits adjacent to its northern coast. Australia was successful in resisting proposals by states advocating extensive coastal state control on passage through straits.[132] Australia's position in relation to archipelagic waters was more complicated. Although it objected to the Indonesian and Philippines archipelagic declarations in the 1960s,[133] primarily because the restriction of navigation to innocent passage would have compromised freedom of overflight,[134] it was also conscious of its responsibility in respect of Papua New Guinea, a former colony with archipelagic aspirations.[135] Thus, Australia reversed its opposition to archipelagic waters early in the negotiations, endorsing the concept in principle in the Seabed Committee in 1972[136] but insisting on a right of transit passage therein in order to protect trade and overflight.[137] Fiji, by contrast, was a strong supporter from the outset of a special regime for archipelagic states and had been working with Indonesia, the Philippines, and Mauritius from 1971 onwards on the definition of an archipelagic state.[138] As rapporteur, Nandan was influential in developing the formulation that ultimately balanced sovereignty and innocent passage through archipelagic waters.[139]

10.4.3 Pollution and deep seabed minerals

Both Australia and Aotearoa New Zealand advocated strongly for coastal state jurisdiction in respect of ocean pollution, although Australia softened its

[131] ibid 408.

[132] ibid 409. It is worth noting the critical diplomatic role played by Fijian Ambassador Satya Nandan during UNCLOS III, alongside the UK representative, in convening an informal working group of 17 states and developing a set of draft proposals that included the concept of transit passage. See Eiriksson (n 11) 41, 44.

[133] Landale and Burmester (n 61) 410.

[134] ibid 411.

[135] David Letts, 'The Development of the 1982 UN Convention on the Law of the Sea: An Australian Perspective' (2020) 17 Indonesian Journal of International Law 455, 459–60.

[136] Landale and Burmester (n 61) 410.

[137] Kaye, 'Australia and the Negotiation' (n 65) 260.

[138] Hasjim Djalal, 'Reflections on Ambassador Satya Nandan' in Michael W Lodge and Myron H Nordquist (eds), *Peaceful Order in the World's Oceans: Essays in Honor of Satya N. Nandan* (Brill 2014).

[139] ibid 26.

strong coastal state position during negotiations to take a more moderate approach in terms of balancing the interests of coastal and flag states.[140] Aotearoa New Zealand actively engaged in the negotiations relating to pollution prevention and control and made particular interventions on the extent of coastal state authority to respond to a polluting event.[141] Australia submitted an influential paper to the UN Seabed Committee in 1973, which set out environmental provisions similar to those embodied in the general obligations under Part XII of UNCLOS.[142] While a proposal—developed by Australia, Aotearoa New Zealand, and Canada—advocating a relatively robust system of port state jurisdiction failed to find support at the 1973 negotiations, some of its suggestions were ultimately incorporated into UNCLOS (with modification),[143] and port state control has, of course, since become a vitally important tool in the enforcement of global rules relating to marine pollution and the safety of shipping.

While the Oceania Group was generally supportive of the development of Part XI of UNCLOS, those states were not significantly engaged in its negotiation.[144] By contrast, Australia did play an important role in the development of the regime. Australian delegates sketched a structure of the International Seabed Authority in 1975 that 'closely resembles the structure finally adopted in part XI of the 1982 Convention'[145] and also contributed to the drafting of Annex III to UNCLOS, setting out the essential conditions of minerals exploration.[146] This notwithstanding, Australia was ultimately 'not satisfied'[147] with Part XI and subsequently became 'an enthusiastic supporter of the "boat paper", the basis for negotiations in the UN secretary general's efforts to resolve the ratification imbalance',[148] which was ultimately resolved by the 1994 Implementation Agreement. It was, in fact, Ambassador Nandan who was chairman of the 'Boat Group'[149] in his role as Under-Secretary-General and

[140] Landale and Burmester (n 61) 439.
[141] Beeby (n 100) 122.
[142] Landale and Burmester (n 61) 440–41.
[143] ibid 449.
[144] Templeton, 'New Zealand and the Development' (n 98) 71.
[145] Shearer (n 60) 27–28.
[146] ibid.
[147] Kaye, 'Australia and the Negotiation' (n 65) 263.
[148] ibid.
[149] David H Anderson, 'Baselines in the Modern Law of the Sea' in Michael W Lodge and Myron H Nordquist (eds), *Peaceful Order in the World's Oceans: Essays in Honor of Satya N. Nandan* (Brill 2014).

Special Representative of the Secretary General of the Law of the Sea and who successfully led the negotiation of the 1994 Agreement.[150] It is worth noting that Nandan continued to influence and develop the seabed regime in his three-term role as Secretary General of the International Seabed Authority from 1996 to 2008.[151]

10.4.4 UNCLOS, Oceania and Pacific regionalism

The adoption of UNCLOS can be considered a major success for the Oceania Group. Michael Powles asserts that '[a]rguably the most successful international endeavour which the countries of the Pacific have ever undertaken together was the achievement of nearly all island state objectives in the near decade-long negotiation of the 1982 United Nations Convention on the Law of the Sea'.[152] Bill Mansfield, a long-serving Aotearoa New Zealand diplomat, has suggested that it is 'highly unlikely that any attempted re-negotiation [of UNCLOS] would produce a result as favourable to New Zealand'.[153] Of equal importance, however, is that during this period, both Australia and Aotearoa New Zealand began to engage more deeply with Pacific regional interests, providing, as noted above, strong advocacy with respect to EEZ issues and fisheries on behalf of Pacific nations.[154] Notably, through persistent advocacy, Aotearoa New Zealand was successful in persuading the Conference to permit the Cook Islands and Niue to become full parties to UNCLOS, even though they were not considered states at that time.[155] The rise of Pacific regionalism contemporaneously with UNCLOS III—and, in part, because of the negotiations and the formation of the Oceania Group—has given rise to one of the most important cultural contributions to the international law of the sea post-UNCLOS: a uniquely collaborative regional approach to fisheries management and, latterly, sea level rise. And it is to this final cultural contribution that this chapter now turns.

[150] Michael W Lodge, 'Satya Nandan's Legacy for the Common Heritage of Mankind' in Michael W Lodge and Myron H Nordquist (eds), *Peaceful Order in the World's Oceans: Essays in Honor of Satya N. Nandan* (Brill 2014).

[151] ibid.

[152] Michael Powles, 'Making Waves in the Big Lagoon: The Influence of Pacific Island Forum Countries in the United Nations' (2002) 2 Revue Juridique Polynésienne 59, 60.

[153] Mansfield, 'Resource Diplomacy' (n 69) 150.

[154] Templeton, 'The Law of the Sea' (n 61) 155.

[155] ibid 155.

10.5 Pacific regionalism and its cultural contribution to the international law of the sea

Pacific regionalism, or Pacific diplomacy, has been defined as 'the diplomacy pursued by Pacific states in global forums, or in multilateral arenas in which the Pacific bloc is negotiating with just one external power'.[156] Pacific diplomacy in the context of the law of the sea arguably began with the adoption of the 1976 Declaration on Law of the Sea Questions[157] by the South Pacific Forum, which committed members to the coordination and harmonization of its law of the sea policies for the benefit of the region as a whole and, more specifically, to the harmonization of fisheries policies and the adoption of a coordinated approach in the negotiation of access to fisheries by distant water fishing nations.[158] The members also agreed in principle to establish a South Pacific Fisheries Agency,[159] which was formally constituted the following year, in 1977,[160] and came into operation in 1979.

The South Pacific Fisheries Agency (now known as the Forum Fisheries Agency or FFA) is open to 'all Forum countries and all countries in the South Pacific with coastal state interests in the region who support the sovereign rights of the coastal state to conserve and manage living resources including highly migratory species in its 200-mile zone'.[161] Australia and Aotearoa New Zealand are members, but the United States is not.[162] The principal purposes of the FFA are the collection, analysis, and evaluation of biological and other data; the provision of support, if requested, to Pacific Island states in their negotiation of access to fisheries with distant water fishing nations; and the facilitation of a regional approach to licensing, including agreement on generally applicable policies and measures, as well as collaboration relating to surveillance and enforcement.[163] The FFA is therefore not a regional fisheries management organization, in that it lacks management and conservation responsibilities; rather, it provides a forum for consultation and collaboration.[164]

156 Fry and Tarte (n 4) 4.

157 'South Pacific Forum' (n 93) 556.

158 ibid paras 1(d), 4(a)–(b).

159 ibid para 5.

160 Declaration on the Law of the Sea and Regional Fisheries Agency (1977) 48 *Australian Foreign Affairs Record* 466.

161 ibid para 7.

162 On the history of the establishment of the FFA, see David J Doulman, 'In Pursuit of Fisheries Cooperation: The South Pacific Forum Fisheries Agency' (1988) 10 University of Hawaii Law Review 137.

163 Declaration on the Law of the sea and Regional Fisheries Agency, para 8(i)–(iv).

164 Transform Aqorau, 'Cooperative Management of Shared Fish Stocks in the South Pacific' (case study prepared for the Norway–FAO Expert Consultation on the Management of Shared Fish Stocks, Bergen, 7–10 October 2002) 4–5.

Nevertheless, it has been successful in terms of its core functions 'because there were no competing interests among the South Pacific countries' and all had a 'common adversary': distant water fishing nations.[165] Within the framework of the FFA, Pacific Island countries have developed a collective approach to providing access to tuna fisheries within the EEZs, to developing common licensing terms and conditions, and to fisheries surveillance and enforcement. These initiatives will be very briefly outlined below. It is, however, important to sound a note of caution around what was undeniably a uniquely collaborative approach to fisheries management in the 1970s and 80s. Aqorau notes, for example, that in more recent years 'the regional configuration and architecture has changed, and that Pacific Island states have a diverse range of strategic interests that are not often amenable to a common approach to their relations with external fishing interests'.[166] He goes on to assert that 'those who advocate a common approach to the management of tuna in the Pacific islands region misunderstand the dynamics at play and the different arrangements that underpin the management of different stocks'.[167] More generally, the South Pacific Forum, established in 1971 and known today as the Pacific Islands Forum, which was the key driver of Pacific regionalism in the 1970s and 80s, became less active in the 1990s in the multilateral arena as it focused on regional integration and responding to the 'war on terror' security agenda.[168] Over the course of the 2000s, the Pacific Islands Forum was less prominent in driving Pacific regionalism, owing to the suspension of Fiji in 2009[169] and the increasing criticism of Australia and Aotearoa New Zealand as members 'making it hard to take strong positions on climate change or trade and decolonization when their positions were antithetical'.[170] Nevertheless, the agreement, in 2017, of a new regional approach to the oceans through the adoption of Our Sea of Islands, Our Blue Pacific[171] and, more recently, the development of the 2050 Strategy for the Blue Pacific Continent[172] demonstrate a resurgence in the work of the Forum in this field. Moreover, the regional collaboration in the context of fixing maritime zones irrespective of the impacts of sea level rise is an issue on which Oceania appears to be united and will undoubtedly

[165] ibid 13.
[166] Transform Aqorau, 'How Tuna Is Shaping Regional Diplomacy' in Greg Fry and Sandra Tarte (eds), *The New Pacific Diplomacy* (ANU Press 2015).
[167] ibid 227.
[168] Fry and Tarte (n 4) 6.
[169] ibid 6.
[170] ibid 13.
[171] Office of the Pacific Island Commissioner, 'Our Sea of Islands, Our Blue Pacific' <https://opoc bluepacific.org/our-sea-of-islands-our-blue-pacific/> accessed 19 April 2024.
[172] Pacific Islands Forum, *2050 Strategy for the Blue Pacific Continent* (2022).

constitute an important Pacific cultural contribution to the twenty-first-century law of the sea.

10.5.1 Access to and management of the Pacific tuna fishery

While Part V of UNCLOS granted Pacific Island states sovereign rights over their coastal fisheries, including tuna as a straddling stock and highly migratory species, most states were in no position to develop their own fishing industries or to individually negotiate fair terms of access with distant water fishing nations, many of which were former colonial states. Moreover, the dispute in the 1980s between the United States—which refused to recognize the sovereign rights of states over migratory tuna within the EEZs—and Pacific Island states proved diplomatically and economically damaging, as the Pacific Island states arrested US vessels for illegal fishing and the United States imposed retaliatory trade embargos.[173] As a consequence, Pacific Island states developed three broad harmonized access arrangements that have, in practice, collapsed 'their EEZs for the purpose of access so that the same degree of limits apply to all vessels operating within the access harmonization regime'.[174] The Nauru group[175] manages access to the skipjack tuna fishery under the auspices of the 1982 Nauru Agreement Concerning Cooperation in the Management of Fisheries of Common Stocks (as amended in 2010).[176] By contrast, the Tokelau Arrangement is a non-binding coalition of states[177] for which Albacore tuna is the dominant species. The third arrangement is the South Pacific Tuna Treaty between the United States and 16 Pacific Island states, originally adopted in 1987[178] and most recently revised in 2016. These three arrangements work within the FFA and the Western Central Pacific Fisheries Commission (WCPFC), the regional fisheries management organization established to conserve and manage the regional tuna fishery, described by Aqorau as 'a

[173] Aqorau, 'The Role' (n 92).

[174] Aqorau, 'Cooperative Management' (n 164) 12.

[175] The Federated States of Micronesia, the Republic of Kiribati, the Republic of the Marshall Islands, the Republic of Nauru, the Republic of Palau, the Independent State of Papua New Guinea, the Solomon Islands, and Tuvalu.

[176] Nauru Agreement Concerning Cooperation in the Management of Fisheries of Common Stocks, 11 February 1982.

[177] The Cook Islands, French Polynesia, Samoa, Tonga, Fiji, Vanuatu, New Caledonia, New Zealand, and Niue. In addition, the Solomon Islands, Papua New Guinea, Tuvalu, and Southern Gilberts, members of the Nauru Group, are also members of the Tokelau Group. See Aqorau, 'How Tuna Is Shaping' (n 166) 225.

[178] Treaty on Fisheries Between the Governments of Certain Pacific Island States and the Government of the United States of America, 2 April 1987, [1988] ATS 42.

coalition of the unwilling, as it provides a forum where stakeholders unwillingly cooperate with one another'.[179]

The 1982 Nauru Agreement (revised in 2010) is the most sophisticated of the arrangements and obliges parties 'without any derogation of their respective sovereign rights, to co-ordinate and harmonize the management of fisheries with regard to common stocks within the Fisheries Zones, for the benefit of their peoples'.[180] It establishes principles for determining priorities among fishing vessel applications (favouring domestic fleets) and for developing uniform terms and conditions for licences and access fees. It also provides for a centralized licensing system and cooperation in monitoring and surveillance activities. The parties to the Nauru Agreement (known also as the PNA) have taken steps to limit fishing activity within the region, first through a cap on the number of vessels licensed to fish (under the Palau Arrangement)[181] and, from 2005, the Vessel Day Scheme (VDS), which controls the number of days a vessel can fish rather than the number of vessels.[182] The VDS, in particular, has resulted in a significant increase in revenue for Pacific Island states[183] and has 'fundamentally transformed the Pacific's negotiating position',[184] being described by Jope Tarai as 'unprecedented' as 'a mechanism owned and driven from within the Pacific, and . . . a crucial marker of the new Pacific diplomacy'.[185] The 1987 South Pacific Tuna Treaty was equally innovative when adopted, resolving the dispute between the United States and the 16 Pacific Island states through a multilateral framework.[186] In addition to facilitating US access to the EEZs of the 16 states in return for licence fees and the creation of a Project Development Fund, the Treaty also provided for relatively far-reaching obligations on flag state responsibility well in advance of more recent multilateral developments in this area.[187] While the Treaty arguably served both US and Pacific interests well for 15 years,[188] PNA states with large tuna fisheries

[179] Aqorau, 'How Tuna Is Shaping' (n 166) 226.
[180] Nauru Agreement (n 176) art 1.
[181] See Transform Aqorau and Anthony Bergin, 'Ocean Governance in the Western Pacific Purse Seine Fishery—The Palau Arrangement' (1997) 21 Marine Policy 173; Transform Aqorau, 'Recent Developments in Pacific Tuna Fisheries: The Palau Arrangement and the Vessel Day Scheme' (2009) 24 International Journal of Marine and Coastal Law 557.
[182] Jope Tarai, 'The New Pacific Diplomacy and the South Pacific Tuna Treaty' in Greg Fry and Sandra Tarte (eds), *The New Pacific Diplomacy* (ANU Press 2015) 244–45.
[183] Revenue increased from US$60 million in 2010 to US$229 million in 2012. See ibid 244.
[184] ibid 245.
[185] ibid.
[186] Transform Aqorau, 'Reshaping International Fisheries Development: Assimilating the Treaty on Fisheries Between the Governments of Certain Pacific Island States and the United States Under the PNA Vessel Day Scheme (VDS)' (2014) 29 International Journal of Marine and Coastal Law 52, 56.
[187] ibid.
[188] ibid.

were increasingly unhappy with the level of the licence fee—particularly after the introduction of the VDS, which did not initially apply to US vessels.[189] Moreover, the overexploitation of tuna, the rapid expansion of Pacific fleets, and the establishment of the WCPFC, which constrained the fishing efforts of states other than the United States, also led to tensions.[190] The Treaty, 'once a symbol of regional cooperative success, [had] become politically divisive, impacting on relations between the US and the Pacific Island states, the PNA and non PNA members, and within the PNA group itself'.[191] The parties, after the best part of a decade of negotiation, nevertheless adopted a set of amendments to the Treaty in 2016, extending its application to 2022 and providing for increased cooperation between the parties, but also an option for the United States to negotiate on an individual basis with Pacific Island states should a collective arrangement fail.[192]

10.5.2 Surveillance and enforcement

The second area of note in terms of Pacific collaboration—and one that also includes Australia and Aotearoa New Zealand—is surveillance and enforcement associated with fisheries. In 1992, the Niue Treaty of Cooperation in Fisheries Surveillance and Law Enforcement in the South Pacific Region (Niue Treaty)[193] was adopted, providing a framework for cooperation whereby parties can adopt subsidiary arrangements permitting the sharing of information and personnel and collaborating in the operation of vessels and aircraft within each other's maritime zones, including a right of pursuit and arrest.[194] Although innovative on paper, this Treaty nevertheless relied on states adopting such subsidiary arrangements; in practice, few did.[195] Thus, in 2012, a further Treaty was adopted, the Agreement on Strengthening Implementation of the Niue Treaty on Cooperation in Fisheries and Law Enforcement in the South Pacific Region,[196] which provides for a 'comprehensive self-contained system'

[189] Aqorau, 'How Tuna Is Shaping' (n 166) 229.
[190] Aqorau, 'Reshaping International Fisheries' (n 186) 68.
[191] Aqorau, 'How Tuna Is Shaping' (n 166) 229.
[192] Amendments to the Treaty on Fisheries Between the Governments of Certain Pacific Island States and the Government of the United States of America, 3 December 2016.
[193] Niue Treaty on Fisheries Surveillance and Law Enforcement Cooperation in the South Pacific Region, 21 December 1982, [1993] ATS 31.
[194] Goodman (n 118) 15.
[195] ibid.
[196] Agreement on Strengthening the Implementation of the Niue Treaty on Fisheries Surveillance and Law Enforcement in the South Pacific Region, 2 November 2012, [2017] ATS 11.

for direct cooperation in enforcement, without the need for specific subsidiary agreements.[197]

10.5.3 Sea level rise and the fixing of maritime boundaries

The final example of Pacific regionalism and collaboration, and the most recent cultural contribution of Oceania to an emerging international law of the sea in the context of climate change, is the fixing of baselines/maritime boundaries irrespective of sea level rise. While a global threat, sea level rise constitutes an existential issue for all Pacific Island nations, with some suggesting that it will 'spell the end of today's Pacific in many ways: a radical change in geography, spawning fundamental changes in settlement patterns and communications infrastructure, subsistence systems, societies and economic development. Breakdowns in the social fabric of the societies of the region threaten their essentially Pacific character. Cultural identities are at risk'.[198] Although the implications of climate change and sea level rise on statehood and cultural identity go well beyond the law of the sea, their effects on maritime zones do fall squarely within the parameters of UNCLOS.

Scholars and practitioners have traditionally regarded UNCLOS as providing for ambulatory baselines, which move as geographical features alter or disappear in light of coastal and environmental change,[199] although recent work from the International Law Commission suggests a less definitive interpretation.[200] Collectively, however, the Pacific Islands states from around 2010[201] onwards have asserted, in increasingly robust terms, that they have a right to fix their baselines in accordance with UNCLOS in a manner that does not take account of sea level rise. Such an assertion was made in the 2015 Taputapuātea Declaration on Climate Change by the Polynesian Leaders Group; by the PNA in the 2018 Delap Commitment on Securing Our Common Wealth of Oceans; and, most recently, by the Pacific Islands Forum in the 2021 Declaration on

[197] Goodman (n 118) 19.

[198] Patrick D Nunn, 'The End of the Pacific? Effects of Sea Level Rise on Pacific Island Livelihoods' (2013) 34 Singapore Journal of Tropical Geography 143, 165. See also Ian Falefuafua Tapu, 'Finding *Fonua*: Disappearing Pacific Island Nations, Sea Level Rise, and Cultural Rights' (2020) 62 Arizona Law Review 786.

[199] See, for example, David D Caron, 'When Law Makes Climate Change Worse: Rethinking the Law of Baselines in Light of a Rising Sea Level' (1990) 17 Ecology Law Quarterly 621; Julia Lisztwan, 'Stability of Maritime Boundary Agreements' (2012) 37 Yale Journal of International Law 153.

[200] United Nations, *Report of the International Law Commission Covering the Work of Its Seventy-Second Session (26 April–4 June and 5 July–6 August 2021)*, UN Doc A/76/10 (2021) para 270.

[201] See Pacific Islands Forum, *Our Sea of Islands—Our Livelihoods—Our Oceania: Framework for a Pacific Oceanscape* (2010).

Preserving Maritime Zones in the Face of Climate Related Sea Level Rise. The majority of Pacific Island states have revised their maritime zones legislation through the use of geographic coordinates,[202] and this process has been robustly supported by Australia and Aotearoa New Zealand through the Pacific Maritime Boundaries Project.[203]

This collective approach constitutes virtually uniform and widespread regional state practice (in the context of developing regional customary law) and appears to have been generally accepted by other states as an appropriate response to maintaining the stability of maritime zones in the Pacific. Frances Anggadi has recently gone further and argued that the 2021 Declaration in particular represents a shift in emphasis from developing state practice and custom to making an interpretive claim about the application of UNCLOS.[204] She asserts that the Declaration emphasizes three elements of state practice—the establishment of baselines in accordance with UNCLOS, the notification of those baselines to the UN Secretary General, and the right to fix said baselines with no legal duty to review them in light of sea level rise—and invokes the 'principles of legal stability, security, certainty and predictability that underpin the Convention and the relevance of these principles to the interpretation and application of the Convention in the context of sea level rise and climate change'.[205] Given that a significant challenge for the law of the sea in the twenty-first century will be whether and to what extent it is able to respond to the fundamental geographical, chemical, and ecological changes in the oceans as a consequence of climate change, the contribution of Oceania to developing a law of the sea fit for the Anthropocene is likely to be as important—if not more so—than its contribution to the law relating to the EEZ and fisheries management in the twentieth century.

10.6 Conclusion

Oceania is a region with an ancient and a modern culture in relation to the oceans. Until the second half of the twentieth century, the rich traditions and

[202] Frances Anggadi, 'Establishment, Notification, and Maintenance: The Package of State Practice at the Heart of the Pacific Islands Forum Declaration on Preserving Maritime Zones' (2022) 53 Ocean Development and International Law 19, 26–29. See also David Freestone and Clive Schofield, 'Current Legal Developments: Republic of the Marshall Islands' (2016) 31 International Journal of Marine and Coastal Law 732.

[203] See Robyn Frost and others, 'Redrawing the Map of the Pacific' (2018) 95 Marine Policy 302.

[204] Anggadi (n 202).

[205] ibid 20, quoting the 2021 Pacific Islands Forum Declaration.

principles of ocean governance of Aboriginal Australians and Torres Strait Islanders, Māori, and Pacific Islanders were largely excluded from the international frameworks of the law of the sea. Even today, their cultural impact is greater at the national level than at the international level. The cultural impact of Oceania on the law of the sea cannot be separated from the colonial history of the region, notwithstanding that from the 1960s onwards the interests of all the states began to diverge to a greater or lesser extent from their former colonial powers. Australia, Aotearoa New Zealand, Fiji, and the Pacific Island states (directly or through the representation of their interests) played an important role in shaping the modern law of the sea through UNCLOS in relation to the extension of maritime zones under the jurisdiction of states, fisheries management, marine pollution, and, more narrowly, the deep seabed. In terms of individuals, while diplomats from Australia and Aotearoa New Zealand played important roles behind the scenes, Fijian Ambassador Satya Nandan made a significant diplomatic and substantive contribution through his representation of Fijian interests, as rapporteur of the UNCLOS III Second Committee, and as an 'honest broker diplomat'.[206] His influence and, by extension, that of Oceania on the law of the sea continued for more than two decades following the adoption of UNCLOS through his roles as Secretary General of the ISA, Chairman of the Conference on Straddling and Highly Migratory Fish Stocks,[207] and Chairman of the High Level Conference on the Conservation and Management of Highly Migratory Fish Stocks in the Western and Central Pacific, leading to the creation of the WCPFC.[208]

After UNCLOS, a distinct Pacific regional culture, which regularly but not invariably included Australia and Aotearoa New Zealand, began to emerge. A unique (at that time) collaborative approach to fisheries management, which involved collapsing EEZs for the purposes of fisheries access, was borne of geographical and economic exigencies and allowed the Pacific states to engage in multilateral fora and to negotiate as a collective. This approach was extended to the surveillance and enforcement of fishing—and included Australia and Aotearoa New Zealand. Most recently, it has been deployed in relation to the fixing of maritime boundaries in the face of sea level rise. Other examples of

[206] S Jayakumar, 'Satya Nandan—The Honest Broker Diplomat' in Michael W Lodge and Myron H Nordquist (eds), *Peaceful Order in the World's Oceans: Essays in Honor of Satya N. Nandan* (Brill 2014). For example, Nandan led the Group of 21 on the rights of landlocked and geographically disadvantaged states in the EEZ.

[207] Lodge and Nordquist (n 9) 2.

[208] Nien-Tsu Alfred Hu, 'Father of the WCPFC Convention: Ambassador Satya N. Nandan' in Michael W Lodge and Myron H Nordquist (eds), *Peaceful Order in the World's Oceans: Essays in Honor of Satya N. Nandan* (Brill 2014).

such collaborative leadership in the development of the modern law of the sea—including the early banning of driftnet fishing,[209] the campaign to include a stand-alone sustainable development goal on the oceans (SDG14),[210] and the 2022 request for a climate change advisory opinion submitted to the International Tribunal for the Law of the Sea[211]—could also have been included in this chapter but for the lack of space. All the states of Oceania recognized the importance of the oceans and the law of the sea to their culture, their prosperity, and, in the case of Pacific Island states, their self-determination as independent states at the time of UNCLOS III, the most important period in the evolution of the modern law of the sea. While the issues and interests of these states have shifted over time, there is no doubt that the oceans and the law of the sea remain as vital to these states now as they were then. All Pacific states remain highly engaged in developing the law of the sea through practice and through contributions in multilateral fora, such as recently concluded negotiations for biodiversity beyond national jurisdiction.[212] As the law of the sea begins to grapple with the effects and challenges of climate change, Oceania is undoubtedly at the vanguard of influencing the next stage of the law of the sea: the law of the sea in the Anthropocene.

Epilogue

In March 2024, Indigenous leaders in Aotearoa New Zealand, the Cook Islands, Tonga, Tahiti, Hawaii, and Rapanui signed He Whakaputanga Moana (Declaration for the Oceans), which recognizes whales as legal persons with inherent rights, in addition to endorsing ocean conservation measures, such as protected areas.[213] While not a legally binding treaty, this is a unique Indigenous transnational initiative from the Pacific region that may provide a precedent and a platform for Indigenous Oceania to contribute to the future development of the international law of the sea.

[209] Aqorau, 'The Role' (n 92) 4–5.

[210] See Genevieve Quirk and Quentin Hanich, 'Ocean Diplomacy: The Pacific Island Countries' Campaign to the UN for an Ocean Sustainable Development Goal' (2016) 1 Asia-Pacific Journal of Ocean Law and Policy 68.

[211] *Request for an Advisory Opinion Submitted by the Commission of Small Island States on Climate Change and International Law* (Case Number 31). Tuvalu (along with Antigua and Barbuda) was an original signatory to the Commission, which also includes Niue, Palau, and Vanuatu from the Pacific among its members. See Richard Barnes, 'An Advisory Opinion on Climate Change Obligations Under International Law: A Realistic Prospect?' (2022) 53 Ocean Development and International Law 180.

[212] High Seas Agreement (n 42).

[213] See Mere Takoko, 'A Descendant's Call for Whale Legal Personhood' (Atmos, 26 March 2024) <https://atmos.earth/a-descendants-call-for-whale-legal-personhood/> accessed 10 July 2024.

11

Conclusion: Historical Legacies and Future Prospects

James Kraska and Hayoun Ryou-Ellison

11.1 Introduction

This book has taken a journey through major civilizations of the world and assessed their cultural influence on the creation and maintenance of the international law of the sea and oceans governance. The cultural influences are entangled with political, economic, and strategic factors. Indeed, culture itself is so multifaceted that it is often hard to disentangle it from these other elements of civilization.

11.2 Western Europe

Chapter 2 explored some of the great names in the development of the law of the sea in the late medieval period. Figures include Pedro Álvarez Cabral, the first European to discover Brazil, Bartolomeu Dias, the first European to round the Cape of Good Hope, Ferdinand Magellan, the first person to circumnavigate the earth, and Vasco da Gama, the first person to discover the sea route from Europe to India via the Cape of Good Hope. These men acted pursuant to the precepts of the Enlightenment and applied the scientific method in navigation. They also came from a world in which papal authority stood alongside secular governance. The Iberian explorers gradually became subsumed within greater Western efforts that included English and Dutch seafarers, encompassing the first large phase in the development of the law of the sea. While the Portuguese and Spanish liturgical traditions provided a more prescriptive governance model, as demonstrated by the Treaty of Tordesillas and the Treaty of Saragossa, all European culture springs from the ancient Greek and Roman world.

James Kraska and Hayoun Ryou-Ellison, *Conclusion: Historical Legacies and Future Prospects* In: *Cultural Influences on the Law of the Sea*. Edited by: James Kraska and Hayoun Ryou-Ellison, Oxford University Press.
 DOI: 10.1093/9780198944140.003.0011

Ancient Greece set the foundation for Western moral and political philosophy, while the Romans were more practically minded and emphasized the importance of the rule of law. Rome spread throughout Europe to include Belgium, England, France, Portugal, Spain, and the southern Netherlands, before its collapse in the West in the fifth century. The culture continued for 1,000 years in Byzantium until the fall of Constantinople in 1453. By then, however, the Renaissance was well underway. Dutch jurist Hugo Grotius and English polymath John Selden offered contending narratives over the division of authority in the oceans.

Western ascendancy in science and technology ignited the age of exploration, accelerating the need for a law of the sea. Measuring and navigating the oceans required mastery of longitude and latitude, and the nautical mile—all inventions of the West. The rise of the Protestant Reformation fused the Dutch and English with the Latin and Catholic, widening the acceptable range of enquiry and creating rapid economic and scientific advances. The Western political culture of investment in regulation, administration, and the rule of law began to form universal rules of the law of the sea, such as seeking universal agreement on the 3-nautical-mile limit of the territorial sea and the allocation of fisheries resources. Although the idea of codifying the law of the sea began in the Roman era, it was not seriously attempted until the twentieth century.

The Western states met in 1930, 1958, and 1960 to develop a universal set of rules for the law of the sea. The International Law Commission adopted a draft instrument in 1956 that formed the basis for the 1958 Geneva Conventions. These were largely Western attempts, but by the Third UN Conference on the Law of the Sea, from 1973 to 1982, many newly independent and non-Western states participated. These conferences were informed by Western European concepts of property law, from the territorial sea to the common heritage of mankind. While these Western European influences on the law of the sea have been direct, the use of Western languages, especially English and French, has been more subtle but just as profound.

11.3 Eastern Europe

Eastern Europe was the focus of Chapter 3. The region has had its own distinct influence on the law of the sea. Tradition in Eastern Europe also traces its roots to Greek and Roman law and the experience of states along the Baltic Sea and Black Sea, including Bulgaria and Romania on the Black Sea and Poland and Lithuania on the Baltic Sea. These states had limited access to the ocean and, therefore, joined the geographically disadvantaged states during the Third UN

Conference on the Law of the Sea. Poland, the largest state, is a transit corridor for the Czech Republic, the Slovak Republic, and Hungary. This geographic position ensured that Eastern European states, especially Poland, insisted on preserving freedom of navigation and access to living resources on the high seas. The people located on the eastern shore of the Baltic Sea were among the last to convert to Latin Christianity, with Poland entering Christendom in the early fourteenth century.

The fall of the Iron Curtain after the Second World War made a hard separation between Eastern and Western Europe. The ocean became a division between these two parts of Europe, with the North Atlantic lending its name to the Western defence organization NATO. The Baltic Sea was a microcosm of the greater contest for freedom of the seas and coastal state control, with Poland, Sweden, and Denmark making various claims to the semi-enclosed sea. Trade by sea was especially important, with the region being a major source of amber, fossilized tree resin. Amber has been traded from the region for a millennium, with a maritime route winding from the Black Sea to Rome. Poland's investment in freedom of the seas continued through the Third Conference. In the contemporary era, states in Eastern Europe have focused on the protection of the marine environment, especially the Baltic Sea. These states have worked through the European Union to protect the Baltic Sea marine environment under the EU marine strategy framework directive 2008/56/EC(MSFD) and the EU Water Framework Directive 2000/60/EC(WFD). Poland has also worked to delimit maritime zones with neighbouring states, including Germany and Sweden.

11.4 Russia

Chapter 4 looked at Russia, which—like Eastern Europe—was heavily influenced by the Viking experience and orthodox Christianity. The oldest historical monuments still surviving in the region commemorate agreements between ancient Rus' and Byzantium. The Roman legal system heavily influenced Russian development. Likewise, Russians concluded agreements with Greeks, which included Slavic and Finno-Ugric tribes on equal terms. The Orthodox Church was an especially strong influence in Russia, as it became the centre of the Orthodox faith after the fall of Constantinople in 1453.

The Russkaya Pravda feudal legal code and church charters began a modern legal system that searched for universal rules or norms. By the thirteenth century, Novgorod had concluded border treaties with Hanseatic cities to regulate shipping. This process accelerated after 1696, with the establishment of the

Russian regular fleet. In 1720, the Statute of Ewers and the Maritime Statute became the first systematized legislation to regulate maritime trade. In the eighteenth century, the tsar was intent on modernization along the Western European model. The tempering influence of Christianity reasserted itself in terms of compassion and justice. Numerous Western legal intellectual figures were translated into Russian, including Samuel von Pufendorf, Hugo Grotius, and Montesquieu. Although some of their thinking was absorbed into Russian legal and political culture, political liberalization was not adopted. Russia remained an absolutist monarchy. While Russia implemented a pan-European legal tradition, the Russian sobornost (spiritual community) contrasted with the individualism inherent in the Western European consciousness.[1] Even with authoritarianism, the pulse of the people was deemed essential for the attainment of justice and order.

11.5 East Asia

As shown in Chapter 5, East Asian cultural values are evident in the law of the sea and reflected in the domestic legal systems and foreign relations law of East Asian states. The Confucian tradition in China and Korea, together with the Buddhist ideals that emerged from ancient Japan, form the core element of East /Asian culture. Confucius extolled the virtues of hierarchy and stability, and this approach reflects a desire to maintain an internal harmony in which participants from the levels of family to sprawling empire understand their place within the system. Confucianism, as a philosophical system, emphasizes respect for authority and the pursuit of harmony within hierarchical relationships. Such values have permeated the region's approach to maritime governance, leading to a quest for harmonious interactions and adherence to mutually agreed-upon rules in oceanic affairs. For China, this means placing Beijing at the centre of the regional security architecture, with surrounding states in a position of subordination or homage. Imperial Japan's 'Greater East Asia Coprosperity Sphere' and China's legal forays into the East China Sea and the South China Sea help motivate this cultural impulse to establish a hierarchal order that facilitates internal regional harmony. Moreover, East Asia's historical emphasis on collective harmony and diplomacy has profoundly impacted the establishment of multilateral agreements and organizations,

[1] СИ Ожегов и НЮ Шведова, *Толковый словарь русского языка* [SI Ozhegov and NU Shvedova, *Explanatory Dictionary of the Russian Language*] (M.O. Wolf 1949–).

shaping the region's cooperative approach to addressing maritime challenges. Beyond philosophical tenets, ancient maritime traditions embedded in East Asian cultures have significantly shaped customs and norms concerning marine resource management. With the encounter with the West, the colonial tradition mixed with these classical Eastern cultural norms. The combination informed nationalist and expansive notions first in Japan and more recently in China. While China was a leader in the Group of 77 (G-77) during the negotiations for the UN Convention on the Law of the Sea (UNCLOS), Japan joined the major Western maritime powers of the United Kingdom, the United States, and France, as well as Russia.

11.6 South Asia

Chapter 6 considered the influence of South Asia. Modern South Asia is the product of a complex ancient Hindu culture with a seafaring tradition. As in the West, shipbuilding, navigation, and extensive maritime trade are widely featured in Sanskrit, Pali, and other ancient sources. Like the Justinian Digest in the Roman era, a treatise from the rein of Chandragupta Maurya created the institution of the Superintendent of Shipping (*navadhyaksha*), responsible for jurisdiction over the coasts, seas, and navigation with control over seagoing ships. The law and ethics were intertwined, requiring, for example, special dispensation for ships in peril at sea. Coastal villages fell within this regulation and were taxed for their position as ports of entry and fish landing sites. Furthermore, fishing was licensed and even the rudimentary beginnings of protection for 'strange or unusual' marine life were recognized in the law. The law also prioritized the suppression of maritime piracy and the maintenance of good order at sea, while a marine insurance regime spread risks of maritime trade. The progressive or advanced elements of maritime law in South Asia also considered protection for maritime refugees fleeing persecution, as demonstrated by a large population of Zoroastrians who fled from Persia by sea and were welcomed into Gujarat during the seventh century.

South Asia's encounter with the West accelerated in the fifteenth century with the arrival of Portuguese mariners and the acceleration of the spice trade. As India became integrated into the competition between the great European powers, it next came under the sway of the Dutch East India Company, which gradually was displaced by the English. This area was the epicentre of the 'battle of the books' and the formation of the two competing paradigms for oceans governance: *mare liberum* and *mare clausum*. During the period of

British dominion from the early eighteenth century to 1945, and especially the region under the Raj from 1858 to 1945, India was subsumed within the Empire. Upon independence in 1947, however, India (and Pakistan and Bangladesh) continued to develop its separate cultural identity. These perspectives became increasingly consequential in oceans law and policy. As a leader of the G-77 and Non-Aligned Movement, India was powerful and influential in advocating for an approach to ocean governance that preferences developing states and the Global South. This approach is most evident in the recognition of the mineral resources of the deep seabed as the 'common heritage of mankind' in UNCLOS. The concern over distant water fishing nations displacing artisanal fishers contributed to the adoption of the High Seas Fish Stocks Agreement and the reformulation of the concept of fishing as a high seas freedom towards a more regulated activity. The position of India and South Asia was also a key factor in the adoption of the 2023 Agreement on the Conservation and Sustainable Use of Marine Biological Diversity of Areas beyond National Jurisdiction (BBNJ), which includes a comprehensive regime for providing access and benefits to developing states for marine genetic resources located beyond national jurisdiction.

11.7 Africa

The influence of Africa was the subject of Chapter 7. Similar to the East Asian view of community, Africa is a continent whose people are focused on collective identity rather than individualism. The importance of collective identity over that of the individual is expressed in the philosophy governing the sub-Saharan African view of life, known as ubuntu. This concept is difficult to translate into a single English-language term, and it is differently worded in several African states, but a concept similar to ubuntu can be found throughout much of sub-Saharan Africa. It means that a true human necessarily belongs to, and should therefore be understood as inherently enmeshed in, a greater series of community, societal, environmental, and spiritual ties. This is the spiritual worldview of one's relationship to the community. Whereas in the Asian notion of collectivism—centred as it is on proper order in society, with hierarchical order being what matters—the African concepts of ubuntu emphasize codependency and interconnectivity, assuming a more egalitarian relationship among people.[2]

[2] Thaddeus Metz, 'Values in China as Compared to Africa: Two Conceptions of Harmony' (2017) 67(2) Philosophy East & West 441, 451.

Like Oceania, Africa has been influenced by its colonial experience. Most of the emerging nations in Africa and Asia that became independent in the mid-twentieth century were not a part of the first and second Conferences on the Law of the Sea, which were held in 1958 and 1960, respectively. However, by the early 1970s, most African states had gained independence and they increasingly demanded to see their views reflected in international law. At the Third UN Conference on the Law of the Sea, African states actively voiced, and took leading roles on, certain issues out of a desire to regain autonomy over their own economic affairs and maritime resources. The Conference's first session began in 1973, and its outcome was the adoption of UNCLOS in 1982. Ubuntu, together with the shared colonial experience, created room for African states to work together on these issues and contributed to the development of the contemporary law of the sea.

Lying outside the reach of any state's national jurisdiction was the issue of deep seabed mining. Their lack of technological capabilities to exploit the seabed concerned African leaders and led African states to take a leading role in shaping the international seabed regime. The unique contribution of Africa to the regime of the sea is its philosophical nature: ubuntu provides other states with alternative angles on understanding resources at sea. While the traditional sea powers focused on the freedom of the seas, the Africans urged countries to look after larger collective interests, in the spirit of ubuntu, and finally ushered in the seabed regime under the notion that it is a common heritage of mankind. This put the focus on the idea of humanity, with its common responsibilities and duties in promoting the general welfare at sea. This values system also influenced advocacy for the rights of landlocked states in terms of their access to the seas.

11.8 South America

Chapter 8 investigated South America's influence on the law of the sea. Like that in Africa and Oceania, the colonial legacy in Latin America has influenced the region's view of the law of the sea. As the earliest area to be colonized by Europeans, from the turn of the sixteenth century through the early nineteenth century, most of Latin America belonged to either the Spanish or the Portuguese empire. The aftermath of independence brought forth strong resentment in the new states concerning their need to protect their maritime claims from interference by foreign powers. The colonial legacy, as well as subsequent interventions by the United States, shaped the views of South Americans, leading to the belief that certain portions of the ocean should fall under the control of a coastal state, as a form of contesting the emphasis of the traditional maritime powers on the freedom of the sea. The importance of independence and security in shaping attitudes towards the sea became influential throughout the continent. One of the most influential figures in these endeavours was Andrés Bello, the nineteenth-century Venezuelan–Chilean intellectual, whose views on the importance of state sovereignty reflected South America's position on regimes at sea, such as those of the contiguous zone and the exclusive economic zone.

Latin America has been an active force in the creation of new institutions in the law of the sea. Following UNCLOS, there have been many ways in which Latin America has made its mark, such as elevating the issue of illegal, unreported, and unregulated fisheries to the global level, as well as advancing the principles governing the continental shelf, which are based on a concept of patrimonial sea. Many Latin American countries even brought their maritime delimitation problems to the international courts that influenced how maritime territories would be divvied up.

Latin American countries and Caribbean states have renewed the historic dialogue over the extent of ocean sovereignty and sovereign rights, adding emerging notions or models, such as shared or common spaces. In practice, the search for certainty and the adoption of nationalist oceanic policies were influenced by concepts such as conservation, the prevention of marine pollution, precautionary approaches to potential marine pollution, due diligence and due regard, and the importance of straddling stocks to coastal states. These views reflect the interconnection between the environmental agenda and the law of the sea. Whereas Latin American nations have initiated international processes to promote the visions of some coastal states, as in the case of highly migratory species, they have also aimed to join other states and regions to form a broader conception of global oceans governance. This shift towards a global approach is underscored by the enthusiasm with which Latin American and Caribbean states embraced the negotiations on the 2023 BBNJ.

11.9 North America

The North American experience was surveyed in Chapter 9. The United States and Canada originated from European culture, derivative of the legacy of Greece and Rome, the Enlightenment, Christianity, and the scientific method. These pillars of Western civilization are broad and complex, mutually reinforcing, and sometimes in opposition. The most compelling norms have focused on the value and advancement of the individual, as expressed through Greek democracy, Roman rule of law, and Christian ethics of the equality of humankind. The Founding Fathers of the United States studied these concepts in the European tradition and animated the ideals of liberty, independence, and classical liberalism most strongly. These norms shaped the national culture and served as the bedrock of politics and the foundation of legal policy in the United States.

In the law of the sea, these norms were reflected in the US policy of free maritime trade and an emphasis on exclusive flag state control, which supported the nascent republic in the face of overpowering English, French, Spanish, and other European naval dominance. The idea of a 'free sea' contributed to the US involvement in the First and Second World Wars and was codified in the Atlantic Charter and recognized in the Charter of the United Nations. The liberal idea of an open order of the oceans has persisted, but in recent decades it is tempered with a more continental perspective born from the Roman tradition of regulatory control and coordinated government oversight. At sea, the impulse has strengthened the coastal state perspective in US lawmaking. This approach is first evident in the US arguments before the Bering Sea Fur Seal Arbitration in 1893, the Truman Proclamation and US recognition of a continental shelf in 1945, and the adoption of the Magnuson–Stevens Fishery Conservation and Management Act in 1976. The United States has attempted to balance a liberal approach that benefits flag states with a regulatory approach that inures to coastal state authority. With President Bill Clinton's attendance at the Rio Summit in 1992, the United States has shifted decidedly in favour of coastal state and regulatory concepts, such as the precautionary approach, marine spatial planning, and the ecosystem-based approach to marine management.

11.10 Oceania

Chapter 10 reviewed the influence of Oceania on the law of the sea. While Oceania consists of thousands of small and large islands scattered throughout the Asia-Pacific region, as well as states surrounded by water, the role of Oceania in the development of the international law of the sea was minimal before the twentieth century due to colonization by Western powers—and, over the first half of the twentieth century, by Japan. In the twentieth century, the colonial legacy retained a leading role in certain countries' understandings of the law of the sea. Some states, such as Australia and New Zealand, largely followed the European approach to the law of the sea. This approach was different from that taken in Africa, where, following independence, the colonial experience inspired the continent's peoples to regain their own voices.

However, in the middle of the twentieth century, in the aftermath of decolonization, instead of approaching issues based on the individual preferences of states, Oceania shifted to enhance regional voices. This was reflected in the creation of the Oceania Group, which was formed to promote the interests of the Pacific Island states, as a forum for sharing their views. For example, New Zealand insisted that all islands, no matter how small, should have an exclusive economic zone. This served New Zealand's own interests as well as those of other Pacific Island states.

Such a collaborative spirit in the Pacific continues to this day, even after the adoption of UNCLOS. In tackling emerging challenges such as climate change, with its attendant sea level rise and consequent impact on the boundaries of Pacific Island states, these countries have begun exercising uniform regional state practices as a source of customary law. Since the text of UNCLOS itself does not address the impact of climate change, as it was adopted before climate change had become a significant threat to the global community, such a highly collaborative regional culture among the Pacific Island states has contributed to the development of the law of the sea.

11.11 Conclusion

This study has identified cultural norms and explored how they are reflected in the development and contemporary application of the law of the sea. These cultures have melded to form the contemporary framework for oceans law and governance. As it is a dynamic body of rules and norms, the law of the sea is dynamic and continues to evolve. The cultures that have combined to shape it have resulted in a regime that balances *mare librum* and *mare clausum*, individual state rights and sovereign equality in the Westphalian state system, with community interests and hierarchical governance models reflected on a global scale. These perspectives are evident in innovations such as Part XI of UNCLOS on deep seabed mining and the BBNJ provisions on marine genetic resources.

Index

For the benefit of digital users, indexed terms that span two pages (e.g., 52–53) may, on occasion, appear on only one of those pages.

The manufacturer's authorised representative in the EU for product safety is Oxford University Press España S.A. of el Parque Empresarial San Fernando de Henares, Avenida de Castilla, 2 – 28830 Madrid (www.oup.es/en or product.safety@oup.com). OUP España S.A. also acts as importer into Spain of products made by the manufacturer.

www.ingramcontent.com/pod-product-compliance
Lightning Source LLC
LaVergne TN
LVHW011821200926
848484LV00005B/1264
* 9 7 8 0 1 9 8 9 4 4 1 3 3 *